Wilfred Owen's Voices

Wilfred Owen's Voices

LANGUAGE AND COMMUNITY

DOUGLAS KERR

CLARENDON PRESS · OXFORD
1993

Oxford University Press, Walton Street, Oxford OX2 6DP
Oxford New York Toronto
Delhi Bombay Calcutta Madras Karachi
Kuala Lumpur Singapore Hong Kong Tokyo
Nairobi Dar es Salaam Cape Town
Melbourne Auckland Madrid
and associated companies in
Berlin Ibadan

Oxford is a trade mark of Oxford University Press

Published in the United States
by Oxford University Press Inc., New York

British Library Cataloguing in Publication Data
Data available

Library of Congress Cataloging in Publication Data
Kerr, Douglas.
Wilfred Owen's voices : language and community / Douglas Kerr.
Includes bibliographical references and index.
1. Owen, Wilfred, 1893–1918—Criticism and interpretation.
2. Language and culture—England—History—20th century.
3. Community life in literature. I. Title.
PR6029.W4Z69 1993
821'.912—dc20 93–13685
ISBN 0–19–812370–1

Typeset by Graphicraft Typesetters Ltd., Hong Kong
Printed in Great Britain
on acid-free paper by
Biddles Ltd.,
Guildford and King's Lynn

For Elaine

Acknowledgements

For personal kindness and professional example I am very grateful to Dominic Hibberd and Jon Stallworthy, Wilfred Owen scholars. Dominic Hibberd has read most of this book in manuscript, and his generous help and valuable suggestions have increased the debt my work already owes him.

It is also a pleasure to thank for their help Piers Gray, Elaine Ho, K. K. Luke, D. S. R. Welland, and Martin Wright. My thanks too to the librarians and staff of the English Faculty Library, Oxford, the Bodleian Library, and the University of Hong Kong Library.

Acknowledgements are due to the following for permission to quote copyright material: the Owen Estate and Oxford University Press for Wilfred Owen's *Collected Letters*, edited by Harold Owen and John Bell, and for Harold Owen's *Journey from Obscurity*; the Owen Estate, the Hogarth Press, and New Directions Publishing Corp., for *Wilfred Owen: The Complete Poems and Fragments*, edited by Jon Stallworthy; and Mr George Sassoon for poems by Siegfried Sassoon.

Earlier versions of parts of this book have appeared in *English Literature in Transition*, the *Modern Language Review*, and the *Review of English Studies*, and I thank the editors for permission to republish these pieces.

Contents

Abbreviations

Citation from the following frequently quoted works is indicated by an abbreviation and page number.

CPF *Wilfred Owen: The Complete Poems and Fragments*, ed. Jon Stallworthy, 2 vols (London: Chatto and Windus, Hogarth Press, and Oxford University Press, 1983)

CL *Wilfred Owen: Collected Letters*, ed. Harold Owen and John Bell (London: Oxford University Press, 1967)

EB *The Poems of Wilfred Owen*, ed. Edmund Blunden, with a memoir (London: Chatto and Windus, 1931)

JFO Harold Owen, *Journey from Obscurity*, 3 vols (London: Oxford University Press, 1963–5)

OTP Dominic Hibberd, *Owen the Poet* (London: Macmillan, 1986)

WO Jon Stallworthy, *Wilfred Owen: A Biography* (London: Oxford University Press and Chatto and Windus, 1974)

I follow *CPF*'s text of Owen's poems, and give page references only when referring to a draft, a variant, or an editorial note.

I

Introduction

Wilfred Owen's short life—a mere quarter-century—was shaped more than most by his experience of communities: the close family among whom he grew up, the Church for whose ministry he once seemed destined, the army in which he served and died, and the company of English poets among whom, like his childhood hero Keats, he hoped to be remembered after his death. Each of these formative communities has its own particular language. My project in what follows is to read and try to understand Owen's writing, in his letters and poetry, in terms of its relationship with the communities, and their discourses, which helped to shape it. Family, Church, army, and poetry were his schools of language, but they also supplied the most important themes of his writing, so there is a kind of dialogue. The words he learned from these communities became in turn the words he used to speak to and of them, and sometimes against them.

Wilfred Owen's language was English. But how many 'Englishes' are to be identified within 'English' depends only on the degree of magnification through which it is observed. Bakhtin, characteristically expansive, finds within every national language an internal stratification, 'into social dialects, characteristic group behaviour, professional jargons, generic languages, languages of generations and age groups, tendentious languages, languages of the authorities, of various circles and of passing fashions, languages that serve the specific sociopolitical purposes of the day, even of the hour (each day has its own slogan, its own vocabulary, its own emphases).'[1] Clearly some of these strata of social heteroglossia are richer and thicker than others; and among the more important are the varieties within a language which serve and define powerful institutions within its culture.

Institutions, involving an identifiable group or activity, express themselves in a particular variety of language to carry out their

[1] Bakhtin, *The Dialogic Imagination*, 262–3.

business. On the most observable level this is a matter of lexis. We would have no difficulty recognizing that counsel, testify, magistrate, and perjury all belong to the discourse of one institution, and aisle, hymn, daily bread, and everlasting to another, though we would also be aware of a good deal of overlapping between the language of different institutions (words relating to judgement being held in common by the special lexis of both court and Church, for example). But the speech of these language communities is not characterized only by a particular lexis, but by other features too. Such features may be syntactic, like the forms of question favoured in cross-examination, or conventional, like the degree of improvisation allowed in different parts of a church service. They may be stylistic like the disc-jockey's hyperbole, or hermetic like family nicknames and private slang. And each community has its own thematic features too, drawn from its own field of discourse, its special topics and imagery. Furthermore, certain relatively stable types of utterance—what Bakhtin calls speech genres[2]—are proper to particular spheres of human activity and communication. An anthem, a letter home, and a report on military action are genres of the discourses of Church, family, and army respectively (though each may be absorbed and digested into genres of the discourse of poetry, as they are in Owen).

Swearing affidavits, singing psalms, telling bedtime stories, giving the order to shoulder arms, are all more or less institution-specific (though once again there will be some overlapping). Uttered by individuals, these language activities also identify their speakers as playing a role within the institution and its discourse. The sergeant-major who hurries from parade-ground to evensong, and then goes home to quarrel with his wife, is one person playing a role in at least three discourses. And as a participant in these acts he is defined for the moment by the role that the discourse assigns to him, a subject position within these speech events corresponding to a subject position within the hierarchy of the institution itself (he speaks or sings or shouts as a non-commissioned officer, a member of a congregation, a husband). Moving from one discursive stage to another, assuming a different role on each, one man in his time plays many parts, and frequently more than one at a time. And in the sense in which you can say that identity is a

[2] Bakhtin, *Speech Genres*, 60–102.

linguistic construction, it might further be said that the human subject *is* his or her discursive roles—not just the sum of them but the interaction between them, which includes the possibility of tension, incompatibility, conflict, and contradiction.

Language is borrowed from the community, though it may be returned with interest. 'The artist,' Vološinov observes, 'receives no word in linguistically virginal form.'[3] Every utterance is related to previous utterances, for all language already belongs to someone. We have to make what we can out of second-hand materials. But though a poet, like any other communicative being, is not at liberty to invent his own language, nevertheless utterances do flow back (if anyone is listening or reading) into the community in which they are made, altering and adjusting it, interpreting and remaking it. If we play roles, we do not play to an immutable script, but can improvise within what Halliday calls 'a shared meaning potential'.[4] The expert performer, such as the poet, can increase the range. Speech is an intervention in the community.

The social institutions that determined the trajectory of Owen's life were also speech communities that formed his language. From an early age Owen was saturated in the language of the Church, and this opened to him a field of discourse (the topics, themes, and ideology of religion, the roles and personnel of its social life), particular modes (such as Christian witness and blasphemy), and genres (special forms of speech and writing, like sermons, prayers, declarations of faith or doubt) and a corpus of texts (including the Bible and liturgy, but also things like temperance parables and tracts). Church discourse became a strong force in Owen's language formation, where it mingled with all the other discourse he was exposed to, and the language formation provides the expressive options out of which comes the style, the verbal resources from which his letters and poems are built. In this sense, the writer is the creature of the language made available to him or her by speech communities, which supply him or her with linguistic resources, but these resources are then used in a series of acts of identity that place the writer in a particular and unique relation to the communities. The writer's own words are derived from, but also modify and extend and may challenge, an order of words he or she has inherited.

[3] Todorov, *Mikhail Bakhtin*, 49.
[4] Halliday, *Language as Social Semiotic*, 2.

Owen is remembered as a war poet. He is indeed one of the great English poets of the army, and army language is thematically prominent in his best-known poems, since they deal with the life and death of soldiers. The army supplied his language formation with a repertoire of imagery, including human types; a body of texts, from songs to instruction manuals; a set of speech genres such as the combat anecdote and the giving of orders; a stylistic propensity for functional, spare, and sometimes violent diction; and an ideological field, where the issues include questions of loyalty, duty, and responsibility, for any institutional speech community has a system of authority and of values. It so happened that it was in the army that Owen made himself most at home. Yet even when he is most deeply immersed in the army theme, his language is still saturated in the experience of the other important communities of his language formation. Just as Lieutenant Owen of the Manchester Regiment does not (could not) cease to be the child of Susan and Tom Owen, so the family theme and its language are never far from the surface. And often his writing is at its most interesting, and at its most highly charged, when two or more strong discourses are present together, jostling for primacy, challenging or reinforcing each other; at moments when perhaps within a line, a phrase, even a single word, army discourse meets a current of family language, or becomes turbulent when it runs into a banked mass of Evangelical ideology. This meteorological figure is a little clumsy, but I want to avoid the idea of the discourses as so many inert strata, laid down one on top of the other in the poet's past. They are not stable, but have life and motion of their own, and are by no means under the absolute control of the poet's consciousness in composition. He navigates as best he can in a restless medium.

The story of Wilfred Owen's life is the story of his movement through (but never beyond) a series of such strong language communities. Sometimes membership of one came into conflict with another. There were times when it seemed difficult to be his father's son—or the son his father wanted him to be—and to be a poet; certainly there were times when the Christian and the combatant soldier found it awkward to share the same voice. And for each of these institutions, which were the most important constituents of his language formation, Owen at one time or another felt something like hatred. He spoke their languages, yet he used his voice to try to change them.

The making of the poet's style is the story of a Yeatsian quarrel with the self. But it is also a small but rich site where some of the history of these institutions—family, army, and the rest—becomes legible as they were tested and to some degree reshaped by the strains brought to bear on them in the poet's lifetime, strains which his own work records and makes articulate. There is something of a dialectical process going on. The particular consciousness and its language are moulded by the configuration of the institutions that produce it; the institutions in their turn are modified to comprehend the experience of the voice that speaks of and through them. An individual style is polyphonic, containing voices or echoes (since each of our words is a quotation) of former uses and forms. In Owen's language can be read his individual history, but as this can be seen in terms of shifting relations with family, Church, army, and poetry, there is a social and cultural history there too, the history of a time in which these institutions came under severe pressure in the crisis of a Great War which they had all helped to bring about.

The question that prompts my enquiry is the simple one of why Wilfred Owen wrote in the way he did, a question not separable from the question of what his writing means. Answering it will involve reading the story of his life which his own language contains: there is a biography, of a kind, in what follows, though it does not take the classic form of a linear narrative. The task is to write the life of a poet's language, something which I think has not been done in this way before. It can be attempted in the case of Wilfred Owen because the circumstances in which his life was lived make it possible to describe and interpret it in terms of these institutions, because his surviving writing is of manageable proportions for this sort of undertaking, and because his work has been well tended by the poets and scholars who have ensured he has been luckier in death than he was in life. In the writing of his brother Harold we have an invaluable second perspective where we need it most, on the poet's family and his most formative years, to supplement or qualify what can be learned from the poet's own letters and poems. With these resources it has been possible to attempt a map of Owen's writing and its relation to its discursive environment.

It is sometimes hard for literary and cultural historians to resist the temptation of exciting and airy gestures in the direction of 'the discourse' of this or that, and these satisfying flourishes can be in danger of coming adrift into a transcendent and cloudy notion of discourse. I have tried to keep in mind that the discourse of the army, for example, exists as a body of actual utterances, and to base my investigations on the specific evidence of these. The risk of sometimes piling up quotations in an unwieldy way was to be preferred to that of generalizing in thin air. Of course selection has been necessary. It has seemed sensible, in looking at the impact of institutional discourses on Owen, to pay particular attention to voices invested with official or unofficial authority, or at least perceived by Owen as being authoritative. Hence, it has been useful to listen not only to the likes of the Bishop of London, but also to Colonel Shirley and Laurie Magnus. These latter two were hardly household names (as the bishop was) but each was important to Wilfred Owen at particular moments as the voice of the orthodoxy of, respectively, the military and the literary establishment. It must also be understood that I do not claim that Owen knew from direct experience all of the items of discourse which are mentioned in this study—all the military training manuals, for example. It is sufficient for my purposes that these items of discourse were in circulation within the institution (the army in this case) at the time when Wilfred Owen was a part of it: they were factors in his discursive environment.

There are pitfalls of particularity as well as of generalization. Although these investigations are sometimes small-scale (I have quite a lot to say, for example, about the words 'I' and 'we'), the issues they deal with are not. It would be a matter of fairly casual interest to examine the way Wilfred Owen picked up habits of speech and writing from the various groups with which he was identified in his lifetime. But discourse—words in use—is impregnated with ideology; it is through discourse, and sometimes against discourse, that values are formed and tested. And so the formation of style—what are judged to be the right words in the right order—comprises a process of decisions which amounts to a judgement about the world. Wilfred Owen said that true poets must be truthful. He had no instruments with which to tell the truth except the words he had heard and read, these words themselves bearing the marks of their own experience in other times and places—some of them (as Conrad complained) defaced by centuries of careless usage, others quite firmly marked as the property of a particular group or interest.

Two moments from the poem 'Exposure' can help to illustrate the presence and interaction of different discourses in Owen's language. It is not a poem that would readily be described as polyphonic, for it seems to be the monologue of a single uninterrupted consciousness, consistent in the sombre mood and language of its description and meditation. Yet even in this sort of poem there is a tangle of voices, and I will pick some of them out by examining two moments, one short and simple, the other rather more complex.

Everyone remarks on the way this poem's opening seems to chime, or rather clash, with the beginning of the quintessential Romantic lyric, Keats's 'Ode to a Nightingale': 'My heart aches, and a drowsy numbness pains | My sense'. Familiar, one would guess, to every single reader of English poetry, the opening of the most famous poem of the man whom the young Wilfred Owen had worshipped above all other poets, these melodious phrases are evoked or provoked by the first line of 'Exposure':

> Our brains ache, in the merciless iced east winds that knive us . . .

Everything Keats's Victorian successors learned from him about writing beautifully seems to have been lost on the author of this compellingly ugly line, with its unlovely vowel-rhyme, its chaotic rhythm, fussy consonants, and the unfortunate neighbouring of 'iced' and 'east'. Worse is to come: 'knive us' is going to be made to rhyme, barbarously, with 'nervous'. And of course we would be quite right to conclude from this that Owen wanted to show that there was nothing beautiful or romantic about the circumstances of modern war.

But the gesture, with its 'ironic echo' of Keats (*CPF* 186), is quite complex in its implications. Keats was Owen's first and for a time his greatest model, kindling in him an enthusiasm which took the form of a romantic identification, to the extent that the adolescent Owen suspected himself (wrongly) of tuberculosis, and also believed, with more justification, that time was always short for him because, like Keats, he was destined to die young. Though he was to move on from the time when he believed 'all Poetry' to be contained in Keats (*CL* 273), many of Owen's juvenilia show him taking Keats as a model and often as a subject for poems of his own. Where would the younger Owen have looked for the best example of how to begin a poem, but to this classic, authoritative voice of the community of English poetry?

'My heart aches' provided a supreme precedent which prints itself into the syntax, tense, and rhythm of Owen's first phrase, but as this almost ritual and as it were ideal opening impacts into the experience and discourse of the army, a surprising mutation or mutilation takes place. The subject becomes plural, the Romantic complaint of dejection metamorphoses into something closer to a literal statement, and the long vowel immediately repeated provides an unpleasing and unKeatsian throb: 'Our brains ache'. Or, perhaps more likely, it happened the other way round: finding a phrase for the sensation caused by exhaustion, eye strain, extreme cold, and nervous tension conjured up a sourly distorted echo of the Keatsian formula. In any case, Owen's placing this phrase at the start of his poem is a deliberate provocation of a head-on intertextual collision.

And it is a confrontation not just with a particular poem that Keats wrote, but also with an aesthetic and a tradition, the institution of English poetry as someone of Owen's generation, class, and education knew it. Palgrave's *Golden Treasury*, of which Owen possessed the very popular Everyman edition of 1906, contains only one poem beginning with the word 'our'. This is Thomas Campbell's 'The Soldier's Dream' (a title Owen was to remember: he drafted his own 'Soldier's Dream' in 1917) which begins 'Our bugles sang truce, for the night-cloud had lowered,' and deals with the theme of a nostalgic vision of home that dissolves with the dawn. But Palgrave's anthology chose no less than nine titles whose first line begins with 'my', including three beginning with 'my heart'. Of course Palgrave confined himself more or less to songs and lyrics in his selection. No such generic limitation was set on at least the title of Sir Arthur Quiller-Couch's magisterial *Oxford Book of English Verse* (1900). This volume has not one poem starting with 'our', but contains twenty-eight which begin with the singular 'my'. This would seem to support a general point (borne out, as we shall see, by an investigation of the critical and literary-historical writing Owen knew) that, in the climate of taste in which Wilfred Owen educated himself, poetry was considered and valued chiefly as the voice of singular, private experience, the voice of the pronoun 'I'. Yet this is a person wholly absent from Wilfred Owen's 'Exposure'. Starting as it does, the poem salutes but at the same time denies (or perhaps blasphemes) what had once been, for Owen, one of the most sacred texts of English verse. Here is a discourse opening that is both a password that seeks entry to the community of English poetry and a challenge that seeks in the same breath to transform it. It is a rhetorical move with some similarity to Owen's plan to declare he was 'not concerned with Poetry', in the preface to a book of his poems (*CPF* 535).

The Thomas Campbell poem favoured by Palgrave uses the military plural pronoun—'Our bugles' meaning the bugles of our army—before settling down to recount the dream dreamed by the first person singular 'while reposing that night on my pallet of straw'. If the singular is the subject of dreams and romantic flights of fancy, the plural is the subject of the activity and attributes of the army: an army cannot say 'I' or 'my'. It is part of both the strength and the pathos of this Owen poem that no special case is made here for the first person singular, who does not break ranks. 'We' suffer together, are perhaps dying together ('Is it that we are dying?'). Even the extreme subjectivity of dream and memory (Campbell's theme, for which it had seemed natural to him to make his subject singular) is shared by Owen's soldiers; they dream of home together, as only brothers could. The private space of Romantic lyricism is commandeered for a plural, communal experience.

The other transformation is of the seat of sensation announced at the beginning of the poem. Keats's heart ached, but it was part of the Romantic inheritance in which Owen had educated himself that the brain was a relatively unpoetic organ. It features in the Nightingale ode as a prosaic embarrassment, 'the dull brain' which 'perplexes and retards' the poetic imagination. Now this implicit invitation to compare 'Our brains ache' with 'My heart aches' is a clue to that declaration of Owen's, in the draft preface, that he was not concerned with (upper-case) 'Poetry', the poetical. The 'ironic echo' of Keats's heartache coaxes the reader to glimpse Keats's words behind or through Owen's. Something—indeed, something polemical—is being said here about literary history. That is what poetry was like, even the best of it: this is how a poem must begin now, in these times and circumstances. The meaning is in the difference. And this moment of dialogue (other Keatsian echoes later in the poem keep that dialogue audible, as Desmond Graham has shown),[5] this double awareness exposes each discourse to the light of the other. The intention or effect in this case at least is not, I think, to diminish either, though the method

[5] Graham, *The Truth of War*, 63–5.

has something in common with mock-heroic—Homeric echoes in Fielding, for example. This type of double awareness is modern, indeed it might be called modernist, and it is by no means either simply satirical at the expense of the modern instance, or simply a cheeky puncturing of an inflated precursor.[6] Here the point is simple and serious. If poetry cannot deal with the modern soldier's experience, what is it good for? And if it is to deal with that experience, it must change its language and its priorities, becoming perhaps a more brutal but a less singular voice, but being still (as it was for Keats) a way of telling the truth.

The second moment I want to examine comes from the seventh and penultimate stanza of 'Exposure', and here I am particularly interested in the transition between the preceding stanza and this one, a change of gear which has always struck me, and I suspect strikes most readers, as jarring and unsatisfactory. After five stanzas evoking the misery of trench warfare in winter, the sixth embarked on the very familiar theme of the soldier's nostalgic dream of home, which is the generic pastoral of war writing. But for the soldiers of 'Exposure' there is no such welcome home as awaited Thomas Campbell's soldier in his dream. Here are stanzas six, seven, and eight:

> Slowly our ghosts drag home: glimpsing the sunk fires, glozed
> With crusted dark-red jewels; crickets jingle there;
> For hours the innocent mice rejoice: the house is theirs;
> Shutters and doors, all closed: on us the doors are closed,—
> We turn back to our dying.
>
> Since we believe not otherwise can kind fires burn;
> Nor ever suns smile true on child, or field, or fruit.
> For God's invincible spring our love is made afraid;
> Therefore, not loath, we lie out here; therefore were born,
> For love of God seems dying.
>
> Tonight, this frost will fasten on this mud and us,
> Shrivelling many hands, puckering foreheads crisp.
> The burying-party, picks and shovels in shaking grasp,
> Pause over half-known faces. All their eyes are ice,
> But nothing happens.

[6] For example: are Leopold Bloom, Odysseus, Joyce, or Homer diminished or enhanced by their textual congress?

In these circumstances it is not surprising that the soldiers' fantasy is focused on an image of warmth: the image itself is also the focus, even the icon, of family domesticity. Hearth means home. This one comes equipped with crickets, which have made their way into the poem from *The Cricket on the Hearth*, one of Dickens's Christmas books, which were among Owen's favourite childhood reading. The story, which ends happily with one of Dickens's most uncompromisingly jovial dramatizations of domestic harmony and fun, is subtitled 'A Fairy Tale of Home', and in it crickets are described as 'the Spirits of the Fireside and the Hearth',[7] the household gods of familial contentment. This imaginative escape of the soldiers' fantasy is to peace, to the past, to a child's world (and Owen's childhood reading) where the playful mice of the proverb are innocent and capable of rejoicing. It is a yearning back to the first world, the family. But only when the vision has formed does it become clear that it is glimpsed from outside—perhaps through a crack in those shutters—and that what seemed a Dickensian idyll is in fact a figure for alienation (equally Dickensian: the outsider, looking in). The dreamers—or are they actually ghosts, already dead?—cannot step back into that innocence: the doors are locked on them (by whom?). At the same time, the house is deserted, its fires sunken. Where is the family who should be there? Where, in the journalists' phrase, is the Nation at Home?

This gesture of the soldiers, in their painful reaching back to home, receives no answer. No communication, no community. There is no one at home. The house is locked and unpeopled, the fire is dying, and as Desmond Graham writes, 'Owen's poem comes to a dead end on the repetition of the word "closed".'[8] There can be no issue along this way. Return is impossible, so they 'turn back' to the activity (inactivity) of their dying at the end of the sixth stanza and then turn into the seventh, which is an attempt to justify or at least explain their predicament as if it were the result of a decision they ('we') have made. Why? Why doesn't 'Exposure' end with the sixth stanza, or move straight from the sixth to the eighth?

'Exposure' (like 'La Belle Dame Sans Merci', another of its intertexts) tells a story of betrayal. It evokes a world in which all systems have failed, a hell in which no action is possible but

[7] Dickens, *Christmas Books*, 183.

[8] Graham, *The Truth of War*, 64.

endurance, no history but duration, no sensation but pain, no knowledge but hopelessness. Although the poem's soldiers utter no complaint (and in his draft table of contents, Owen listed the motive of this poem simply as 'Description' (*CPF* 539)), they are almost completely unsupported by those systems of community and values, that culture which ought to be relied upon to give their suffering some meaning and their lives some hope. Now, at this point of the poem and for the moment, Owen was not prepared or was not able to be so uncompromising. The poem flinches, and accedes to an ideological pressure encoded in its own language (a pressure, that is, not from without, but from within) demanding a sort of right of reply. The poem's faltering, its temporary loss of nerve before its own appalling implications, is a moment of great interest and pathos, but the seventh stanza's attempt to rescue itself from these implications only tightens the knots.

It is a forlorn prospect indeed that this poem discloses—a dark, entropic, God-forsaken end-game of a world, from which energy, value, and life itself have all but completely leaked away. The official values (so to speak) of the communities in which Owen's language is formed, values on which 'we' in 'Exposure' might draw to make some sense of their experience or just to derive some comfort from it, these values are bankrupt. The beauties of the natural world and the transforming power of the imagination; the sustaining love and loyalty of people at home; a loving or at least sane providence, visible in its operations; the possibility of victory or at least of some kind of an end to the war—all these are wanting, and their failure leaves a gaping absence, a sort of vacuum which the sorry language of the seventh stanza rushes in to fill:

> Since we believe not otherwise can kind fires burn;
> Nor ever suns smile true on child, or field, or fruit.

The image and proximity of 'home . . . fires' from the previous stanza conjured up, for the beginning of the seventh stanza, a ready-made formula from the popular Ivor Novello song 'Keep the Home Fires Burning', a formula which came already primed with an appropriate emotion (sentimental, but stoical) and an explanation of what the war was about:

> Keep the Home Fires burning,
> While your hearts are yearning,

Though the lads are far away
They dream of home.

The cosy economics of the song's message to civilians—their job is to win the war: your job is to keep the home fires burning—provides a kind of answer to the question 'we' asked in the second stanza of Owen's poem, 'What are we doing here?' The answer is defending our loved ones at home who have not forgotten us. And this line seems to endorse that explanation; 'we' are willing to face death, it says, 'since we believe not otherwise can kind fires burn'. This is, as it were, the official position on the war of patriotism in its domestic and familial clothing, the patriotic rhetoric that speaks not about king and country but about hearth and home. And it is simply enough stated here, seemingly unembarrassed by the way it has been contradicted in advance by the previous stanza, in which the soldiers saw the home fires untended and dying. The home side has not carried out its very unexacting division of the war's labour. Where is the family that should be keeping faith with the soldiers, watching the kind fire? Are they asleep, like the disciples in Gethsemane who had not the strength to watch through the agony of Christ as he prepared to die for them? Have they gone away? Are they perhaps dead? Dominic Hibberd suggests they 'have locked up and gone to bed oblivious' (*OTP* 168). How can 'we believe' we suffer exposure to keep the fires alight, when we have already seen that the fires of home are dying? The language of home can only muster a weak counter-attack here, supported in the next line by a rounding-up of some of the usual icons of English pastoral imagery: 'Nor ever suns smile true on child, or field, or fruit.'

A similar pattern of unconvincing defence is to be seen when religious discourse comes overtly into the poem:

For God's invincible spring our love is made afraid;
Therefore, not loath, we lie out here; therefore were born,
For love of God seems dying.

Some kind of spiritual regeneration (mindful perhaps of Rupert Brooke's *1914* sonnet sequence, or Owen's own sonnet of the same title) is naturalized here and guaranteed in a Romantic metaphor, for if winter has come then spring cannot fail to be close behind. Yet the declared invincibility of God's spring is immediately undermined by doubt: 'our love is made afraid' for it.

Here the official position of the Anglican Church on the war, that to fight for one's country was a Christian action,[9] is accepted by the soldiers, who say they will not shirk doing their duty as Christians. The grim disclaimer—'not loath, we lie out here'—may also have a meaning in family discourse, as a dialogic response to or defence against the imagined reproach of 'you have made your bed and you must lie on it,' a 'depressing proverb' which, according to the poet's brother Harold, their father 'was very fond of using' (*JFO* 2. 221). However, it is immediately clear that acceptance of this duty is seen not as a matter of obeying and serving God, but of replacing him. The divine love that used to ensure the renewal of life is now itself enfeebled and not adequate to the task. An assertion of faith in the invincibility of God the Father has stumbled into a declaration of no confidence, for the love of God 'seems', in a line over which Owen hesitated for some time (*CPF* 365–70) 'dying'. The love of God, like the fire of home, is almost spent; and if the soldiers are like Christ now, going about their father's business—and here too Church discourse and Owen family politics flow together—they are blasphemous and soon to be orphaned redeemers. If, on the other hand, the grammatically ambiguous 'love of God' is read as referring not to the Creator's love of the world but to humankind's love of the Creator, the results are the same. The contract between God and men has been breached, the lines are down, men must shift for themselves in the dark and can expect no help from above. The grammatical ambiguity has a lot to say about still unresolved tensions in Owen's uneasy relations with his father and with the Church.

This most overtly ideological of the poem's stanzas is full of anxiety and contradiction. Its attempt to justify and explain exposes the difficulty of justification and explanation. The stanza which begins with the proposition 'we believe' contains the proposition 'we lie', and ends with something close to a denial of the first tenet of the Creed. The contradictions and confusions are open to inspection, yet there is no satire here of the sort Owen elsewhere brings to bear on the war's apologists, nor are there signals of irony of a knowing kind.

[9] In November 1915, however, the Archbishop of Canterbury drew the line at Lord Derby's request that the clergy should appeal from their pulpits for men to enlist (Barrow, *The Flesh is Weak*, 185).

The presence of these confusions might be traced not to this or that deliberate rhetorical intention of the author, but to their presence already in the tissue of the language his culture made available to him, so that the strain under which Wilfred Owen's style comes in this stanza may be read as a symptom of the crisis being suffered in 1917–18—the testing to destruction of beliefs, loyalties, institutions—in the society of which it is one of the voices. Sometimes in Owen's stylistic choices we can observe a paradigm of the tensions within and between the communities whose voices can be heard in his writing, as here, where the imagery of a popular music-hall song, a symbol of Romantic millenarianism, and an unorthodox version of the Evangelical theology of substitutionary atonement are assembled to contend with the voice (borrowing accents from the family malcontent and the rebellious agnostic) of an embittering and estranging experience, the experience of front-line troops, in a deadlocked winter campaign, in a war which had long since begun to seem endless. And no doubt these features are not brought into contact deliberately, in the way that the opening phrase had deliberately confronted the Nightingale ode. They are the fingerprints of history as it lives in the language, testimony to contentions going on in the larger community to which Owen belonged, and imprinted within its language, out of which the poem is made.

The essays which follow will be an investigation of the social determinations of a poet's creativity. Admittedly the idea of determination and the idea of creativity consort uneasily together, but although creativity is mysterious I do not think it is ineffable. And although discourse is certainly socially determined, the utterance is always unique. In thinking about Owen's writing as both a product and an enactment of his relations with the important social institutions of his experience, the challenge has been to do justice to both the individual poet and the communal institutions, both the creativity and the discourses. The ideas of language and society on which this study of Wilfred Owen's English rests are themselves shaped, of course, by other voices, particularly by Bakhtinian notions of social discourse, heteroglossia, and intertextuality. But such ideas need not lead to the kind of austere dismissal of creativity formulated by Vološinov, who declared that 'What is usually called "creative individuality" is nothing but the expression of a particular person's basic, firmly grounded, and consistent line of social orientation.'[10] This gives the impression of assuming that social orientation is simple and stable, whereas experience would suggest that it is complex and always shifting, each utterance indeed being an adjustment of orientation towards one or more than one group, institution, even culture. An individual's social orientation is created and trimmed continuously by their speech and writing.

By their 'everyday acts of meaning,' says Halliday, 'people act out the social structure, affirming their own statuses and roles, and establishing and transmitting the shared systems of value and of knowledge.'[11] This idea of discourse as drama is a fruitful one; but certainly for the complex acts of meaning that are literary discourse it is necessary to add that language can question, as well as affirm, social statuses and roles and established values. Wilfred Owen did not choose to be a speaker and writer of English. He did not choose his family, the kind of education he received at school, the Church into which he was baptized, or the arbiters of taste from whom he learned to read and write poetry. His enlistment in the army was not a free choice either. His immersion in these institutions, and their role in forming his own language, were largely matters outside his control. But his feelings about them shifted, sometimes violently, as his individuality developed (itself polyphonic, a development through the social), and so did what he had to say about them in the language they had given him. To say that his writing is the creature of the discourses is not to say that it is their prisoner. There is to be found in his writing a playing—a playing-up, even a playing-off—of roles, themes, and values from different discourses, though it is to be sure a serious, even a tragic play. And in the negotiations, combinations, and conflict which this play produces, the author's creativity is at work, and it is unique. Only one middle-class subaltern, with an Evangelical upbringing and a taste for Keats and Shelley, wrote the letters and poems of Wilfred Owen. If his social orientation determined his style, as it did, it has to be acknowledged that that social orientation—acted upon by so many changing loyalties and revulsions—was a needle that was never still.

[10] Vološinov, *Marxism and the Philosophy of Language*, 93. Though it is often attributed to Bakhtin, the translators of this work suggest that its author should continue to be identified as Vološinov 'since it has not been conclusively proved otherwise' (Vološinov, p. xi).

[11] Halliday, *Language as Social Semiotic*, 2.

I

Family

2

Hearth and Home

> Everything that pertains to me enters my consciousness, beginning with my name, from the external world through the mouths of others (my mother, and so forth), with their intonation, in their emotional and value-assigning tonality. I realize myself initially through others: from them I receive words, forms, and tonalities for the formation of my initial idea of myself . . . Just as the body is formed initially in the mother's womb (body), a person's consciousness awakens wrapped in another's consciousness. Only later does one begin to be subsumed by neutral words and categories, that is, one is defined as a person irrespective of *I* and *other*.
>
> (M. M. Bakhtin, *Speech Genres*, 1986.)

Two remarkable sources are the site from which the language used in the Owen family has to be pieced together. The *Collected Letters* of 1967 has 673 items, of which 631 are letters to members of the poet's immediate family (554 of these are addressed to his mother). And the three volumes of *Journey from Obscurity* tell the story of the family as remembered, in his sixties, by Wilfred Owen's brother Harold. There are grounds for being suspicious of Harold's memory at some points.[1] I draw heavily on both the *Collected Letters* and on *Journey from Obscurity*, without claiming that either gives an objectively accurate picture of the Owen family, supposing such a thing were possible. They are items, not receptacles, of evidence.

Wilfred Owen's parents began their marriage under the same roof as her father, at Plas Wilmot, Oswestry, leaving that house to set up on their own after the old man's death in 1897. Harold Owen chooses this moment to begin his *Journey from Obscurity: Memoirs of the Owen Family*—his first chapter is entitled 'Leaving

[1] See Dominic Hibberd's scepticism about Harold Owen as family historian (*OTP* 199–201) and Simcox, *Wilfred Owen*, 1–3.

Plas Wilmot 1897'—four years after the birth of the eldest child, Wilfred, and six months before his own birth. Harold Owen's story begins here, with a retreat, a defeat, a losing of paradise:

> Plas Wilmot, on the outskirts of Oswestry, was the house of my mother's family: it was here that she herself had been born; it was from this house that she went to be married to my father. It was back to this house that she returned as the bride of my father . . . It was to this house, four years after the birth of Wilfred, that my father and mother had to say goodbye and leave all its warm pleasantness, its gardens, fields, and coach-houses, and the gracious way of living that had seemed to them, although their own lives were not at all affluent, to wrap about them, not only a warm happiness, but a sense of security. (*JFO* I. I.)

Harold Owen himself never lived at Plas Wilmot, and there is no way of telling how much, if anything, Wilfred Owen actually remembered of the house where he spent his first four years. But the meaning of the place, as part of the family's imagery, a myth, speaks through the rather conventional language of Harold Owen's imaginative recreation—the maternal site, 'the house of my mother's family', pastoral, sheltering, privileged, nurturing, and warm, but all too soon to be lost, and so one of the first constructions of an image-complex, and an idea, that appears with variations through Wilfred's own writings.

> So sharply defined was the division between those first years and the times that were to follow after leaving Plas Wilmot, that this short era became—as such things will in families—a legend, much talked of amongst ourselves, and most likely, as legends do, gaining enhancement with the years. Wilfred built up, by questioning my mother and father, a romantic picture of these early years, which became an actual part of his experience. As a family we all in our different ways tried to hold on to the imagery of these more generous times, as something which was a part of ourselves and to which we belonged. (*JFO* I. 12.)

If this theme of a lost domain, an almost obligatory convention of the drama of the romantic memory, can be construed at the same time as a womb-like space and a Garden of Eden, it also has in this case a class meaning, indicated by Harold Owen's allusions to a 'gracious way of living' and to 'more generous times'. The years of Wilfred Owen's infancy and early childhood—incidentally the crucial years of his language acquisition—were spent in the spacious and genteel surroundings of 'this largeish country house . . . with its large gardens, orchards, and paddocks' (*JFO* I. 9), a place of nature certainly, but of nature as property. The place was a guarantee as well as the visible form of social rank. But it was also an economic millstone. The grandfather had been in financial difficulties for years, and upon his death Plas Wilmot, its grounds, and most of its contents had to be sold immediately to pay his debts. Tom and Susan Owen and their two elder children started their own independent life as a family 'houseless . . . and with little except a large quantity of linen and silver' (*JFO* I. 16). Important consequences flow from this early reversal of fortune. Leaving the house of the mother's family meant stepping out or down from a sanctuary of graciousness into a sometimes squalid and altogether less fine world where, it was important for them to remember, they did not really belong. The linen and silver salvaged from Plas Wilmot were a relic of that lost but desirable world, a reminder of what home ought to have meant.

A few months after the sale of Plas Wilmot, Harold Owen was born in what he characterizes as 'a small, rather shabby little house in a long street of other mean little houses', on the fringe of Shrewsbury. The family had slipped yet further by the time Colin Owen, the fourth and last child, was born 'in the smelly July heat of a slum area of the vast seaport of Birkenhead' (*JFO* I. 13). Accommodation was difficult, and they had to move house several times. One of Harold Owen's earliest memories was of one of their arrivals in a new home—a word that was taking on less gracious meanings for the family.

My next moments of consciousness came to me as I was being unloaded from a dark and dripping cab onto a black wet pavement in a dank and evil-smelling street outside one of a long line of small, squalid, and near-slum dwellings. Our cab driver, who was terribly drunk, threw off our boxes and bags, somehow regained his seat and drove away, cursing and singing very loudly. When we had groped our way into the house, and my father had made a light, the floor and walls of the passage and the small room leading from it appeared to surge and lift as if covered with a simmering treacle. We had been welcomed to our new home by armies of black beetles. The disgusting crunching as our feet pressed down on these horrible insects, the loathsome smell of the air in the house, following as it did the nightmarish crossing from Ireland, with the wet cold blackness of my arrival in the slummy street, was more than my small body could withstand. I was immediately and very violently sick, and the last impression I had before consciousness once again drifted away from me, was of Wilfred's protective rush towards me, the feel of his arms around me, and the fearful sight of the racing heaving black mass of beetles converging upon what I had thrown up. (*JFO* 1. 19.)

This is quite a way from the secure and comfortable backgrounds of the officer poets with whom Owen is usually grouped. But it also explains why it was important to keep alive that myth of the warm, clean, fine place they had come from, 'the house of my mother's family' to which they properly belonged. Plas Wilmot was gone. But Wilfred, aged fifteen, told his mother that she was 'home (personified)' (*CL* 46) and was later to write to her, in 1917, 'By your love, O Mother, O Home, I am protected from Fatigue of life and the keen spiritual Cold' (*CL* 424).

Although Harold describes them as living still 'on the borderline of poverty' in 1913 (*JFO* 2. 192), it was the years in Birkenhead, which came to an end when they moved back to Shrewsbury early in 1907, shortly before Wilfred Owen's fourteenth birthday, which were rendered most difficult and anxious by ill health and 'the perpetual struggle against poverty and the threat of debt' (*JFO* 1. 21). The children, badly nourished though never actually having to go hungry, developed 'a pinched and rickety look', like 'the hundreds of other children living around us who somehow survived in the dirty little houses and smelly streets': but at the same time they were 'in a rather worse plight than these others in the neighbourhood, as, unlike them, we were not indigenous to it and were never allowed to become a part of the district' (*JFO* 1. 21).

They had almost no friends, and held themselves aloof from their neighbours, refusing to admit that their circumstances had really altered. There is a linguistic as well as a social dimension to the family's self-imposed ostracism. The neighbours and their children were not to be associated with, or spoken to.

The immediate effect was that every emergence by us children from the house held a hunted and nightmarish quality, as of course we were the natural prey of the stevedores' and dock labourers' children, who lay in wait for us and with jeers and screams of laughter set upon us, egged on with ribald encouragement by the slatternly women who seemed perpetually to fill the dark doorways. Another consequence was that we had to go far afield, and get right away from our own neighbourhood, before we could feel safe to start playing. (*JFO* 1. 21–2.)

And after the Owens moved to Shrewsbury they took with them this notion of the family as existing within a linguistic and social *cordon sanitaire*. Harold Owen remembers that it was an ordeal for the Owen children to pass through the neighbouring working-class streets, risking 'verbal abuse' from 'the rough, ill-reared, untrained children who swarmed around them'.

The real trouble was the women who were an idle, blowsy, dirty, and vindictively resentful collection who neither troubled nor cared about seeing that their unwanted children were kept clean either in mind, habits, or bodies, so that the children were not just healthily grubby but visibly unclean, always scabrous and dirty. It was no uncommon thing for us to see tiny toddling children not only soaked with their own urine but smeared about with their own excreta. These women would stand in their doorways and as we passed hurl extraordinarily foul invective and horribly disgusting references to our anatomical parts and what they would do to them if we were their children. It must have been the sight of our well-kept little suits and stockings and clean bodies that exasperated them to such fury and brought forth the streams of senseless abuse. Occasionally, one more infuriated than the rest would lunge out at us with some vague idea of fouling our cleanness, but they were grossly cumbersome and very slow. I was always quick and became clever at avoiding these encounters. (*JFO* I. 180.)

Here then is a powerful image of the family, in its cleanness, being threatened with contamination by actual and verbal foulness ('extraordinarily foul invective . . . horribly disgusting references . . . streams of senseless abuse'). Sixty years on, Harold Owen's feeling of revulsion is still very strong indeed; yet, perhaps because he had absorbed 'some urchin craft', become streetwise in Birkenhead, he was more capable of braving this ordeal, he remembers, than his fastidious elder brother.

Wilfred Owen in his writing would often return to questions of purity and impurity. Years later, when he was assistant to the vicar at Dunsden, he found himself counselling a village boy who was afflicted by swearing.

His chief difficulty is *Language*. So is mine. In *his* case, *Bad* Language though one would never have thought it. He hates it, and he cannot escape it.

In *my* case, *Fine* Language, to yield wholly to the glamours of which would be accounted 'of this world' by those who aver they are not of this world.

I love it, and I cannot escape it. (*CL* 123.)

There was bad and impure language, and there was good and pure language. Good language was spoken inside the family and must be protected from contamination by its surroundings. The best language, Fine Language, was poetry, which was the glamorous language of beauty. Bad Language was dirty and ugly. After he had been for a month in the trenches, Owen complained in a letter to his mother about 'the universal pervasion of *Ugliness*', which for him included 'foul language and nothing but foul, even from one's own mouth' (*CL* 431).

Here conditions did not seem propitious for purifying the dialect of the tribe; and it was only when that aesthetic of purity was revised and overturned that a new space was to be created for the war poems, a poetry of impurity, much of which *is* bad language—dirty, bloody, blasphemous, insulting. But to reach that point would mean a transgression of those boundaries of manners, sympathy, and knowledge, within whose somewhat stifling limits the family had experienced itself and language had been learned. It was to mean, in a different sense now, leaving the propriety, safety, and cleanness of Plas Wilmot, 'the house of my mother's family'.

3
Fathers and Sons

Harold Owen says he first attempted a straight biography of his brother, but soon discovered that 'by separating him from the rest of us I found I was beginning to distort the picture' (*JFO* 3. p. ix). My own study takes its cue from Harold Owen's belief—the foundation on which *Journey from Obscurity* is raised—that the poet could best be represented and understood in the company and the history of his family.

It was a family constituted in loss and retrenchment, with a memory (or at least a myth) of better days, but economically and socially anxious. At the time of his marriage in 1891, Tom Owen was a clerk in the Oswestry branch of the Great Western Railway, earning a salary of seventy-five pounds a year (*JFO* 1. 9). In 1900 when his fourth child was born, his salary was still less than a hundred pounds a year. As the children grew up, Harold Owen reports, the family was 'short of money all the time' (*JFO* 2. 192). Tom Owen's job with the railway offered the most unsatisfying of prospects, but he could not take the risk of giving it up to look for something better.

> It was this I saw that made everything so difficult; except during moments like this [an outing to church] when our general appearance of comfortable well-being helped us all to forget and smothered a little the everlasting anxiety my father and mother had to contend with, we were in a state of perpetually living on the borderline of poverty. It was the constant necessity for make-believe . . . which made my mother lethargic to ambition for us and my father hopelessly despondent about any projects which were not immediately wage-earning. (*JFO* 2. 192.)

They were absolutely dependent for survival on the barely adequate salary Tom Owen earned from the job he clung to from 1891 until his retirement, in a career which, says Harold Owen, he not only disliked intensely but knew that he would go on detesting more and more as the years went on (*JFO* 1. 14).

The portrait of Tom Owen which emerges from *Journey from*

Obscurity is of an unhappy man. And Tom Owen's disappointment, his sense of entrapment, was made deeper and more poignant by an idea or myth of its own past conditional, the promise made and then broken of a fulfilling, adventurous, and romantic life.

Tom Owen had had little formal education, and went to work as a junior clerk on the railways at the age of fifteen. When he first met Susan Shaw he was earning a few shillings a week and, having few expectations, turned like so many of his class and age to the great Victorian romance of empire. He managed to secure a post with the Indian Peninsular Railway in Bombay, signed on as an ordinary seaman in the ship *Benalder*, 1330 tons, and worked his passage to India. The story of that voyage, embellished in frequent retellings, became Tom Owen's own myth of the possibility of the heroic. It had its own holy relic.

This seaman's 'Certificate of discharge' he was to treasure all his life: it was, I know, one of his most prized possessions. During the dullness of his later life it became emblematic of early adventure, and a signal mark to him of real manhood . . . he had at least once been a sailor before the mast. (*JFO* 1. 5.)

While he was in Bombay, Tom Owen and Susan Shaw wrote to each other twice or three times a week.

He did well during these four years in Bombay, and had established himself so securely that his prospects for a career that might have been spectacular, and anyway would have been of real importance, with work that he liked, were very bright indeed. The lure of a foreign land and, especially to him, the glamour of the East, did much to reconcile him for his disappointment in not being embarked upon a seagoing career. (*JFO* 1. 6.)

It was Tom's intention to bring his fiancée out to India to join him to be married. But he fell dangerously ill, and, after some months in hospital, was recommended for leave in England. At the same time a letter arrived from England: 'Susan wrote that her mother was dying, her brother Edward was drinking and gambling more wildly than ever, and her father was worried about his financial affairs. There could be no question of her joining Tom in Bombay, so he immediately decided to return to England (*WO* 7). He arrived to find that Mrs Shaw had died, Susan's drunkard brother had disappeared (to America, as they later discovered), and her father's finances were dangerously drained by her brother's gambling excesses and the cost of keeping up Plas Wilmot. Harold Owen reports:

The dissolute behaviour and now the final loss of Edward caused my grandfather disappointment and bitter sorrow, which in his ageing grief he found difficult to support. In his frailty, he welcomed the youthful strength of my father; his one wish and hope now seemed to be that his favourite daughter, Susan, should marry Tom Owen as soon as possible, and that they should set up house with him in Plas Wilmot. If this happened he felt that happiness might return to him for his few remaining years, and that my father would help somehow to straighten out the financial difficulties. My father decided that in all these circumstances a return to India was quite impossible, and that the only thing to do was to marry his Susan and reconcile himself to employment in England. To secure this end, he hid his disappointment and, abandoning all hope of an adventurous career in the East, obtained for himself a post with an English railway; and with a salary of only seventy-five pounds a year, married my mother. (*JFO* 1. 8–9.)

These melancholy declensions speak the language of duty and renunciation: 'a return . . . quite impossible . . . reconcile himself . . . hid his disappointment . . . abandoning all hope . . . married my mother'. The seeds of Tom Owen's difficult and sad relations with his family are sown here. Did they appreciate what he had given up for them, and in any case, how could they ever compensate him? The presence of this brooding disappointment and reproach, sometimes expressing itself in irritability or just glumness, but always an immanent presence even when silent, was one of the facts of the household environment in which the Owen children grew up. It is the voice of a man who has put himself in a cage for the sake of others. And while a great deal of Wilfred Owen's poetry is a protest against the hostile demands of that voice—in other words, language against the father—it is sometimes also an echo of that voice, speaking in the father's own tones of disappointment, reproach, anger, resignation.

You could trace this important ambivalence by following the complicated history of sacrifice as a topic with a family meaning. Harold Owen remembers that it was a word often heard in this hard-pressed household. Tom Owen's touchiness was, like his seaman's certificate of discharge, a constant reminder of his own sacrifice (though one made willingly) in entering the marriage and subsequent family obligations. Here is a scenario which will also be found in the poetry of his son: the sense of colourful, romantic possibilities which have to be renounced; a sacrifice in youth, of youth, undertaken for the security of others who sometimes seem neither to appreciate nor deserve it, and at a cost which Wilfred Owen would articulate as 'fields half-sown' in 'Futility' and, in 'Strange Meeting', 'the undone years, the hopelessness'.

Sacrifice is one of the principal topoi of Owen's war poetry, but it had been in the repertoire of family discourse from the beginning. It makes an interesting appearance in Harold Owen's account of being taken by his father to look at Wilfred's school, the Birkenhead Institute. As they walked along, Tom Owen told Harold that it was possible that he too might one day be allowed to enter this great school, provided he showed a little more aptitude and worked very hard (*JFO* i. 31).

> It was while walking down the hill that ran alongside the main building that my father, still holding me by the hand, commenced to deliver his peroration . . . I was to learn many years later that [his] diffident shyness was so great a handicap that when he had occasion to talk seriously, it was only by previously rehearsing what he wished to say over and over again that he was able to express anything at all, and then, of course, it came out with the pre-thought-out effect of a speech. It was in this stilted way that he delivered his ideas to me while we were walking around the school, the main theme being the difficulty of affording the fees which sending me to school would entail, and that to do so he and my mother, if they decided to give me this start in life—I was only six or seven years old—would have to make large sacrifices. The impact of this word on my small mind caused it to fill with an imagination of Isaac stretched out and bound to a slab on the mountain-side, with his father standing over him all ready to plunge a long and gleaming knife into him. My father, continuing his peroration, told me that of course I must do my best to emulate the brilliance of Wilfred . . . I gathered from all this that . . . everything now depended upon my own efforts. If these were insufficient, then I might embarrass if not disgrace Wilfred and the rest of the family. Should this happen, I would be placed in the Free Board School and after the allotted period there I would be put out into the world and left to devise my own existence. This horrifying picture froze my small heart, and the horrid word sacrifice my father still kept using kept alive the vision of Isaac lying bound below the dazzling knife; but this was now being replaced by another one of myself standing alone in an unfriendly world with nothing to eat and nowhere to go. (*JFO* i. 32–3.)

It is certainly possible that Harold Owen's memory had been supplied retrospectively with an image from the poem 'The Parable of the Old Man and the Young', or that Harold may have told this story to his brother, thus providing a trigger for the poem. More likely, I think, is that both visions derive from a book illustration or a church window or simply from a memorable reading of the Bible story. Tom Owen's forbidding manner, even at moments like this when he was actually doing a kindness to his favourite child, and his real expressive ineptitude, do the rest and ensure the already inviting identification; the image of the patriarch is laid over the image of the father. Tom Owen, speaking of his own self-sacrifice (and the mother's), gets cast in the role of executioner: the supposed beneficiary of the sacrifice suspects that he himself is the intended victim. There is confusion here, in the six-year-old Harold's comic misunderstanding of what he is being told, but it is at the same time a serious confusion, stirred up by a real ambivalence, and this ambivalence makes itself felt when this topos returns, as it does importantly, in Wilfred Owen's war writings. The topos of sacrifice, familiar to him from an early age from family discourse and supplied of course with Christian imagery, does not enter the war writings in fixed form but as something plastic and capable of variation, an object of serious play in which roles may be split, exchanged, reversed, doubled; the youthful figure being sometimes the sacrificial victim of a man, or of a woman, or of himself, and sometimes the executioner, and sometimes the voice which, in the poem at least, tries but fails to intercede in the murderous business.

> When lo! an Angel called him out of heaven,
> Saying, Lay not thy hand upon the lad,
> Neither do anything to him, thy son.
> Behold! Caught in the thicket by its horns,
> A Ram. Offer the Ram of Pride instead.
>
> But the old man would not so, but slew his son,
> And half the seed of Europe, one by one.

Harold Owen's account of his father is a good deal more sympathetic than Wilfred's; and the father's sacrifices on behalf of his children were indeed many, and lifelong. Rather pathetically, he never gave up his bitterly avowed determination that as soon as the children were all safe and settled, 'he would take himself out of this dull and dreary England and go back to the Far East or voyage round the world' (*JFO* 1. 249). But meanwhile, every penny and every pleasure had to be scrimped. I think it is a factor of great importance in the linguistic formation of Wilfred Owen that circumstances determined that the voice of his father should have been so often the voice of denial and even antagonism. While a psychoanalytical account might be given of this, it has to do with both their socio-economic circumstances and the politics of the family. Susan Owen was indulgent, at least to Wilfred her favourite, and in any case usually took the view that God would provide. In the meantime it was always her wish to advance the family socially and let the money look after itself, while Tom Owen's instinctive plan was always to remain socially stationary and try to save money for a margin of security (*JFO* 1. 39). He was a chronic worrier and a pessimist, and his familiar refrain was that what his children wanted was beyond the family's means.

Journey from Obscurity suggests that the gloomy speech about sacrifice made to the young Harold was fairly typical of the paternal voice. It was Tom Owen's function and certainly his misfortune to be the voice of caution, the disappointment of hopes, the assertion of bleak necessity. When first Wilfred, with his mother's encouragement, became bookish and vague, and then Harold showed symptoms of talent in drawing and painting, Tom Owen became increasingly restive, having no illusions about the earning potential of either inclination.

He became hard and brittle, and seemed to have lost any real interest in either of us, showing us only his reserved and angry side, and seeming over-anxious that somehow we should be got away from home and be earning our own livings—in what manner he did not at that time seem to care. (*JFO* 2. 25.)

This hostility over the question of his sons' education and careers was in the case of Wilfred an extension of difficulties caused by Susan Owen's passionate possessiveness of her eldest and favourite child, which, according to Harold Owen, 'embittered my father's love for him and explained the cold and antagonistic attitude he took, not so much towards Wilfred, but more towards his future ambitions and endeavours' (*JFO* 1. 53). Harold Owen recalls a conversation with Wilfred in 1910:

He often seemed—although he was actually talking to me—to be really talking at himself, chafing at the restrictions that he felt beset him. He had exaggerated in his own mind the conviction that my father was opposed to him. In muttered asides, he unburdened himself to me about the way he felt father persistently discredited his desire for learning, and how much he knew he despised all mental ability and was concerned only with physical prowess. (*JFO* 1. 196.)

What begins to emerge here is a discursive polarization, a male and female voice within the field of what Harold Owen calls the 'gravitation' (*JFO* 1. 77) of the family. On one hand is Tom Owen, with his own all too brief manly adventure behind him, showing a brusque and even philistine contempt for intellect, sensibility, and the arts, a voice impatient and uncomfortable with language but urging to duty and action. On the other hand is the feminine voice, Susan Owen's, who 'rarely disagreed with Wilfred and never reprimanded him' (*JFO* 1. 24), the voice of delicacy, sensibility, refinement, and enervation. The feminine is the voice of feeling, of long private confidences at home or by letter, a voice which is never raised. The masculine seems the voice of insensibility, easily moved to anger, but its flashes of tenderness 'unbelievably rare' (*JFO* 1. 162), the voice of a small, violent man, irritable and impatient with his family and especially with his eldest son (given to the irritating formula 'Take more exercise, my boy, and play some games' (*JFO* 2. 265, 3. 61)), having a nervous, blustering manner, 'inclined to intersperse his conversation with platitudes and clichés' (*JFO* 2. 56), wretchedly inadequate with the language of feeling. 'How extraordinarily badly my father always managed to present his thoughts and feelings! Words were a trap and a menace to him, so ineptly did they interpret his emotions' (*JFO* 2. 57).

If Tom Owen was incapable of the language of feeling in its accents of solicitude, concern, and love, Susan Owen in contrast spoke it fluently in her dialogue with her eldest son, who responded, as the letters show, with a sometimes cloying stream of lover-like language. The masculine is the voice of authority (and is usually heard as such in the war poetry), but the feminine has a power of its own. Masculine and feminine discourse gather to themselves certain clusters of imagery, most obviously human imagery, the men and women who populate the poems; but also the masculine discourse seems to come with exposure, instruments, threatening weather, the sun, whereas feminine discourse is often attended by imagery of enclosure, warmth, flowers, sleep. 'Exposure' is the poem where the contention of these discourses is most obvious in its imagery, and this might be the time to point out that, in that poem as elsewhere, it is not simply a matter of favouring one discourse over the other. The two voices and their attendant themes, as they appear in Wilfred Owen's writing, can be seen as reproducing discursive configurations he had learned about in his first school of language, the family.

Paternal discourse is the mode of those dangerous fathers, compounds of age and authority, so frequently pictured in Owen's war poems and his letters as being responsible for the war and the suffering it causes. It is to be heard in the unyielding pride of the filicide Abram in 'The Parable of the Old Man and the Young', and in the vexation of God the Father in 'Soldier's Dream', who loses his temper and pulls rank on his compassionate Son, answering the healing 'smile' and 'tears' of 'kind' Jesus with a brusque command that the war should go on.

> And there were no more bombs, of ours or Theirs,
> Not even an old flint-lock, not even a pikel.
> But God was vexed, and gave all power to Michael;
> And when I woke he'd seen to our repairs.

In 'Greater Love', 'God seems not to care', and in 'Exposure', 'love of God seems dying', while in one early draft of 'Apologia pro Poemate Meo' Owen wrote and then cancelled 'For God forgets Christ then, and blesses murder' (*CPF* 279). These are all occasions when the heavy father of the family scenario merges with the bloody-minded patriarch of the Old Testament. And while they are all scenes when the language of denial and death freezes out the word of love, and I have been trying to show that the word of love is the word of the mother, the situation is further complicated when you remember Owen knew that moments like these would be deeply disturbing to his pious Evangelical mother when she read them: so the modality of these moments becomes quite dramatic. Another variation of paternal callousness is specifically dialogized in 'S.I.W.', the poem about a suicide in the trenches, which starts:

Patting goodbye, doubtless they told the lad
He'd always show the Hun a brave man's face;
Father would sooner him dead than in disgrace,—
Was proud to see him going, aye, and glad.

and later:

'Death sooner than dishonour, that's the style!'
So Father said.

The same bluff insensibility is stretched further to parody in the stilted and mendacious voice of the politician's speech reported in 'Smile, Smile, Smile':

Peace would do wrong to our undying dead,—
The sons we offered might regret they died
If we got nothing lasting in their stead.
We must be solidly indemnified.

'The sons we offered': the style is the style of Horatio Bottomley, but the voice is the voice of the patriarch with the knife.

As I have suggested, fatherly discourse does not adhere only to human images. The sun in 'Futility' is a procreative power which has awakened life on the planet, and has roused the young soldier to consciousness and warmth through the days of his youth. Surely it has not given him life only to connive at his murder.

Move him into the sun—
Gently its touch awoke him once,
At home, whispering of fields half-sown.
Always it woke him, even in France,
Until this morning and this snow.
If anything might rouse him now
The kind old sun will know.

Think how it wakes the seeds—
Woke once the clays of a cold star.
Are limbs, so dear achieved, are sides
Full-nerved, still warm, too hard to stir?
Was it for this the clay grew tall?
—O what made fatuous sunbeams toil
To break earth's sleep at all?

The sun is first characterized—or cajoled, flattered, appealed to—in motherly language. Moving the soldier into the sun is an attempt to move the sun to compassion and so to help, to move the soldier into the role of the sun's son and so into its sphere of protection and responsibility. A scenario is offered in which the helpless soldier plays the part of the child and the sun is implored to protect and restore him. The sun is prompted with maternal discourse, which is the speech of protection, quiet, private, and loving, contained in the nursing constructions 'move him . . . awoke him . . . woke him . . . rouse him', and in 'gently', 'home' (the mother-word *par excellence*), 'whispering', and 'kind'. The procreative sun is wooed to behave like a mother, but it does not accept the invitation. It will not take the part. It remains unmoved, and will not stir itself to perform an act of love which should surely be within its life-giving and life-preserving powers. It withholds the saving word of love, and responds to its child's needs with a silence which is eloquent of damnation. Nothing then remains but a gesture of belittlement and insult: if the generative sun has failed to be 'moved' in a motherly way, it can only be dismissed with contempt as 'fatuous' sunbeams whose fatherhood is a bad joke. The sun is past it. After his clumsy and laboured impregnation of the earth, he shrinks to impotence, suffering a failure of power which is a failure of feeling. The doubleness of sun/son, paternal and filial, adds I think an entirely characteristic uneasiness to what is, overtly, a pattern of mutual contraversion or turning against.

Harold Owen incidentally reports Wilfred's fondness, in family quarrels, for 'invective and the sardonic reply' (*JFO* I. 24). Another recourse was certainly complaint. On home leave in November 1917 Owen wrote to Siegfried Sassoon: 'I am spending happy enough days with my Mother, but I can't get sociable with my Father without going back on myself over ten years of thought' (*CL* 506). And in July 1918, when a medical board pronounced him recovered from his shellshock neurasthenia and now 'G.S.' (fit for General Service) again and therefore liable to be posted back to France, he reported at the end of a letter to Osbert Sitwell: 'I very much look forward to meeting you again, and if it be in Scarborough the pleasure will be that of all snatched joys . . . This is the beginning of decadence. As is proved by my Father's message on hearing I was G.S.: "gratified to know you are normal again"' (*CL* 562).

'Normal' meant fit to kill and be killed, a status on which it was certainly bizarre for a father to congratulate his son. A paternal discourse with the accent of these values was deadly indeed. And there is certainly a grim satisfaction in Owen's describing such an attitude as 'the beginning of decadence', 'decadence' being a word of such connotations, since the spectacular career of Oscar Wilde, as to make it a particularly sweet (if private) revenge on the father who had often complained of his son's unhealthy antipathy to manly pursuits.

It was not, of course, that the accidents of family circumstance gave Wilfred Owen exclusive rights on the figure of the heavy father, as his correspondent Osbert Sitwell could very well testify. The unfeeling or even criminally negligent father-figure was in any case already one of the conventions of the 'trench poetry' which Owen quite deliberately set out to write from August 1917 onwards, with the example of Siegfried Sassoon before him. That callous voice was one that had been dramatized in several of the poems in Sassoon's *The Old Huntsman*, for example, in 'They' and 'Arms and the Man'. There are obvious reasons why old men in general get a very bad press in the literature of the Great War. A large-scale and protracted war, which made of younger able-bodied men a community literally apart, with overwhelming grounds for a communal self-consciousness, had a far-reaching and profound effect on relations between the generations (and, of course, between the sexes). Owen's writing articulates an important moment in the history of fatherhood and filiality, and of the modern family in general. In this context it is of some interest that when on 6 January 1921 the *Times Literary Supplement*—that anonymous Olympian voice of authority—passed judgement on Sassoon's edition of Owen's *Poems* (1920), it felt the need to deliver a patriarchal reprimand. The reviewer was Basil de Selincourt. 'And what shall we say finally of the strange intimation that the old men sacrifice the young? As if any father would not face death sooner than send his boy to face it for him.'[1] But it would be a simplification to suppose that in Owen the voice of the father is the voice of the villain, and the voice of the son that of the victim. This does happen in some of the poems, but more often we have to look not at a fixed tableau, but a space in which different voices contend and collaborate, infiltrate or impersonate each other.

In 'The Dead-Beat', a poem written soon after Owen's first

[1] *Times Literary Supplement*, 6 Jan. 1921: in Hibberd, (ed.) *Poetry of the First World War*, 56.

meeting with Sassoon at Craiglockhart, and an exercise 'in Sassoon's style' as he told his cousin Leslie Gunston (*CL* 485), the first-personal subject, who is an officer, speaks in jeering and brutal terms of the soldier in his charge:

He dropped,—more sullenly than wearily,
Lay stupid like a cod, heavy like meat,
And none of us could kick him to his feet;
—Just blinked at my revolver, blearily;
—Didn't appear to know a war was on,
Or see the blasted trench at which he stared.
'I'll do 'em in,' he whined. 'If this hand's spared,
I'll murder them, I will.'
                                        A low voice said,
'It's Blighty, p'raps, he sees; his pluck's all gone,
Dreaming of all the valiant, that *aren't* dead:
Bold uncles, smiling ministerially;
Maybe his brave young wife, getting her fun
In some new home, improved materially.
It's not these stiffs have crazed him; nor the Hun.'

We sent him down at last, out of the way.
Unwounded;—stout lad, too, before that strafe.
Malingering? Stretcher-bearers winked, 'Not half!'

Next day I heard the Doc's well-whiskied laugh:
'That scum you sent last night soon died. Hooray!'

There are four voices here, three reported speeches folded into that of the unsympathetic or at least uncomprehending officer narrator. It is a quiet voice, separated from and enclosed by this language of authoritative insensibility, which is assigned the counterpoint, digging beneath ('sapping', to use the appropriate terminology) the first voice's assumptions about courage, loyalty, and proper behaviour. But the officer who duly reports it seems not really to hear this 'low voice', or not to care, as he sends the dead-beat down 'out of the way', at the same time dismissing him from consideration (and from compassion) as a malingerer. It is a disowning or disinheritance; his officer and his doctor feel no obligation to him; the dead-beat is no longer one of 'us'; so much the better if he and his whining are out of the way for good. And so the officer's voice finishes the poem blended with the voice of his class ally, his fellow-professional the doctor, this emotionally anaesthetized familiar who is glad to have seen the last of that disorderly threat to discipline, that 'scum' or, in earlier versions, 'that dirt' (*CPF* 299–300).

Owen wrote this in hospital where he himself, to all appearance unwounded, was being treated as a neurasthenia case. Furthermore, he had (or believed he had) been accused of cowardice by his commanding officer (*OTP* 76–7). The point here is that as a junior officer with a job to do (like the officer in 'The Dead-Beat', who *acts* correctly when faced with a serious and perhaps capital breach of discipline), Owen found himself in a painful though ultimately creative way discursively compromised, the miscast juvenile lead having to speak or rather improvise the lines of the heavy father or master of discipline.

There is another instance in the poem 'Inspection', which begins dramatically with an officer's speech in an early version, '"Rear rank one pace step back, March!" | I shouted; and inspected the Platoon' (*CPF* 240), but though this was dropped, the new beginning retains some of the blurting brusqueness that recalls the doctor's monosyllabic brutality in 'The Dead-Beat':

> 'You! What d'you mean by this?' I rapped.
> 'You dare come on parade like this?'
> 'Please, sir, it's—' ''Old yer mouth,' the sergeant snapped.
> 'I takes 'is name, sir?'—'Please, and then dismiss.'
>
> Some days 'confined to camp' he got,
> For being 'dirty on parade'.
> He told me, afterwards, the damnèd spot
> Was blood, his own. 'Well, blood is dirt,' I said.
>
> 'Blood's dirt,' he laughed, looking away,
> Far off to where his wound had bled
> And almost merged for ever into clay.
> 'The world is washing out its stains,' he said.
> 'It doesn't like our cheeks so red:
> Young blood's its great objection.
> But when we're duly white-washed, being dead,
> The race will bear Field-Marshal God's inspection.'

'Inspection' was originally entitled 'Dirt', which is what the soldier is treated like, his attempt to enter into dialogue refused as officer and sergeant settle his fate between them. And when finally he *is* allowed to speak, the officer's blustering retort—'"Well, blood is dirt," I said'—is left to resonate in the empty space of the stanza division, ample time for the speaker to consider the implications of the words he has just spoken, the part he is playing, spokesman and executor (lieutenant, 'place-holder') for the power of the heaviest father of them all.

But here too the officer is only doing his job, interpreting the requirements of army discipline to the men under his command, mediating orders which travel right down the hierarchy from, theoretically, Field-Marshal God at the top to the wretched offender at the bottom of the heap. But if the officer is the medium for that discourse of power, his utterance here—the poem of which he is the controlling speaker—also mediates the protest of the victim as it struggles upwards, mediates rather than reports. For whose language does the final speech speak? Though enclosed in quotation marks, it cannot pretend to be a verbatim report or a naturalistic representation of the kind of speech you might hear in the ranks. Compare it with the sergeant's lines. Its diction is not exactly pure—indeed it is a plea against purity—but it belongs to the very elaborated code of poetry none the less, and in that code it will bear inspection for prosody, correctly aligned rhymes, metaphor, even conceit. It is a discursive encounter, the officer *I* improvising a performance of the speech act of the man, in what amounts to a collaborative utterance; it is the voice of *us*, the pronominal antagonists of the first line ('"You! . . ." I rapped') now at the end merged into a first person plural ('when we're duly whitewashed, being dead').

In the institutional context of this encounter, the controlling speaker's position of intermediacy is a function of his military rank, which places him at the contact point between the officer corps and the other ranks. But intermediacy was a territory entirely familiar to Wilfred Owen, a place in which he was, if never comfortable, at least always at home. He occupies a sort of dialectal no man's land within the major discursive fields which make up his linguistic formation: the institutional languages of family (the eldest son, who used to refer to his sister and brothers as 'the children' (*JFO* 1. 89)); of the Church (as junior lay assistant, and agnostic quasi-candidate for holy orders); of the army (Second Lieutenant—a position which is already intermediate—but also 'conscientious objector with a very seared conscience' (*CL* 460)); and finally of poetry itself (as the idolater of Keatsian luxuriance, who didn't want, he said, to write 'anything to which a soldier would say "No Compris!"' (*CPF* 193)). This intermediacy or doubleness shows itself, I believe, in discursive features that include dialogue itself, and code-merging, paradox, and irony (and perhaps even, in the uncomfortable doubling of his prosodic signature, pararhyme). It seems this pattern, like everything else, begins at home, in the network of family relations.

4
Brothers in Arms

I have already dwelt on the fact that this was a family which grew up on its own resources. The children were largely insulated from others of their own age except for friends of their mother's choosing, 'usually clergymen's or other religiously active persons' offspring, often spotty and always dull,' Harold Owen remembered; 'we did not like them very much' (*JFO* 1. 223). The Owen children played no organized games, and were encouraged to find and improvise their own entertainment (*JFO* 1. 222). Tom Owen was out at work for long hours each day, and Susan Owen, especially after the birth of her fourth and youngest child, Colin, was often ill and sometimes bedridden, so that the daughter Mary, herself 'frightfully delicate', was 'all the same constantly active over the household chores and with concern for the comfort and well-being of [her] mother' and indeed Mary was to develop an 'obsessive devotion' to Susan Owen, and never married or left home (*JFO* 3. 46).

These circumstances left the boys a good deal together, first Wilfred and Harold, and later Wilfred, Harold, and Colin.

During the period which foreran my going to sea a remarkable companionship did exist between Colin and myself—so much so that we shared not only our time but our every possession . . . We were never antagonistic in spirit; the slight superficial hostility which, unbidden, seemed to creep between Wilfred and me never came between us . . . This in itself is unimportant except to throw into relief the really too mature unsociability and lack of co-operation which was so evident in Wilfred at that time, so that in spite of his very deep love for the small Colin and his affection for me, companionship from him—in its more recognised form—was unknown to us, and during the occasions when we did all three go out together while enjoying each other's company, we never even remotely made a trio. In many ways it was as if he was a third parent and, like a parent, unpredictable. Some days he would join in with our high spirits, sometimes overreaching us in gaiety, but mostly he would ignore our frivolity and disapprove of any natural levity. (*JFO* 1. 214–15.)

It was a tight family group and until 1911, when Wilfred went to Dunsden, the six of them remained as a complete family unit, always living together under the same roof. But within that unit, as Harold Owen recalls, ran a line of difference; the gap in age between Wilfred and the other children was very noticeable and came to be accepted as the demarcation between him as the eldest and responsible child, and the other three as the small children. This, in Harold Owen's memory,

> very often threw undue responsibility—for so young a boy—upon Wilfred, and did account in great measure for his early gravity, and made him mature far beyond his years. My mother encouraged this, indeed with her indifferent health she had little choice, which meant that in the beginning Wilfred was very often in sole charge of us three. This established an early bond between her and Wilfred, and had the tendency to separate Wilfred further from us three. It was also, I think, the beginning of a fixed feeling in Wilfred's own mind that he really belonged to and shared the responsibility of the parental side. (*JFO* 1. 23.)

The junior elder took his responsibilities as 'third parent' seriously, especially when delegated to shepherd his charges on expeditions. *Journey from Obscurity* describes him making some reins out of thin clothes-line, and driving Harold and Mary tandem or abreast through the (to them) dangerous streets of Birkenhead. 'In the evenings he used them to help to drag us through the last streets on our journey home, for sometimes Mary and I were so exhausted that he could only get us home by dragging us with the lines and by endless coaxing and persuasion' (*JFO* 1. 26). Here, fifteen years before the Somme, we can see Owen unwittingly in training for the shepherding function of the infantry officer; and indeed the incident of 'Dulce et Decorum Est'—with its feelings of anguished responsibility—is perhaps oddly prefigured in an occasion when Wilfred ('by some fluky mischance') tied the rein to Harold's arm with a slip-knot, causing agonizing pain to Harold, and anxiety and shame to Wilfred (*JFO* 1. 25–6). But it is not particular incidents, but a pattern, that I want to draw attention to, the pattern, very early established and encouraged by his mother, of being with but above his siblings, particularly his two brothers.

Wilfred was it seems devoted but not particularly close to his younger brother Colin, and apt to speak of him with an idealization (sometimes teasing and sometimes sentimental) which also makes its way into that considerable proportion of his poems, including some war poems, devoted to the beauty of boys. With Harold Owen the relationship was at once closer and much more difficult and important; for it was in this brotherhood above all that the early social and discursive moves were learned, and these two boys were each other's first and formative school of friendship and enmity.

The generational division drawn between Wilfred and his brothers is also an isogloss. By general consent, Harold was cast from an early age as 'the rather commonplace child of the family', because he was clumsy and inarticulate. This relegation, he says, 'often not only made me childishly angry but set up a harmless sort of hostility between Wilfred and me, the effect of which was to make me exaggerate my own Philistinism and thereby to accentuate Wilfred's disbelief in me' (*JFO* 1. 24). In the dialogues between the brothers that *Journey from Obscurity* recreates, Harold's difficulties with expressing himself (or at least with getting a hearing) most often result in sullen silences on his part, punctuated by the occasional petulant outburst. Wilfred on the other hand (if Harold Owen's account is anything like accurate) habitually addressed his brother in an appallingly patronizing and elaborate manner, a 'ponderous form of address' which 'often included some stuffy quotations' and plenty of 'long words and heavy-sounding phrases', which used to make Harold cross, but which he retrospectively excused as being used by Wilfred 'in the form of an exercise in order to accustom himself to the sound and feel of unusual words' (*JFO* 1. 94). Like his quasi-parental status and obviously related to it, these habits of speech were established very early on, and most of these brotherly utterances recreated in *Journey from Obscurity* are either monologic rehearsals of this kind, or 'slightly hectoring lectures' (*JFO* 1. 184).

These exchanges are rarely on the level. The younger brother, as listener rather than interlocutor, is placed firmly in the stalls (or on the carpet), his function being to attend, which indeed he cannot choose but do, since he does not command the language to reply in kind. In any case he could not have anything of interest to say, in view of that lumpish insensibility of which he was always being reminded by 'Wilfred's jibes and assumption of my crass, unimaginative, stolid stupidity' (*JFO* 2. 7–8). Incidentally

Harold Owen also confesses with some dignity that the family was united in the opinion that he was very ugly.

As late as 1916, when Harold visited his brother at his army training camp, he had to submit to one of these 'dissertating spells' and another taste of the 'tutorial' or 'professorial' manner (*JFO* 3. 144). But things were changing. Harold Owen suggests that in the last years of Wilfred's life, 1916 to 1918, the relationship between the two brothers became close, confidential, loving, at last an equal relation of friends. Whatever the actual course of this brotherhood—and meetings between the two in wartime were of course very rare and very brief—it does seem that the time of his army service saw a change in the discursive scenario laid down in Wilfred's relation with Harold, which was an important paradigm for his relations with 'lads' junior to him.[1]

Wilfred Owen joined up with the romantically named Artists' Rifles but was commissioned into the unromantic Manchester Regiment, joining its 5th (Reserve) Battalion in camp in Surrey, in June of 1916. He reported in letters to his mother the complete unfamiliarity of this new world—'the country, the people, my dress, my duties, the dialect, the air, the food, everything'. Being with the Manchesters felt more foreign than being in France, and he wrote uneasily of feeling 'marooned on a Crag of Superiority in an ocean of Soldiers' (*CL* 395). He began to form some first impressions. 'The generality of men are hard-handed, hard-headed miners, dogged, loutish, ugly. (But I would trust them to advance under fire and to hold their trench;) blond, coarse, ungainly, strong, "unfatigueable", unlovely, Lancashire soldiers, Saxons to the bone' (*CL* 395). He soon settled into a pretty familiar mode with these Saxon Calibans, the mode of leading and instructing, and started to speak of parties under his command as 'my little Family' (*CL* 403, 414). They had not much charm—'my men are rather rough Lancashire Lads' (*CL* 397)—but were of course obedient and were a challenge to the teacher in him: he took a pride in his lectures to them, and meanwhile undertook to coach his young servant in French (*JFO* 3. 152), an office he had offered to perform for his

[1] 'Lads' in the army are not necessarily youthful, of course; but in the last years of the war the army was growing younger, for what might be called natural reasons. For 'lads', see Fussell, *The Great War and Modern Memory*, 282–99, and Martin Taylor's anthology *Lads: Love Poetry of the Trenches*.

brother Colin (*CL* 330) and indeed for all his family (*CL* 232). Some of the 'lads' under his command had already seen action (as he had not) and some had been wounded. 'It gives me a great deal of pain to speak severely to them, as now and again need is' (*CL* 398).

On his being posted 'overseas' to France at the very beginning of 1917, at first the same themes persist. But it was now more difficult to hold aloof from the earthiness of the Manchester soldiers and their language. He wrote in his second letter from France to his mother:

> After those two days, we were let down, gently, into the real thing, Mud.
> It has penetrated now into that Sanctuary my sleeping bag, and that holy of holies my pyjamas. For I sleep on a stone floor and the servant squashed mud on all my belongings; I suppose by way of baptism. We are 3 officers in this 'Room', the rest of the house is occupied by servants and the band; the roughest set of knaves I have ever been herded with. Even now their vile language is shaking the flimsy door between the rooms. (*CL* 422.)

This moment is a paradigm of its own. That flimsy door, which here does not succeed in shutting out either the dirt or the impure and ugly language from the poet's sanctuary, is related to the language and class barricades that provided shelter and identity in Shrewsbury, Birkenhead, and perhaps already in Oswestry; and it is also related to the lofty parapet of fine and elaborate language which so often had relegated Harold Owen to inferior discursive status and rendered him speechless. At this point, the flimsy door still holds: on the inside the junior parent in his sanctuary, and on the outside his loutish and unlovely charges, who speak a different and coarser language, the restricted code of stunted sensibility. While 'On all the officers' faces there is a harrassed look', the men 'are just as Bairnsfather has them—expressionless lumps' (*CL* 422). As yet no sense of irony, as far as I can see, links that word 'expressionless' with the information given a couple of sentences later in the letter that 'I censored hundreds of letters today.' Not everyone had free or equal access to expression; and in the last month of his life Owen became worried that his own letters were liable to the attention of the censor (*CL* 587). But by that time he had long come round to a revised view of the soldiers, as 'men, that have no skill | To speak of their distress, no, nor the will!'

('The Calls'), and of his own duty towards them. 'I came out in order to help these boys—directly by leading them as well as an officer can; indirectly, by watching their sufferings that I may speak of them as well as a pleader can. I have done the first' (*CL* 580).

The transgression of that barrier, social and linguistic, in the months that followed, is the decisive move in Owen's poetic career and therefore an important moment, or part of an important moment, for English poetry. It meant for him breaking the habits of a short lifetime, allowing traffic or dialogue across those discursive frontiers of difference which he had patrolled within the family, between the family and its neighbours, and between the fine language of his earlier notion of poetry and the bad language, the language of dirt, which in the army he came to know and speak. 'Apologia pro Poemate Meo' shows that the mud—'the real thing, Mud'—was a revelation to Owen, as that poem steps down from the Latin of its title,[2] to sink into 'the real thing'.

> I, too, saw God through mud,—
> The mud that cracked on cheeks when wretches smiled.

Dirt could make poetry and, in a satisfying reversal, poetry became a dirty word ('Above all, I am not concerned with Poetry'). And the inexpressive 'lads' at first so fastidiously separated from 'us' are now attended to, for

> I have perceived much beauty
> In the hoarse oaths that kept our courage straight;
> Heard music in the silentness of duty;
> Found peace where shell-storms spouted reddest spate.

Bad language and even 'silentness' have been discovered to be beautiful, and 'Faces that used to curse me' now recognized as 'Seraphic for an hour; though they were foul'. As in the extraordinary unrecognition scene in the last chapter of Barbusse's *Le Feu* (where the battlefield has become a quagmire in which exhausted French and exhausted Germans are indistinguishable) 'the

[2] Latin was the great shibboleth of the classically educated governing class, and it is not irrelevant to note that after Owen had chosen a title for this poem, 'Apologia pro Poema Mea', Siegfried Sassoon corrected his faulty Latin grammar. See *CPF* 125.

real thing, Mud' obliterates differences of status and provenance; dirt is a great leveller, a brotherhood.

And so the turning from an aloof and cultivated aesthetic of fine language and fine feeling to a committed realism and an impure diction ('the true poets must be truthful') is also something of a revision of the old family pattern. The ode 'Insensibility' begins with a dismissal of motherly language.

> Happy are men who yet before they are killed
> Can let their veins run cold.
> Whom no compassion fleers
> Or makes their feet
> Sore on the alleys cobbled with their brothers.
> The front line withers,
> But they are troops who fade, not flowers
> For poets' tearful fooling:
> Men, gaps for filling:
> Losses, who might have fought
> Longer; but no one bothers.

And it execrates patriarchal cruelty—'dullards whom no cannon stuns', hard-hearted and mean-minded and at a safe distance from the fighting—in its last stanza. It is the poem of brothers. And while it is certainly an apology to and for the 'expressionless lumps' of the January 1917 letter, it is possible to see in it too a kind of reparation to Harold Owen, the brother so often sneered at in the past for his insensibility.

> We wise, who with a thought besmirch
> Blood over all our soul,
> How should we see our task
> But through his blunt and lashless eyes?

But here too the situation is not a simple one. That 'tearful fooling' despised and rejected at the beginning of 'Insensibility' makes some kind of reappearance in the Tennysonian grandeurs of the end.

> By choice they made themselves immune
> To pity and whatever moans in man
> Before the last sea and the hapless stars;
> Whatever mourns when many leave these shores;
> Whatever shares
> The eternal reciprocity of tears.

Realism in Owen's poems is never unmixed, or not for long, with 'fine language', and 'Insensibility' is a highly literary production.[3] If Owen at last makes common cause with his inarticulate brothers, it is not to imitate their voice but to interpret it, mingling it with his own—to reciprocate (Latin *reciprocare*, to move backwards and forwards), as with the 'eternal reciprocity of tears'.

[3] It is, for one thing, in sophisticated dialogue with Wordsworth, Shelley, and the genre of the Romantic lyric; see *OTP* 137–40.

5
Susan

Susan Owen was the family's still point. It revolved around her. Leaving England for what was to be the last time, at the end of August 1918, her son Wilfred wrote to her: 'You are at home; yet you *are* home; | Your love is my home, and I cannot feel abroad' (*CL* 570). She represented not only the refuge of home, but a sort of home within home, an inner sanctuary. As the children grew up, their mother lived an increasingly indoor existence. If she ventured out, she usually had to be carefully wrapped up, and sometimes supported by her husband or sons or pushed in a Bath chair. Often she was bedridden. The house was her element and her domain. She was what her husband and children came back to. Wilfred's early gravitation to her—and his antipathy towards his robust and vigorous father—showed in his distaste for outdoor activity, a disinclination which his mother encouraged. 'In this way it was inevitable that he should be drawn to look to her to provide his quieter interests and this undoubtedly made him—in those early years—unduly dependent upon her' (*JFO* 1. 77).

Tom Owen liked to read aloud to his children and these readings were a special event in the household, a minor ritual; but Wilfred soon began to withdraw from them, gradually dissociating himself from the gathering, and preferring his mother to read to him alone (*JFO* 1. 60–1). Susan Owen was to tell Edmund Blunden that her reading to her son was the greatest pleasure of his childhood (*EB* 5). A pious woman but not well-educated, she encouraged him in his school-work and took great pride in his successes; meanwhile, through Bible-reading and praying together, she did her best to look after his soul. The two of them were united (he was to tell her) by an 'unconfinable sympathy' (*CL* 204). She encouraged him to confide in her: mother and son apart from the others would talk quietly together for hours on end, and it was to her that he confessed his ambition to become a poet.

She presided over his private life, for him at least the cherished domestic angel of the Victorian stereotype, providing refuge and reassurance to her favourite. Illness particularly guaranteed him her solicitude, which he courted and seems to have innocently relished as a quasi-erotic, quasi-aesthetic pleasure. Two years after the event, he looked back with a kind of excited nostalgia to an illness of early 1913.

It must be getting near the date of my pneumonia-time. I have only to think of you as you were then to me, and I immediately get into a kind of sweet anguish, an ecstasy, (very difficult to describe, but something like the effect of a great music). I hope you will think of those times, and let that memory bring its sheaves with it. (*CL* 322.)

In Owen's writing motherhood is often associated with sickroom nursing, as in the paradise imagined in 'A New Heaven' (written in 1916) where 'our own mothers' tears shall heal us whole', and more sourly in 'S.I.W.' the following year, in which a recruit's mother 'whimpered how she'd fret | Until he got a nice safe wound to nurse'. His letters to Susan Owen, especially those from Bordeaux, have a running sub-plot of symptoms and ailments, and these may be seen as the relatively trivial and personal precursors of the war poems to come, which would detail the sufferings of a generation in a plea for or a challenge to love. But if the letters court verbal nursing, they also administer it. Susan Owen is plied with earnest enquiries about the state of her health, and all sorts of advice about looking after herself, avoiding excitement, drinking tonics, and what not. For if Susan was a devoted nurse, she was also herself a permanent semi-invalid, and, in a letter written when he was fourteen, Wilfred told her he knew why: 'We went to Grandpa's to tea on Saturday. They were talking about you, how you didn't take enough fresh air [*several words illegible*] & denouncing your habits of staying in! They don't know that its your self-sacrifice for us, I do though' (*CL* 32). Self-sacrifice was a phrase she was 'inordinately fond' of using, Harold was to remember (*JFO* 1. 120). Here Wilfred has picked up the phrase, like a student eager to please, and returns it to her as a compliment. He is assuring her at once that son and mother speak the same language, and that he recognizes that self-sacrifice is a bond of love.

In July 1917 she was to travel to Edinburgh to visit Wilfred when he was a neurasthenia patient at the War Hospital at Craiglockhart.

The reunion of frail mother and damaged son was emotionally supercharged. He told her later he had only once experienced the same 'exultation' as when he had come unscathed through the barrage, four months before on the Somme battlefields.

> The 'only once' was when I saw you gliding up to me, veiled in azure, at the Caledonian [Hotel]. I thought you looked very very beautiful and well, through the veil, and especially on the night of the concert. But without the veil I saw better the supremer beauty of the ashes of all your Sacrifices: for Father, for me, and for all of us. (*CL* 479.)

This moment seems in Owen's mind to have snagged onto a memory of Keats's *The Fall of Hyperion*, where the veiled, beautiful, and wasted figure of Moneta is just such an object of worship, awe, and pity. But there is a mutuality of pathos about this reunion of mother and son, which has a bearing on his poems. If it was a pleasure to be cherished and nursed by his mother, there was satisfaction too in devotedly performing these services for her, in easing her burden and giving her comfort. It had often been the responsibility of the eldest child to minister to his mother when she was unwell, to look after her and keep her company, and to see that the younger children did not disturb her rest (*JFO* I. 23–5). This theme, in family discourse, of a mutual care and compassion was to provide some of the genetic material for the war writing, with its insistence on 'the eternal reciprocity of tears'.

The romantic poet that the young Owen wanted to be was a sort of professional invalid. In his early invocation 'To Poesy' he imagines himself groaning, stretching out his arms for help, begging a female muse to pity him. The poet as romantic dreamer was a fever of himself, his professional sensitivity a kind of illness; and yet (and this too came with the romantic inheritance) he was also himself a nurse, his words could soothe and heal his fellow-sufferers. In 'On My Songs', drafted early in 1913, the poet's words can fill the space and the function of the lost mother, for himself and others:

> 'Tis then I voice my own weird reveries:
> Low croonings of a motherless child, in gloom
> Singing his frightened self to sleep, are these.
> One night, if thou shouldst lie in this Sick Room,
> Dreading the Dark thou darest not illume,
> Listen; my voice may haply lend thee ease.

His poems to come (he wrote in 1915) would be a harvest of poppies, 'poppies wherewith many dreams may be fed, and many sores be medicined' (*CL* 322). This narcotic language goes back to Keats's 'Sleep and Poetry', but for Owen sleep is most strongly associated with the mother who was most emotionally vivid to him as either his nurse or his invalid charge. And if the poet is the victim in pain, a romantic sufferer, he is also at least potentially a quasi-maternal comforter, cleanser, and healer, gathering up and restoring his charges when the time of action is over—like the voice of Poesy in 'Science has looked', inviting the distraught child to nestle and suck his fill of joys; like sleep itself, which 'mothers' its children at nightfall in 'Disabled'; or like the speaker in 'Strange Meeting':

> Then, when much blood had clogged their chariot-wheels,
> I would go up and wash them from sweet wells,
> Even with truths that lie too deep for taint.
> I would have poured my spirit without stint.

In the circumstances this vocation, as nurse of the spirit, remains unfulfilled for the former aesthete who is the half-recognized 'strange friend' of this poem; but the last thing he can and does offer is sleep. Owen's intimacy with his mother was his first school of pity. It is pity that is the ruling passion of the war poetry, and with Susan Owen he experienced it from both sides, as subject and object. This rehearsal of the roles of patient and devoted nurse, the debtor and the creditor of self-sacrifice, was to have a shaping effect on Wilfred Owen's understanding of both what it meant to be a soldier and what it meant to be a poet. Once again, patterns of discourse first learned in the family were to become a way of construing and representing the unfamiliar experience of war.

It is, in any case, in this relationship that the source of his poetry is to be found. Susan Owen was the focus in the household of the intimate languages of prayer, private reading, and confession. Tom Owen inhabited a bustling world of action, but Susan's was the quieter realm of ideas, sensations, and feelings, and (as Harold Owen recalled grudgingly) of the arts:

> My mother was always accorded the right to sit in final judgement upon all matters of intellect and art, for had she not taken painting lessons as a girl and did not her still-life studies of cut and juicy melons, dripping with ropes of seeds, and her Highlandic shooting scenes of pointing pointers

and rigid setting setters even now adorn our sitting-room walls? My father, in his deep humility, never sought to usurp this untrue intellectual superiority but rather, out of his profound loyalty, built it up to secure her eminence. (*JFO* I. 269.)

Accomplishment in the arts for domestic consumption, such as piano-playing and water-colours, were for a woman of Susan Owen's upbringing the equivalent of sporting prowess for a young man. Her brother, indeed, had become an international footballer. And so her taste for painting and music, her delicacy and fastidiousness, her own beauty (of which Wilfred often reassured her), their private confidences, and her propensity to encourage and praise anything her favourite set his mind to—these were all factors associating her in her son's mind with artistic activity and the expression of feeling. And her faith, too, played a curious part in this. For though her own Evangelical upbringing had taught a suspicion of the arts as trivial and in some manifestations actually wicked, in the relatively repressed and tongue-tied household of Tom Owen it was in the area of religion—presided over by Susan Owen—that feelings could be fluently voiced, and emotionally exciting language tasted every day in the Bible, hymnal, and prayerbook. Wilfred Owen's own expressions of love for his mother never lost the accent of the Church.

His own artistic endeavours, then, were bound up with his feelings for Susan Owen, and she was from the start a sort of mascot or muse for his poetry. His earliest poetic ambitions seem to have stirred when he and his mother spent a holiday from Birkenhead alone together in a country cottage in the Cheshire hills near Broxton, in 1903 or 1904 (*WO* 27–8). But she was already established in the mind of her devoted child as a sort of totem of beauty, to whom tribute could be brought. On an earlier holiday in Ireland, he enjoyed picking flowers—for which she had an almost ritualistic passion—to strew thickly in the path where she would walk, or to arrange in profusion around the rooms. 'My mother usually rested during the afternoons, lying on an old-fashioned sofa, and Wilfred discovered a special enchantment by persuading her to feign sleep, then covering her completely with masses of the wild blossoms' (*JFO* I. 77–8).

She was to remain the only woman he knew intimately. His letters to her are love-letters. At nineteen, he wrote to her from Dunsden:

Now I *do* think you should have had yourself 'snapped' before you sent the camera. Oh how do I stand (yes and sit, lie, kneel & walk, too,) in need of some tangible caress from you.

Ink-slung ones are all very well in their way, and no one appreciates them more than I do; but my affections are physical as well as abstract—intensely so—and confound 'em for that, it shouldn't be so.

What if I feel 'strange' in your company after all this time apart; as I have done before after but a fortnight—surely that was the same *I* and the same you. (*CL* 137.)

He was careful to reassure her from time to time that she had no female rivals for his love. 'All women, without exception, *annoy* me,' he told her in a letter from France early in 1914: 'In fact I was never so absolutely free of "heart trouble" within these ten years past. This will no doubt give you immense satisfaction. But it *should* not . . . You ought not to discourage too hard' (*CL* 234). It was true: for better or worse, she was all women to him, and the love of women would continue to mean, for him, the love of his mother. I have no idea whether the closeness with Susan Owen was a determining factor, or a factor of any kind, in Wilfred Owen's homosexuality. Jonathan Cutbill has claimed that Owen was 'out as gay to his mother early on',[1] but he offers no evidence of this and I can find none. My guess is that he did not speak of his homosexuality to her, but nor did he disguise the homoeroticism of many of the poems he gave her to read. Meanwhile he did what he could to give her the reassurances she needed. The letters speak to her with an unfailing tenderness. 'Taking the world as it really is,' he wrote a few months before his death, 'not everybody of my years can boast (or as many would say, confess) that their Mother is absolute in their affections . . . Next time I come, we must have a very long and very deep talk' (*CL* 569).

For one function of that love, perhaps the most important, was the confidences they shared, in talk and in writing. He called her his 'dear willing Hearer' (*CL* 81). More than 80 per cent of his surviving letters are to her. His news was to be relayed to the rest of the family, he told her, but 'I always make my salutations to you alone because some things I say are not meet for an audience' (*CL* 260). 'I pine spiritually for need of talk with you, my dear Mother, I like no audience but either the whole world or You.

[1] Cutbill, 'The Truth Untold', 22.

There is no other, with enough sympathy or understanding' (*CL* 322). She was the young poet's ideal audience, 'either the whole world or You'. And yet because she was a woman and his mother, there were boundaries to his confessions. One aspect of his devotion to her had been a willingness, or obligation, to protect her from distress. She who had been a refuge and resort for her children had to be sheltered in her turn. Her upbringing seems to have left her profoundly ignorant of the world, to an extent hardly possible in today's conditions but perhaps not so uncommon among people of her time, place, class, and sex. She had not an inkling, for example—though Tom Owen must have known from his own youthful experience—of what the realities of life might be like for a boy sailor in the merchant marine; and inevitably Harold censored out the violences, the whore-houses, the heat and dirt and venereal diseases, in telling her of his life at sea.

> Gone at these times was her more natural critical disapproval and in its place had come a tender compliance, the yielding gentleness of which played happily on my growing ego, flattering my sense of adultness, until I became responsive and eager to please her and vie with her in gentle solicitude, and expanding thus would talk lengthily but speaking only of the things that I knew would please her; and as she sought to penetrate into my life at sea, I would—under the spell of her—unconsciously adapt my mood to hers, choosing carefully the things of which I spoke, holding back the ugliness, the brutality and the stark truth; for I knew now that into these dark tunnels of actuality she could not and did not wish to travel with me, preferring always to escape from what she did not wish to acknowledge. (*JFO* 3. 47–8.)

The passage is of particular interest as a tribute by the usually unsusceptible Harold to the effect of his mother's confidence. That '[vying] with her in gentle solicitude' is a feature of Wilfred's letters to her. She must be sheltered and not upset by brutalities and stark truths. Just before going into front-line trenches for the first time, at Bertrancourt in early January 1917, Wilfred received a letter from her. 'It seems wrong,' he wrote back immediately, 'that even your dear handwriting should come into such a Gehenna as this' (*CL* 424).

A year and a half later, on 30 July 1918, Wilfred Owen finished a poem in the Decadent manner which he entitled 'The Kind Ghosts':

She sleeps on soft, last breaths; but no ghost looms
Out of the stillness of her palace wall,
Her wall of boys on boys and dooms on dooms.

She dreams of golden gardens and sweet glooms,
Not marvelling why her roses never fall
Nor what red mouths were torn to make their blooms.

The shades keep down which well might roam her hall.
Quiet their blood lies in her crimson rooms
And she is not afraid of their footfall.

They move not from her tapestries, their pall,
Nor pace her terraces, their hecatombs,
Lest aught she be disturbed, or grieved at all.

'Presumably the sleeping figure is Britannia, representing the Nation at Home,' Dominic Hibberd suggests, and goes on to show how she is a variation of the image of the languid *femme fatale* beloved of poets of the Decadence (*OTP* 161). To these political and literary-historical dimensions of the figure we can add a gloss which brings her closer to a particular home. Trapped out in Gothic properties, this is a poem about the woman of the house, whose rest her boys are not allowed to disturb. This placid and indoor creature, a beauty sleeping among the miraculous flowers provided for her, remains unaware that her peace is guaranteed by the death and mutilation of others, the shades who well might (but they are too kind) haunt her like the ghosts of the soldiers shut out from home in 'Exposure'. But these shades not only shelter the lady of the house (her wall, like some ghastly trench parapet, is built of bodies), they even shelter her from the knowledge and the guilt of their sacrifice for her sake. For all her late-Romantic glamour it is clear who this woman is, resting indoors, with her blossoms provided, and her peace of mind protected, by boys.

Some further light can be shed on this mysterious but important poem by turning to one of Owen's favourite books, Ruskin's *Sesame and Lilies*, which he had recommended often to his sister Mary, most recently earlier in the month he wrote this poem (*CL* 556, 563). *Sesame and Lilies* contains two lectures, the second of which is called 'Of Queens' Gardens' and is addressed to women, and at one point accuses womankind of being responsible for all war and injustice—not as a result of any action of theirs, but because of their inaction.

There is no suffering, no injustice, no misery, in the earth, but the guilt of it lies with you. Men can bear the sight of it, but you should not be able to bear it. Men may tread it down without sympathy in their own struggle; but men are feeble in sympathy, and contracted in hope; it is you only who can feel the depths of pain, and conceive the way of its healing. Instead of trying to do this, you turn away from it; you shut yourselves within your park walls and garden gates; and you are content to know that there is beyond them a whole world in wilderness—a world of secrets which you dare not penetrate; and of suffering which you dare not conceive.[2]

Woman as mother—'the tender and delicate woman among you, with her child at her breast'—had the power to call a halt to 'the myriad-handed murder of multitudes': why did she not use it?

This is wonderful—oh, wonderful!—to see her, with every innocent feeling fresh within her, go out in the morning into her garden to play with the fringes of its guarded flowers, and lift their heads when they are drooping, with her happy smile upon her face, and no cloud upon her brow, because there is a little wall around her place of peace: and yet she knows, in her heart, if she would only look for its knowledge, that, outside of that little rose-covered wall, the wild grass, to the horizon, is torn up by the agony of men, and beat level by the drift of their life-blood.[3]

And the next sentence asks the reader to consider the meaning of 'our custom of strewing flowers before those whom we think most happy'. There are too many echoes here to be accidental. 'The Kind Ghosts', in claustrophobically compressing Ruskin's parable so that the wall itself and its roses contain (rather than just obscuring) the agonies of men, and in the added twist of the victims' gentle refusal to complain, is a powerful indictment; and the associations—indoors, sleep, flowers, the privileged and protected figure—hint strongly at the identity of the unnamed accused.

I think that what happened was this. A few days after the letter deploring that even her 'dear handwriting' should come into the Gehenna of the front line, Owen's baptism of fire plunged him into a horror for which nothing could have prepared him. His mother at home must at least be made to understand what had happened to him. 'I can see no reason for deceiving you about these last four days. I have suffered seventh hell' (*CL* 427). This letter goes on to relate the experience which would later become the basis for 'The Sentry':

[2] Ruskin, *Sesame and Lilies*, 136. [3] Ibid. 137–8.

My dug-out held 25 men tight packed. Water filled it to a depth of 1 or 2 feet, leaving say 4 feet of air.

One entrance had been blown in & blocked.

So far, the other remained.

The Germans knew we were staying there and decided we shouldn't.

Those fifty hours were the agony of my happy life.

Every ten minutes on Sunday afternoon seemed an hour.

I nearly broke down and let myself drown in the water that was now slowly rising over my knees.

Towards 6 o'clock, when, I suppose, you would be going to church, the shelling grew less intense and less accurate: so that I was mercifully helped to do my duty and crawl, wade, climb and flounder over No Man's Land to visit my other post. It took me half an hour to move about 150 yards.

I was chiefly annoyed by our own machine guns from behind. The seeng-seeng-seeng of the bullets reminded me of Mary's canary. On the whole I can support the canary better.

In the Platoon on my left the sentries over the dug-out were blown to nothing. One of these poor fellows was my first servant whom I rejected. If I had kept him he would have lived, for servants don't do Sentry Duty. I kept my own sentries half way down the stairs during the more terrific bombardment. In spite of this one lad was blown down and, I am afraid, blinded.

This was my only casualty. (*CL* 427–8.)

Only those two small domestic touches, the mother's church-going and the sister's canary—the merest glimpses of the terrible disparity between women at peace and men at war—give any hint of reproach. The next letter declares that the people of England need not hope: 'They must agitate. But they are not yet agitated even' (*CL* 429). And from this point onwards the letters mount an extraordinary and brilliant campaign to wring his mother's heart, to educate her in the realities and the pity of war. Though the letters are sometimes shocking they are never unkind, and they invariably address Susan Owen as an ally. They often scornfully lose patience with Tom Owen but never with her. She is courted and coaxed through a long course of lessons (Owen was an experienced teacher by the Berlitz direct method) towards the point where she will be able to speak in his language. His writing about war uses a language in large measure learned from home, but now in the letters his project is to reverse the dialogic gradient: the child must now teach the mother how to talk. 'Did you speak your mind at Alpenrose?' he asked her in July 1918, when she had visited her pro-war relatives, the Gunstons (*CL* 565). And in October, when he was back in France: 'I am glad you are finding courage to speak. In a previous letter you said you kept quiet. I was not proud of that' (*CL* 584–5).

The poems, however, are not so kind. In them can be found—in coded but legible form—reproach, anger, a desire to wound. In February 1917 in France he found time to draft a sonnet on the theme of 'Happiness'. One version begins:

> Ever again to breathe pure Happiness,
> The happiness our Mother gave us, boys? (*CPF* 229.)

He wrote to tell his mother that 'Happiness' was dedicated to her, but added cheerfully that the sentiment was 'all bilge' (*CL* 437). It was the last of his poems written directly for her; the next phase of his writing is primarily for the more critical inspection of Siegfried Sassoon. But though he told his mother in a letter in 1918 that he could no longer write a poem for her (*CL* 569), a number of the war poems address her obliquely, as subject if not as audience; and as the letters speak to her directly as an ally, these poems contain and conceal the anger, the reproach, the accusations of betrayal, which could not be admitted in the open, perhaps even to himself. The politics of the letters, in which an alliance of mother and son is so tenderly cultivated, are contradicted in the poems, for there the figure and the associated imagery of woman and mother can be treated with the same bitterness as is given to old men and fathers. What was repressed from the exchanges of family discourse turns up, disguised and admitted to the language of poetry.

The misogyny behind Owen's war poetry is not unique among writings about a war in which the most spectacular sufferings were borne almost exclusively by men. Sassoon's poems and Aldington's *Death of a Hero*, for example, furnish plenty of instances of soldiers' hostility towards women. Women in Owen stand accused of desertion, a dereliction of duty which is a failure of love. The mother in 'S.I.W.' sends her son off to his death in an ignorance almost as complete as that of the statue of the 'Virgin still immaculate', in 'Le Christianisme', still smiling and expecting to be worshipped when surrounded by the ruins of war. In 'The Send-Off', women collude with railway signals and a guard's lamp (father imagery, for the stationmaster's son) to despatch their soldiers to the front, decking them with flowers; but the send-off is a conspiracy, the men are being sent to be buried 'like wrongs hushed-up'. (Whose wrongs?) The flowers the women gave them were really funeral tributes, no one expects them to return home, and no loving celebration will greet the few survivors who may 'creep back, silent, to village wells, | Up half-known roads,' to a home which has become foreign and unwelcoming.

'The Send-Off' has obvious links in this respect with 'Exposure', where the spirits of the soldiers seek refuge, warmth, and safety from the exposed and painful (masculine, in Ruskinian terms) world of war. The deadly snow is metamorphosed into a littering of blossoms, a strong maternal association recalling the mother's body strewn with flowers, and enabling the transition to home in the soldiers' dream—but again there is no maternal welcome here. Home is deserted and empty of love, its fire dying (a female earth in the earlier apocalyptic sonnet 'The End' had confessed 'My fiery heart shrinks, aching'). The assurance of 'A New Heaven' that when the spirit returns home, 'our own mothers' tears shall heal us whole' has been lost. Even the matronly 'Hospital Barge', with her soft crooning voice, her gentle movements, and 'bulging amplitude', has no remedy for the agony of her wounded passenger. The cripple in 'Disabled' went to war for women, 'to please the giddy jilts': now he has lost his legs, women cannot bear to look at him, and the nurses (here, as in that other sickroom poem 'Conscious') seem to neglect their patient. His injury has taken away his manhood, so that now, like an infant, he needs to be put into bed: the person who should do this for him is not there.

> Now, he will spend a few sick years in institutes,
> And do what things the rules consider wise,
> And take whatever pity they may dole.
> Tonight he noticed how the women's eyes
> Passed from him to the strong men that were whole.
> How cold and late it is! Why don't they come
> And put him into bed? Why don't they come?

It is no good looking to women to provide for the men in the war poetry comfort, shelter, confidence and love. How could they? Self-sacrifice—which Susan Owen was inordinately fond of mentioning, and for which her son expressed his thanks to her—is an exclusively male prerogative now. The self-sacrifice of the mother has been succeeded and eclipsed by that of the son. 'Greater Love', an exercise in comparative anatomy which declares the face, body, voice, and heart of woman (those icons of romance) to be inferior to those of men, was at one stage to be entitled 'To any Woman' (*CPF* 339), and ends with an allusion to Christ's *noli me tangere* ('Woman, why weepest thou? . . . Touch me not; for I am not ascended to my Father' (John 21:15–17)).

> Heart, you were never hot
> Nor large, nor full like hearts made great with shot;
> And though your hand be pale,
> Paler are all which trail
> Your cross through flame and hail:
> Weep, you may weep, for you may touch them not.

The greater love was of a kind passing the love of women. And the tenderness of that greater love, of which the war poems and letters are full, manifests itself in the way the soldiers try to provide for each other ministrations that Owen had first had at the hands of his mother—protection, food and warmth, medical help, sleep; encouragement, pity, confidence, admiration; devotion, example, and faith. Feminine language in the war poems is spoken by men.

So while the letters go on insisting on the 'unconfinable sympathy' between them, Owen's poems begin to tell a different story, an oblique accusation of his mother's betrayal, her failure to prevent, understand, or provide remedy for what started to happen to her child on that Sunday afternoon in January 1917 at a time when she was going to church. There could be no direct and perhaps no really conscious reproach; but it is displaced onto women in general, coded into the imagery associated with Susan Owen, and voiced too in the poems' impieties, uncouth language and subject-matter, brutality and squalor and violence—features introduced to educate and 'warn' the gentle (and genteel) reader but also, surely, to punish.

He was moving beyond her, as years before he had moved beyond his father. A month before his death he wrote to tell Susan that he had been in battle again. 'Of whose blood lies yet crimson on my shoulder where his head was—and where so lately yours was—I must not now write' (*CL* 580). Something else had literally taken her place, demanding and offering a greater love. In recent weeks he had found some time to revise a poem probably begun at Scarborough in July, and drawing on his combat experience in the spring of 1917. It was 'Spring Offensive'.

Halted against the shade of a last hill
They fed, and eased of pack-loads, were at ease;
And leaning on the nearest chest or knees
Carelessly slept.
                But many there stood still
To face the stark blank sky beyond the ridge,
Knowing their feet had come to the end of the world.
Marvelling they stood, and watched the long grass swirled
By the May breeze, murmurous with wasp and midge;
And though the summer oozed into their veins
Like an injected drug for their bodies' pains,
Sharp on their souls hung the imminent ridge of grass,
Fearfully flashed the sky's mysterious glass.

Hour after hour they ponder the warm field
And the far valley behind, where buttercups
Had blessed with gold their slow boots coming up;
When even the little brambles would not yield
But clutched and clung to them like sorrowing arms.
They breathe like trees unstirred.

Till like a cold gust thrills the little word
At which each body and its soul begird
And tighten them for battle. No alarms
Of bugles, no high flags, no clamorous haste,—
Only a lift and flare of eyes that faced
The sun, like a friend with whom their love is done.
O larger shone that smile against the sun,—
Mightier than his whose bounty these have spurned.

So, soon they topped the hill, and raced together
Over an open stretch of herb and heather
Exposed. And instantly the whole sky burned
With fury against them; earth set sudden cups
In thousands for their blood; and the green slope
Chasmed and deepened sheer to infinite space.

Of them who running on that last high place
Breasted the surf of bullets, or went up
On the hot blast and fury of hell's upsurge,
Or plunged and fell away past this world's verge,
Some say God caught them even before they fell.

But what say such as from existence' brink
Ventured but drave too swift to sink,
The few who rushed in the body to enter hell,
And there out-fiending all its fiends and flames
With superhuman inhumanities,
Long-famous glories, immemorial shames—
And crawling slowly back, have by degrees
Regained cool peaceful air in wonder—
Why speak not they of comrades that went under?

It is a poem that could hardly seem more remote from concern with the family. And yet there is a strong familial subtext, and this poem about a terrible transition is not just anecdotal but autobiographical in the fullest sense: it can be read as the story of Wilfred Owen's life, a poem about growing up. The lovingly detailed valley, on which the soldiers eventually turn their backs, is saturated with childhood associations although ostensibly it is in the war zone.[4] Dominic Hibberd finds the landscape 'recognisably Salopian'; Owen had been letting his mind dwell on his native border country, and no doubt also remembering the steep heather-topped hill at Broxton (*OTP* 186). The boots yellowed with buttercups were remembered from a family walk back to Shrewsbury from Uffington church in 1907 (*JFO* 1. 176), but floral blessings may also carry a memory of the flowers and ferns he had heaped with equal devotion on his mother and on the homemade altar he used to set up in the sitting-room at Shrewsbury with her encouragement and help (*JFO* 1. 77–8, 151). For 'Spring Offensive' is full of parental imagery. The fatherly sun, at first kind but later estranged and hostile, is familiar from 'Futility'. But the gentle landscape where the soldiers rest is maternal. Though an outdoor scene, it is a sheltered valley, and they can be at their ease there, shielded from (but by the same token unable to see) what awaits them beyond the last hill. This hollow is a place for quiet domestic activity, intimate contact, eating and sleep. The air itself nurses them, relieving their pains, in a place of warmth and flowers. But this maternal safety is soon to be lost, as it was in 'Happiness', where 'No nestling place is left in bluebell bloom, | And the wide arms of trees have lost their scope.' An earlier draft of 'Happiness' declared: 'Happy are they

[4] It is an odd fact that the attack in the poem is set in May, but in May 1917 Owen was not in action. His long hospitalization with shell-shock began on the second of that month and his battalion went into action without him (*CL* 453).

who see not past the scope | Of mother-arms. I loosed them, broke the bond' (*CPF*, 228). The soldiers spurn the 'sorrowing arms' that would detain them. These men 'like trees' are soon to be uprooted; and Dominic Hibberd, again, is surely right to adduce the legend—the subject of Owen's fragment 'The Wrestlers'—of Antaeus, the warrior who could come to no harm unless he broke contact with the earth, his mother.

But the soldiers will not or cannot stay. 'So, soon they topped the hill': when the time comes they move over the ridge and plunge terribly into the world beyond, an act of violation that immediately sets them at enmity with the landscape that had nurtured them. Why? Desmond Graham, one of Owen's most sensitive readers, is interested in the way he offers at this point 'an extraordinary reduction of a term normally expressing logical continuation: "So, . . ." '.

'So' is almost a jaunty quickening of narrative pace leaving a pause between itself and what went before, the kind of space we leave when telling something we cannot explain and hopefully, but without true conviction continue, 'So . . .'. The single simple word leaves behind it all Owen will not write directly of here—the questions about the purpose of the action, the connections between whatever nature means to man and what these men are doing, the whole meaning of their being carried along in these events.[5]

That 'So', that Larkinesque shrug, is a naturalization. It says: it goes without saying. So one chapter of an autobiography succeeds another; so a child grows up, moves on, comes to grief; so family ties are stretched and broken. So men go to war, even when they know what they are doing.

In suggesting that 'Spring Offensive' is, among other things, a poem about growing up, I do not mean to trivialize it. On the contrary, its language enacts (like Keats's 'On sitting down to read King Lear once again') a growing up from idyll and romance to tragedy and epic, and at the same time a historical growing up from a certain nineteenth-century security ('Tennyson, it seems, was always a great child') to a century more brutal for the English ('So should I have been, but for Beaumont Hamel' (*CL* 482)). It is a poem of the modern world, in more than one sense a coming of age. Owen's family experience is built into many, perhaps

[5] Graham, *The Truth of War*, 75.

all, of his poems, but this does not restrict their scope, interest, or importance. The narrow world of family was for him both a rehearsal of wider adult experience and a means of understanding it: his relations with his father and mother were the school, and in some ways the paradigm, of his relations with institutions and traditions.

One factor in his growing up—though it is not possible to tell how much it was a cause and how much an effect—was his gravitation in 1917 to his new friend, Siegfried Sassoon. It was a *coup de foudre*. 'Know that since mid-September, when you still regarded me as a tiresome little knocker on your door, I held you as Keats + Elijah + my Colonel + my father-confessor + Amenophis IV in profile. What's that mathematically?' (*CL* 505). He should perhaps have added his mother to this list, for Siegfried Sassoon unwittingly took over from Susan Owen the important function of being the ideal audience and judge of Owen's work. Anyone who compares Owen's poetry written before and after August 1917 can see just how decisive and liberating for his creativity was this breaking of the magnetic field. Of course the history of his relations with his family does not end at this point, nor even with his death in November 1918. First his mother and later his brother sought to become the guardian and shaper of his memory, and to move him back into the orbit of the family as each of them understood it. That discursive struggle between the version of the mother and the version of the brother, a kind of Homeric tussle over the body of a fallen hero, is another story, with its own fascinations.

II

Church

6
Praying Together

In June 1911 Wilfred Owen visited the Revd Herbert Robson, vicar of Kidmore End in Oxfordshire, where his cousins the Gunstons lived. It was an informal interview that had been set up by Owen's mother, who had already discussed her son's future with this clergyman (*CL* 68). She wanted him to enter the Church; but the eighteen-year-old Wilfred wanted to try for a university scholarship, and for this he would need time and probably help to study. Mr Robson, who 'had prepared some notes to aid him in his discourse', took some time to come to the point of his advice, but finally revealed what he had in mind for the young man.

> It is:—to become the 'assistant' of some hardworked or studiously inclined parson, helping in parish work, correspondence etc. and being generally companionable to a lonely country-sequestered bachelor, such as himself. *Not* to himself actually, however, one reason being—that it would never do to have one *with relations in the parish*! He had heard, however, that 'Wiggan of Dunsden' wanted help in the parish this winter, and suggested applying to him, especially as his views coincide with ours. (*CL* 75.)

Wilfred Owen did indeed become assistant to the Revd Herbert Wigan at Dunsden near Reading, thus entering into a phase of crucial importance for his formation as a poet. Mr Robson knew Mrs Owen and her sister, and had been able to recommend Wigan 'especially as his views coincide with ours'. It was an important and perhaps decisive guarantee. This coincidence of views folded Mr Wigan in to the same community of belief and worship as the Owen family: he was a Church of England minister of Evangelical convictions and practice. Susan Owen had arranged that her son's first step into the adult world would take him from an Evangelical household to an Evangelical vicarage.

Fifteen months later and in a mood of nervous depression, he was to make his 'escape from this hotbed of religion', having, as he told his mother, 'murdered [his] false creed' (*CL* 157). But although he quit the household of Mr Wigan, and departed from anything Wigan would have recognized as Christian faith, those twenty formative years in an atmosphere of Evangelical seriousness and respectability had made Owen the man he was and they were shaping the writer he was to become. Jon Stallworthy and Dominic Hibberd both emphasize the great importance not only of the Dunsden episode but of the atmosphere at home which prepared Owen for it and propelled him to it: from the beginning of his life he was involved in the culture and language of Evangelical piety. To see what that involvement meant, and how vital an element it was in the formation of the poet's language, we must look first at the phenomenon of Evangelical Anglicanism and listen to some of its voices.

'In his early years he was very bookish and devout, belonging entirely to the nineteenth century' (*OTP* 1). And if Owen's early literary education was in a tradition that upholstered its approved writers in the reassuring fabric of orthodox Victorian tastes and values, his early devotion too was in a tradition that was above all respectable, and had mislaid, perhaps as the price of its very success, much of the vitality of its earlier heroic ages. Kenneth Hylson-Smith explains that Evangelicalism at the turn of the nineteenth century was in something of a trough; although still a large and growing constituency with literally worldwide ramifications, the movement was inclined to fits of disputatiousness and arrogance, a little unsure of itself but none the less hostile to fresh ideas.

> At the dawning of the twentieth century the Evangelicals were wrestling with a crisis of confidence. After the invigorating years of the eighteenth century, the crusading era of the Clapham Sect, and the pioneering social involvement of the mid-Victorian decades, the latter part of the nineteenth century can justifiably be viewed as a period of decline . . . [B]y the time Edward VII ascended the throne they were quite seriously dispirited, uncertain of their role within the church and in society, and without that cohesion, purposefulness and energy which had characterised them in the halcyon days of the past. It is significant that the leaders among them were almost exclusively of the older generation.[1]

Some of the awkwardness and irritability of this passage in Evangelical history certainly exacerbated Owen's difficulties at Dunsden and, as we shall see, at Keswick in 1912. But meanwhile, although the movement might not now have been in a particularly

[1] Hylson-Smith, *Evangelicals in the Church of England*, 227.

inspirational phase, there was plenty in its history to impress a bookish and devout youth. Evangelicalism had its beginnings in the 1730s, when George Whitefield and the Wesley brothers proclaimed their new-found faith and began preaching in what was rapidly to become a national crusade for revival, gathering an ever-expanding number of converts. Mistrusted by the established Church, and more often than not excluded from its pulpits, what had begun as a movement for renewal within the Church of England progressively assumed the characteristics of separation.[2] There were, however, devout and energetic clergymen who shared most of the Methodists' convictions but none the less preferred to remain and work within the Anglican communion: these became the nucleus of the Evangelical wing of the Church of England. It was a sometimes uneasy confederacy of nonconformist and Anglican Evangelicals that fixed its extraordinary stamp on the spiritual, cultural, and political life of the English nineteenth century.

The most signal achievement of Evangelicalism was certainly the emancipation movement, whose most eloquent leaders were Evangelicals, which finally triumphed in 1833. It was chiefly adherents of 'vital religion' who achieved the abolition first of the slave trade and then of slavery itself within the British Empire. Evangelical fervour also propelled the legislative campaigns of Shaftesbury and others in the cause of factory workers, and a great deal of Victorian philanthropy besides. Most of the famous humanitarian ventures of the nineteenth century had Evangelical inspiration and leadership. The movement later lost some of that generosity, which was eclipsed by its less attractive tendencies to bigotry, self-righteousness, anti-Catholic hysteria, and snobbery. But it had known what it was to be a religion of compassion, and a generous if paternalistic indignation; and while these are qualities of Owen's later poetry, it should also be noticed that much of his criticism of the establishment at Dunsden, naïvely though that criticism is sometimes expressed, is of the way that vigorous spirit of Evangelical charity had been betrayed or forgotten, leaving behind only a husk, or a corpse, in 'the Silence, the State, and the Stiffness' (*CL* 104) of the vicarage. I have no intention to try to reclaim Wilfred Owen for the Church. His loss of faith was in

[2] For the history and culture of Evangelicalism I have drawn on Bradley, Rosman, and Hylson-Smith.

some ways quite a straightforward matter and, once the Dunsden crisis was over, there are no signs that he ever regretted or doubted it; but from his earliest complaints about Mr Wigan, his attacks on the Church are mounted from the grounds that it is not Christian. And his later savage indignation at the war is sharpened by the gross contradiction between what the European nations were doing and the religion they all professed. He has the apostate's outrage at what he was to call 'the unchristian ways of Christendom' (*CL* 461).

If nineteenth-century Evangelicalism had an honourable history of work in alleviating suffering and pleading for the powerless, it also had eloquent critics, who anticipated the sort of complaints Owen was to make at Dunsden. Dickens satirized its hypocrisy; Mill thought it a cause of Victorian conformism and the deadening cult of respectability; Arnold regarded it as being responsible for the narrow philistinism and puritanism of the middle classes. Certainly, its high sense of duty and its air of self-righteousness were vital ingredients of the public and private life of the English nineteenth century. Ian Bradley's list of eminent Victorians who had an Evangelical upbringing and who remained profoundly influenced by it for the rest of their lives (even when many of them renounced its creed) includes many famous names. Among them are Lord Macaulay, Sir Robert Peel, W. E. Gladstone, John Henry Newman, Henry Manning, Archbishop Tait, Sir Henry Havelock, the legendary defender of Lucknow, General Gordon of Khartoum, George Gilbert Scott, the architect, the philosophers F. H. Bradley and T. H. Green, John Ruskin, Charles Kingsley, Samuel Butler, George Eliot, Wilkie Collins, Elizabeth Barrett Browning, and the Brontë sisters, not to mention Queen Victoria herself.[3] A list of only those children of Evangelical families who deserted the Evangelical fold would be impressive enough; and this is a point of some importance too. Those who were unable to retain the religious faith of their Evangelical parents commonly did not relinquish the ethical and moral beliefs that had gone with that faith, and the profound sense of duty it had imposed. Deserters like George Eliot took with them the seriousness of their Evangelical upbringing, as they took with them the habits of its language. There was apostasy, but not forgetting.

[3] Bradley, *The Call to Seriousness*, 13–14.

Evangelicalism is not a faith of great theological sophistication. To the common basis of Protestantism, Evangelicals added a fundamental belief in the necessity of individual repentance and conversion; the spirit of revival lay in the need to be, in the familiar modern phrase, born again. They preached salvation by faith in the atoning death of Christ. Men were 'bad, estranged from God and under his condemnation'.[4] Only through the substitutionary atonement of the Cross could they be saved from the evil, of Satanic origin, which was their birthright of original sin. C. H. Spurgeon, the great Victorian preacher, reminded his flock that the fear of the Lord was the beginning of wisdom:

> A man experiences a dreadful paralysis in his soul when he is really and thoroughly awakened . . . The dying man shudders at the awful future, and so does the awakened sinner. He dares not go forward; he is afraid, and a dreadful sound is in his ears. I, myself, before I obtained mercy, was afraid lest every tuft of grass I trod on should open before my feet and swallow me up . . . Thus does many a sinner feel the sorrows of death compass him.[5]

Guilt and fear were, for an Evangelical, the gateways to salvation.

They held that regeneration was not given to the individual in the sacrament of baptism; and this brought them into conflict with High Churchmen, who said that the Prayer Book declared that it was. Evangelicals were 'low': they mistrusted ritual, and laid supreme emphasis on preaching and on study of the Bible, in whose literal authority many of them were to entrench themselves in the long controversy about evolution. To be Evangelical meant to be imbued with the spirit of the gospels.[6] In church and at home, the Bible was paramount. 'There is no church in Christendom,' wrote the prominent Anglican Evangelical Griffith Thomas, 'which uses so much of Scripture or gives it so prominent a place in its services.'[7] From the 1850s onwards, biblical fundamentalism lost vital religion large numbers of its more sensitive adherents: the number was to include Wilfred Owen. Evangelicalism also did itself considerable harm by an increasingly strident anti-Catholicism, and the espousal by many of its adherents of the doctrine of the Second

[4] Rosman, *Evangelicals and Culture*, 11.

[5] Spurgeon, *Sermons*, 265–6.

[6] Owen was still sometimes attending Bible classes in Bordeaux in 1914, a year after the 'bust-up' at Dunsden (*CL* 227), though his motives may well have been mostly sociable and linguistic.

[7] W. H. Griffith Thomas, *The Work of the Ministry*, 126.

Coming. But although he lost his faith, there was no unremembering the scriptures which had been Owen's daily reading for the best part of two decades, and which continue to reverberate throughout his writing. Sometimes he engages directly with them:

> So Abram rose, and clave the wood, and went,
> And took the fire with him, and a knife.

The first part of 'The Parable of the Old Man and the Young' renders the biblical story of the sacrifice of Isaac into blank verse with facility, but then the poem proceeds to break open the benign closure of this patriarchal myth, by changing the ending to show Abram choosing to slaughter his son rather than sacrifice his pride. In hospital in May 1917 after his shell-shock, Owen had amused himself by writing a fantasy in the style of the Authorized Version of the Bible. Authoritative language is here 'carnivalized', in Bakhtin's terms, with a hilarity that is of considerable psychological interest:

> And they put him upon his own ass and took him to an inn.
>
> And in the process of time, he saithe unto him that kept the inn 'I will drink a little wine for my stomach's sake. Fill me seven barrels full.'
>
> And they filled them unto the brim.
>
> And there was silence for the space of half an hour.
>
> And when he understood the meaning of the seven stars, he lifted up his voice, and cried 'Fill them a second time.' So they filled them a second time. Till there was no room for him in the inn.
>
> And his face shone with the brightness of the sun. (*CL* 459.)

And so on. 'I did it without any reference to the Book, of course,' he told his mother rather sheepishly, 'and without any . . . detraction from reverence', adding: 'I think the big number of texts which jogged up in my mind in half-an-hour bears witness to a goodly store of them in my being' (*CL* 461). It was an unexpected testimony to an education in Evangelical piety.

Ian Bradley calls it 'a highly introspective religion'. '[Their] perpetual fear of being found wanting when the Day of Judgement came led the Evangelicals into agonizing sessions of self-examination and soul-searching.'[8] It also made them acutely aware of the passing of time, and the dangers of wasting it. At Dunsden

[8] Bradley, *The Call to Seriousness*, 23.

Owen had a minor accident, riding his bicycle at speed on the way back from reading to a housebound parishioner.

Further, I was riding away from an old man to whom I had been reading Spurgeon—and the burden of the Sermon was the fact that our lives are 'leased by seconds—not by seventy years, thirty years, five years.' 'Not more frail are flowers, more fragile moths . . . or more fleeting meteors than human life.'

I was even moralising on this when I tried to put it into practice! (*CL* 154.)

What is here a rueful joke about the pressure of time is a recurring theme in more serious form in Owen's letters, where it meets and is made more poignant by a Romantic presentiment of early death. The letters express an anxiety about time which is largely secular and Keatsian, the impending judgement being a matter not of salvation but of fame; but Owen had learned early in his life to keep an eye on the clock, from the Evangelical conviction that Christians were accountable to God for every minute spent. Adam Clarke, a redoutable commentator on the Bible, 'noted that by giving up tea and coffee over some four decades he had saved several years of time',[9] and Evangelical literature, sermons, and hymns are full of urgent recommendations to improve the shining hour.

Related to this is the Evangelical habit of keeping an account with the Almighty in the form of diaries, in order to 'assist in the task of self-examination and to chart . . . spiritual progress';[10] and in many cases, in order to monitor a child's development, parents 'required detailed accounts from absentee sons of their companions, of how they spent each hour of the day, of their reading, and of their use of Sunday.'[11] If there is 'a discipline of intensive reading' at the heart of Evangelical practice (*OTP* 5), there is also a place for writing, providing that writing is useful. Owen did not keep up his teenage habit of informing his mother, when separated from her, of his Sunday attendances at church, the choice of hymns and the theme of the sermon. But he never ceased to be a faithful, frequent, and often highly confessional correspondent: 'because they are my only diary,' he reminded Susan Owen in 1917, 'I

[9] Rosman, *Evangelicals and Culture*, 59.
[10] Bradley, *The Call to Seriousness*, 23.
[11] Rosman, *Evangelicals and Culture*, 100.

humbly desire you to keep these letters' (*CL* 495). Owen's letters are, in many ways, as remarkable as his poems. His chief model here was Keats; but some of the reflective richness of his letter-writing is likely to derive from the religious culture of his upbringing, with its encouragement of self-examination in writing.

It would not in the end be possible to extricate the contributions to Owen's language formation of his religious and his domestic upbringing: these were in the early years indivisible, and religious and family values supported each other to the point of identity. 'Evangelicalism was above all the religion of the home,' says Ian Bradley. 'It idealized and sanctified family life.'[12] The Victorian parlour scene, like the Victorian deathbed, had been a genre of the Evangelical imagination; and vital religion took very seriously indeed the question of the formation of young minds and the cure of young souls. To address these responsibilities, Evangelical worthies promoted institutions like Sunday schools and mothers' meetings which were based in the church or the parish hall, but everyone agreed that it was in the bosom of the family that the child must meet its first and most important intimations of God's love, and also of his law. Serious-minded parents saw themselves as missionaries to their children—just as missionaries, in the African jungle or the industrial slums, habitually spoke of their parental duties and feelings towards the savages, or the poor, whose souls they wanted to win; and just as Owen the army officer was sometimes to speak of his men in the same terms, as his 'little Family' (*CL* 403, 414). Evangelical children were frequently exposed to intense or oblique parental pressure well into maturity, from parents determined not to neglect their pastoral responsibilities, and '[i]t is clear', says Doreen Rosman, 'that in exercising their priestly role, Evangelicals sometimes resorted to something perilously close to religious terrorism.'[13]

In Birkenhead and Shrewsbury it was Susan Owen who willingly took charge of the religious upbringing of her children, Tom Owen playing a supportive but mostly silent role in this drama. And in Harold Owen's memoir, which is shot through with loathing of the religion of his mother's family, there are traces of something indeed close to religious terrorism. When as a young man Harold

[12] Bradley, *The Call to Seriousness*, 179.
[13] Rosman, *Evangelicals and Culture*, 101.

thought of his mother's idea of heaven, he conjured up 'the picture of God himself sitting like some awful hanging judge, stern and terrifying' (*JFO* 3. 36). An earlier incident from *Journey from Obscurity* gives a quite detailed impression of Susan Owen in action. It takes place when the family is on holiday in Ireland, and Harold, aged about five and accident-prone as ever, has dashed into the road and only just, by an adroit manœuvre, avoided being run down by two jaunting cars travelling at great speed. I must quote here at length: it is Harold Owen at his best, describing vividly an incident a good sixty years after the event, and whether or not it is in every particular true to a vanished actuality, it is true to his memory of it.

My mother had been sitting in the cottage window and seen everything and of course was really frightened. Hurrying across the road, she collected me and, holding me by the hand and scolding me very severely, dragged me back to the cottage. I was now in angry tears for I did not want to leave my boat, but my mother was adamant and continued to impress upon me how impossible my naughtiness was becoming. Once in the room of the cottage my mother changed and became very sweet and gentle and with great tenderness tried to impress upon me how Jesus had saved my life, but my glorious moment had been ruined by her severity so that I did not somehow feel in the mood for Jesus. In any case I thought it most unfair—if there was any praise going at all—that Jesus should have it; I was quite certain myself that it was not Jesus but my own superb letter 'S' manœuvre which had got me safely across the road. My mother's crossness must have made me aware that I had done something wrong, but her description of what might have happened to me, instead of frightening me, only made me think even more highly of my own agility. My mother, perhaps perceiving now that she was only causing me to compete with Jesus for the honours, tried another tactic, painting a frightful picture of what might have happened to me if God had not been watching over me . . . I should have now been a small mangled child, cut everywhere and covered in blood and laid out in a sort of little bundle at the side of the road . . . I was a bit frightened about God being brought into it. It seemed to me I had quite a fellow-feeling about Jesus, but I did not much like the sound of God; this misgiving, though, was swamped by the vividness of me spread out on the road. I became absolutely entranced and could see myself quite clearly lying there in a sort of splendid importance of mangled bloodiness. I remember I added a good many more pools of blood myself just for good measure . . . this vision was so splendid to me, I was enjoying looking at myself so much, that something of this pleasure must have appeared in my face and bearing. This my mother misinterpreted and she became terribly distressed and very angry with me. She was of course—so deep was her religious feeling—genuinely frightened for me. I was made to get down on my knees, my mother doing likewise, in order to beg forgiveness from God and Jesus. This I was quite agreeable to do as long as I could leave God out of it, for I badly wanted to get back to my boat. We had just got our knees comfortably settled when in burst my father demanding to know what on earth we were doing in a stuffy room on an evening like this when we ought to be down by the sea . . . I was sent out of the room, and later on my father joined me by the boat. He gave me a gruff homily about upsetting 'your mother' so often, told me to look where I was going in future, and then dried up. (*JFO* 1. 71–2.)

Here in the robust comedy of this scene we can catch a not altogether sympathetic glimpse of Susan Owen in the role of Evangelical parent. As her tone swings from anger to tenderness to morbidity and back to distress and anger, she brings to bear on her child the whole armoury of godly didacticism. There could be no question of her limiting herself to the sort of excellent advice that her husband later gives Harold, 'to look where I was going in future'. Her own beliefs and upbringing, her own conception of motherhood, childhood, and the depravity of human nature, all oblige her to treat the event as essentially a moral and ultimately a soteriological crisis (that is, one in which the salvation of the delinquent's soul is at stake). Harold's narrow escape prompts his mother to a lesson in theology rather than, as might have seemed more appropriate, in road safety. Susan speaks in a discourse that mixes tender appeal to the gentler feelings with moral challenge and terrifying imagery. It is a rhetorical combination whose constituents will be heard later in the didactic poetry of her son; and the likelihood is that both of them had heard it first, and frequently, in the preaching of ministers who took Spurgeon and his like for their models. The mother's sermon comes with the characteristic Evangelical mixture of parental love and what Rosman calls terrorism. If Harold cannot be softened out of his tendency to stray, he may be shocked out of it by a display of the consequences. Like a seasoned preacher, Susan Owen balances an Old Testament threat with a New Testament promise. She cajoles with Jesus and frightens with God. Since it seems Harold cannot be persuaded to be grateful for the mercy of Jesus, he can be reminded to be afraid of the disfavour of God. And at the centre of Susan

Owen's warning lies the vivid image of the child's mangled body in its own blood.

It is worth pausing a moment over this since Wilfred Owen's own warnings too are often accompanied or dramatized by imagery of vulnerable or stricken bodies. We have already seen how Harold Owen's imagination was possessed by the image of the boy Isaac, 'lying bound below the dazzling knife' (*JFO* 1. 33). Years later, returning to consciousness in a Calcutta hospital after very nearly dying of heat apoplexy, Harold Owen was aware of his own almost naked body: 'I remember thinking rather dreamily as I noticed my jutting ribs, laid-out legs and arms and caved-in tummy with the white band across it, how much I resembled the biblical pictures of my infant days—of Jesus being taken down from the cross' (*JFO* 2. 145). Although the sacrifice of Isaac and the deposition from the Cross are almost certainly remembered by Harold from illustrations of the Bible or biblical stories, Susan Owen's dramatic homily shows that the imagery of the suffering body was familiar to the Owen children in verbal as well as iconic form, and that their mother was quite capable of improvising it to striking effect, to point a moral.

She had sufficient precedent. The tortures of hell as the punishment for wickedness formed an essential part of the Evangelical curriculum. And to dangle before a child an image of death was in any case a favourite theme of the vast body of tract fiction that improved so many Victorian Sundays. The tactics of tract fiction ranged (like Susan Owen's) from terrorism to pathos; from *The Death of the Liar* with which Charlotte Brontë has her Evangelical school principal threaten Jane Eyre, to the gentler tales, sober in content, spiritually instructive, and invariably including an edifying death, of Hesba Stretton, who had written for Dickens's *All the Year Round* and was still publishing her stories in 1908.[14] More will be said later about the image of the dead or suffering body which is so important in Owen's writings. It should be noted that it entered his imagination not from his experience of battle, but from the Christian iconography which was inculcated literally at his mother's knee, and for this reason it retains traces of the sacramental even in the unholiest of contexts. And the effect of the

[14] For tract fiction, see Margaret Nancy Cutt's *Ministering Angels*. Cutt reports that Hesba Stretton's stories were still popular with children in the 1930s.

image of mutilation and death on the young Harold deserves attention too. His mother introduced the image as a didactic device intended to appal, but instead Harold remembers being thrilled by this splendid vision; he is 'absolutely entranced' by it, and cannot conceal the pleasure, aesthetic and narcissistic, which it gives him, and for which he is then punished. This little comedy points, in an almost allegorical way, to serious and difficult issues about the pleasures of Wilfred Owen's war poetry.

The Christian discourse which the Owen children first heard in their mother's voice could speak almost in the same breath (as we have just seen Susan Owen speaking to Harold) in tones of solicitude and dangerous anger, of pity and terrorism. That strange Evangelical mixture of tenderness and brutality reappears in Owen's own adult language, and has its implications for the sado-masochistic strain sometimes to be found in his work. His fascination with the infliction and suffering of pain is only partly to be explained as a consequence of his taste for Swinburne and the poetry of the Decadence. If his religious upbringing taught him about virtue and love, it also introduced him to a vocabulary of oppression and terror. One aspect of this sentimental education bears fruit in the remarkably adult lovingness of his childhood letters to his mother. Harold Owen himself reaches for religious language to describe the 'devotionalism' (*JFO* 1. 78) with which Wilfred did not cease to treat Susan Owen, and her 'adoration' of him (*JFO* 3. 17, 60). But the darker and as it were more gothic side of a religion which, after all, emphasized human depravity and the terrors of hell, took an equal grip on Wilfred Owen's imagination.

At one point this found a kind of expression in his fondness for bringing about dramatic situations in the home, 'nearly always of a deep melancholy and often adult eeriness', to terrorize the younger children. Harold Owen in retrospect sees these games as experiments in which 'it was as if he must test out his own power of make-believe'. They 'always took the form of bringing us into a state of fear, and sometimes to a state of unnatural religious fervour; this last, of course, was directly influenced by my mother' (*JFO* 1. 49). Harold would be locked in a dark room or cupboard and visited by a 'ghost' or spirit from another world, draped in a sheet and mumbling incantations with a terrifying solemnity. The terrors which these performances produced in the children were real enough, and threatened to get out of hand and deteriorate into 'a dangerous hysteria' (*JFO* 1. 50). All Evangelical children knew about the dread of being damned to hell. Here is an example of Wilfred Owen putting to the test a lesson of that upbringing, about the histrionic power of shock and horror.

The most direct descendant of these experiments is 'Mental Cases', written in May 1918, in which a visitor to a hospital (or to hell) is shown its inmates:

> Who are these? Why sit they here in twilight?
> Wherefore rock they, purgatorial shadows,
> Drooping tongues from jaws that slob their relish,
> Baring teeth that leer like skulls' teeth wicked?
> Stroke on stroke of pain,—but what slow panic,
> Gouged these chasms round their fretted sockets?
> Ever from their hair and through their hands' palms
> Misery swelters. Surely we have perished
> Sleeping, and walk hell; but who these hellish?

Much of the opening stanza of 'Mental Cases' comes almost word for word from 'Purgatorial Passions' (*CPF* 455), a substantial fragment drafted in the first half of 1916 and so before Owen's experience of combat or of its possible mental costs. 'Purgatorial Passions' accumulates horrific detail in its description of the damned, but has no apparent structure or direction; it gets nowhere, but it must be counted another experiment—descended from those childhood performances of 'deep melancholy and often adult eeriness' that scared the young Owen children—with an idea that had long drawn the poet's curiosity. When in 'Mental Cases' this theme met his own experience of war's mental casualties, and his recent reading of Dante, and his new conception of the poet's duty and function, then the image of the stricken body and damned soul returns with great power in that complex of terror, guilt, and fascination in which it had first been encountered.

> —These are men whose minds the Dead have ravished.
> Memory fingers in their hair of murders,
> Multitudinous murders they once witnessed.
> Wading sloughs of flesh these helpless wander,
> Treading blood from lungs that had loved laughter.
> Always they must see these things and hear them,
> Batter of guns and shatter of flying muscles,
> Carnage incomparable, and human squander
> Rucked too thick for these men's extrication.

Therefore still their eyeballs shrink tormented
Back into their brains, because on their sense
Sunlight seems a blood-smear; night comes blood-black;
Dawn breaks open like a wound that bleeds afresh.
—Thus their heads wear this hilarious, hideous,
Awful falseness of set-smiling corpses.
—Thus their hands are plucking at each other;
Picking at the rope-knouts of their scourging;
Snatching after us that smote them, brother,
Pawing us who dealt them war and madness.

W. H. Griffith Thomas, in his 1911 manual called *The Work of the Ministry* and intended for those considering entering the priesthood, had named forcefulness as one of the essential requirements for every sermon.

Let us never fail to drive home our message and make it as personal, direct, and definite as possible . . . It [the conclusion] should be pungent. That is to say, there must be a direct, personal appeal. Each hearer must feel the force of the words, as though the preacher were saying to him, 'thou art the man!'[15]

Whether or not he read these words while he was unofficial curate at Dunsden, Owen had learned for himself years before, from example and experience, about the rhetorical and didactic force of shock. It was the experience of the war (and of the war hospital) that had enabled 'Purgatorial Passions' to be revised and completed as 'Mental Cases'. The powerful reproach of its closing lines gives it its point and its passion: it is an anti-war poem. Yet both the imagery and the rhetorical shock of 'Mental Cases'—and incidentally of 'Strange Meeting', with its infernal setting, and its chilling variation ('I am the enemy you killed, my friend') on 'thou art the man'—were in Owen's repertoire before he went to war. He had absorbed them from the Evangelical vocabulary of hell which terrified and excited him as a child, and from the aggressive tactics of dramatic warning and alarm disseminated through Evangelical discourse by the example of preachers like the great Spurgeon.

Flee, sinner, flee! The avenger of the blood that thou hast shed pursues thee with hot haste; with feet that are winged, with a heart that is athirst for blood, he pursues thee. Run, man, run! The refuge city is before thee!

[15] W. H. Griffith Thomas, *The Work of the Ministry*, 214.

It is there, along the narrow way of faith. Fly, man, fly, for unless thou reach that city ere he overtake thee he shall smite thee, and one blow shall be thine everlasting ruin.[16]

The language of his family's faith had other and gentler resources too, which Wilfred Owen as a boy brought into serious creative play. Like many another Evangelical child, he experimented with predication.[17] Around 1907 and coinciding with a very pious phase in his letters, there came into being what was known in the family as 'Wilfred's Church'.

Aided and encouraged by my mother, Wilfred would on Sunday evenings arrange our small sitting-room to represent a church. The table would be moved away, all available chairs collected and arranged for pews, an armchair turned backwards making a pulpit and lectern . . . Wilfred would spend a long time arranging the room, after which he would robe himself and, looking very priestlike in his surplice and mitre, would call us in to form the congregation. He would then conduct a complete evening service with remarkable exactitude and would end by reading a short sermon he had prepared with great care and thought. (*JFO* I. 150–1.)

Here, in a fine instance of semiotic play, the furniture and members of one institution were translated and pressed into service as the trappings and personnel of another. The parlour turned into a candlelit church, the armchair reversed was a pulpit, the sideboard masqueraded as an altar heaped with masses of wild flowers and ferns. The family anagrammatized into a congregation with the son as its pastor. 'The whole of these unusual proceedings,' Harold Owen remembered, 'were conducted with absolute reverence throughout.' These services seem to have become increasingly baroque with Wilfred's 'mounting demands for more embellishment'—an instance, I dare say, of the return of the repressed, since ritualism was deplored by the Evangelicals and banished from their churches as a papist practice. Harold Owen thinks that this Roman tendency was the reason why his mother eventually caused these performances to cease. But he himself, characteristically, is reluctant to allow much religious significance at all to the proceedings. As the young Wilfred translated a family occasion—Sunday evening at home—into a church ritual, the chronicler Harold Owen nearly

[16] Spurgeon, *Sermons*, 88.

[17] Ian Bradley (p. 190) quotes John Ruskin's sermon, delivered standing on a chair at the age of three: 'People, be dood. If you are dood, Dod will love you; if you are not dood, Dod will not love you. People, be dood.'

sixty years later reaccentuated the ritual as chiefly an aesthetic event, a sort of rehearsal. 'It was of course the obtaining of the effective setting and his own unconscious acting in his role as priest which really intrigued him, and not the religious value or importance' (*JFO* I. 151). Thus do the institutions of which he was a part continue to fold into and contend with each other. What Susan Owen certainly saw as evidence of a vocation for one institution—the Church—is retrospectively interpreted, by Harold, as evidence of a vocation for another—the arts.

Translating the speech and imagery of one community into that of another is one of Owen's favourite rhetorical turns, nowhere more deliberate than in 'Anthem for Doomed Youth'. Here in the octave the mad and mechanical voices of the battlefield supply the only available or appropriate funeral rites for butchered soldiers.

> What passing-bells for these who die as cattle?
> —Only the monstrous anger of the guns.
> Only the stuttering rifles' rapid rattle
> Can patter out their hasty orisons.
> No mockeries now for them; no prayers nor bells;
> Nor any voice of mourning save the choirs,—
> The shrill, demented choirs of wailing shells;
> And bugles calling for them from sad shires.

In the sestet, ornaments and embellishments, redundant and perhaps a mockery (for this poem, in eschewing outward trappings and rituals in favour of undemonstrative piety, is impeccably low Church), are transformed to become the tearful eyes and pale faces of sorrowing children:

> What candles may be held to speed them all?
> Not in the hands of boys but in their eyes
> Shall shine the holy glimmers of goodbyes.
> The pallor of girls' brows shall be their pall;
> Their flowers the tenderness of patient minds,
> And each slow dusk a drawing-down of blinds.

'Wilfred's Church' had metamorphosed the private space of the family home into a place of worship. The 'Anthem' repeats the pattern, interiorizing the business of the Church (as the poem appropriates its language) and handing it over to the quiet sincerity of family grief and memory. Funeral furnishings may be beside the point; it is (as Keats believed) the heart's affections that are 'holy'.

And the poem reaches into silence on the eloquent sign of a family in mourning, the house with drawn blinds, beautifully naturalized as a figure for dusk. Soldiers, the Church, family relations: the missing discourse, poetry, is of course the omnipresent one; the anthem is a Romantic sonnet, and positions itself in relation to (among other voices) Sassoon and Laurence Binyon, Keats and Housman, and the classical elegists.

Religion began at home. The language of Christianity for Owen had always been strongly bound to that of the family and accentuated by family voices, especially his mother's and his sister's. Church and home seconded each other, their values very largely overlapped, each invested in the other's language. After Owen had quit Dunsden, having revealed to his mother the existence if not the scope of his doubts, she continued to send him religious texts, messages, and prayers. And he responded, if not in kind, then with a stream of declarations of devotion to her. From training camp in March 1916:

> Your Note arriving on the 17th gave me the comfort and renewing of a sacrament. Thereby I had communion with those things which are now passed behind a cloud out of sight, but which shall come to us in like manner again . . . Yes, I take and read these your words with thanksgiving. (*CL* 386.)

This profession of love is pentecostally possessed, as it were, by the sacramental and apostolic language of his lost faith. The religious idiom can serve as an appropriate expression of his devotion to his mother, as easily as the family parlour had become a church. It was to remain for him one of the chief dialects of the language of love.

Religion began at home, but did not end there. To examine further the sort of religious speech and writing that Owen was exposed to and participated in, we need to begin to move out of the small and rather claustrophobic circle of the Owen family. Ahead lay his crucial fourteen months as the Revd Herbert Wigan's assistant at Dunsden, months in which Owen's discursive experience was to be saturated in the language of the Church and the work of the ministry. But before following Owen to Dunsden I want to take a shorter step, hardly a step out of the Owen family at all, and begin by considering the poet's childhood exposure to the language of the temperance movement.

7
Drink and the Devil

Susan Owen was an energetic worker for the Temperance Society and for the British and Foreign Bible Society (*WO* 39–40). The temperance movement was second only to missionary activity as an arena for Evangelical good works. Drink was a serious social problem, most visibly appalling among the poor. Efforts to combat it in the early nineteenth century with the formation of teetotal societies were overwhelmingly Nonconformist in inspiration, but later the movement was espoused and eventually came to be dominated by the Evangelical wing of the Church of England.

The Church of England Temperance Society (to which Susan Owen belonged) acquired Queen Victoria as its patron in 1875, but the character of the temperance movement had significantly shifted some time before. By the 1850s the old 'experience meetings', at which usually working-class former drunks were paraded to declare their reclamation for sobriety, were being replaced by drawing-room meetings, which, according to Brian Harrison in *Drink and the Victorians*, signalled the development of 'a temperance movement with no personal experience of the drunkard's miseries, and which merely passed the time listening to itinerant lecturers who spoke about them'.[1]

Marx in the Communist Manifesto had already included 'temperance fanatics' in his contemptuous list of bourgeois reformers, 'desirous of redressing social grievances in order to secure the continued existence of bourgeois society'. Certainly as the nineteenth century drew on, temperance work acquired more middle-class habits and middle-class respectability. There were no more public processions of reformed drunkards. The movement was attracting support from the genteel, whose money built the temperance halls which are its monument. And it was raising its voice in the centres of Victorian power. To great Tory opposition, sponsored by the brewers, a Liberal government introduced public-

[1] Harrison, *Drink and the Victorians*, 191.

house licensing laws. Losing the subsequent election in 1872, Gladstone declared, 'We have been borne down in a torrent of gin and beer.'[2] More than twenty years later but apparently none the wiser, the Liberals entered the 1895 general election pledged to bring in some temperance legislation. The Unionists were returned with a majority of 152.

But there was in any case a large section, perhaps a majority, in the temperance movement itself which believed that its business was to change not the laws of the nation but its moral character: 'moral suasion' ought to be its watchword, not 'legislative suppression'. In this debate, its history recorded at length in Henry Carter's *The English Temperance Movement: A Study in Objectives*, can be seen a detail of the wider picture of Evangelical uncertainty about the desirability, and the perils, of becoming directly and practically involved in social issues and political action. This question was an important one for Wilfred Owen. One way or another, the movement never brought about the social revolution which its early Nonconformist crusaders had hoped for: those hopes flowed instead into an increasingly powerful labour movement, maintaining links with temperance but purporting to have a commitment to tackling not just the symptoms but the causes of social misery.

Meanwhile, as the temperance movement became more Anglican and respectable in its outlook and personnel, it seems also to have become increasingly characterized by the Victorian Evangelical tendency to look after its own. In *Drink and the Victorians* Brian Harrison traces a developing complacency in the movement, whose beginnings he finds in the first Victorian decade. 'Far from initiating a national reformation, teetotalism from the 1840s gradually became a way of drawing the line between the righteous and the unrighteous.'[3] Temperance discourse was finding it more congenial to congratulate the sober than to convert the inebriate. A symptom of this favouring of the 'preventive' over the 'redemptive' arm of the crusade is to be found in the movement's increasing concentration on the indoctrination of children.

The original Band of Hope was founded in 1847 in Leeds, its object being to persuade children of the evils of drink and to get them to sign the pledge. Other bands quickly proliferated and,

[2] Turner, *Roads to Ruin*, 98. [3] Harrison, *Drink and the Victorians*, 194.

after a meeting chaired by Lord Shaftesbury, the United Kingdom Band of Hope Union was formed in 1855 to unite the various separate societies. By the end of the century the union had some 26,000 bands with more than three million registered members.[4] Temperance reached into the secular classroom, where Dr Benjamin Richardson's *Temperance Lesson Book* started to become required reading in many schools soon after the foundation of the Band of Hope Union,[5] and into the family home, where many a Victorian Sunday was lent a melancholy drama by the ghastly warnings of temperance tracts and tract fiction.[6] But for the child with a teetotal parent or minister, the most sustained exposure to temperance rhetoric was in the form of the weekly meeting, under the auspices of the local Band of Hope or any of the smaller but similar associations. Large meetings would take place in a temperance or church hall, but smaller bands often met in private houses.

When Wilfred Owen was considering the possibility of becoming assistant to the Revd John Morgan in his new parish in Bordesley, he was told that one of his duties would be 'to start and organise meetings and unions, bands, and so on' among the children of the parish (*CL* 174). He himself had been recruited by his mother at a very early age in Birkenhead into the Young Abstainers' Union, and used to sport its badge in his buttonhole. For a short period (until Tom Owen put his foot down) Susan Owen not only wore the blue ribbon of the pledge herself, but also decorated her four infants with them (*JFO* 2. 175). Brian Harrison notes that the growth of the Band of Hope and its popularity among middle-class parents 'represents the increased self-consciousness of temperance reformers as a community, as an élite whose children must be protected against the snares of a wider world.'[7] To be sure, the induction of her children into the temperance movement at an early age afforded Susan Owen the gratifying coincidence of reinforcing the family's social standing at the same time as its righteousness, for as Jon Stallworthy observes,

[4] Hylson-Smith, *Evangelicals in the Church of England*, 205.

[5] Turner, *Roads to Ruin*, 97.

[6] Two million copies of Hesba Stretton's cautionary tale *Jessica's First Prayer* (1866) had been printed at the time of the author's death in 1911. It was distributed, as was its sequel *Jessica's Mother* (1867), by Temperance Societies all over the country, as well as becoming the basis for a magic-lantern programme for the Band of Hope, and a Service of Song. See Cutt, *Ministering Angels*, 135.

[7] Harrison, *Drink and the Victorians*, 194.

'Lectures on the dire consequences of involvement with the Demon Drink were held in certain of the better-class homes in the Tranmere area, another factor commending the [Young Abstainers'] Union to Mrs Owen' (*WO* 22).

And it was not only lectures that young abstainers were treated to at such meetings. The rhetoric of temperance designed for the ears of the young expressed itself in a fairly limited stock of themes, but across a considerable variety of forms, and these ranged from the sort of sermon you might hear in church to a wide repertoire of songs, poems for recitation, courses of instruction, dialogues, catechisms, dramas, and different sorts of games. Its discourse can be examined in the publications of the Band of Hope, the largest of the temperance organizations for children, which had the parental blessing and often the imprint of the Church of England Temperance Society (CETS). This kind of language was among the earliest discourse Wilfred Owen learned outside the family; and while it is a discourse which may seem quaint or sometimes ludicrous from this distance, Owen's experience of it was neither eccentric nor trivial. At the turn of the century, as we have seen, the Bands of Hope numbered their child-members in millions. The perils of drink were an obsession with his mother, and although in maturity both Wilfred and Harold broke the parental taboo on alcohol, it was in the nature of an almost biblical transgression, a step taken 'only with awe amounting to superstitious dread' (*JFO* 2. 175). Susan Owen made sure her children were steeped very thoroughly in the rhetoric of Christian temperance.

The world into which the temperance child was inserted by this rhetoric, reinforced by the addresses of his adult mentors (more than likely his own parents or schoolteacher or minister) and by the various performances and activities enjoyed at meetings, was essentially a simple one in its moral organization. Drinking was bad, abstinence was good. To combat the brewers' and distillers' claims that drink was nourishing and health-giving, the temperance movement had assembled a baleful medical case against the effects of alcohol on the body, brain, and blood; and surprisingly detailed accounts of the physiological depredations of alcohol made their way into model addresses intended for delivery to even quite young Band of Hope children. Still, the overwhelming weight of the attack on drink was moral and religious rather than medical or even social. Children who had already heard a good deal about evil at home, in church, and in Sunday school, were told that alcohol was the very devil. 'Realise, then, that you are members of one great army, in the church, banded together to protect yourselves and others from one great enemy—drink.'[8] The temptations of the 'one great enemy' were a total explanation. No more needed to be said about the reasons why a person might take to drink, nor is there much curiosity (still less, of course, knowledge) about what it might be like to be a drunkard, or to try to stop being one. The drinker may be pitied; but he—it is almost always he—has succumbed to evil, and has suffered a moral and spiritual failure. His condition may be materially harmful to society and to himself, but above all it is a sin. Later a similar attitude was being taken, in some quarters, towards the victims of shell-shock.

Young abstainers, then, were encouraged by a great emphasis on solidarity in the rhetoric and activities prepared for them, to see and congratulate themselves as a tightly knit moral community, banded together for protection in an unwholesome world. Obviously the paradigm for this was the Church itself, and particularly the beleaguered if sometimes complacent self-image of the Evangelicals as a communion of saints. It will also be clear that temperance was in more senses than one a continuation of the family for the Owen children. In a Tranmere drawing-room their integrity, purity, and social status could be confirmed more confidently than on the doorstep in Birkenhead. In temperance discourse, drunkenness is invariably associated with dirt and leads to poverty; but abstinence is respectable, polite, civilized, and (it is strongly hinted) affluent. In one of the more spirited of the Band of Hope's entertainments, *The Downfall of King Drinka: A Fairy Play for Children*, his alcoholic majesty is dressed in rags and so are his grubby attendants Vini, Brandi, Whiski, Gini, etc.: but the stage directions declare, 'Queen Sobrieti, her Lieutenants [Will Wellpledge and Tilly Touchnot] and Band of Hope should be neatly attired, and as far as possible in a uniform style of clothing.'[9] If there is a subtext of class distinction here, there is also one of racial superiority. The uniformed and well-disciplined army of the queen use superior weaponry—squirts and syringes of water—to defeat the savage King Drinka and his tribe with the comical

[8] *Band of Hope Outline Addresses*, 2nd series, 49.
[9] *The Band of Hope Entertainer*, 23.

names. Clearly this temperance allegory borrows a paradigm narrative from the discourse of empire, a story the children would all have been familiar with. One of many examples of the paradigm was the exciting victory, a generation before, in the Ashanti war against the monarch known to the British public as King Koffee.

The sense of community and community pride into which temperance culture sought to bind its children found its models, as might be expected, in the universally recognizable paradigms of family, Church, and army. The army is the most curious case of the three, and has always been available as a sometimes uneasy metaphor for the community of the godly. 'I am a recruiting sergeant,' declared C. H. Spurgeon in his last sermon, in 1892, 'and I would fain find a few recruits at this moment.'[10] In late Victorian times Britain's professional soldiers—always excepting a number of heroic generals—had not been very affectionately regarded at home, but the great displays of military might for Victoria's Jubilee in 1897 seemed, as James Morris says, to signal or confirm a change.

> In support of it all a new militarism was popular in Britain. Kipling had touched up the Army's shoddy image and military similes and models were very much in vogue. *Onward Christian Soldiers* was the hymn of the day. The Salvationists called their new movement an Army, and when they set up a mission in a new country were said to have 'occupied' the place. The boys were organised in Brigades, the Anglican church was more than ever militant.[11]

Two years after the Jubilee, the South African war brought the army to the centre of national attention again, and managed to confirm the impression, though only after some severe embarrassments, that the British Army won all its wars in the end. The Band of Hope liked to tell its children they were fighting for Captain Christ in the wars against King Alcohol, and taught them to sing their battle song 'We are Soldiers of Temperance'. The Revd J. Isabell produced for them a series of twelve addresses called *Lessons from the Boer War*. 'From ancient times this realm has been subjected to an invasion more disastrous in its effects than the Boer invasion of Natal and Cape Colony . . . The enemy has even sought to annex the Empire and call it his. *This invader*

[10] Spurgeon, *Fifty Most Remarkable Sermons*, i.

[11] James Morris, *Pax Britannica*, 404.

is Intemperance.[12] And the war then becomes an extended metaphor for the struggle against alcohol, an elaborate 'object-lesson' in the manner familiar from Evangelical sermons. There are sections on weaponry, on prisoners, on the wounded, and so on.

> A wounded soldier is a sad sight, but a dead soldier is a sadder sight still. If all the graves of persons killed in England every year by alcohol were placed one after another in a long line, they would stretch across the country for a hundred and forty miles; and if you started from one end and walked to the other, and walked twelve hours a day without stopping, it would take you three days to reach your destination.[13]

Mr Isabell had even perfected the war correspondent's rhetorical technique of the unchallengeable detail. A hundred and forty miles! Others too could command this militant rhetoric. 'We are fighting Germany, Austria and Drink,' Lloyd George declared in March 1915, 'and, as far as I can see, the greatest of these deadly foes is Drink.'[14]

To be in the temperance movement was to belong to a family, a Church, an army. A corporate identity was constructed for young abstainers in a discourse that made capital out of what children knew to be their duty to their parents, religion, and country. They belonged to a community of purpose which, in its language and its personnel, overlapped their family and their Church and reinforced the loyalty and the values both these institutions were teaching them. Although Wilfred Owen in later years was not a teetotaller, and was to face more formidable antagonists than King Drinka, he retained a strong sense of a community of obligation and of moral action. For all his dramatization of himself as a romantic solitary or 'a mad comet' (*CL* 557), his imagination was fully mobilized only when its isolation was broken, and his language became most powerful as the voice of a moral community. It was the poet's duty to warn, but he was not speaking for himself. And while he had good polemical reasons for claiming (in the draft preface) that his poems were 'not about heroes', there are groups, companies, fellow-sufferers, brothers in arms—though never individual soldiers—who can without irony be described as heroic. Heroism exists in Owen as a plural, communal quality.

The illocutionary tendency of temperance rhetoric is overwhelmingly towards warning, which the preface Owen drafted in

[12] *Band of Hope Outline Addresses*, 3rd series, 42.
[13] Ibid. 60. [14] Marwick, *The Deluge*, 65.

1918 was to claim as the only admissible function of the poet in wartime. But if his discursive experience in the Young Abstainers' Union gave him an early taste of some of the varieties of didacticism, it must also have given him, if only in retrospect, a strong example of the power of language, especially over children. Children are one of Owen's master images, and their susceptibility to persuasion was something he knew a good deal about. The vulnerability of the young and impressionable is a theme for indignation in 'S.I.W.', 'Arms and the Boy', 'Disabled', and 'Dulce et Decorum Est'. Much of his work at Dunsden consisted in spreading the Christian gospel to children, and after his faith in that gospel foundered, he realized he had the power not only to inculcate what he considered to be the truth but also to expose and uproot a lie. For a moment he seems to have toyed with the idea of undoing what he had done. He remarked in a letter to his mother on the good Christian behaviour of the children at Dunsden school, all of whom he knew well, but he continued:

> Now is there after all some region of their natures which I shall never fathom? Is there a definite relation between them and the unseen, into which my curiosity, my jealousy may never pry? I think not.
>
> I believe this sweet piety of theirs has reference to present environment only. Environment was the cause of it. Alter the environment and it will go. For already I grieve to say (though *why I grieve* is not very patent, considering) that 'impressions' are 'wearing off' in some cases, already. In fact I am convinced that I hold under my tongue, powers which would shake the foundations of many a spiritual life. (*CL* 179.)

Owen knew nothing of Nietszche, but this was a giddying moment —'This is speaking boldly, and terribly'—because the children were glimpsed as completely in his power, having no inner integrity his words could not reach and mould. Their piety was entirely the creation of language; and what the tongue had given, the tongue could take away. From the other side of the exchange he could see that the power of language over the vulnerable was the power of life and death. Words are the most deadly weapons in the war poems, but words are also the only hope.

If his career as a young abstainer was Owen's introduction to didacticism, polemic, and propaganda, it planted other seeds too, which I believe bore fruit in the later writing. I shall deal with three of these: one stylistic, one mythopoeic, and one thematic.

The discourse of temperance was Wilfred Owen's introduction

to naturalism, that is, to that material realism which is prepared to dwell in detail on physically, morally, and socially unsavoury subjects in the interests of scientific accuracy or didactic intent. Nothing else in his discursively sheltered early life approached the boldness and vehemence with which temperance writers and speakers described the awful consequences of drink. And even Susan Owen, chronically disposed to pass over unseemly or distressing subjects as if they did not exist, made an exception when it came to this, as Harold Owen remembered.

All of us had been brought up to regard the drinking of alcohol as absolute sin. My mother had been both rigid and persevering in her teaching of this; concerning 'drink' she would allow no qualifications whatsoever. Upon all of us her influence had been powerful, partly because the evils of it were so constantly being impressed upon us but mostly, I think, because, on this subject, my mother would always enjoy speaking with undisguised frankness, as opposed to her guarded and camouflaged disquisitions upon all the other 'sins'. So horrific were some of her portrayals of the certain consequences of any divergence from absolute abstinence that, when I was small, on the few occasions when I saw anybody drinking, I more than half expected to see them fall down dead. My mother was on committees of several temperance societies and had all the terrifying patter always ready to turn on. (*JFO* 2. 174–5.)

With what sometimes looks very like relish, temperance tracts and the Band of Hope dossier drummed into children the physical and moral degradations of alcoholism, as it led its victims down the slippery path to one or more of its inevitable destinations: the prison, the hospital, the madhouse, the graveyard. There is sometimes an odd instability of tone, attributable probably to a writer's uncertain aim at the youthfulness of his target audience, as the jocular mixes with the horrifying. 'Lost! Lost!! Lost!!!', exclaimed 'The Band of Hope Bellman':

Lost! Lost!! Lost!!! Countless noble and beautiful intellects . . . Now, alas! by the continual use of strong drink, these fine and beautiful intellects have been degraded and ruined, so that their owners no longer think noble, or kindly, or sweet, or holy thoughts, but are mad or foolish with violent or silly ideas, so much so that many of these said owners are now in lunatic asylums, as hopeless imbeciles or raving maniacs![15]

The Bellman's message is blunted by his efforts to shock the children and patronize them in the same alcohol-free breath: was he

[15] *The Band of Hope Entertainer*, 55.

warning them of insanity or silliness? More often the warnings were, appropriately, more sober. There were harrowing accounts of the squalor, disease, and crime that lay in wait for a family when all the money went on drink. Another favourite theme was the physical appearance of the drunkard and his family, dressed in ragged and dirty clothes and with 'red eyes, staggering walk and shaking hand'[16]—all features faithfully, or coincidentally, bequeathed to the exhausted patrol, 'drunk with fatigue', in 'Dulce et Decorum Est'. And the cold eye of temperance did not confine itself to outward physique. Children were regularly and emphatically treated to descriptions of the whole physiological process of alcohol-induced collapse in a series of medical talks that made no concessions to squeamishness. And these lessons could be illustrated, and no doubt made more memorable, by a variety of available lantern-slides and pictures. You could send away, for example, for 'Four Anatomical Diagrams in Colours, showing the Injurious Effects of Alcohol upon the Internal Organs of the Body: produced in the highest form of chromolithography' and issued by the Church of England Temperance Society by arrangement with the Swiss Patriotic League against Alcoholism. Temperance is not an intrinsically very gripping topic, but this Swiss map of the internal organs, and in colours too, no doubt recalled some wandering attentions.

The effect of these things on the imagination of a child of eight may be pondered; the effect on the imagination of that child in his adult creativity is also worth thinking about. It is tempting to adduce here the story that Owen used to carry photographs of mutilated soldiers, with which to shock civilians; this would mark him a true child of temperance methodology, but Dominic Hibberd gives reasons for doubting this 'legend' (*OTP* 129, 220). It is possible, I think, to see such language and images speaking to a morbidity already present in the child's temperament, and giving it as it were a moral, didactic justification. This is certainly the impulse behind an account (complete with illustrations) of a visit to an improvised war hospital in Bordeaux, in a letter to Harold in September 1914.

> The hospital is in the building of the Boys' *Lycée* and appliances are altogether crude. First I saw a bullet, like this  cut out of a Zouave's leg. Then we did the round of the wards; and saw some fifty

[16] *Band of Hope Outline Addresses*, 3rd series, 141.

German wretches: all more seriously wounded than the French. The Doctor picked out those needing surgical attention; and these were brought on stretchers to the Operating Room; formerly a Class room, with the familiar ink-stains on floor, walls, and ceiling; now a chamber of horrors with blood where the ink was. Think of it: there were eight men in the room at once, Germans being treated without the slightest distinction from the French: one scarcely knew which was which. Considering the lack of appliances—there was only one water-tap in the room—and the crowding—and the fact that the doctors were working for nothing—and on Germans too—really good work was done. Only there were no anaesthetics—no time—no money—no staff for that. So after that scene I need not fear to see the creepiest operations. One poor devil had his shin-bone crushed by a gun-carriage-wheel, and the doctor had to twist it about and push it like a piston to get out the pus. Another had a hole right through the knee; the doctor passed a bandage thus:

Another had a head into which a ball had entered and come out again.

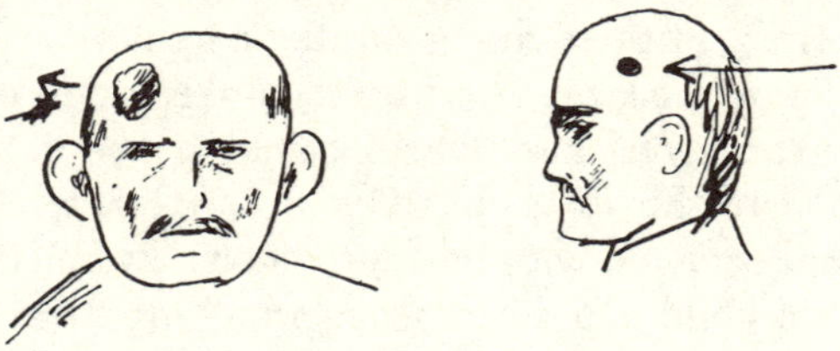

This is how the bullet lay in the Zouave. Sometimes the feet were covered with a brown, scaly, crust—dried blood.

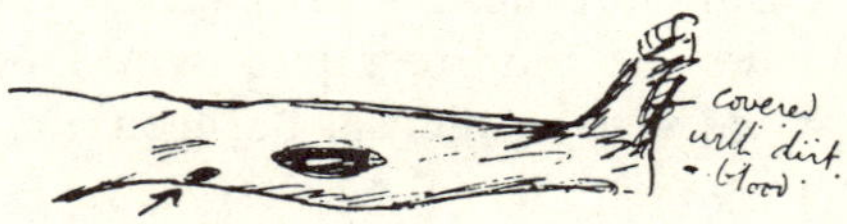

I deliberately tell you all this to educate you to the actualities of the war. (*CL* 284–5.)

That was a little self-regarding, in both senses. In more mature form, and now without smugness since the speaker himself is implicated, the same impulse can deliver a moment like this, from 'Dulce et Decorum Est':

> If in some smothering dreams you too could pace
> Behind the wagon that we flung him in,
> And watch the white eyes writhing in his face,
> His hanging face, like a devil's sick of sin;
> If you could hear, at every jolt, the blood
> Come gargling from the froth-corrupted lungs,
> Obscene as cancer, bitter as the cud
> Of vile, incurable sores on innocent tongues,—
> My friend, you would not tell with such high zest
> To children ardent for some desperate glory,
> The old Lie: Dulce et decorum est
> Pro patria mori.

The pious words of the poet Horace—that it is sweet and seemly to die for one's country—are brutally discredited by this illustration of the facts of the matter. I have already discussed the sensational or gothic shock as one feature of Owen's stylistic repertory. Complementing and sometimes (as here) merging with it is the naturalistic or photographic shock. The face 'like a devil's sick of sin' is sensationalist gothic (and indeed, Decadent); 'the froth-corrupted lungs' are clinical realism, with a moral accent. In temperance lessons about the ravages of drink Owen first met that unsparingly realist didacticism that is one of the weapons of his own documentation of the ravages of war.

The language of temperance also seems to have left an imprint on Owen in mythopoeic terms. It was a discourse which constructed an identity for young abstainers by telling them a story about themselves and the world. The Band of Hope's underlying myth is repeated in full or in fragments in the songs, stories, dramas and dialogues, addresses, catechisms, ballads, and games that made up its culture. You could reconstruct it just from the list of the *dramatis personae* of 'His One Fault: an Original Dialogue' (in *The Band of Hope Entertainer*), as a palaeontologist might build an image of a dinosaur from a bit of bone.

John Takesome	A Workingman
Mrs Takesome	His Wife
Lena	Their Little Daughter
Mr Caller	A Rent Collector
Mr Speakman	A Scripture Reader

It is a myth, as you would expect, of loss and redemption. First there is the happy man. Then the man takes a drink, which is poison. Alcohol actually becomes a serpent in the allegory 'The Worm': 'The symptoms of its *bite* are terrible. The eyes of the patient become red and fiery, his tongue swells to an immoderate size, and obstructs his utterance; and delirium of the most horrid character quickly follows.'[17] It corrupts his body, damages his family; he goes to the devil. He will die, unless he can be brought back to the path of righteousness and shown the error of his ways. The agent of redemption may be an adult Christian, but in the stories it is just as likely to be a child who persuades the drinker to take the pledge and live happily and sober ever after. The latter version, in which it is a child who saves the day, was more popular with an audience and, for dramas, a cast of children. In the dialogue 'His One Fault', mentioned above, the scripture reader and the little daughter together save John Takesome. The drinker is reclaimed through the word—the Christian word of the gospel and the temperance word of the pledge. Optional or implied at the end of the story is a choric rendering of 'We are Soldiers of Temperance'.

The motifs of this myth are of interest. The stricken man is saved by the untouched (innocent) child (or Redeemer). He is corrupted and deluded by drink: he must be cleansed and counselled. The alcohol in his mouth must be replaced by the word (the pledge, the gospel), administered by its acolyte. The structural pattern of the myth could be represented as the following opposition: *man/drink/alcohol/poison/madness: child/speak/word/healing/truth*.

If young abstainers were encouraged or flattered to see themselves as, potentially at least, young redeemers, this myth of the redeeming word was one which continued to compel Wilfred Owen. It led him at one point seriously to consider devoting his life's work to the Church. And when he turned his back on the Church, he took with him the myth of a healing redemption through speech.

[17] *The Band of Hope Entertainer*, 65.

The war poems are really an attempt to reclaim people from self-destruction and insanity by speaking the truth.

> Then, when much blood had clogged their chariot-wheels,
> I would go up and wash them from sweet wells,
> Even with truths that lie too deep for taint.

But in 'Strange Meeting' it is too late. The redemption is a story never to be told because the young redeemer has been killed, the hope he represented turning to hopelessness, the truth untold even as he finds a name for it, pity. Other poems insist even so, as 'Dulce et Decorum Est' does, that there is only one antidote to poison and madness.[18] There the soldier's body is ruined, his lungs 'froth-corrupted', because of the lies he has ardently imbibed. The only way to stop the ruin of countless bodies is by stopping corruption at its verbal source, 'the old Lie', which is why the true poets must be truthful.

A third point in which temperance discourse leaves its print on Owen's later language concerns a reaction to, rather than an adaptation of a feature of discourse. The human body is the central image and focus of temperance speech. It becomes too the central theme of Owen's poetry, and it is to the treatment of this theme that I now want to turn.

The 'Band of Hope Examination' is a catechism (a speech genre borrowed of course from the prayer book) in which young abstainers were drilled in the damage alcohol did to drinkers.

EXAMINER. What effect has it then?
SCHOLAR. It greatly *weakens* them by lowering their systems.
EXAMINER. But how is it that persons after drinking heavily appear to be lively, strong and brave?
SCHOLAR. They are *maddened* or goaded to their *seeming* hilarity, strength or bravery by the power of the drink. It is a *false* strength or bravery, such as is caused by goading or spurning a jaded horse.
EXAMINER. What effect has drink on a person's moral system?
SCHOLAR. It also *lowers* his or her *moral* system.[19]

[18] The poison which is a curious motif of some of the earlier poetry—'A Palinode' for example—may have entered his imagination from temperance warnings in one direction and from the image repertory of Romantic poetry in the other—'the poisons of self-harm' in Coleridge, for instance. There was also a plentiful pharmacopoeia of poisons in Decadent writing. After the trenches, there were more unequivocal poisons to write about.

[19] *The Band of Hope Entertainer*, 70.

Warnings against drink were warnings against the body, for the body's stupid pursuit of its own satisfactions could imperil moral character and sanity, as the Bellman warned. Evangelicals tended to feel that the body lacked seriousness. There was an ascetic emphasis in most Evangelical theology, and a suspicious attitude was taken to most bodily pleasures and recreations, at least indoor ones. The body had to be policed, if not bruised, to safeguard soul; for the body was a weak line of defence. 'Alcohol and its Effects', one not untypical group of temperance addresses, was headlined: '1. The Body 2. The Mind 3. Moral 4. Spiritual'.[20] And into the breach made by drink in the system, children were told, other sins of the flesh could infiltrate, among them gluttony, idleness, impurity, and 'false manliness'.

For children, the further dangers of the flesh could only be hinted at in blood-curdling but often completely unenlightening warnings. Adult temperance discourse could be more frank about the links between alcohol and promiscuity, disease and illegitimacy. Henry Carter, in *The Church and the Drink Evil*, quotes the Royal Commission on Venereal Diseases which reported, in 1916, that 'the communication of disease is frequently due to indulgence in intoxicants, and there is no doubt that the growth of temperance among the population would help to bring about an amelioration of the very serious conditions which our enquiry has revealed.' In a population of forty-six million it was estimated that there may have been as many as ten million who had either gonorrhoea or syphilis, and the Commission was told that about 80 per cent of venereal disease was acquired under the influence of alcohol.[21]

These were not matters for the ears of young persons. But although it seems neither parent gave their sons any direct guidance about sexual matters—Owen seems to reproach his mother for this in a 1914 letter (*CL* 234)[22]—Susan Owen did dispense, along with her temperance tracts, some 'extraordinarily puerile pamphlets' which only succeeded in alarming Harold (teenaged and about to go to sea but still 'profoundly unaware' in these matters) 'because they conveyed to me nothing but the conviction that even to think would be sufficient to bring down on me an unnamed but apparently most loathsome disease' (*JFO* 2. 58).

The temperance discourse that taught a fear of the body was part

[20] *Band of Hope Outline Addresses*, 1st series, 65–76.
[21] Carter (ed.), *The Church and the Drink Evil*, 20.
[22] See also Hibberd, 'Wilfred Owen's Letters', 280.

of a wider Evangelical campaign against the flesh, which was seen as essentially antagonistic to the spirit. The doctrine was to be found uncompromisingly stated in St Paul's Epistle to the Galatians, 5:17: 'For the flesh lusteth against the Spirit, and the Spirit against the flesh: and these are contrary the one to the other: so that ye cannot do the things that ye would.' Paul's blacklist of the works of the flesh starts with various sexual misbehaviour and ends with drunkenness and revellings, while his catalogue of the fruits of the Spirit runs from love and joy to temperance. This chapter had always been a favourite text among Evangelicals, whose views about bodily indulgence might be epitomized in the example of Sir James Stephen, who once smoked a cigar and found it so delicious that he never smoked again.[23] St Paul concludes (5:24): 'And they that are Christ's have crucified the flesh with the affections and lusts.'

As Wilfred Owen grew up he heard these denying words often enough to come to dislike them profoundly, for he had no wish to be recruited into this war which spirit had declared on flesh. St Paul was to make an appearance in the strange poem 'The time was aeon', begun at Dunsden. It gives a vision of the world as 'one vast deformity', which is nevertheless made lovely by a mysterious Presence:

> For as the morning sunshine sanctifies
> Even the ordure of a sordid town,
> So all this wreck was glamoured by some charm
> A mystery of music. For, a Presence there
> Created low, rich music, endlessly.

The name of 'that strange regnant Presence' is 'the Flesh', and it presides over the scene in the shape of the statue of a beautiful naked boy, which the poet says he cannot describe, or even think about, without being overwhelmed by a passion which seems to be both erotic and idolatrous. This is where St Paul comes in, and his words to the Galatians:

> Then watched I how there ran towards that way
> A multitude of railers, hot with hate,
> And maddened by the voice of a small Jew
> Who cried with a loud voice, saying 'Away!
> Away with him!' and 'Crucify him! Him,
> With the affections and the lusts thereof.'

[23] Bradley, *The Call to Seriousness*, 28.

'The time was aeon' seems to rest on a fairly straightforward contention. The flesh redeems the ugliness of the world, but the Church, to which beauty is a criminal, denies the flesh and kills it. It was almost certainly at Dunsden that Owen began to acknowledge to himself his homosexual feelings, and this predicament can only have sharpened his awareness of the way the flesh was treated as an enemy by St Paul's successors. But from what source, in dialogical terms, does the poem construct the discourse of the flesh which is set against the mortification of the body? Dominic Hibberd has identified the influence of 'Two Visions', the opening poem of Harold Monro's *Before Dawn*, and so (at second hand) of the 'liberalising and liberating views' of Edward Carpenter (*OTP* 26–7). But before this and more generally, Owen had found a counter to Evangelical asceticism in poetry, and there is no doubt that he saw the beauties and pleasures of the body as among the chief topics and attractions of poetry. There could be few better answers to temperance prohibitions and Evangelical denials than the enjoyment and imitation of a poet as sensational and as oral and throaty as Keats. Poetry itself was a counter-discourse to the commands and interdictions of authority.

The claims of the life of sensations and of bodily pleasures and beauties had to be defended more urgently as these things were more repressed, curtailed, and threatened—especially, then, in wartime. The greatest enemy of the body was war itself. As for Blunden the dreadfulness of war is most powerfully measured by what it does to a countryside, in Owen's poetry it is the body, in its terrible vulnerability, that takes the measure of war's cruelty. Indeed in 'The Show', a nature poem for the end of the world, the countryside has become one ruined and disgusting body, putrefying in war. The 'vast deformity' of the landscape imagined in 'The time was aeon' became actual in Flanders, and so did the punishment and torture of the flesh. But that landscape could still be 'glamoured', made lovely, and redeemed by the presence of the flesh, even (as in 'Greater Love', 'Beauty', 'Apologia pro Poemate Meo') when the flesh had indeed been insulted, defiled, and crucified by its enemies. For the 'multitude of railers' who hated it, the body was an alias, or an ally, of the devil. But in Owen's poems the body is innocent: he speaks in its defence. He had grown up listening to denunciations and suspicions of the flesh, delivered in the accents of the Church or under its auspices. But he was to realize that his own vocation lay in a different speech community, that of English poetry, in which he could find (and contribute to) a discourse that did not distrust and despise the physical life, but celebrated it, loved it, and could pity it.

Owen was no ascetic by temperament. Although most of his life was lived in conditions which did not allow of much physical pleasure, he had a strongly sensuous imagination and he believed he had a gift for enjoyment, a gift he had found abundantly present in the poems and letters of his early hero Keats. He even had a theory about this, which he playfully developed in answer to a letter in which his mother seems to have complained of suffering from 'nerves':

> Ah me! Nerves! Well, *my* philosophy teaches that those mortals who have nerves exquisitely responsive to painful sensation, have a perfect right to use them, when time serves, *to respond equally keenly to enjoyment.* I know I have a tingling capacity for pleasure on occasion, and if such be the operation of a tense nerve, then must I content me with nerves' foolish ado when things offend and lacerate them. Foh! how many things in this room, in this land, on this earth offend my senses! But I am willing to pay this price, to purchase the delight to the full, when delight is possible. (*CL* 167.)

Susceptibility to 'nerves' was the concomitant of bodily sensitivity to both pleasure and pain. Owen's nerves were a matter of more than 'foolish ado' when in 1917 he was diagnosed as a shell-shock neurasthenic. But before it acquired a military meaning this sensitivity was something simply to be prized, since he considered it a token or badge of artistic temperament. The artist was a specialist of the senses. Owen believed himself to be an artist, before he had much to go on except that belief. It was all very Romantic. Aged twenty and alone in France, he confided some of his ambitions and hesitations to his mother.

> My Temperament I have now no right to doubt. That I believe infallible; though it remains to know which, if any, Music, Painting, Sculpture, or Verse, is the most possible. Witness, to confirm what I believe of my composition, on one side the Tragedy of Uncle Edward Shaw, torn up by the roots by a perverted appetite; and on my other side, the Comedy of Aunt Emily Owen, who literally palpitates with excess of physical sensation.
>
> These are the natures which, labouring for self-expression, produce Art; and which rolling in retrogression produce Nothing or Crime. (*CL* 256.)

This confidence contained a signal which Owen must have known would be disturbing to his mother. He announces his artistic temperament as an inherited characteristic, citing as part of the evidence an affinity with the sensitivity of his Uncle Edward Shaw, Susan Owen's brother. This man, the cause of her obsession with drink and her immersion of her children in the prohibitions of temperance propaganda, was a drunkard who left the family home in 1891 and was never seen by them again.

8
The Work of the Ministry

At the Pan-Anglican Congress of 1908 the Revd W. H. Griffith Thomas delivered an address on the subject of *The Training of Candidates for Holy Orders*. Few people were better qualified to speak of what was required of a priest in the Church of England in the Edwardian era. Griffith Thomas was at the time Principal of the theological training college at Wycliffe Hall in Oxford, a respected scholar and teacher and, in the judgement of Kenneth Hylson-Smith, 'one of the most intellectually competent Evangelicals of his generation'.[1]

He began his talk by taking for granted that a candidate for the Anglican priesthood would be a university graduate or the equivalent, and already possessed of 'all that that means of general educational preparation'. One thing it meant was that clergy were normally recruited from the class that could afford a university education, the same class that supplied, for example, officers for the regular army. Scholarships were available (though not enough of them, in the speaker's opinion) but the most important resources a candidate would need were not material ones, for he would have to be prepared to be tested spiritually, intellectually, and pastorally. Spiritually, nothing could be done without a vocation: 'Do you think in your heart that you be truly called . . . to the Order and Ministry of Priesthood?' is the first and most vital question put to candidates in the service of ordination. Intellectual strengths would be needed for the interpretation of scripture and the study of doctrine, and unflagging energy in pastoral work would have to be devoted to the welfare of the flock. The address, published subsequently as a pamphlet, deals succinctly with all three of these aspects.

There was not much to be said about vocation except that any amount of training without it was a waste of time. Full-time training took a year, and Griffith Thomas reckoned that something like

[1] Hylson-Smith, *Evangelicals in the Church of England*, 274.

two-thirds of the student's time and attention would be taken up by the study of the Bible. As we have already seen, he was proud of the fact that no other church in Christendom used so much of scripture, or gave it so prominent a place in its services.[2] 'This study will naturally proceed along three lines. 1. The contents of the Bible, critically and devotionally studied; 2. the interpretation of the Bible, with constant reference to the closest and most accurate exegesis; 3. the application of the Bible to all the complexities of modern life.'[3] The student's curriculum would also need to include a study of the history of the Church, and of the standards of Anglican doctrine, contained in the Creeds, the thirty-nine Articles of Religion, and the Book of Common Prayer, and illustrated by homilies, an understanding of the Church of England's relation with other churches, and finally the 'evidences of Christianity', the arguments on which the true faith reposed.

More practically, it was important that the candidate should acquire 'the principles and art of speaking and preaching', since by these above all he would be assessed.[4] Teaching skills would also be needed, mainly but not only for work with children. And intending ministers would also certainly benefit from exposure to what life was actually like in the front line of Church work, in the parishes. However, in the matter of the Church's social role there was a line to be drawn. 'If no reference is made in these suggestions to the relation of the ministry to modern social problems it is not because these are deemed unimportant,' Thomas told his audience, but 'fundamental principles' had to come first. 'Nor must we forget that social ethics can never dominate religion. Christianity is far wider than society or any form of socialism, and it is never to be identified with the better provision of better conditions of living and with the relations of man to man.'[5] Finally, Griffith Thomas asked what sort of person was fitted for the great task of Christian ministry, and answered, in an arresting phrase, 'The call is for men of reality', elaborating, 'men who, notwithstanding their comparative youth, realise something of the unspeakable responsibility involved in standing between the living and the dead, of being ambassadors to a sinful world, of being watchmen for the souls of men, of being instant in season and out of season.'[6]

[2] W. H. Griffith Thomas, *The Work of the Ministry*, 126.
[3] W. H. Griffith Thomas, *The Training of Candidates for Holy Orders*, 4.
[4] Ibid. 5. [5] Ibid. 6. [6] Ibid. 8.

All of the themes of *The Training of Candidates for Holy Orders* are dealt with more fully three years later in Griffith Thomas's *The Work of the Ministry*, to which I will return; but already in the little 1908 pamphlet is an epitome of most of the issues which will be examined in this section, on Wilfred Owen and the ministry.

He was eighteen when he joined the Revd Herbert Wigan as lay assistant in his parish at Dunsden near Reading in October 1911, and he was to leave the vicarage in February 1913, the month before his twentieth birthday. It is not possible to say how long or how seriously Owen considered a career in the Church of England. Harold Owen maintains that before accepting the 'unofficial curacy' at Dunsden, his brother told Mr Wigan it was extremely unlikely that he would ever enter the Church, and his accepting the Dunsden post must be without prejudice to his choice of a career (*JFO* 1. 255–7). But it would be prudent to remember that this conversation, reported in detail fifty years after the event by a man who was not there, has its part to play in Harold Owen's running battle with his mother's religion, whose claims on Wilfred he is constantly playing down.

For a while in August 1910 Wilfred Owen had considered trying to get in to St Aidan's Theological College in Birkenhead. Susan Owen must have encouraged and perhaps even suggested this move, but the seventeen-year-old Wilfred was making no promises at this stage. 'Certainly, if it is possible, it is my wish to get into such a college. As to whether I mean [to] be a clergyman is a different matter' (*CL* 65). Nothing came of this project, and the following year steps initiated by his mother were taken which led Owen to the door of Mr Wigan. Harold Owen claims that Wilfred did some theological reading to ready himself for Dunsden, but gave up this preparation before he ever got there. Yet he was reading enough theology the following June to complain about it in what he himself described as an 'important letter' to his mother.

> One thing I may state, and that is—I definitely abandon the *thought* of Divinity Training *till* at least an Arts Degree is won. Such at present is my resolve. All Theological lore is growing distasteful to me. All my recent excursions into such fields proves [*sic*] it to be a shifting, hypothetical, doubt-fostering, dusty and unprofitable study. Such a conclusion at my time of life is not to be wondered at. It may change hereafter. All I can do now is to groan with Meredith:

'Ah what a dusty answer gets the soul
When hot for certainties in this our life.' (*CL* 141.)

That dialogic move is characteristic of the Dunsden period. Owen answers theological lore with a poetic utterance, a text which becomes a key of doubt to let him out of the closures of dogma. Probably this rejection of the idea of an ecclesiastical future is presented as a postponement only to soften his mother's disappointment, for there is no doubt that she had set her heart on a Church career for her favourite son, and she may not have given up this dream even after the 'bust-up' (*CL* 175) at Dunsden.

It is most likely in my judgement that Wilfred Owen took up the post of Mr Wigan's lay assistant primarily because it seemed to offer him an opportunity to further his secular studies with the aid of some tuition from the vicar, in exchange for help with parochial work, and that his intentions in the longer term (like the extent of his duties in the parish) were never clearly spelled out. In a sense, however, it is no vital loss that we do not know precisely what Wilfred Owen thought he was doing when he arrived at Reading station that October. For the next year and a half he was treated by the vicar—and would certainly have been regarded in the parish—as if his credentials and function were no different from those of his predecessor as lay assistant, Alfred Saxelby-Kemp, whose stay at Dunsden overlapped with Owen's until May 1912, when he left for the London College of Divinity and eventually a Church of England career.

From October 1911 to the new year of 1913, Owen lived in the vicarage, helped in the church, and worked hard in the parish at Dunsden. He studied the Bible, tracts, and some theology (begrudging the time lost to botanical studies and poetry), composed sermons for children's services, visited the sick and needy, and did more than his share of parish administration. He attended innumerable meetings and, in the summer of 1912, the great annual Evangelical gathering at Keswick. At the end of this time Wilfred Owen was not a Christian in any conventional sense, but during it he was as immersed in the language and affairs of the Church as if he had been a prospective candidate for holy orders without a doubt in the world. He was living in the usually placid ideological mainstream of Anglican Evangelicalism, and his function in that institution was a role, or a series of roles, in the institution's discourse. For Owen between the ages of eighteen and twenty—a time when, he was sourly aware, if his family had been richer or luckier he might have been studying at university—this discursive experience was very important indeed.

It is a well-documented experience. This was the first time Owen found himself away from home for an extended period, and he wrote copious letters describing his day-to-day activities, his work in the parish, and life at the vicarage. The vicar was a believer in delegation and, especially after Kemp's departure, Owen seems to have had to do all the work that an ordained curate might have been given, except presumably for officiating at the sacraments, though there was one occasion when he thought he would have to take a marriage service in Mr Wigan's absence (*CL* 139). According to Kemp, Wigan 'took little interest in the parish, and rarely seemed to go out' (*CL* 91). Owen was to become resentful of the way it sometimes seemed he was expected to do the work of the ministry in Dunsden, virtually single-handed and virtually unpaid. But when he first arrived to take up his post, he liked what he saw.

For reasons I have already discussed, Owen had an acute sensitivity to signals of social class. His first impressions of Dunsden are contained in a highly satisfactory report to his mother on the size of the vicarage, the opulence and gravity of its domestic life, the excellence of its unobtrusive servants. The early Dunsden letters are cheerful: this was the life, or so it seemed, a long way from the actuality if not from the aspirations of Monkmoor Road, Shrewsbury. 'In fact every[thing] is on the scale of a fine country *manor*, and my only sorrow is that you are not in a like man(ner)or established!' (*CL* 92). Owen's fellow-assistant Kemp thought Mr Wigan 'rather lordly', and he remembered the village women curtseying to him (*CL* 91). The vicar was a bachelor with an interest in his own genealogy, and his establishment was rather aloof and grand. His junior lay assistant was paid only pocket-money and he sometimes had to ask his father to supplement this, although (he told his mother cheerfully) 'I do feel ashamed of begging thus when I live as if my income were £500, and sit on a chair worth £20!' (*CL* 117).

But as he started to find Dunsden increasingly irksome, Owen began to apply to it language appropriate to describing a dead body. The vicar himself was rigid and cold, 'the Silence, the State and the Stiffness' of the vicarage became oppressive, its atmosphere was 'putrid' (*CL* 157, 104, 171). After-dinner conversation at the vicarage was obligatory but without spontaneity; it was joyless and stilted, with great yawning chasms of silence that were first embarrassing, then just tedious. And there were different levels of constraint. There was what Owen called vicarage life proper—'Oh very proper indeed'—from which he escaped as often as he could into the privacy of his own room. There was secondary vicarage life, consisting of his intercourse with the servants, more relaxed, but hardly familiar, for he had had no real experience of dealing with trained professional domestic servants. And there was '*Super-Vicarage Life*' when there were guests in the house, evening dress was *de rigueur*, and Owen was expected to be (and professed himself) amused by a story about 'a big Oxford savant appearing to a dinner with black coat but *grey* trousers!' (*CL* 156–7).

All this became oppressive, though not for completely straightforward reasons. His life in the lofty gentility of Dunsden vicarage can be linked to the imaginary barricades of class behind which the family crouched in Birkenhead, as it can be linked forward to his uneasy self-consciousness, on joining the Manchester Regiment in June 1916, at finding himself 'marooned on a Crag of Superiority in an ocean of Soldiers' (*CL* 395). This world of privilege and inhibition was neither altogether foreign to Owen nor altogether distasteful. He enjoyed physical comfort. He thought and spoke of himself as a gentleman. His upbringing had given him a deference to authority and a sense of the importance of status. He was a conformist and a snob. If Wigan's style was stiff and pontifical, he seemed at first 'on a higher plane than myself' to the eighteen-year-old Owen (*CL* 92), who was in any case himself inclined to be highly pompous in manner on occasion. In fact Owen's increasing dissatisfaction was a function of his awareness of an uncomfortable contrast between life inside the vicarage and life in the parish which it served. Since the vicar, as Kemp remembered, took little interest in the parish and rarely seemed to go out, his assistant's involvement in the life and problems of the village was necessarily in direct proportion to Wigan's distaste for these things. It was in delegated pastoral duties, and especially among Dunsden's children, that Wilfred Owen was most involved in the work of the ministry, and from that perspective that he became most indignant about the shortcomings of religion and its ministers. At Dunsden vicarage a new meaning was laid over the figure, important and recurrent in the history of his imagination, of a division drawn between shelter within and exposure without.

Owen's parish work took him among the children, the sick, and the poor of Dunsden. Since he was given just those duties which Mr Wigan had not the time or the taste for, it is not surprising that the sympathy and pity these cases aroused in Owen were accompanied by resentment and anger that they were being neglected by those who should have felt professionally responsible for them, and could have helped. So the emotional repertory and the polemical stance of the trench poems were prepared here, as the young unofficial curate trudged round the cottages of the poor with a pocketful of tracts. There were not exactly beggars at the gates of Dunsden vicarage, but the village parish had its share of ill-paid agricultural labourers in tied cottages, and long-term unemployed; and Owen alarmed his mother by telling her that consumption was 'all around us here', adding that 'Scarlet Fever and Diphtheria are at work near by' (*CL* 109). The sense of contrast was heightened by the fact that the vicarage was a bachelor establishment. Wigan's two young assistants were addressed jocularly as Brother Kemp and Brother Owen, but there were no women in this artificial family, except below stairs, and there were no children—in fact it seems to have been forbidden to invite village children into the house.[7] Speech in the vicarage was lofty, ponderous, stilted, and cold; outside there were other voices, more spontaneous, warmer, and more urgent. Owen himself moved, listened, and spoke in both worlds. The village life he knew, however, was no carnival of Bakhtinian heteroglossia, but a stiff hierarchy of discourses, with little dialogue between them.

The fairly full picture of parochial work in Owen's Dunsden letters can be usefully supplemented by Griffith Thomas's book *The Work of the Ministry*, published in 1911 and intended for young men just embarking, or intending to embark, on a career in the Church of England. There is no evidence that Owen knew this work, though it is not unlikely: the book was newly published

[7] Jon Stallworthy suspects that the 'furore' alluded to in the incompletely preserved letter of 4 January 1913 might have been caused 'by Wigan finding Vivian Rampton [a village boy befriended by Owen] smuggled into the vicarage'. (*WO* 83).

when he came to Dunsden, and Thomas was well-known as a pillar of the Evangelical establishment, editor of the *Churchman*, and one of the stars of the Keswick convention (where Owen was to hear him preach in 1912), besides being a man whose speciality was the preparation of young men for the Church. Whether or not *The Work of the Ministry* was put into the hands of Mr Wigan's new assistant, it is an authoritative and contemporary account, from a man whose views coincided with Susan Owen's and Herbert Wigan's own, of the world that Owen entered when he went to Dunsden. In Thomas's book you can listen to the Church of England talking to and about itself.

Readers of *The Work of the Ministry* were told that the single most important function of the clergyman was to speak to his people. 'Where the spiritual life has been greatest there the preaching has been strongest,' for from a low-church Anglican point of view the focus of the church was the pulpit, rather than the altar, which went with ritualism and with Rome. 'Wherever the priest goes up the prophet goes down.'[8] Thomas's advice on preaching is much to the point. As the letters show, Owen had been something of a connoisseur of sermons since childhood. His duties at Dunsden entailed hearing Mr Wigan preach every week, and no doubt he listened with the critical interest of an apprentice. There were also quite frequently visiting preachers, speakers at numerous Christian meetings in the parish, in Reading, and in London—not to mention the occasional political speech (in June 1912 he heard F. E. Smith speak at a Conservative fête, noting proudly that he was 'an old B[irken]head school boy' (*CL* 139)), and, whenever there was time, literary lectures to be attended. So the Dunsden months brought Owen into continual contact with public speaking in different modes, as a listener but also as a speaker. It was not his job to preach at regular Sunday services, but he had to organize and attend (and complained of) innumerable meetings at which he was expected to take the lead—his letters are full of accounts of Scripture Union meetings, Saturday prayer meetings, Bible classes, Sunday school, parish meetings, mothers' social evenings and the like. But speaking to children was among his first duties, and it became a regular and enjoyable one. In November 1911 he wrote about it to his sister Mary:

[8] W. H. Griffith Thomas, *The Work of the Ministry*, 202.

I addressed the Children's Service in the Parish Hall on Sunday Afternoon. I am also booked for the Scripture Union on Thurs. I enjoy speaking very much. I use no notes, and spend no great time in preparation; but I use no high falutin' words, but try to express myself in simple, straightforward English. I believe the children are impressed for the time being. I hope they will really benefit, for, of course, I give them the Messages, with one Purpose, and not with any idea of displaying my own bumptiousness. (*CL* 94.)

And in the following paragraph he is telling her he has been with the vicar to 'Earley Court, the fine residence of some of the Suttons' Seeds people', to hear Bishop Ingham, who was Home Secretary of the Church Missions Society. 'I need hardly say that the Address more than justified the great praise which I heard of him from you at Shrewsbury.'

Kemp and Owen, student assistants at Dunsden, would have been well aware of the paramountcy of speaking in the Evangelical ministry. As the descendant of the Old Testament prophets, according to Griffith Thomas, the minister's functions were those of messenger, witness, pleader, comforter, and herald, all speech roles which, incidentally, point to a set of speech acts that cover quite fully Owen's later idea of the function of the poet in wartime—warning, truth-telling, advocacy, consolation (of those who deserved it), prediction. The Romantic poet in Owen would also have approved of 'the classic definition of preaching', which Thomas gave as 'truth through personality'.[9] Preaching is a very clear line connecting the Dunsden lay assistant with the author of the war poetry and the draft preface. Dominic Hibberd observes that a knowledge of what happened at Dunsden contributes to an understanding of Owen's later poems. 'The public role to which he aspired in 1918 was that of an evangelising preacher against hypocrisy, false creeds, oppression and lack of pity' (*OTP* 13). This is certainly true, and one could go further. Dunsden was Owen's school of rhetoric. It was there, and in ways whose later outcome could never have been foreseen, that he first encountered as a practical question the issue of the power of language and how it could be harnessed to best effect, and the relation created between a speaker or pleader and those he wanted to move by his speech. The parish of Dunsden was a very small world indeed, but it

[9] Ibid. 202.

introduced Owen quite literally to something he had neither met nor considered before: a public for his words. This is an issue which Griffith Thomas can help to illuminate, because of his emphasis on the importance of rhetoric in the work of the ministry, on speaking, and on the variety of factors that determine it.

Thomas's book contains excellent practical advice for the beginner. 'Let us beware of saying "Finally" until we are really at the close of our sermon' is obviously sound, as is 'It would be particularly wise to avoid preaching from the Song of Solomon while we are young in the ministry.'[10] More seriously, he advises speakers always to consider the audience and circumstances of their speech. Of the regular sermon, he says:

> It is an address to a mixed class, and therefore ought not as a rule to deal with any speciality, still less with any technicality. 'I do admire the vicar's sermons, mum; 'E's so wonderful fluid.' 'I'm so glad you like them, Mrs Smith; do you understand them?' 'Me, mum? Oh, no; I wouldn't presume to hunderstand 'em, mum.'[11]

This little dialogue is unmistakably in the idiom of a *Punch* cartoon. Yet the serious point behind it (and the mimicry too) find an echo in the reservations Owen was to express when he paused in the writing of the late poem 'Spring Offensive', telling Siegfried Sassoon he did not want 'to write anything to which a soldier would say No Compris!' (*CPF* 193). Both preacher and poet must recognize themselves to be privileged beings; but for their words to be most widely effective, they had to find a common tongue.

This involved, Griffith Thomas suggested, trying to give the sermon the spontaneity of speech. But that did not mean that he disapproved of rhetorical artifice. 'No one can doubt that the extemporaneous ideal is the true one . . . But we know that unless a sermon obeys the laws of art, and is the result of genuine work, it will be of no value whatever.'[12] A good speaker could improve by studying other preachers, the Bible, history, and literature. Milton, Wordsworth, and Tennyson were held up as models of lucidity and grace, George Eliot and Froude were recommended 'because of their simplicity, force, and directness'.[13] Owen started to read George Eliot at Dunsden, beginning appropriately with *Scenes from Clerical Life*.

[10] Ibid. 219, 225. [11] Ibid. 204. [12] Ibid. 205. [13] Ibid. 214.

An address had four essential elements, Thomas considered. The first was definiteness of aim. The second was simplicity and precision of language: style must be cultivated but all 'high-flown language' should be carefully avoided. A lesson could be learned from the late Bishop Ryle of Liverpool, who abandoned the florid language of his earlier sermons and 'to use his own expression, determined to "crucify his style"'.[14] Third, the address should be clearly arranged with a coherent structure of narrative or argument. And lastly, it should have forcefulness of application. As we have seen, Griffith Thomas believed that a sermon's message should be made 'as personal, direct, and definite as possible', for the object was nothing less than to change people's lives. The model preacher was Christ himself, but the *locus classicus* of the 'direct, personal appeal' was the parable preached by the Old Testament prophet Nathan to King David in 2 Samuel 12, whose devastating rhetorical shock Thomas quotes admiringly: 'Each hearer must feel the force of the words, as though the preacher were saying to him, "Thou art the man!"'[15] This rhetorical turn on the second person is a move Owen was to use, with variations, at the ends of 'Dulce et Decorum Est':

> My friend, you would not tell with such high zest
> To children ardent for some desperate glory,
>   The old Lie—

of 'Apologia pro Poemate Meo':

>   These men are worth
> Your tears. You are not worth their merriment—

of 'Mental Cases':

> Snatching after us who smote them, brother,
> Pawing us who dealt them war and madness—

and (with a dramatic twist) of 'Strange Meeting': 'I am the enemy you killed, my friend.'

Now if it were a case of trying to identify a single precedent for this single rhetorical tactic, then Owen might as easily have found the move anticipated in, say, Baudelaire's 'Au Lecteur' (which he

[14] Ibid. 214. [15] Ibid. 214.

almost certainly knew) as in Griffith Thomas or the prophet Nathan. I am not arguing the case for seeing direct influence here, but a sense of discursive potential: this is the move of someone who has an audience in mind, and definite and even aggressive designs upon it. Owen's experience and some of his studies at Dunsden had taught him to think in this way. And in this respect, Thomas's other 'essential requirements' for speaking are also to the point of the poetry Owen was soon to write. We have already glimpsed his views on simplicity and clarity; as for definiteness of aim, Owen is the only poet I know whose table of contents lists not only the title but also the 'motive' of each poem.[16] The draft preface declares the aim of his poems: 'My subject is War, and the pity of War', an aim so definite and urgent as to make him impatient with his own medium: 'Above all I am not concerned with Poetry' (*CPF* 535). C. H. Spurgeon, himself a rhetorician of genius possessed by the urgency of what he had to say, had expressed the same sort of apparently paradoxical impatience in a sermon: 'Words, words, words; we have so many words, and they are but chaff, but where is THE WORD that in the beginning was God and was with God?'[17]

What Owen learned at Dunsden about preaching and public speaking, from observation, study, and his own practice, made him think about uses of language quite different from the Keatsian rhetoric he admired, with its lyric language of sensation and natural expression, devoted to beauty and what might be termed the private feelings, a language mistrustful of what Keats called a palpable design.[18] But for the preacher, everything was subordinate to that design. The Evangelical address was a public utterance, audience-orientated and determined to convert, to save souls, for Thomas urged his readers to remember that there would always be unconverted and sceptical members of any congregation, and even the devout needed to have their faith renewed. 'Every preacher

[16] The motives include such things as 'How the Future will forget', 'The unnaturalness of weapons', 'Foolishness of War' (*CPF* 539). The existence of this draft does not mean that Owen intended that the list of motives should be published in the eventual book, but their motives seem to have been a factor in his choosing the order in which the poems should be printed.

[17] Spurgeon, *Sermons*, 247–8.

[18] 'We hate poetry that has a palpable design upon us.' Keats, Letter to J. H. Reynolds, 3 Feb. 1818.

should have a definite aim . . . All the brilliance of our sermons will count for nothing unless we are enabled to "save some".'[19]

By the end of his time at Dunsden, Owen was hostile to the clerical public voice. He knew its tricks too well from observation and practice, he was alert to its hypocrisies (especially Mr Wigan's (*CL* 126)), and sceptical about its assertive dogmatism—whereas by now his own treatise on philosophy, he said, 'would be a succession of interrogations from beginning to end' (*CL* 178). But above all, the clerical voice and vocation seemed to him to be inimical to the poetic voice and vocation, and he would have to choose between them. The clash of those discourses is the great running theme of the Dunsden letters. Owen's understanding of both the preacher and the poet would have to develop in as yet unforeseeable ways before the two discourses could become one, in his didactic poetry. In a letter from France a month before his death, he told his mother: 'I came out in order to help these boys—directly by leading them as well as an officer can; indirectly, by watching their sufferings that I may speak of them as well as a pleader can' (*CL* 580). As a soldier and a poet, he found himself doing the pastoral and the preaching work of another kind of ministry. Among the lessons of the Dunsden period then remembered with a new aptness might well have been what Griffith Thomas, concluding his advice on speaking, called 'The Deepest Secret of All'. 'The most important factor of everything is the man behind the sermon. "Thou must thyself be true, if thou the truth would'st teach".'[20] The true preachers must be truthful.

As well as insisting on sincerity—and he makes the interesting enough point that 'moral honesty' is especially required in speaking to children,[21] a point with which the author of 'Dulce et Decorum Est' was to agree—Thomas stressed that the clergyman's sympathy must be catholic enough to reach any audience (a group of poor women, for example), even though he himself was sure to be middle-class and male.

> We must neither lecture, nor hector the women who come to Mothers' Meetings, for it is not our place and province, and we shall inevitably do

[19] W. H. Griffith Thomas, *The Work of the Ministry*, 236.
[20] Ibid. 273. I have not been able to identify the quotation.
[21] Ibid. 246.

harm rather than good if we attempt it. One thing will always be welcome and admits of universal application. Our addresses at Mothers' Meetings should not fail to contain the note of comfort in them. The joylessness and monotony of life among the poor, especially among poor women, should not be forgotten.[22]

There was no pretence that the speaker at mothers' meetings, a job usually delegated to the curate or assistant, suffered the hardships of real poverty. He was being asked (as Siegfried Sassoon in his protest was to ask the nation at home) to have the imagination to realize sufferings he did not share, and to use his voice to try to alleviate them. The reciprocation of tears was part of the work of the ministry, even though the tears of the minister must of necessity flow *down* to his poorer parishioners. In 'The Calls', Owen's poem about vocation, the speaker's voice is an answer to the speechless sighs of the soldiers in his charge: it is also a secular affirmative to the first question in the ordination ceremony, which asks the candidate if he thinks in his heart that he is 'truly called'. At first, he is unstirred by the sights and sounds of the world going about its business.

A dismal fog-hoarse siren howls at dawn.
I watch the man it calls for, pushed and drawn
Backwards and forwards, helpless as a pawn.
    But I'm lazy, and his work's crazy . . .

Then sometimes late at night my window bumps
From gunnery practice, till my small heart thumps
And listens for the shell-shrieks and the crumps,
    But that's not all.

For leaning out last midnight on my sill,
I heard the sighs of men, that have no skill
To speak of their distress, no, nor the will!
    A voice I know. And this time I must go.

This vocation is not the call to the Church—the speaker has already been summoned by bells to church in the third stanza, and declined to go—but it is a call to the work of ministry, and it is one that will bring the poet down (and out) from his lofty indoor vantage, to the unprivileged level of a common distress. The call was for men of reality.

[22] Ibid. 250.

And the pulpit too was rather like that window-sill: you could lean out from there and see and hear the whole world without being touched by it. Evangelical clergy in Owen's lifetime knew that their most important duties were performed in the pulpit, but they were not at all clear just how far they should step down from it. Mr Wigan, as we have seen, took little interest in his parish. Griffith Thomas, to whom we can turn for something like the official Evangelical line on this, is interestingly indecisive about the clergyman's social dealings with his flock. He notes that the ordinal lays very little stress on regular house-to-house parochial visitation, which he says is a comparatively recent practice, and one not shared by Nonconformists who visit only their own people, or by the Catholic clergy who wait in the confessional for the parish to come to them. He does say the authority of a preacher depends on his social visibility. But preaching itself must be the priority. 'A man who visits morning, noon and night, will find himself at the end of the week physically fagged, and intellectually unfit to brace himself for the effort required to prepare a proper sermon.'[23] And in any case, the clergy 'must beware of gaining a reputation for attending afternoon teas'.[24] He does give advice on visiting, but he is not very enthusiastic about it. He warns that visitation, whether of rich or poor, requires a large expense of time for an indifferent return. There are exceptions. 'The visitation of the sick,' he says perhaps unguardedly, 'is a rare opportunity.'[25] For the clergy's calls were business calls, and their real business lay in guarding and increasing the trophy of grace. 'It is very essential to have at hand a supply of suitable tracts and booklets which we can leave when paying calls.'[26]

What is implicit here is later brought into the open in Thomas's section on social work. Ultimately, the work of the ministry was with the soul and not society.

Christianity emphasises sin, but the social reformer is only concerned with selfishness; and yet it is when the latter is seen to be due to the former that we shall get men and matters right. Christianity urges personal reform, Socialism cries out for corporate action. One emphasises regeneration, the other legislation. Now the latter is great and important, but the former is still greater. We must insist on both.[27]

[23] Ibid. 277. [24] Ibid. 279. [25] Ibid. 287.
[26] Ibid. 296. [27] Ibid. 348.

We have already heard temperance Evangelicals speaking just like this.

> We must be particularly careful not to identify Christianity with any ideas and schemes of social and economic reform . . . At the risk of being misunderstood, we must call attention to the fact that Jesus Christ Himself was not a Reformer, and He did not organise men to bring about a reconstruction and improvement of human life.[28]

He is treading cautiously here because he knows he is in a minefield of controversy. Thomas allowed that it was all right for a clergyman to do voluntary work with the Christian Social Union, because it 'does not pledge itself to any particular scheme of social improvement, still less to any attempt at revolution', and with the temperance movement, though even there, there was 'the risk of being regarded as political or prejudiced'. These were fairly safe areas of social work, as was 'active co-operation with the Peace Movement' on behalf of international arbitration. But apart from these uncontroversial worthy causes, Thomas advised that men of the cloth should not meddle in 'industrial conditions, the treatment of pauperism, protective legislation for workers, the housing of the people, and above all, the land question', for fear of what he calls 'the charge of politics'.[29]

The subtext of this strangely familiar call for the clergy to keep out of politics is an anxiety about alienating the Church of England's preponderant conservative constituency. Nonconformists might agitate for radical reforms, but the Church of England should not rock the establishment vessel in which it was a weighty passenger. Holding an authority vested in them by a national institution, the Anglican clergy could not (so this argument went) be seen to be partial. This meant they should not involve themselves in what everyone called 'the Social Question'; and this inaction was described as non-political. Clerics were therefore encouraged to see themselves as above or outside or exempt from politics. This argument, vigorously pursued, but also challenged, among Evangelicals at the time Owen was at Dunsden, is important for two reasons. One is the congruence, of which Owen was well aware, between the roles of priest and army officer. The officer was the creature of a national civil and military authority whose

[28] Ibid. 348–9. [29] Ibid. 350.

orders it was unlawful for him to question. But by the same token he was responsible for men under the wheels of the same juggernaut. This dilemma was not completely unfamiliar to him, after Dunsden. The second consequence of the social question was a more immediate one: it became the focus of Owen's growing disgust with Dunsden and the Church of England. In April 1912 he wrote: 'I am increasingly liberalising and liberating my thought, spite of the Vicar's strong Conservatism' (*CL* 131). But it was that summer, at the Keswick convention, that the crisis came.

9
Troublesome Voices

Wilfred Owen brought to the Keswick convention a grievance and a doubt. The grievance had its root in Christian attitudes (and especially Mr Wigan's) to social misery. Evangelical theology laid great emphasis on the doctrine of original sin. Evangelicals urged submission to suffering, because suffering was the consequence of original sin and was therefore inevitable: there was not much to be done about it since you could not change fallen human nature. 'Self cannot be improved, it must be crucified,' declared E. W. Moore, an original pillar of the Keswick conventions and one of Susan Owen's favourite clergymen.[1] He later added dishearteningly: 'Life is not a struggling after ideals; it is a clinging to Jesus.'[2] Looking at the texts annotated with Wilfred's name in Susan Owen's Bible, Dominic Hibberd remarks that the mother was already showing her child 'that passive endurance was the way to deal with unhappiness' (*OTP* 6). Harold Owen was taught the same, though he was a less tractable pupil, especially when the point of the lesson was that he might as well forget his ambitions to become a painter.

An approach to my mother—I made one or two tentative ones when I found her in a tender and receptive mood—always brought forth the grave injunction that 'all was in God's hands' and that interference on my part was wicked and irreverent and was the tempting voice of the devil and must be eschewed at all costs; this would always be followed by a beseeching that I would be content with what God ordained, no matter how lowly and humble that lot might be; to wish for anything else was profane, and she would finish off by saying that ambition and success were all right for people in their right place, but were not meant to be

[1] Owen himself knew Moore. He reported listening 'with delight' to Moore's preaching in 1911, and the following year, when the old man came to stay at Dunsden, a letter to Susan Owen gives a long and quite funny description of his oratorical manner (*CL* 82, 120–1).

[2] Moore, *Wanted, a Man!*, 15, 59. For Moore's association with the Holiness movement and with Keswick, see Hylson-Smith, *Evangelicals in the Church of England*, 191f.

indulged in by us. To strive for things that we were not meant to have was wrong. (*JFO* 2. 55.)

Things could not be changed, and must be endured; this was the burden of the pamphlets and tracts Owen left behind after visiting the cottages of the poor in Dunsden. Mr Wigan was fond of deprecating the things 'of this world' (*CL* 123), and a profession of unconcern for the things and the affairs of the world was a position with a long history in Evangelical discourse. As Doreen Rosman puts it: 'The belief that this world was but "the antechamber to the next", and the accompanying conviction that eternal life was essentially a future experience, caused many evangelicals seriously to devalue secular activity.'[3] Some secular activities were easier to devalue than others. It is strongly hinted in the letters that Mr Wigan was more interested in his antiques than in his parishioners; Owen unkindly juxtaposes the vicar's sermons on otherworldliness with his passion for buying and selling furniture. The other face of otherworldliness was selfishness and insensibility.

In the previous month, the *Christian* reported (on 12 February 1912) an address by the Bishop of Oxford in which he deplored 'the blank, and, as it seems to me, the simply stupid, refusal of church-people to recognise their social duties'. The *Christian*—to give it its full title, *The Christian, with which is incorporated 'The Revival': a Weekly Record of Christian Life and Testimony, Evangelistic Effort, and Missionary Enterprise*—had to hand just the right Evangelical answer to the bishop's outburst. 'Wealth has a terrible tendency to blind its possessors. It is when riches *increase* that we are warned not to set our hearts upon them. But we are always driven back to the living Christ for the solution of the social problem: a changed spirit would soon result in changed conditions.'

Owen's own attitude to 'the social problem' is consequent on his beginning work in Wigan's parish, and makes its first textual appearance in an interestingly muddled way in a letter of 7 November to his sister Mary, the same letter from which I have already given a quotation about his visit to Earley Court.

From such mansions as these, I pass, next afternoon, to the wretched hovels of this Parish, and carry myself with equal ease in the crazy,

[3] Rosman, *Evangelicals and Culture*, 55.

evil-smelling huts of the poor, as in the wide, luxurious chambers of the rich.

Numbers of the old people cannot read; those who can seldom do so. Scores of them have passed their whole lives in the same stone box with a straw lid, which they call their cottage; and are numbed to all interests beyond it. Those who have within them the Hope of a Future World are content, and their old faces are bright with the white radiance of eternity. Those who, like the beasts, have no such Hope, pass their old age shrouded with an inward gloom, which the reverses of their history have stamped upon their worn-out memories, deadening them to all thoughts of delight.

There is one poor creature who cannot be said to live—she exists and no more: She can neither speak, hear, nor see; I suppose she can taste, smell, and feel. But alas, all her feeling must be that of pain, for she has a disease of the bone; all her smell must be the smell of a foul cottage; all her taste, the taste of bread and of tea. What a life! Why am I telling you these dreadful things? Simply to let them educate you, as they are educating me, in the Book of Life, and to make us rejoice in our own happy state. (*CL* 95.)

But it is not clear just what lesson Owen thought this chapter of the book of life was teaching him. Here is the Evangelical insistence that what really mattered was the next world, with a painterly illustration of the pious poor, their faces transfigured (an important image for Owen) by a radiance which his sister would probably not recognize as a reflection from the atheist Shelley's *Adonais*.[4] And here too, in rather carefully poised prose, was the dumb and squalid suffering of the hopeless.

Some months later there is real anger as well as pity for a girl of five suffering from consumption, her father perennially out of work and her mother half starving for the sake of four children. This time Owen is not prompted to talk about long-suffering serenity.

Isn't it pitiable? She is going to a hospital (weeks hence *of course*), and may be beyond reach of doctors by that time . . . This, I suppose, is only a typical *case*; one of many *Cases*! O hard word! How it savours of rigid, frigid professionalism! How it suggests smooth and polished, formal, labelled, mechanical callousness! Even the gaunt Selwood [another dying consumptive in the parish] is not yet provided for; and is not likely to be. (*CL* 126.)

[4] 'Life, like a dome of many-coloured glass, | Stains the white radiance of Eternity.' *Adonais*, stanza lii.

It is not a coincidence that this comes in a letter that also complains about Mr Wigan. The epithets Owen chooses (rigid, frigid, formal) to denounce insensitive professionalism suggest strongly whom he had in mind as its personification. By this time the book of life was becoming more alarming.

From what I hear straight from the tight-pursed lips of wolfish ploughmen in their cottages, I might say there is material ready for another revolution. Perhaps men will *strike*, not with absence from work; but with arms at work. Am I for or against upheaval? I know not; I am not happy in these thoughts; yet they press upon me. I am happier when I go to '*distribute dole*

To poor sick people, richer in His eyes,
Who ransomed us, and haler too than I'. (*CL* 131.)

But he did not follow Tennyson's *Guinevere* into its next line, 'And treat their loathsome hurts and heal my own.' The social question, and the Church of England's failure to answer it (at least in the parish of Dunsden) was a grievance which was already compacting with a doubt, by the time Owen arrived to take part in the convention at Keswick in July 1912.

A combination of factors had raised the social question for the Church in the first decade of the century—the development of socialism and the Labour movement, the 1906 general election and the subsequent Liberal programme of social legislation, and the birth of the Church Socialist League with its challenging slogan coined by Lewis Donaldson, 'Christianity is the religion of which Socialism is the practice.'[5] This last was alarming to the many people in the Church who believed religious and political loyalties should be kept separate. Spurgeon had warned, a generation before, that churchmen should keep out of the sphere of politics altogether. 'The bride of Christ comes not into the world to toy with the politics of princes, hers is a higher work. She leans upon the Lord alone, and yields allegiance to none else. Remove worldliness and you will see bright days.'[6] There were many who agreed that the Church's business was not with 'things temporal' or affairs 'of this world', two of Mr Wigan's favourite themes (*CL* 126, 123). In the years before the Great War, the Church of England was quite bitterly divided on this question, but its Evangelical wing tended to disapprove of any Church involvement in

[5] See Hylson-Smith, *Evangelicals*, 256–63. [6] Spurgeon, Sermons, 256.

social problems, which, as we have already seen, they were disposed to regard as among the inevitable effects of man's sinful nature. Kenneth Hylson-Smith says of the Evangelicals: 'Their primary doctrinal emphasis equipped them well for coping with individual spiritual matters, and even individual behavioural problems, but it was less helpful in the theological understanding of such questions as bad housing and sweated industries.'[7] And the 25 July 1912 number of the *Christian*, which carries extensive reports of the first part of the Keswick convention, has an editorial comment on the social question written in a temper that is wearing thin.

There is no more misleading error afoot today than the notion that the Millenium is automatically to usher itself in by way of social betterment and reform. Such an idea is entirely un-Scriptural; but it is taught more or less directly from hundreds of pulpits, and the Christian Church is thus divided into two opposing camps, neither fully understanding the other's point of view.

Some people at the convention may have wished the social question away, with other worldly matters. '"Love not the world" is the Keswick slogan', wrote Mr Daniel Crawford, a cheerful-sounding missionary 'of Luba-land, Africa', in his impression of Keswick in the *Christian* of 1 August. But the world, in the form of the social question, was hard to ignore in 1912, a year in which there was to be a total of 857 industrial disputes involving 1,233,016 workers, including a full-scale national miners' strike earlier in the year. Even as the Keswick convention was going on, as the *Christian* reported gloomily on 1 August, a prolonged dock strike was drawing to a bitter end. There had been riots in the London docks on 24 July.

With its terrible entail of suffering [said the *Christian*], not only for the men, but also for the women and children, the conflict is one which, for long years to come, will bring to the minds of masters and men alike, reflections suggestive of mistake rather than of victory. The merits of the case are outside the sphere of our enquiry; but the lessons are obvious to all. That such lessons should be learned at so heart-rending a cost, is quite sad to contemplate.

[7] Hylson-Smith, *Evangelicals*, 261.

The 'merits of the case' were not the business of the Christian (or at least the *Christian*), it seemed; but one lesson to be learned was in 'a striking [*sic*] display of generosity on the part of the Christian community' in the alleviation of distress and want. In just such a way, in the letter quoted above, Owen had found distributing dole preferable to thinking uncomfortable thoughts about the issues of industrial unrest.

'The poor and suffering occupied a large place in the thoughts of all,' says the *Christian*'s report on Keswick. But in fact the emphasis of the 1912 convention was on overseas missionary work, a theme not calculated to appease Owen's grievance about the Church's neglect of the responsibility on its doorstep. Later, writing from the shell-shock hospital in 1917, Owen was scornful of his mother's voluntary work for the Foreign Bible Society, and he reached back interestingly for names from his childhood reading to tease her (jealously?) about her self-sacrifices on behalf of 'Mowgli-Mowgli of Fiji, or whoever it will be that will receive the much fine gold of Israel's literature through your hands', and later, more bluntly, to tell her: 'Leave Black Sambo ignorant of Heaven. White men are in Hell' (*CL* 478, 483).

The Keswick convention was a camp, and Owen found himself sharing a tent with three divinity students from Durham. 'Socially, I suppose they are the pick of the Camp, but they are really not at all interesting' (*CL* 151). Writing home from the tent and literally surrounded by the sound of praying, he has nothing but hostility for Griffith Thomas and the other 'sleek' Keswick speakers. And for an intriguing moment, he seems to glimpse a more true Christian witness in an image quite different from that of the pulpit professionals.

There is, in a tent remote from mine, a Northumberland lad who works in the pits, whose soul-life and Christianity is altogether beyond my understanding. He has absolute peace of mind; faith before which mountains not only sink, but never become visible; and most other virtues of which the Keswick Platform speaks. The watching of his conduct, conversation, expression of countenance during meetings, bids fair to speak louder to my soul than the thunderings of twenty latter-day Prophets from their rostra upon these everlasting hills.

While your sleek [Griffith] Thomas, Hopkins, Dixon, Holden, Scroggie, and the rest of these double-barrelled guns, whose double-barrelled names I refuse to write, while they, I say, preach that preaching is no witness of a Christian Soul, your scar-backed mining-lad *acts* that acting *is* efficient. Scar-backed, I say, through running along subterranean 'roads' four feet high, and scraping against its jagged roof. And while my guide to Edinburgh [John Bulman, a medical student and family friend] would calmly send people to the Devil for no greater provocation than say having an ugly face, this youth lets no profane word pass his lips, tho' pricked with piercing pain and surrounded by the grossest human mud that ever sank to a pit's bottom.

Another interesting thing, a good antidote to student-superciliousness, is that this pit-lad is wrestling with a Class-book of Physics—and taking Correspondence Tuition in the Arts of Mining. He has no holiday and during this week, his pay is stopped. (*CL* 151.)

It is a pity we know no more than this about the scar-backed mining-lad, and Owen's relation with him. He flashes across the poet's life like a comet, momentary but illuminating. It may be that even at the time his importance was more emblematic than personal. Certainly Owen's account of him touches on a large number of the current and potential issues of his imagination. The scar-backed mining-lad is a prototype for the master theme which Owen was to find in the image of the young soldier. But even in the war years Owen's compassion was not reserved for those in uniform. Mary Newboult remembered him in Edinburgh in 1917 arguing with her father about the rights and working conditions of the miners (*WO* 230).

The lad is anonymous, set in discursive contention with a list of the names of Griffith Thomas and the rest of the Keswick orators. The entirely characteristic set-up, in which youthful long-suffering is more eloquent and more true than patriarchal or institutional bluster and fuss, has its roots in the Owen family. Here is another instance of the way the poet's later writing can rework structures of discourse from his earlier experience to interpret new circumstances. This is a pattern repeated in many of the war poems—'S.I.W.', 'Inspection', 'Smile, Smile, Smile', 'Insensibility', 'Anthem for Doomed Youth', and the specifically anticlerical 'At a Calvary Near the Ancre'. The discourse position of authority in these instances belongs, respectively, to 'father', the officer (and Field-Marshal God), the government and the press, civilian 'dullards', and the priesthood. In 'Inspection' and 'The Dead-Beat' (as in 'Strange Meeting') the autobiographical speaker himself is at first guilty of a lofty insensibility, not realizing the nature of the suffering before his very eyes. As a junior officer in command of front-line troops, Owen was both the agent and the victim of the orders under which that suffering took place.

It happened that the men of the Manchester Regiment whom Owen was to command were many of them coalminers in civilian life; but the scar-backed lad is in any case a forerunner of the underground men of the trenches and the trench poems, working in dangerous and degrading conditions, and of course of those other lads in 'Miners' who risk their lives to keep others comfortable. These last the poet conjures, as he stares at a dying coal fire in the hearth:

> But the coals were murmuring of their mine,
>   And moans down there
> Of boys that slept wry sleep, and men
>   Writhing for air.
>
> And I saw white bones in the cinder-shard,
>   Bones without number.
> Many the muscled bodies charred,
>   And few remember.
>
> I thought of all that worked dark pits
>   Of war, and died
> Digging the rock where Death reputes
>   Peace lies indeed.
>
> Comforted years will sit soft-chaired,
>   In rooms of amber;
> The Years will stretch their hands, well-cheered
>   By our life's ember;
>
> The centuries will burn rich loads
>   With which we groaned,
> Whose warmth shall lull their dreaming lids,
>   While songs are crooned;
> But they will not dream of us poor lads,
>   Left in the ground.

Here the singular voice of the speaker becomes inhabited—or possessed: he is their medium—by the voices (which no one else hears) of the miners who in turn have merged into soldiers. The guilty distance between poet and miners seems to be abolished; somewhere along the way and imperceptibly, they and 'I' have become 'us'. The speaker who warmed his hands at this holocaust is also its voice, its memorial. There is a clear link between this and the underground man encountered in 'Strange Meeting', who all but claims identity with the poet-dreamer ('Whatever hope is yours, | Was my life also') but is also his victim ('I am the enemy you killed, my friend'); the poet has killed him, yet it is only to and through the poet that he can speak. And 'Spring Offensive', one of Owen's last poems, leads to another subterranean agon which leaves the privileged survivors with a duty to perform for the speechless victims underground.

> But what say such as from existence' brink
> Ventured but drave too swift to sink,
> The few who rushed in the body to enter hell,
> And there out-fiending all its fiends and flames
> With superhuman inhumanities,
> Long-famous glories, immemorial shames—
> And crawling slowly back, have by degrees
> Regained cool peaceful air in wonder—
> Why speak not they of comrades that went under?

In the person of the scar-backed mining-lad is also to be found, its flesh stigmatized if not crucified, the image of the stricken body which always excited Owen. The lad's unimaginative placidity will be met again in 'Insensibility', his physical vulnerability in 'Arms and the Boy', but his quietness and refusal to protest against suffering (a theme returned to in poems as various as 'Exposure', 'The Kind Ghosts', and 'Spring Offensive') quite clearly relate him to the Redeemer foretold in Isaiah 53, who 'was bruised for our iniquities' and 'yet opened not his mouth', and to the scourged but all-patient Christ. This unsuspected saint and martyr cannot be seen or heard by the loud-mouthed ministers in their high places on the Keswick platform; yet his actions, his life, speak louder to Owen than all their thunderings.

Coalmining of all trades had a specific social meaning in a year, 1912, which had seen the mineworkers' union bring about a million men out on strike against a continuing drop in real earnings, in a dispute which brought much of the nation's transport and industry to a halt, and forced the government to legislate for a minimum wage.[8] Here was indeed the social question in person—the industrial North with its low pay, its dangerous and demeaning working

[8] See Dangerfield, *The Strange Death of Liberal England*, 195–294.

conditions, the obstacles in the way of a hard-working and gifted young man who wanted something better. Owen's reaction is of great interest. He sees the case as a 'good antidote' to snobbery, his own and others'. He also uses the contrast to suggest that the well-fed and high-and-mighty Evangelical patriarchs—these 'latter-day Prophets'—were speakers and nothing more, their lofty rhetoric all words, both neglectful and ignorant of the real business of Christianity. But beyond this Owen does not go. He says the scar-backed miner's actions speak louder to him than the words of all the preachers, but these actions are in practice inactions—not doubting, not questioning, not complaining. The lad is commended as a model of Christian submission.

In other words, Owen falls awkwardly between the two sides of the debate on the social question. He is indignant about the Church's complacency and blindness to remediable suffering and inequity, but all he finds to recommend is a model of stoical passivity. This has serious implications for the war writings but it also has, I think, a straightforward explanation. In 1912 Owen had no political language that might enable him to imagine things otherwise.

His upbringing in a family devoted to minding its own business seems to have given him no interest in political issues, which in any case, as an aspiring aesthete, he did not consider his concern. But the Owen children were brought up with a Victorian insistence on respect for authority. Harold Owen recounts how this family instillation of an 'unreasonable application to duty' (*JFO* 2. 128) almost cost him his life in Calcutta, when he continued to obey without question a careless command, working for hours in the full tropical sun until he collapsed with heat apoplexy. If he had been ordered to be in the sun, in the sun he must remain.

> All of this when recorded seems dreadfully priggish and unbearably over-conscientious but inasmuch as it is so fundamentally true, and as Wilfred himself came under this same terrific influence from our parents and our family life, it is important that it should be noted. Always our creed had been the unimportance of 'self', and the stressing of the rightness of carrying out what lay under our hand with the utmost inflexibility, irrespective of gain or loss, or even detriment to ourselves. (*JFO* 2. 127.)

One consequence, Harold Owen thought, was 'a too easy persuasion to accept what was offered'. Questioning established authority went against the upbringing instilled by the Evangelical mother and the father who was a railway bureaucrat and a lifelong company man. Protest, agitation, social discontent, a refusal to accept what was offered—there was plenty of this sort of language in the England of the great labour unrest of 1910–14, but it was a foreign tongue which Wilfred Owen did not speak. And so when the issues of injustice and social misery touched him, as they did in the Dunsden period, they touched him more as religious and aesthetic issues than as political ones; that is to say, they were for him *private* matters.

A moral is drawn from the scar-backed miner which is not fundamentally different from the one extracted by Wordsworth from the leech-gatherer in 'Resolution and Independence'. And the pretty schoolchildren, the stoical poor, and the pathetic consumptives of the Dunsden letters are also observed with an eye trained on Wordsworth as the Victorians read him, Wordsworth the sentimental rural Christian moralist. I do not at all mean to challenge the sincerity of Owen's feelings for these people: but he felt for them in the discourses that he knew. And such rebelliousness as is expressed in the Dunsden period, against oppressive authority and injustice and in the name of the downtrodden, that too has a literary precedent. For the letters show that Owen's tastes were shifting from Keats towards Shelley. In April 1912 he had been reading Laurie Magnus's *Introduction to Poetry*.

'The Revolutionary Ideals, crossing the Channel into England, inspired the British School of revolt and reconstruction in Burns, Shelley, Byron, Wordsworth, Coleridge and Tennyson, *till its fires have died down today.*' Have they! They may have in the bosoms of the muses, but not in my breast. (*CL* 131.)

What follows—the passages I have already quoted, in which he talks about liberalizing his thought and hearing wolfish ploughmen mutter about revolution—is really a trying-on of a new poetic stance, a rewritten Romantic tradition in which he places himself, and in which the emphasis no longer falls on Keats. This is not to impugn Owen's generous indignation. After all, his turning to Shelley was not arbitrary; he found in Shelley something he was looking for, but the indignation probably has as much to do with literature as with social conditions. And even the decision to quit Dunsden, when it came, was written up in literary-historical discourse. 'This flight of mine from overbearing elders, if it comes off, will only be my version of running away from College (Shelley, Coleridge)' (*CL* 175). Owen's feelings on the social question ultimately had their issue in *poetic* discourse, his dissatisfaction aestheticized as part of the equipment of the Romantic poet.

When the social question was rewritten with the front-line troops as the war's proletariat, Owen's response again came in poetic discourse. It is as a poet that he is remembered, not as an agitator or mutineer. His eventual decision to enlist was not without an element of poetic careerism. He had found in Belloc a quotation from Alfred de Vigny: 'If any man despairs of becoming a Poet, let him carry his pack and march in the ranks' (*CL* 342). Yet combat experience, with all its horrors, provided no material for poetry until the example of Sassoon showed him how poetry might take a stand on public issues. And even then, Owen's war poems have no political programme. They excoriate the callousness of authority but they make no proposals; and they do often portray the troops as patiently submissive and uncomplaining, and the war as a misery as inevitable as the weather. In these respects they are continuous with Owen's pre-war writings about the English poor. But his position as a junior officer implicated him deeply in the misery around him in Flanders at the same time as making him share it, as he had not really shared or been implicated in England. And one result was poetry that did have a programme, a definite aim, though not the sort of aim to express itself directly in calls for a negotiated peace or a revolution or better conditions of service. The aim was to rewrite the language of war. He believed war was possible and perhaps inevitable so long as wars were lied about. A poet could change the meaning of war by changing its language. This would also involve changing the language of poetry, although poetry itself was something with which, he said, he was not concerned.

All that was still to come. In 1912, apart from his uncertainties over the social question, Wilfred Owen was in more fundamental trouble. His impatience with the shortcomings of the Church of England and its ministers was beginning to blur into difficulties with the very foundations on which the Church rested, the doctrines of resurrection and redemption. These doubts start to find a voice in poems written after Keswick.

One such poem is 'Deep under turfy grass', written after Owen attended the double funeral of a mother and a four-year-old child in Dunsden churchyard in October 1912. 'Owen's reaction to this village tragedy,' says Jon Stallworthy (choosing a Wordsworthian phrase), 'moved him to a more direct and genuine poetic utterance than any hitherto' (*WO* 80). This poem begins:

> Deep under turfy grass and heavy clay
> They laid her bruisèd body, and the child.
> Poor victims of a swift mischance were they,
> Adown death's trapdoor suddenly beguiled.
> I, weeping not, as others, but heart-wild,
> Affirmed to Heaven that even Love's fierce flame
> Must fail beneath the chill of this cold shame.
>
> So I rebelled, scorning and mocking such
> As had the ignorant callousness to wed
> On altar steps long frozen by the touch
> Of stretcher after stretcher of our dead.
> Love's blindness is too terrible, I said;
> I will go counsel men, and show what bin
> The harvest of their homes is gathered in.

The church is a place for callousness, ignorance, illusion. The poem raises the possibility of rebellion and of some new and realistic language of warning. But neither the rebellion nor the resolution come to anything. Both remain potential and, as public discourse, speechless. For at that moment a group of children is seen to approach the graveside of their playmate, and there is 'one Child with them, whose pale brows | Wore beauty like our mother Eve's'. This vision of innocent life not only replaces but seems to redeem the preceding vision of disfigurement and death, and the poem weakens into a secular and aesthetic variant on the redeeming Child story (the capital letter is significant) and seems to forget its indignation over the fate of 'our dead'—this 'our' being, I suppose, the parochial possessive—and the way their fate is ignored.

> And there stood one Child with them, whose pale brows
> Wore beauty like our mother Eve's; whom seeing,
> I could not choose but undo all my vows,
> And cry that it were well that human Being
> And Birth and Death should be, just for the freeing
> Of one such face from Chaos' murky womb,
> For Hell's reprieve is worth not this one bloom.

Yet the 'blindness' that first roused the poet's indignation is not the same as the blindness of the pulpit professionals who could not see the sufferings and the saintliness at their feet. It is a blindness to death, the blindness of those who cannot see what the issue of their loving union must come to, those who, in the delusion of faith, do not realize death and are therefore callous, immune to pity. From 1912 onwards Owen was very much possessed by the finality of death, and 'Deep under turfy grass' is an early example of a genre, elegy, with which he was to engage for the rest of his life. How do you write an elegy to perform its traditional function of consolation, when you do not have faith in any kind of survival after death? The war poems, as we shall see, have plenty to say to this question. 'Deep under turfy grass' essays one answer, and it is an aesthete's response: suffering and even eventual extinction are a price worth paying for human beauty.

'Deep under turfy grass' is one of a series of poems of teleological doubt, written or drafted after the Keswick convention and before Owen's move to Bordeaux the following year. Other poems in the series are 'The Dread of Falling into Naught', 'Science has looked', 'Unto what pinnacles', 'Impromptu' ('I have none other thought of peace'), 'Sonnet' ('Daily I muse on her'), 'But it is not enough', 'O World of many worlds', 'The time was aeon', and 'The Unreturning'. Their common theme is a sense of loss and anxiety produced by the fear that heaven is empty, and death therefore final and life unredeemable. 'Impromptu' tells the story:

> One time, the world contained great store of friends,
> Mother and Brethren, Teachers, Holy Guides,
>
> All tender to my foolishness; all dear to me;
> But this last woe they would not understand.
>
> I once had hopes of heaven, whereon I slept and smiled,
> But a cold hand awoke me from that dream.

This group of poems seeks, with more or less success, to fill that void with faith in the power of human love and bodily beauty, and of the poetic imagination. 'Uriconium', the archaeological poem in which the dead city is restored to life by a sympathetic imagination, is also in the series. These poems—one of them really does end 'O cruel world . . . Farewell!'—are perhaps of more interest than merit. They are the traces of a kind of revolution that Owen was undergoing, and for quite a time trying to conceal, at Dunsden. And jejune though they may be, some of the best of the later poetry would not have been written without them. These forebodings of extinction, with their roots in Tennyson and Arnold, are unwitting rehearsals for 'Strange Meeting', 'Futility', 'A Terre', and 'Asleep', all denials of the resurrection; and for this, 'The End'.

> After the blast of lightning from the east,
> The flourish of loud clouds, the Chariot Throne;
> After the drums of time have rolled and ceased,
> And by the bronze west long retreat is blown,
> Shall Life renew these bodies? Of a truth,
> All death will he annul, all tears assuage?
> Or fill these void veins full again with youth,
> And wash, with an immortal water, age?
>
> When I do ask white Age, he saith not so:
> 'My head hangs weighed with snow.'
> And when I hearken to the Earth, she saith:
> 'My fiery heart shrinks, aching. It is death.
> Mine ancient scars shall not be glorified,
> Nor my titanic tears, the seas, be dried.'

With a pathetic brilliance, Susan Owen reaccentuated this in the inscription she chose for her son's gravestone in the cemetery at Ors (*WO* 288):

'SHALL LIFE RENEW
THESE BODIES?
OF A TRUTH
ALL DEATH WILL HE ANNUL'

Owen's rejection of Christian faith—he called it the murder of his 'false creed' (*CL* 175)—was the first independent action of his life. It cost him great anguish over a number of months, and a breakdown of health at the end. To follow its traces in the letters and poems is to read a story in some ways quite familiar, the story of Victorian doubt.

Were the claims of religion compatible with the statements of science? Spurgeon had said he did not care. 'We are not at all wishful to make our beliefs appear philosophical or probable: far from it! We do not ask that men should say, "That can be supported by science." Let the scientific men keep to their own sphere, and we will keep to ours'.[9] The faith should be kept separate from scientific as from political discourse. But Owen could not practice this mental segregation. In March 1912 he was busy 'reading, analysing, collecting, sifting and classifying Evidence'; in September he announced to Harold that he was grappling as never before with 'the Problem of *Evolution*', but could not form a conclusion (*CL* 122, 73).[10] The difficulty met Owen, as it had met plenty of earnest young Victorians before him, on the opening pages of the Bible. There were Anglican Darwinists who allowed that the Garden of Eden might be a parable or something; but Evangelicals insisted on the literal truth of all the Bible and on this rock Owen's faith was not the first to come to grief. In the matter of the authority of scripture it had to be all or nothing, said Evangelical theologians, and Owen agreed; if the Fall was a myth, so must be the Redemption. In January 1913 he had an argument about this with his cousin Dorothy Gunston, who had also attended the Keswick convention the summer before.[11]

Her position is extraordinary, and wholly illogical. She has no decided belief in the *first man Adam*; and cannot help regarding the talking-serpent interludes as not adapted to present-day needs, etc. How, then, can she attach any importance to the precise words of St. Paul (?):

'*As* in Adam all die,
So in Christ shall all be made alive'?

If all have *not* died in Adam, where is the possibility of all being 'made alive' (whatever *that* means) in Christ? More, where is the need? To me, if there be no 'As' there is no 'So'; no Adam, no second Adam. Yet the more I read early Genesis, the more does it appear the work of a Hebrew sage (Moses, or somebody else of the same name!!) recording his own notion of the beginnings of things; so that 'the Fall' is a myth. This is only one difficulty, taken from the Science Instances; itself only *one* of the troublesome voices. (*CL* 176.)

This was dangerous, and forces were mobilized to bring the straying sheep back to the orthodox fold. Wigan made arrangements to send his assistant to London to see the Revd Dr J. Stuart Holden, one of the 'sleek' heavyweights from the Keswick platform.

[9] Spurgeon, *Fifty Most Remarkable Sermons*, 472.

[10] Letter 82 (*CL* 72–5) misdated June 1911, was written from Dunsden in late Sept. 1912. See Hibberd, 'Wilfred Owen's Letters', 278.

[11] Dorothy had shocked E. W. Moore with her own 'apostasy' in Mar. 1912; but she was later to become a missionary (*CL* 121).

On her own initiative or prompted by Susan Owen, his pious sister Mary wrote to him. He replied politely—'I cannot tell you, dear sister, how glad I was to hear of your experience in spiritual matters'—but firmly (*CL* 180). And Susan Owen sent him a pamphlet written by E. W. Moore. This must have seemed a good move. Owen liked and admired the old man, numbering him, he said, 'among the chiefest prophets in my . . . *Theogony*' (*CL* 121). It is not known what 'pamphlet' of Moore's Susan Owen prescribed for her son, but the vigorous reassurance that Moore had to offer the doubter can be gauged from the sermons collected in *Wanted, a Man*! which had just been published by the Religious Tract Society in 1912. Here is E. W. Moore on the prophet's encouragement, in Isaiah 40, to a people who have lost touch with God. Even the youths shall faint and be weary, and the young men shall utterly fall, says Isaiah; but they that wait upon the Lord shall renew their strength. Moore glosses:

> Their strength was failing them. Circumstances were against them. No doubt the enemy was assailing them, and they gave way to despondency. 'God has forgotten me,' they seem to say. 'He does not seem to care.' That was the temptation. [But the prophet counters temptation with reassurance.] 'Who is it that keeps this mighty universe in the perfect order and harmony that you see? . . . How is it that the seasons revolve in their harmonious order? Spring gives place to summer, and summer fades into autumn, and autumn yields to the desolation of winter. All things serve him. Seed-time and harvest, cold and heat, summer and winter, do not cease. Why is all this? Why? Because of the faithfulness of God.'[12]

Whether or not Owen had read these actual words of Moore's, he was certainly familiar with the terms of the argument, for it is exactly the argument that we have seen proposed, and deconstructed, in the penultimate stanza of 'Exposure':

> Since we believe not otherwise can kind fires burn;
> Nor ever suns smile true on child, or field, or fruit.
> For God's invincible spring our love is made afraid;
> Therefore, not loath, we lie out here; therefore were born,
> For love of God seems dying.

But in any case, in January 1913 Owen's doubts were not to be met by the reassurances of 'old E. W. M'. He told his mother he had given the pamphlet a conscientious reading but that it was

[12] Moore, *Wanted, a Man!*, 143. In 'Greater Love', 'God seems not to care'.

'now quite beside the mark' for him. 'Discussions which *take it for granted the reader believes in Adam's getting outside some fruit or other! and then going off into occult matters of retributive dogma, are not what I want*' (*CL* 176).

He had been brought up to understand Christianity as a faith grounded on the absolute authority of the scriptures. For the Evangelical fundamentalists, there could be no dialogue with Darwinian science: there was really nothing to talk about, simply a choice to be made. But for Owen with his Romantic ambitions, science was not the only discourse to challenge scripture's absolute authority. It was only one of the 'troublesome voices'. 'On my other hand, but pulling the same way, is "Literature", and all it means; and ways of life that will have to be changed, as well as habits of thought' (*CL* 176). And here he registers the strain of finding himself a battleground of competing discourses, not just 'The Two Voices' of faith and doubt, as in Tennyson's poem of that name, but several troubling voices asking for his allegiance. (The predicament was larger than Owen's individual case, of course; it was the momentum of late nineteenth-century art, religion, and science marching off in different directions.) There were a number of painful interviews with Mr Wigan in January 1913. At first the vicar prescribed tracts; but as it became clear that Owen was not going to 'get right', they agreed to differ and Owen left Dunsden vicarage on 7 February, at the beginning of Lent. He returned to the family home at Shrewsbury and took to his bed, suffering from congestion of the lungs, an illness which his brother believed 'came just in time to prevent a nervous breakdown' (*JFO* 2. 263).

To the physiological and psychological accounts of the collapse, I want to add a discursive one, and to begin it I must return to the summer of 1912. After the Keswick convention Owen had had some time at home before returning, depressed and jumpy, 'flabby and unstable' (*CL* 152), to Dunsden. On 16 August he wrote to Susan Owen in some distress:

> On Saturday I have to give some account of my Impressions of Keswick. It will be something of an ordeal: If they want, as I imagine they do, a relation of my personal feelings, I am *not* going to give them such. Some of my impressions were made with an instrument so sharp, so quick, that they should be called *wounds* rather than *impressions*.[13]

[13] This figure seems to have been produced out of a memory of the scar-backed miner.

These I have no intention of laying bare. On the other hand it will not do to give them an inkling of my unorthodox theology. So that I simply daren't be sincere; hence the preparation will cost a lot of thought. (*CL* 155.)

Owen was in a fix. The conspiratorial tone of this letter strongly suggests that in the aftermath of Keswick he had confided to his mother at least some of his unhappiness with his position, and some of his 'unorthodox theology'. But it is very unlikely that he had revealed to her the radical doubts that were to find expression in 'The Dread of Falling into Naught' and the other poems that followed. A week after telling Susan Owen that he dared not speak sincerely about Keswick at the meeting at Dunsden, he was writing to complain that he now lived in 'so many distinct worlds', and had to play 'a corresponding number of roles' (*CL* 156). As we have seen, this referred immediately to degrees of formality in the domestic life of the vicarage. But there was also a wider applicability to this condition of selective inhibition. His discursive world had started to fragment.

The strain may be imagined of masking his 'personal feelings' on religious matters for the six more months that he stayed at Dunsden, in a state that could accurately be described as 'bad faith'. The Church took a serious view of anyone doing its business without sharing its faith. 'Amongst all who will need eternal compassion, surely the unfaithful, unholy, unearnest minister of Christ will be the most pitiable. What did I say? Nay, rather the most contemptible, the most despicable, the most accursed!'[14] He tried to keep his state of mind a secret. Mr Wigan was not the only hypocrite at Dunsden in these months. The language Owen spoke to Wigan and to all those parochial meetings was different from the anxious and tentative doubts expressed in letters to Susan Owen, and different again from the more faithless and anticlerical pronouncements of the teleological poems, which he kept to himself. At the height of the crisis in February 1913, he told his mother she too must be shut out. 'I will say no more. I *don't want* to communicate my calm frenzy to anybody—let alone you' (*CL* 181).

To enter the vicar's lordly presence was to 'banish *candid expression*' (*CL* 119), but it was more than a matter of being on one's

[14] Spurgeon, *Sermons*, 76.

best behaviour. Owen was concealing from Mr Wigan not only his doubts but also, apparently, his secret meetings and continuing friendships with village children, particularly Vivian Rampton. The doubts, these friendships, and his passion for poetry all seem to have come out into the open in the painful negotiations with Mr Wigan in the new year of 1913, and Owen concluded—had he been given an ultimatum?—that if he stayed at Dunsden to 'become a religious devotee', he would have to give up these friendships and give up writing poetry (*CL* 181).

It was a discursive crisis because the different fields of discourse he lived in could not speak to each other. If science pulled against religious faith, faith it seemed was also incompatible with poetry. Owen had first thought 'dear Mr Wigan' well-disposed to the arts, citing, as rather pathetic evidence to this effect, his discovery that Wigan was a sixth cousin of William Morris, had been to a lecture by Ruskin, and claimed acquaintance with the original of Dickens's Sam Weller (*CL* 92). But it soon became clear that Wigan regarded poetry with the indifference and even hostility Evangelicals reserved for worldly amusements. His 'compositions' were another thing Owen kept secret at first at the vicarage. Kemp reported that he had no idea that his fellow-assistant was writing poetry at Dunsden though he did remember, he said, that Owen wrote home a good deal (*CL* 91). The opposition and competition between the claims of poetry and of religion run through the Dunsden letters to the end, when after murdering the 'false creed' of fundamentalist Christianity, he declared in the last letter sent from Dunsden a creed fetched from the fountainhead of the discourse of poetry—unacknowledged quotation being, in this case, the sincerest form of intertextual tribute: 'For the rest, I have not the slightest feeling of humility for anything in existence, but the Eternal Being, the Principle of Beauty, and the Memory of Great Men' (*CL* 181).[15]

This was the breaking-point of an accumulated tension which had as much to do with speech as with the nervous system. It is most likely that the crisis was precipitated at Keswick and brought to its painful resolution at Dunsden, when Owen felt most strongly pressed, by revivalist rhetoric from the Keswick platform and later from Kemp's replacement, Clyde Black, to make some open declaration of what he believed in. Almost as soon as he arrived at

[15] The quotation is from Keats's letter to Reynolds, 9 Apr. 1818.

Dunsden in October 1911, Owen had been told of Mr Wigan's 'hope of a Revival in the place' (*CL* 93), and in late 1912 revival came, bringing to Dunsden parish a small-scale cultural revolution. Kenneth Hylson-Smith explains the phenomenon:

With a revival there is a sudden, spontaneous, noteworthy and sustained increase in the extent and intensity of the commitment of a number of individuals in a particular area to the beliefs and practices of their faith. The corporate life of those concerned is rapidly and significantly energized, and there is a renewed sense of fellowship. Accompanying this is an increased concern for the conversion of those who do not share the same faith; and a wave of conversions among both 'outsiders' and 'nominal' believers.[16]

Revival at Dunsden seems to have driven one 'nominal' believer into the open with all his doubts.

The special speech genre of Evangelical revival was a public declaration of faith. On the last Friday of the 1912 Keswick convention, according to the *Christian* of 1 August, 'opportunity was afforded for those to stand, who had consciously entered into "the rest of faith". But on Saturday the testimony to blessing received during the week came as a flood.' Owen did not get to his feet with all those others at Keswick; but he did not escape the pressure of revival either, for by the end of the year it was confronting him again at Dunsden. There is a critical and unprecedented silence of three full weeks during which he wrote no letters home. Then on 10 December 1912, he wrote again to his mother, apologizing:

If I must face the question, there may have been a moral reason for witholding my speech; just that I may not speak unadvisedly.

Now, For many months, in fact ever since I have been here, the Vicar has been praying, now hotly, now coldly, for *Revival.*

It has come.

At least, is coming.

Here is the Organist converted; the 'blower' and numbers of others 'under conviction'; here is Jack Dear writing to the Vicar of how he is completely healed of his backsliding, and has made a wholesale surrender of his will to God.

Here is a woman saying to our last Prayer Meeting: 'I should like help', and being 'prayed through'.

[16] Hylson-Smith, *Evangelicals*, 186. For Evangelicalism and revival see Hylson-Smith, ibid. 186–94. For Clyde Black and the Dunsden revival see *OTP* 11–22, 193.

Here is a man, B__ himself, accepting Christ last night at Black's Bible Class for men.

Here is Vera B__, the same evening at another mtg. being asked by Black whether she took Christ as her Saviour, answering Yes.

Here is a woman of the parish writing from Reading Hospital to say she has found Christ there.

Here is Willie Montague, being cornered by Black on Sunday afternoon, making his (second) profession of Christianity.

Here are women shedding tears in Church every Sunday night.

Here am I, halting between two, aye, more than two opinions, till sense deserts my mind, and strength my body. (*CL* 170.)

After two days comes another very anxious letter, in which he says his nerves are in 'a shocking state', his breast 'continually "too full"'. This may have been the onset of congestion of the lungs but it was also a feeling of oppression, as at Keswick, by the voices of revival all round him, urging him to make his declaration.

I have just heard that at the Mothers' Meeting this afternoon, Milly's Mother yielded herself to God, and was brought to the point by the visible happiness of her child. Is it cowardly to be influenced by the doings of others; I mean, being willing to follow if others will lead?

That is how it strikes me, if I at this juncture, were to make *my* sacrifice—of Reason. (*CL* 171.)

A declaration of faith would be a denial of reason, yet he had been tempted to it.

But the discursive disintegration went beyond this. His feelings of love for his favourites among the village children—his first emotional adventure outside the family—had to be disguised from Mr Wigan. If there was a sexual element in these feelings, that too had to be repressed or at least hidden. To embrace the religion which it was his job to profess every day in the parish was, he considered, to fly in the face of science, in which he had a Victorian's faith. To reject that religion seemed a denial of his love for his mother. Poetry spoke with a voice equally contrary to religion and science. He spoke one language in his rounds in the parish, another in the vicarage, a third and fourth in his letters and poetry. There was now literally no one to whom he could speak openly. He had tried to deal with these discursive contradictions by secrecy and repression, building walls between different discourses to keep their spheres separate and to prevent their challenging each other in speech. He had remained silent when the vicar sneered at

Wordsworth (*CL* 118), he would not reveal his true impressions of Keswick, he tried to keep his child favourites to himself, his more doubtful poems were private, and at the end he would not communicate his 'calm frenzy' to anyone. He had also tried to relieve his anxieties by bathing them in a solution of Romantic aestheticism. Neither expedient was much good. Divided, uncertain, and unhappy, he fled from Dunsden. The religious crisis, which was also one of language, precipitated a social displacement and an existential check. His estrangement from the Church, now out in the open, gave him the obligation and the opportunity to find himself elsewhere. By the next new year he had put behind him the Protestant faith, England, and his family, for the time being. The move to France had the romantic glamour of a fresh start, a new life. Yet he did not in any important way leave Shrewsbury and Dunsden behind, for he carried his twenty-year history imprinted in the language he took with him.

And after all, though the discursive configuration of his crisis was unique, all of its elements were common enough. Millions of Wilfred Owen's generation had had a pious upbringing, millions were familiar from childhood with Evangelical and temperance warnings and prohibitions about the devil and the body. Middle-class children of the Protestant imperial nation were reared to do their duty and know their place; they had an inculcated respect for order and equity, and were unsure how to react when one seemed threatened in the name of the other. Genesis and evolution had wrestled to the point of banality over countless consciences, and the outcome of that conflict in Owen's case happened, as often as not, in others. He had no monopoly either on what Yeats called 'the distress | Of boyhood growing into man', on impatience with his Victorian elders, on feelings that became articulate in accents borrowed from Keats and Shelley and Tennyson and Ruskin, or for that matter on discreet but guiltless homoeroticism. If in the spring of 1913 he was at check, confused and unhappy and lonely, it was a confusion and unhappiness very much of its time, a tangle whose strands each linked him to a community and a culture even when he felt most utterly alone.

III

Army

10

The Disciplines of the Wars

Owen's move to Bordeaux in September 1913 came after seven ill-tempered and pointless months in England. After his flight from Dunsden and the illness which followed it, he did not know what to do. He could not decide on a career and he could not afford to go to university. He sat for a scholarship to University College, Reading, and failed it. He was ill again in the summer. Bordeaux did not seem very enticing, and at first the omens did not look too good for this Daedalian flight. He knew no one in France and was inclined to acute homesickness, the Berlitz school in Bordeaux worked him very hard and paid him miserably, and he was still anxious that his health would break down again. And yet the move to France did prove to be a success, and the following summer the cheerful tone was characteristic, in which he reassured his family that he continued to be 'immensely happy and famously well' (*CL* 273). These words are in a letter dated 8 August 1914.

It had not been easy. The teaching could be exhausting, money was always a worry, and he seems to have made few confidential friends. But he worked hard, and developed a wide acquaintance which provided him with enough private pupils to enable him to quit the Berlitz school and become a freelance teacher of English. That increased self-confidence was not as yet bearing much fruit in his writing. The poetry he wrote in France is mostly poor stuff and the letters do not often have the sharp neurotic edge of the later Dunsden period. But Bordeaux was as decisive in its way as Dunsden had been. For the first time in his life, in France Owen created happiness for himself. He had a skill by which he earned a living, he knew numbers of interesting and lively people, he was at home in a milieu which was foreign, even cosmopolitan, and (especially when the outbreak of war brought the French government to Bordeaux and Parisian society with it) stirringly romantic. In March 1914 he had celebrated his twenty-first birthday.

The name of this new contentment was independence, and it

seemed to Owen that he had achieved this victory like a giant-killer of romance.

If not greatly happier than I was this time last year, I am infinitely more comfortable. And the feeling that I am under obligations to no man, is as sweet as it is new. For the moment I have neither schoolmaster nor taskmaster, neither patron nor boss. I have slain—so far as I am concerned four tyrants: first, Timpany, who taxed his subjects with grievous work; next Lightbourn, a bullying boss; next Wigan, who essayed to dominate one's entire being; next Aumont, unmercifully grinding, being goaded by avarice. These men are not my enemies (except perhaps the last); but they are not the masters I feel called to serve. Indeed, though I look up and down the world, I see no man whom I could serve without a suffocated feeling of captivity. (*CL* 289–90.)

Two headmasters, his old antagonist the vicar of Dunsden, and the director of the Berlitz school in Bordeaux: it is in a letter to his mother that he boasts of his liberating slaughter of these patriarchs with their taxing, bullying, domineering, and grinding. This can also no doubt be read as an episode in Oedipal romance, but its manifest content is more to the point. When he resigned from the Berlitz school at the end of July 1914 Wilfred Owen was for the first time in his life independent of hierarchical institutions in which he had a subordinate rank. He had moved on from his family home, the schools where he was a pupil and later for a time a pupil-teacher, the vicarage at Dunsden, and the Church to which he had been an ambiguous apprentice, and the language school which had dictated his timetable and teaching method and chosen his pupils. He was free. Less than two weeks after this declaration of independence began the war that was to draw him into a more exacting institution and discipline than these from which he had freed himself.

But at first it seemed to have little to do with him. For Owen, the greatest excitement of August 1914 was his meeting with 'a great French Poet' (*CL* 278), Laurent Tailhade.

Quite apart from the prospect of this Friendship, I am, for quite an appreciable length of time, imbued with sensations of happiness. The war affects me less than it ought. But I can do no service to anybody by agitating for news or making dole over the slaughter. On the contrary I adopt the perfect English custom of dealing with an offender: a Frenchman duels with him: an Englishman ignores him. (*CL* 282.)

He had decided against 'agitating for news' or 'making dole over the slaughter'; he did not even consider the possibility of going back to enlist. Owen did not join the army until 21 October 1915. Edmund Blunden's memoir says the date of his enlistment was controlled by his tutorial engagement (*EB* 10–11). This statement (whose source must be Susan Owen) is misleading. When Owen's work in the Léger family came to an end, in the autumn of 1914 he went round looking for people likely to take English lessons. By 14 October he had found just enough, he thought, to justify his 'staying on a while' in Bordeaux (*CL* 287). The great gush of patriotic militarism that washed over the British press and public that autumn was several hundred miles away, but it reached him in the form of news and press cuttings from home, and continental editions of British newspapers were readily available in Bordeaux. The *Daily Mail*'s attack on young men who shirked their duty to King and country caused him 'a good deal of shame' on 2 December 1914 (*CL* 300), yet within a week he had accepted another assignment, tutoring the young English nephews of Miss de la Touche at Mérignac, which was to keep him until September 1915. Mérignac turned out to be something of an idyll and although, at Christmastime, 'One thinks of the "trenches" with guilty feelings, in the midst of my surroundings' (*CL* 311), it was to be another ten months before he joined the army. He did not do so earlier because he did not want to.

In May 1915 he sailed to England to perform a business commission at the British Industries Fair for one of his pupils, a scent manufacturer, and then had some weeks at home in Shrewsbury, returning to France in June. M. Peyronnet hoped to persuade Owen to travel in the East later in the year as a representative of his perfume company. The Dardanelles campaign ruled this out for the time being, and Owen told him that, if the way were still blocked in September, he would return to England and join the army. It was even now not an unconditional decision, nor was it an enthusiastic one. 'I don't want the bore of training, I don't want to wear khaki; nor yet to save my honour before inquisitive grand-children fifty years hence. But I *now do* most *intensely want to fight*' (*CL* 341). He may have found resistible the appeals to honour and glory of the enlistment campaign, which was busy urging fit young men to do their bit in what was already being called the Great War ('What did you do in the Great War, Daddy?'), and which his poems were to treat with such anger. But battlefield casualties in 1915 were unprecedented, and as he read the bulletins Owen confessed, on 5 July, to feeling '*traitorously* idle: if not to England then to France' (*CL* 345). He left for England again on 14 September, to escort his two pupils to Downside school. Then he had a month's holiday at Shrewsbury. Even now there was a late flurry in which he considered becoming a munitions worker, which could earn him five pounds a week (*CL* 359), but finally on 21 October 1915, in London, he enlisted with the Artists' Rifles.

Of course the private decision has to be understood in its public setting. To fight a war on the European mainland for the first time in a hundred years, Britain's small professional army had to be swollen by hundreds of thousands of temporary soldiers. The regular army, 200,000 strong in 1914, had lost 80,000 killed or wounded by Christmas. These losses were made good largely by reservists from the Territorial army, and they bore the brunt of the 1915 fighting, culminating in the very expensive autumn offensive at Loos. The third wave consisted of the new armies of wartime volunteers, 'Kitchener's Army'. Many of these completed their training in time for the Somme battle which began at the start of July 1916, a campaign which was to cost 300,000 casualties. The fourth and last wave was drafts of conscripts. By 1918 the army had absorbed over five million men.

Unlike all the other combatant nations, the British had never had compulsory military service, which was alleged to be alien to the national character. Volunteers came forward readily enough: 298,923 in August 1914, 462,901 in September. By September 1915 the monthly recruitment had dropped to some 71,000. Partly in response to the news of serious losses in the autumn offensive at Loos, the numbers went up for the next two months—113,285 in October 1915 (Wilfred Owen was one of these), 121,793 in November—but they fell back to 55,000 in December.

Lord Kitchener, the Secretary of State for War, had been advised that there was in the country an effective pool of two and a half million potential volunteers. Such was the casualty rate that, once that limit had been reached, conscription would have to follow, un-British though it might be. The two and a half million mark was indeed reached in December 1915, and in January 1916 the government introduced the first Military Service Act, which 'deemed that all single men and childless widowers between the ages of eighteen and forty-one had enlisted'.[1] When it came, conscription was no surprise (and it met with less resistance than the government had feared). Compulsory service had been a matter of debate in parliament and press since the early days, and the casualties of the 1915 fighting had made it inevitable if Britain was to stay in the land war. From very early on, the press had muttered or shrieked about shirkers (football players and spectators seem to have represented the greatest affront).[2] By the autumn of 1915 fifty-four million posters had been issued, eight million letters sent, and 12,000 meetings organized.[3] The writing stood out most clearly on the wall when, after considerable debate, the Derby Scheme was brought into operation in October 1915. A. J. P. Taylor calls it 'a genteel form of conscription':[4] single men in the civilian population were asked to indicate if they would be willing to serve if called upon to do so. The scheme was already in operation when Wilfred Owen joined the army. It seems likely that the higher enlistment figures for the first two months of the scheme may contain numbers who preferred to jump now with credit rather than be pushed later. But to take this plunge in the autumn of 1915 was a world away from the jump Rupert Brooke had famously volunteered for, in his *1914*, as of 'swimmers into cleanness leaping'.

Owen's volunteering in October 1915 was not, to use another of Rupert Brooke's words, 'glad'; nor was it in an uncomplicated way voluntary. Brooke's *1914* sonnet group, which Dean Inge had read from the pulpit of St Paul's in 1915 shortly before Brooke's death, treats soldiering as pastoral—fresh, natural, youthful, simple, a relief after the shame and boredom of civilian life. But for Owen, pastoral was what he was having to leave behind, in the warm south of France:

[1] Beckett and Simpson eds., *A Nation in Arms*, 13.

[2] See, for example, illustrations 5 and 6 in Hibberd and Onions eds., *Poetry of the Great War*, and the *Daily Mail*'s attack on 'ten thousand lusty louts playing football' which Owen alluded to in Dec. 1914 (*CL* 300).

[3] Winter, *Death's Men*, 29.

[4] Taylor maintained that conscription was introduced unnecessarily, since 'more volunteers were still coming forward than could be equipped'; but this is probably more an indication of inefficient supply than sufficient manpower. See A. J. P. Taylor, *The First World War*, 114, and Ian Beckett's essay 'The Nation in Arms 1914–18', in Beckett and Simpson eds., *A Nation in Arms*, ch. 1.

Bees
  Shaking the heavy dews from bloom and frond.
Boys
  Bursting the surface of the ebony pond.
Flashes
  Of swimmers carving through the sparkling cold.
Fleshes
  Gleaming with wetness to the morning gold.
A mead
  Bordered about with warbling waterbrooks.
A maid
  Laughing the love-laugh with me; proud of looks.

Looking back in 1917 to the time before the war touched his life, he constructs here in 'From My Diary, July 1914' a pastoral list which is a menu of fleshly delights, forever to be enjoyed in the non-time of idyll, where all the verbs are suspended in participle form. Yet the title's July was timed to explode into August 1914, when history was to invade this paradise and would have to be met with a brave face.

So Wilfred Owen joined up and went into training in the uniform of the next of the institutions that shaped his life, entering a world whose atmosphere and language were quite alien and struck him as much more foreign than France had ever been (*CL* 395). He was immersed in and set to learn the army's language in what must have seemed the most blatant discursive clash with what he wanted language to be. The poetry to which he aspired was romantic self-expression, and the poet for him was a hypersensitive individual prized for his originality, the celebrant and creator of beauty and pleasure. There had been epic swashbuckling times when military and poetic speech consorted comfortably, but not Wilfred Owen's idea of poetry and his idea of the army. The British army, he opined in the first month of the war, were 'all Tommy Atkins, poor fellows' (*CL* 282), and he was to describe his Manchester Regiment soldiers in June 1916 as coarse, loutish, and ugly (*CL* 395). They would be poor company and no subject for the aesthetic poet, the priest of beauty. In any case, had not Keats remained 'absolutely indifferent to Waterloo and all that commotion' (*CL* 349)? Poets had their own world, a separate universe of discourse which could have little to say to the life of a military camp. Harold Owen visited him in camp and listened as his brother complained, scraping the two discourses together to show that they did not fit. 'What does Keats have to teach me of rifle and machine-gun drill, how will my pass in Botany teach me to lunge a bayonet, how will Shelley show me how to hate or any poet teach me the trajectory of the bullet?' (*JFO* 3. 144). It seemed to be the familiar story of discursive separations. Army experience was none of poetry's business, just as in the Dunsden world religious discourse had been sealed off from social intervention and from scientific investigation, which in turn had no connection with the language of poetry.

One of his reasons for rejecting a career in the clergy had been the incompatibility of Evangelical Christianity with literature, which Mr Wigan, it seems, dismissed as 'artificialised life' (*CL* 273). But Owen had quit Dunsden rather than give up his writing. Poets acknowledged no discipline but that of beauty. Misunderstood by society and (especially if French) in rebellion against it, the poet Owen wanted to be was heretical and singular—to use his own epithets from 'O World of Many Worlds', 'fast, eccentric, lone, | Lawless'. His career had been in his own eyes a series of struggles to free himself from tyrannical authority; this was an essential prelude to poetic success, finding his own voice. But now he had bound himself over to a discipline of absolute obedience, in the most unpoetic and unlovely company, in an institution whose first actions included giving him a number and a uniform. It was a multiple transformation—the poet became a soldier, the expatriate a patriot, the teacher a trainee, the elder a cadet. To his family he had seemed supremely inapt for the army, with his bohemian affectations, his vagueness, his disdain for the practical and disinclination for the athletic. 'The very idea of him soldiering,' says Harold Owen, 'seemed to us all too fantastic to think seriously about' (*JFO* 3. 118).

But there was plenty to read in the army. A cadet or young officer could learn from any number of printed sources, which he would also hear endlessly paraphrased by his own instructors. In these fascinating publications, you can hear the British army of the Great War talking to itself. They are of particular interest to the student of Wilfred Owen, not only as the syllabus of his military training, but as the written records of the language he heard, spoke, and thought every working day of the last three years of his life. The textbooks ranged from frankly technical booklets like

How to Instruct in Aiming and Firing by Quartermaster-Sergeant-Instructor J. Bostock (which cost Owen a shilling in 1916), through the many War Office manuals with titles like *Infantry Training*, *Notes for Infantry Officers on Trench Warfare*, and *Notes on Field Defences*, to the more informal advice offered in '*Out There!' or the Platoon Commander in Warfare* by 'One of Them', and the admonitions of the dug-out Lieutenant-Colonel E. G. Mackenzie's intimidating *Notes on Mess Etiquette* ('Never draw a sword in the Mess'). Officers were issued with the indispensable *Field Service Pocket Book* (1914, amended 1916) in which they could look up everything from the weight of the Lee-Enfield .303 rifle (9lb10oz with bayonet) and the dates of the full moon, to the maximum punishment for falling asleep on sentry duty (death). The staff also compiled a handy digest of the official textbooks and training manuals, published in 1915 as *What Every Soldier Ought to Know*. These official and semi-official publications were the law and the prophets of the army, and about the word that they preach there was no question.

> By taking the oath of allegiance, a man binds himself, of his own free will, to submit to military discipline. *Discipline* is the living force which turns a crowd of men into an army. It is absolutely necessary for the efficiency, safety, and comfort of all ranks. The essence of discipline is instant and cheerful obedience, not only to commands given by word of mouth, but to all rules and regulations duly issued by proper authority.[5]

Challenging words for the would-be 'lawless' individualist in his new uniform. He had exchanged his hard-won liberties for what Fluellen, the Welsh captain in *Henry V*, calls the disciplines of the wars. Discipline is the great capital theme of army discourse and I shall examine it here in three modes, as it relates to the body, to speech, and to mental organization.

The first disciplines of the army were registered on the body. Exchanging civilian clothes for the uniform marked an epoch, as did the issue of a weapon. All the manuals agree that the prime aim of training was to inculcate the soldierly spirit. But the right spirit in turn depended on the training of the soldier's body to physical fitness, a task given new emphasis in the army since its embarrassing performance in the South African war had given rise

[5] *What Every Soldier Ought to Know*, 4.

to fears that an industrialized society was making the British puny and effete.[6] The army undertook to make the recruit strong; preserving his health was his own affair and the manuals, believing that if a man is fit and self-disciplined he will not fall sick, are unsentimental about illness. 'Given the knowledge as to what is right, every man must stand or fall by his own actions' and 'A sick man is not only a rifle lost to the firing line, but an actual encumbrance requiring special food, housing and transport.'[7] Constant exercise, drill, marches, and 'manly games' would ensure physical fitness and reinforce self-discipline.[8]

This would have been familiar enough to the majority of officer cadets who remembered the sportive regime of their public schools, but not to the unathletic Owen who had always scorned his father's chivvying to take exercise and play games. Yet in another sense it was familiar indeed. It brought back the old theme of the dependence of the spirit's welfare on the discipline of the body, a theme that had been drilled into the young abstainer in temperance discourse that often borrowed military forms and language. And it was also related to the Evangelical propensity to deny the body in obedience to Pauline warnings to crucify the flesh, against which 'The time was aeon' was a protest. Now the army had its prohibitions too. Officers were recommended to lecture their troops on the advantages of moderation, sobriety, and physical fitness,[9] and Lord Kitchener himself, in a message to the troops which every soldier was rather optimistically advised to learn by heart, warned that 'temptations both in wine and women' should be entirely resisted.[10] However, there was a vital difference in the way these institutions regarded the body. Temperance and Pauline rhetoric demanded bodily discipline because the body was a potential enemy or traitor, but the army spoke of disciplining the body to enhance the soldier's efficiency and his morale; his body was a potential weapon, to be cared for, even to be proud of.

The day of his enlistment gave Owen his first close-up sight of

[6] An Interdepartmental Committee on Physical Deterioration was appointed to investigate. A more long-lasting consequence of this anxiety was the foundation in 1907 of the Boy Scout movement.

[7] *What Every Soldier*, 8, 10. [8] *Infantry Training*, 3.

[9] Ibid. 241. Owen gave a lecture on 'Discipline' in August 1916 (*CL* 406).

[10] *What Every Soldier*, 32.

British soldiers, on medical parade—'fine, healthy animals' he thought them, and, in spite of a typhoid inoculation, 'I feel so physically happy,' he wrote that day, 'that it might have been Morphine injected' (*CL* 360). This theme of physical happiness continues in the letters. Polishing the buttons of his new uniform was a bore, but the Artists' Rifles reckoned themselves 'as smart as anything except the Guards', and in the streets, he found, 'one is the admiration of all little boys, and meets an approving glance from every eye of eld' (*CL* 362, 363). (The young man in 'Disabled' enlisted because people told him 'he'd look a god in kilts.') Early training was exhausting, with its 'physical drill' and route marches, but exhilarating too in the demands it made, and the new kind of attention it drew to the body.

After his enlistment the bodily consciousness of Owen's poems becomes more substantial. In his early work the human body had been largely constituted of pale skin, lips, cheeks, hands, hair, and eyes. But with his changed way of life (and perhaps too the example of the heartier Georgian poets) the represented body evolves, developing muscles, teeth, back and thighs, and a tanned skin. It is not at all a paradox that the disciplines of army life, as John Brophy remembered, gave soldiers 'a renewed zest in animal pleasures'. Brophy found this physicality inscribed in army slang itself, for 'the exhilaration which most men felt in the hardening of their bodies and the sharpening of their physical faculties is clearly to be traced in the imagery, the onomatopoeia and the sensuous fidelity of many of these words [of soldiers' slang].'[11] Owen greatly enjoyed the circumstances of physical activity shared with large numbers of fit young men, and the homoeroticism already present in his pre-war poetry looked for and found worthy and (as it were) legitimate subjects in the army. In June 1918 at Scarborough, he cast a veteran's eye on a new draft of conscripts, 'awful specimens, almost green-pale, another Race altogether from the mahogany swashbucklers who have finished their training' (*CL* 559). It could be added that the well-trained body was the dearer for the danger that awaited it. 'Training', a strange poem written in the same month (June 1918) apparently after a cross-country run (*CL* 561), seems narcissistically enthralled by the beauty of the body preparing for sacrifice:

[11] Brophy and Partridge, *The Long Trail*, 21, 210.

Not this week nor this month dare I lie down
In languor under lime trees or smooth smile.
Love must not kiss my face pale that is brown.

My lips, panting, shall drink space, mile by mile;
Strong meats be all my hunger; my renown
Be the clean beauty of speed and pride of style.

Cold winds encountered on the racing Down
Shall thrill my heated bareness; but awhile
None else may meet me till I wear my crown.

It seems that solitary pleasures and sexual partners alike must be renounced while the body in action perfects itself for apotheosis, but these pleasures, denied, immediately return diffused into space, speed, and air; the exercise is as erotic as the languor or the kiss.

This was not quite the sort of outcome the army had in mind in its designs on the body. It was important for morale that a soldier should be 'smart', but the whole purpose of training was to make his body useful. Physical training improved his strength, stamina, and reflexes; exercises and drill harnessed them. He must be taught 'to execute certain movements as a second nature', and to develop 'the habits of absolute and instant obedience to the orders of a superior'.[12] Drill could be 'a most excellent sedative to the nerves in warfare', advised a platoon commander; 'a few minutes ordinary arms drill every day, whenever possible, has a most extraordinary steadying effect both on the officer conducting it, and the men undergoing the exercise.'[13] A stylist from the General Staff summed it up as follows, in one of the training manuals:

> The first and greatest aim of all training should therefore be the establishment of the strictest discipline. To attain this there is no other method than constant and precise drill, strict enforcement of march discipline, insistence on a rigid exactness in the performance of even the dullest details of camp and barrack routine, and unceasing attention to apparently trifling detail in time of training. Without such previous preparation the silent and thorough execution of work and performance of duties, in darkness and in danger, in the presence of the enemy, and often without direct supervision of a superior, which distinguish good from bad troops and spell success, are impossible of attainment.[14]

[12] *Infantry Training*, xvi, 2.
[13] 'One of Them', '*Out There*!', 15.
[14] *Notes for Infantry Officers*, 9.

This is the authentic voice of disciplinary power making its claims on the body; and Foucault's excavations in the discourse of correction and training are much to the point here.[15]

The disciplines of war train and manipulate the soldier's body (or, to be accurate, the civilian's body) to perform certain functions as if they were 'a second nature'. Drill exercises make him more efficient by instilling rhythms that by repetition become habitual, and unbreakable even by fear. The body becomes reliable when its actions can be safely predicted, but this is dependent on 'unceasing attention to apparently trifling detail' (for army discipline has to be totalitarian) and a rigid exactness of routine.

Training aimed to create the desired combination of maximum efficiency and complete obedience. The army hardened the soldier's body and at the same time made it docile. To borrow Foucault's formula, discipline 'increases the forces of the body (in economic terms of utility) and diminishes these same forces (in political terms of obedience)'.[16] The army took away a man's power while it increased his strength and perhaps his beauty. Strength without power is a formula for tragedy in 'Spring Offensive'; the body deprived of both is a theme for pathos in many poems. The force of the soldier's body should be the force of an instrument, rhythmic and reliable and interchangeable with others in a uniform series—a machine, but also a part of a larger machine. The dream of the army's training manuals was of a totally controlled, totally efficient society, in which each soldierly body performed the tasks for which it had been moulded, so reliable an instrument that ideally the whole thing could still function (as the *Notes for Infantry Officers* anticipated) without supervision. It was an industrial ideal not to be realized in Owen's lifetime.

Owen grumbled, like any other soldier, about the mind-numbing succession of drills, inspections, and parades—'enough to send crazy any thinking being' (*CL* 385)—but he was not above boasting, in a letter from training camp, that he had scored full marks in an exam on drill (*CL* 387). Fastidious and a conformist by upbringing, he was anxious not only to be a good soldier but also, as an officer, to turn out good soldiers under his command. As an administrator of the disciplines, he had an investment in the

[15] Foucault, *Discipline and Punish*, 135–94. [16] Ibid. 138.

formation of uniform instruments which was the work of the army on the body. 'Inspection' shows the inflexibility with which a (first-personal) platoon commander deals with a deviation from discipline: the soldier's tunic is blemished with a stain of his own blood, and the army (through the officer) treats as a scandal this maculation of the texture of the uniform by the body which it contains. Soldiers must appear identical to the army because the army has to be able to treat them as interchangeable. Dead or maimed bodies in the army's language (endorsed in the first stanza of 'Insensibility') are 'losses, who might have fought longer'; their usefulness gone, they are mere empty space, 'gaps for filling'.

There is even a kind of interchange between the bodily and the instrumental. Weapons in 'The Last Laugh' and 'Anthem for Doomed Youth' provide a metallic and chemical commentary on the slaughter, in the absence of human voices to mourn. In 'Arms and the Boy' too, weapons live as bodies must die:

> Let the boy try along this bayonet-blade
> How cold steel is, and keen with hunger of blood;
> Blue with all malice, like a madman's flash;
> And thinly drawn with famishing for flesh.
>
> Lend him to stroke these blind, blunt bullet-leads,
> Which long to nuzzle in the hearts of lads,
> Or give him cartridges whose fine zinc teeth
> Are sharp with sharpness of grief and death.
>
> For his teeth seem for laughing round an apple.
> There lurk no claws behind his fingers supple;
> And God will grow no talons at his heels,
> Nor antlers through the thickness of his curls.

The human body is hopelessly under- or over-evolved for survival against these rapacious predators. Bayonet and bullet have desires and powers and even knowledge of which the boy (who has not yet grown up beyond the pleasure principle, so that for him the fruit of knowledge is still a laughing matter) is innocent in both senses. He is not made to be a soldier: his body is hopelessly unarmed; it will always be a civilian. Into this gap, between what the body is and what the army asks of it, flows much of the irony and the pathos of Owen's war poems. It is a pathos sharpened by irony: the army enhances and exposes the beauties of the body, only to dehumanize and destroy it. Beauty could be glimpsed, as freedom had been, before its promise was broken. The pattern is like pararhyme itself.

If the training manuals exhorted discipline of the body, they also enjoined discipline of speech, although this was of different kinds. 'When you first join,' cadets and young officers were advised by 'Regular', 'be careful not to talk too much, or to hold too strong opinions.'[17] Many officers had had identical advice on arrival as new boys at their public schools, and in both cases it was a reminder that the institution they had joined was a hierarchy and a discourse in which they would have to watch their language. For the officer, it was not only speech pitched up the hierarchy towards his seniors that was constrained. Discipline forebade too close a contact with the men under him. 'Get to know each one of them,' 'Regular' counselled, 'but never be familiar with them.'[18] Communications outside the army were restricted too. Under King's Regulations 453, no officer or soldier could publish any military information, or his views on any military subject, without special authority. In letters, parcels, or private diaries sent from the theatre of operations, no reference was allowed to details of place, military dispositions, casualties (previous to the publication of official lists), the effects of hostile fire, and the like. 'Criticism of operations is forbidden, as are statements calculated to bring the army or individuals into disrepute.'[19] A platoon commander was expected to censor his men's letters to ensure these rules were obeyed; and in fact Owen almost never broke them himself, in letters or poems. He was in an atmosphere where speech was not free, though after Dunsden this was not a novel experience for him. His *Field Service Pocket Book* reminded him that all his correspondence should be 'in clear', but it could also teach him methods by which secret messages could be enciphered. There were more ways of telling the truth than spelling it out.

The army sought to discipline speech as it disciplined the body; and in the event these constraints the army imposed on language were much to the benefit of Owen's writing. Not too much, perhaps, need be made of the fact that at about the time of his enlistment

[17] 'Regular', *Customs of the Army*, 18. [18] Ibid. 10.
[19] *Field Service Pocket Book*, 216.

he began a set of exercises in poetic composition, joining his cousin Leslie Gunston and a friend, Olwen Joergens, in writing on agreed themes in the discipline of the sonnet form. But experience of the army does seem to have coincided with a tightening-up of style. Discipline and precision, the army virtues, had never been among Owen's desiderata for poetry; he did not even much like to find these things in discourse where they might more commonly be supposed to belong, confessing in 1914 that 'I am only conscious of any satisfaction in Scientific Reading or Thinking when it rounds off into a poetical generality and vagueness' (*CL* 254). Music and feeling are what the early poems are after—'De la musique avant toute chose'—and these were commodities which writers of an aesthetic tendency liked to wrap in the tasteful or suggestive blur that enraged Ezra Pound. When the army became available to Owen as a literary subject it gave his writing a field of material observation and at the same time a new quality of terseness, where before he had tended to luxuriance. The effect is not so much a metamorphosis as a widening of stylistic range. In 'S.I.W.':

> One dawn, our wire patrol
> Carried him. This time, Death had not missed.
> We could do nothing but wipe his bleeding cough.
> Could it be accident?—Rifles go off . . .
> Not sniped? No. (Later they found the English ball.)

Subject-matter aside, this kind of movement would have been inconceivable in a pre-1916 Owen poem. This is a new accent, economical of feeling and not concerned with music, the voice of that military pronoun. And you may search for hours through the manuals for a first-person singular. Owen learned to vary pace and accent by moving between this spare and functional language and the foliate romanticism he had from his earlier reading. 'Insensibility' refuses music and feeling through five increasingly tense stanzas, to release them in a great wash at the end of the sixth. The monologue in 'Strange Meeting' moves in the other direction, when the romantic autobiography—'I went hunting wild | After the wildest beauty in the world'—reaches an unadorned conclusion in the matter-of-fact 'I am the enemy you killed, my friend.'

The army had little time for personal difference: much of its special language is encoded in fixed ritual form, and belongs among those speech genres classed by Bakhtin as the least conducive to reflecting individuality in language.[20] There was no room for variation or elaboration, for example, in the standard military command, an entirely automated utterance. 'All the activity of the disciplined individual,' says Foucault, 'must be punctuated and sustained by injunctions whose efficacy rests on brevity and clarity; the order does not need to be explained or formulated; it must trigger off the required behaviour and that is enough.'[21] Individual variation among a very severely restricted range of parameters was possible in the Field Service postcard (Army Form A2042), on which nothing could be written except the date and the signature of the sender, whose message was composed by deleting options appropriately.

I am quite well.

I have been admitted into hospital.

{ sick	and am going on well.
wounded }	and hope to be discharged soon.

And so on. It was an interesting challenge,[22] and there were others. The army's bureaucracy produced an endless supply of forms for officers to complete. With the Reserve Battalion in Scarborough in 1918, Owen was familiar with the duties of the subaltern of the day, illustrated (in Captain Hood's *Duties for All Ranks*) in a specimen report.

Form of Report
I inspected rations yesterday, and saw them weighed and issued. They were of . . . quality.
I visited the breakfasts and found them . . .
The men were . . . properly dressed. There were . . . complaints.
I inspected all the guards coming off duty and found them . . .
I visited the soldiers-in-arrest in the Detention Room and found them . . .

And so on. The pro forma accountability of bureaucratic utterances like this could be brought face to face with the language of

[20] Bakhtin, *Speech Genres*, 63.

[21] Foucault, *Discipline and Punish*, 164.

[22] On at least one occasion Owen rose to the challenge, cheerfully adapting a Field Service post card to read: 'I am quite well and am going on well to be charged soon. I am base.' The card, which Jon Stallworthy reproduces in his biography (*WO* 271), was sent to Conal O'Riordan, who later published it in an article entitled 'Poets are Cheerful!', in *John O'London's Weekly*, 6 June 1941, 224–6. I am grateful to D. S. R. Welland for correspondence about this document.

a quite different field of discourse, with a different idea of what responsibility might mean. It is one of Owen's most studied discursive confrontations.

For 14 hours yesterday I was at work—teaching Christ to lift his cross by numbers, and how to adjust his crown; and not to imagine he thirst till after the last halt; I attended his supper to see that there were no complaints; and inspected his feet to see that they should be worthy of the nails. I see to it that he is dumb and stands to attention before his accusers. With a piece of silver I buy him every day, and with maps I make him familiar with the topography of Golgotha. (*CL* 562.)

Above all, military training inculcated a certain kind of mental organization. The most effective discipline, it was agreed, was discipline introjected and normalized so as to become 'a second nature', and this was greatly dependent on the creation of a group identity and loyalty. Self-discipline was a social virtue. 'An organization with a strong *esprit de corps* powerfully influences the conduct of its members. Discipline becomes natural.'[23] Discipline was moralized as unselfishness. As the soldier's uniformed body merged ideally into the file, so too individual interests became indistinguishable in a hierarchy of larger interests—chums, battalion, regiment, possibly nation. If the soldier's personal interests were subordinate, his sympathies too had to be rationed where kindness was not compatible with efficiency. First things had to come first, and the army's handbooks agreed that the first thing was to win victory through attack.

Denis Winter makes this point in his discussion of training in *Death's Men*:

'All ranks must be taught that the aim and object is to come to close quarters with the enemy as quickly as possible so as to be able to use the bayonet. This must become a second nature.' The words were written into training manuals at the close of the Somme campaign, and repeated with just one significant exception the official handbook of 1914. Missing were the words 'close with the enemy, cost what it may'. This was the only minor adjustment made in battle training in Britain after the disaster of 1 July 1916, the first day of the Somme.[24]

[23] Baynes, *Morale*, 184.
[24] Winter, *Death's Men*, 39–40. The 'missing' words can be found in *Infantry Training* (1914), 134.

The army's obsession with what *Infantry Training* calls the doctrine of 'the primacy of the advance to close quarters' is inscribed all through the manuals and deserves a study of its own. Denis Winter adds that skill with the bayonet was supposed to distinguish the British, with their professional military traditions, from the amateur Germans. But the bayonet was a virtually redundant weapon on the western front; just 0.03 per cent of wounds on the battlefield throughout the war were inflicted by bayonet, and Winter says that 'the "discipline" required by bayonet work was thought of as an end in itself.'[25] This nostalgic yearning for close-quarter fighting was magnified in the strategic insistence of the British and French generals on attack. But an attentive reader of *Trench Warfare: Notes on Attack and Defence* (1915) could not fail to notice that that handbook's case histories told stories of comprehensively successful defensive actions, while in its one 'Description of a Successful Attack' it is clear that the attackers suffered considerable losses and succeeded only in establishing themselves in a new front line some forty yards from the enemy's original front line, which the enemy continued to hold: not very cheering news for proponents of the offensive spirit. Bayonets are phallic in a fairly obvious way (a phallicism hinted at in 'Arms and the Boy') and it is hard to resist the conclusion that aggression was insisted on because it was manly.

The army that Owen joined was in every way a masculine community, speaking masculine language; the disciplines of war were essentially Victorian masculine disciplines. Ruskin, one of Owen's literary heroes, had explained gender difference in *Sesame and Lilies* fifty years before. Men, he had said, 'by their nature are prone to fight',[26] whereas women are the adepts of sympathy, imagination, beauty, and peace. 'The man, in his rough work in open world, must encounter all peril and trial;—to him, therefore, must be the failure, the offence, the inevitable error: often he must be wounded, or subdued; often misled; and *always* hardened.'[27] Ruskin's masculine world was rough, exposed, dangerous, hardening; the feminine was soft, enclosed, sheltered, sensitive. This sexual geography coincided with the imagery and discourses of Owen's own upbringing, and poetry for him had hitherto been

[25] Ibid. 40. [26] Ruskin, *Sesame and Lilies*, 136.
[27] Ibid. 108.

preponderantly a feminine discourse. The masculine disciplines of war extended the register of his writing. He never lost the lyrical and private tones which, I have suggested, have their earliest origins in communings with his mother. The repertoire was now increased by the mixing-in of the voice of the good soldier.

The good soldier's body was disciplined to uniformity and use; his mind too had to be partially automated and concentrated to an end. Training in the soldierly spirit set great store by manliness and impersonality, and kept a severe check on sentiment. Here is some advice on attack, from the manual *Infantry Training*:

> The paramount duty of all leaders in the firing line is to get their troops forward . . . [Troops] must be imbued with a determination to close with the enemy . . . If incapacitated from advancing, the soldier's first duty is to place his ammunition in a conspicuous place, ready to be picked up by other men . . . No man is permitted to leave his platoon in action to take wounded to the rear, or for any other purpose, without special orders . . . A commander must demand the impossible and not think of sparing his men. Those who fall out must be left behind and must no more stop the pursuit than casualties stopped the assault.[28]

Owen's lyric compassion has power because he can command this brisk and dispassionate voice too. It can be the voice of the villains of his war poetry, satirized and condemned for their callousness, but it is also the voice of the soldier at work, for without the disciplines the work could not be done, and, so long as the work was to be done, personal feeling might have to be deferred, the only allowable elegy an automatic gesture. In October 1918 he told Sassoon that his battalion had been in the fighting and suffered serious losses, including 'the boy by my side, shot through the head, [who] lay on top of me, soaking my shoulder, for half an hour'. He continued: 'I shall feel again as soon as I dare, but now I must not. I don't take the cigarette out of my mouth when I write Deceased over their letters' (*CL* 581).

'Insensibility', a concourse where so many of Owen's concerns meet, explores these matters of the mental disciplines of the wars. It invokes for its own grim purposes the classic formula of beatitude and pastoral idyll.[29]

[28] *Infantry Training*, 143, 145, 147.

[29] Jon Stallworthy thinks 'Insensibility' may be a reply to Wordsworth's 'Character of the Happy Warrior' (*WO* 261).

1

Happy are men who yet before they are killed
Can let their veins run cold.
Whom no compassion fleers
Or makes their feet
Sore on the alleys cobbled with their brothers.
The front line withers.
But they are troops who fade, not flowers,
For poets' tearful fooling:
Men, gaps for filling:
Losses, who might have fought
Longer; but no one bothers.

2

And some cease feeling
Even themselves or for themselves.
Dullness best solves
The tease and doubt of shelling,
And Chance's strange arithmetic
Comes simpler than the reckoning of their shilling.
They keep no check on armies' decimation.

3

Happy are these who lose imagination:
They have enough to carry with ammunition.
Their spirit drags no pack.
Their old wounds, save with cold, can not more ache.
Having seen all things red,
Their eyes are rid
Of the hurt of the colour of blood for ever.
And terror's first constriction over,
Their hearts remain small-drawn.
Their senses in some scorching cautery of battle
Now long since ironed,
Can laugh among the dying, unconcerned.

Here is an anatomy of what the 'second nature' of discipline means in battle. Feminine discourse is banished; virility and realism discard flowers and tears and poetry, for they are useless. The good soldier, cold-blooded, insensible of self and unconcerned with others, embodies that soldierly spirit which, the manuals said, 'will produce such a high degree of courage and disregard of self that, in the day of battle, he will use his brains and his weapons coolly and to the best advantage.'[30] He is man-machine, or dead man erect, his body anaesthetized and hardened to terrible deeds, his heart shrunken and unresponsive. In order to function, that is, in order to work efficiently, a kind of disintegration has taken place within him. To avoid breakdown he is broken down, mentally dismembered. The relation of this poem to Owen's neurasthenia is obvious though complex. Those faculties that are no use have been discarded like a cumbersome pack—pity, sensibilities, comradeship that is merely nostalgic, care about the future (he is doomed anyway from the first line), memory, imagination, speech, even seriousness. The result is a monster: brute, machine, corpse, madman: but it is also the good soldier, and he is still alive, that is, the poem is not to be mistaken for satirical grotesque. It is not *The Dunciad*, but an apology for dunces. After the 'sheer' fighting of early October 1918, Owen told Siegfried Sassoon: 'I cannot say I suffered anything; having let my brain grow dull: That is to say my nerves are in perfect order' (*CL* 581). His nerves had broken down in 1917; now his terrible composure among the dying had to be construed as evidence that he had recovered and was functioning properly as a member of the military community. It was proof that he was, in his father's words, 'normal again' (*CL* 562).

'Insensibility' continues:

4
Happy the soldier home, with not a notion
How somewhere, every dawn, some men attack,
And many sighs are drained.
Happy the lad whose mind was never trained:
His days are worth forgetting more than not.
He sings along the march
Which we march taciturn, because of dusk,
The long, forlorn, relentless trend
From larger day to huger night.

5
We wise, who with a thought besmirch
Blood over all our soul,
How should we see our task
But through his blunt and lashless eyes?

[30] *What Every Soldier*, 3.

Alive, he is not vital overmuch;
Dying, not mortal overmuch;
Nor sad, nor proud,
Nor curious at all.
He cannot tell
Old men's placidity from his.

6
But cursed are dullards whom no cannon stuns,
That they should be as stones.
Wretched are they, and mean
With paucity that never was simplicity.
By choice they made themselves immune
To pity and whatever moans in man
Before the last sea and the hapless stars;
Whatever mourns when many leave these shores;
Whatever shares
The eternal reciprocity of tears.

Not one, but several kinds of insensibility then. In stanza four there is the insensibility of the simple. I mean the word to retain something of its class sense; these are clearly the private soldiers, young men without much education and without military responsibilities, presumed to have a short imaginative range. I think 'the lad' belongs to the conscript drafts of 1917, though the poem doesn't say this; he is surely different from the battle-hardened veterans of stanza three. What then of 'we wise'?

We can follow Jon Stallworthy's gloss of this as 'we poets' (*CPF* 147). Poets are the specialists of sensibility, which means they are able to drown their imagination in blood with just a thought. But that way lay only madness, the crippling sensibility of the 'Mental Cases' on whose traumatized sense 'Sunlight seems a blood-smear; night comes blood-black; | Dawn breaks open like a wound that bleeds afresh.' In these circumstances the poet like the soldier must discipline his mind if he is not to break down. His function, mere hysterical fooling in the first stanza, is now spoken of as a task, a piece of work that has to be done; it is work that requires the poet to be cool and impersonal, to keep his nerve. It is a position in which the army's discipline of subordinating the individual to the interests of the group meets the Evangelical insistence on usefulness, with which Owen had grown up and to which the army's ethic is obviously related. Only by subordinating the imagination to the point of view of the anonymous soldier can poetry *work*. Poetry had a task to perform in wartime, might indeed be instrumental as a weapon with which to flay the insensibility of civilians. In this way in the last stanza (and of course this is the rationale for the poem itself) the discourses of army and of poetry, estranged in stanza one, are reconciled, the lyricism and the tears inhibited earlier flow at last and are answered.

To read the 'wise' as poets need not, however, lead to a closing-down of the other possibilities in the pronoun. If 'we' makes sense as 'we poets', that does not cancel its more immediate function as a continuation of the pronominal subject marching taciturn to the end of stanza four. 'We' in stanza four are silent: they are afraid of the dark, they know and care (as the lads do not) where they are going, and what may be in store. So 'we' seem to be experienced soldiers, combat veterans and survivors.[31]

Experienced soldiers, only too aware of the blood on their hands and of what may await them in the next battle, can only go on with their task if they cultivate insensibility, deliberately becoming casual, unthinking, uncaring, as the most placid lad seems to be. Efficiency is automatic: too much feeling is inefficient. 'Insensibility' confesses to the consequences of the disciplines of the wars. The good soldier has to be economical with his humanity, even if this reduces him to the level of a simpleton, an animal, an automaton. Placid, unconscious, his vitality inhibited, his sensibility killed with his nerves, he has disciplined himself to a kind of willed death. He is properly in the end an object of horror. But at least he is not as inhuman, nor as dead, as the civilian whose hardness of heart is voluntary.

Vigny's ambiguous advice—'If any man despairs of becoming a Poet, let him carry his pack and march in the ranks' (*CL* 342)—had borne a strange fruit. The war did not make Owen a poet, but it made him a particular kind of poet. In giving him a subject, it also decisively formed his style by making available to his repertoire a discourse—disciplined, concrete, masculine, impersonal—at odds with the qualities he had previously thought of and cultivated as poetic, qualities of the upper-case Poetry with which, he said, he was not concerned now. Army language did enrich

[31] You could at the same time make out a case for 'we officers', 'we shell-shock neurasthenics', perhaps 'we cowards'.

Owen's poetry, as army experience widened its range, by interrupting it with an unfamiliar and unromantic way of speaking, seeing, and judging. This new voice, the voice of his working life in his last three years, challenged the softer and more lyrical voice in Owen, though it did not drown it. They speak to each other, the language of the two communities no longer separate but in dialogue, for poet and soldier had much to say to each other after all.

The army made Owen a modern poet. In an eerie way, the army itself was a modernist in its language, and belongs in company or relationship with contemporary modernizers—Yeats who wanted his writing to be more masculine, Pound cultivating an exact spareness, Lewis and T. E. Hulme variously dismantling individualism to expose the inhuman, Eliot setting a rigorous training programme in tradition and disciplined impersonality for the recruit to poetry, and all of these perhaps in their distance from what might be called the civilian public or nation at home. But while the army taught Owen the uses—the necessity, sometimes—of a new toughness, an 'insensibility', a curb on personal feelings, it also showed him how (as some modernist writing was soon to demonstrate) these things could breed monsters of indifference and authoritarian brutality; these perils, too, became his subjects. The poet, like the soldier, knew what he was doing in accepting the disciplines of the wars.

11

Wilfred Owen's England

The soldier served the army and the army served the nation and empire. The Great War to which Wilfred Owen went was a war between nations, yet the nation as an entity was not an existentially strong community for him, as family and Church were. He declared his priorities when he said, more than half-seriously, that he would sooner fight to safeguard English literature than for England. 'Do you know what would hold me together on a battlefield?: The sense that I was perpetuating the language in which Keats and the rest of them wrote! I do not know what else in England is greatly superior, or dearer to me, than another land and people' (*CL* 300). But the best way to perpetuate the language was not by dying, which enabled him to point out that 'my life is worth more than my death to Englishmen.' This was not necessarily the way the nation saw things.

Owen grew up under the zenith of British imperial power, and whatever the economic statistics were beginning to say, there were not many people in pre-war Britain who doubted that they belonged to the greatest nation on earth. No one could remember a time when the British had lost a war, and few could imagine that the still wider-increasing bounds of empire might also be capable of shrinking. This sense of relative security meant that the voice of British patriotism was not particularly shrill. French and German patriots, for their different reasons less satisfied with the hand that history had dealt their nations, were subjects for mockery in Britain, for example, in *Punch* or on the music-hall stage. Strutting and ranting were not considered the British way. The Englishman, Owen himself said smugly (*CL* 282), dealt with an offender by ignoring him. But British patriotism did run deep, and when it was deeply stirred—on 'Mafeking Night' (which lasted five days) or in August 1914—was capable of just as much fervour, and just as much vulgarity, as any foreigner could manage.

Patriotism seems to have been pretty evenly spread across the social classes. It flourished among the poor, some of whom had not much to be patriotic about. In large parts of working-class Britain in 1914, says Jay Winter, there were 'conditions of poverty and ill-health which today we associate with countries of the Third World'. The life expectancy for British men in 1911, for example, was equal to that in Iraq in 1970–5 (51.5 years).[1] And millions of the working population had been involved in the widespread and divisive labour unrest of the early Georgian years. Yet industrial militancy and patriotism were complementary sentiments. When war came in 1914, one-fifth of the industrial labour force joined the forces in the first year, so many that numbers had to be returned to civilian life to keep essential industries running.

The response of the middle and professional classes was as prompt, though this was more predictable, for these were the people who had been educated to administer and police the empire. It was the patriotism of this class that Ruskin had confidently appealed to, a generation before, in his inaugural lecture as Slade Professor of Fine Art at Oxford in 1870:

> Will you, youths of England, make your country again a royal throne of kings; a sceptred isle, for all the world a source of light, a centre of peace? . . . There is indeed a course of beneficent glory open to us, such as never was yet offered to any poor group of mortal souls. But it must be—it *is* with us, now, 'Reign or Die' . . . And this is what [England] must either do, or perish: she must found colonies as fast and as far as she is able, formed of her most energetic and worthiest men;—seizing every piece of fruitful waste ground she can set her foot on, and there teaching these her colonists that their chief virtue is to be fidelity to their country, and that their first aim is to be to advance the power of England by land and sea.[2]

Admirer of Ruskin though he was, Owen was never moved by this vision of ravening national destiny, and least of all when, in the trenches, it took the form of the doctrine of maintaining ascendancy in the entirely unfruitful 'waste ground' of no man's land. 'They want to call No Man's Land "England" because we keep supremacy there,' he told his mother in January 1917, and

[1] Beckett and Simpson (eds), *A Nation in Arms*, 195.
[2] Ruskin, *Lectures on Art*, 36–7.

added that he would as soon christen his child Chlorina-Phosgena (*CL* 429). But Ruskin's strangely vulnerable omnipotence fantasy was in any case pitching things rather high. More to most people's taste was the unostentatious, technocratic, self-sacrificing supremacism that was to find a voice in Kipling, articulating the destiny of the work of empire to those at home. Kipling spoke for and about the imperial workforce, people like Wilfred Owen's father, who spent his happiest years in India, as a young man working for the Great Indian Peninsular Railway, and would probably have made his career there if circumstances had not dragged him back to England. Both parents impressed upon their children the paramountcy of self-denial and patience, virtues in which Christian humility and the service ideal of empire met and agreed.

The European dimension of British supremacism in the pre-war years was to be heard again most eloquently in Kipling, in warnings about the challenge of upstart Germany. There were a number of invasion scares between 1900 and 1914 (it was a popular theme in fiction, from Buchan and Saki to Erskine Childers) and consequently a certain amount of military awareness—and of course naval awareness—if not, in Kipling's view, enough military readiness.

There was a well-trained Territorial army. By 1914 some 8 per cent of the male population had had some form of military training, according to Ian Beckett; but he further estimates that as many as 41 per cent of all male adolescents may have belonged to some form of youth organization.[3] There was a diffused and mild militarism, operating in schools and parishes in the form of Officers' Training Corps, Boy Scouts, Boys' Brigades, sporting organizations, and some church groups. We have seen its spirit infiltrating even the Band of Hope. If in 1914 Britain was (as Beckett puts it) mildly militaristic, it was also partially and informally mobilized. Many of these organizations were not nationalistic in their *raison d'être*; but many were also transformed easily and sometimes wholesale to a military purpose. Militarization was not a complete shock to a nation that dressed up in childhood in the uniform of sailors and soldiers.

There was then a network of institutions, as well as an ideology, a network of habit and assumption, all set to be mobilized and

[3] Beckett and Simpson (eds), *A Nation in Arms*, 5.

pressed into service when the nation went to war in 1914. It was a patriotic culture, from its music-hall and children's books to Elgar and Captain Scott. Following the lines drawn up over the issue of the South African war at the turn of the century, patriotism might take an aggressive form, banging the imperial drum abroad, or it could be more defensive and home-based, the Little Englandism whose literary expression is in countless Edwardian and Georgian registrations of the charms of the countryside. When the nation called, in its appeal for the war effort, it found an answering voice of patriotism. Yet that voice—the voice of Britain or of 'England'—is strangely muted in Wilfred Owen.

It is not just that he was living abroad in 1914, absorbing and enjoying French life. His reasons for being there had as much to do with a dislike of England as with a fascination with France. England had disappointed him. Its universities were closed to him because his family had not enough money (which was grounds for resentment of both the educational system and his family). It offered no palatable employment or prospects to an aspiring poet in provincial obscurity. Its Church was a nest of hypocrites, its social conditions a festering sore. And in England he had no real friends. He had 'exhausted his immediate environment', says Harold Owen, and knew he had to seek a fresh country.

> With bitter disappointment he faced the truth—that his hopes that he might have three years in Oxford or any university were now quite impossible of fulfilment and, realising this, he felt adolescent resentment against England and fostered a passionate hope that what England refused him, France, if he embraced her, might in some measure offer him—and not solace alone, but also intellectual friendships and the encouragement he so sorely needed. (*JFO* 2. 206.)

Once settled in France, he was in no hurry to return. After his one-month visit in May–June 1915, he spoke warmly of the family home, and of London (which he loved), but these experiences are never articulated into any sense of enthusiasm for England, or Britain, as an idea, a nation. At most, it seems to have come to represent to him a debt, to which his freedom and happiness in France would sooner or later have to be paid. He was not the most likely of patriots or militarists.

But the voices of patriotism and militarism were all round him. They clamoured from the English papers he read regularly in France, and from the recruiting posters he saw everywhere on his visit to England, during which he also managed to get a ticket to attend a great meeting at the Guildhall, organized by the Central Committee for National Patriotic Organizations. He heard Asquith and Bonar Law there, and thought he saw Kipling. There were harder and softer forms of patriotic discourse. *Punch*, for example—which was faithfully sent to him in Bordeaux, at training camp, and later at the front—was not as crassly jingoistic as *John Bull*, but may have been just as persuasive. It specialized in priming the satisfying legend that the British were the more formidable soldiers and patriots because they had a sense of humour, something unknown to the Germans.

The army took patriotism seriously. Patriotism had brought the recruit to the colours, and it was an essential ingredient of the soldierly spirit. The trainee was instructed in the deeds which had made the British army and his regiment famous. Furthermore, 'The privileges which he inherits as a citizen of a great Empire should be explained to him, and he should be taught to appreciate the honour which is his, as a soldier, of serving his King and country.'[4] Ideological education in direct form was pretty rudimentary. The patriotism of volunteers in the New Armies was largely taken for granted; it was discipline and skills that they needed. It was perhaps a different matter for the conscript levies of the later years, and when Owen came to the 5th (Reserve) Battalion of the Manchesters at Scarborough at the end of 1917, some attention was being paid to the instillation of correct thinking in the teenaged new recruits.

> There is much talk of Education for the 'A4's' of the Battalion, that is the tender younglings. I have been 'approached' on the subject, but I shall not consent to lecture on Militarian subjects. The scheme either comes of a desperate feeling that the race is going to perdition intellectually or else it is a Jesuitical movement to catch 'em young, & prepare them for the Eucharist of their own blood. (*CL* 516.)

Patriotic militarism did have a respectable intellectual ancestry, though there may have been few in the British army who knew or cared much about it. One such was Lieutenant-Colonel W. Shirley, who began a lecture to new recruits in the following arresting manner:

[4] *Infantry Training*, 2.

The words which I have to speak to you this afternoon are the most important you will hear during this course—I even venture to think that they are the most serious you will ever hear in all your lives, for my object is to convince you, now you have entered upon the service of your Country, that you must proceed to serve her with all your heart and with all your soul and with all your mind and with all your strength.[5]

He goes on to quote at considerable length Ruskin's exposition of the duties of her children to England, garnishing this with Horace's 'Dulce et decorum est pro patria mori' (it is sweet and seemly to die for your country). 'If you have done your best and yet must fall, you may take comfort in the thought that you will have suffered for a cause greater and more noble than that for which any man has ever yet sacrificed his all.'[6] In this war against 'the inhuman Hun' Colonel Shirley urged his listeners 'to go forth as the Champions of Right, not as the Avengers of Wrong'. He quoted Burke's claim that Britain was 'the tutelary genius of the human race', and Ruskin again—'I tell you that war is the foundation of . . . all the high virtues and faculties', and his praise of 'the creative or foundational war' as the highest expression of a nation or indeed mankind. 'To such a war as this all men are born.' He also adduced Bacon's view that 'the greatness, stability and wealth of nations depends upon a race of military men.'[7] This fascinating lecture (to which I shall return) was published in 1916 under the title *Moral: The Most Important Factor in War* (see page 183). The lecture formed the introduction to the Officers' Course with the Artists' Rifles.[8]

While literary discourse was able to provide this sort of ammunition for a national war effort, the imperatives of service to the nation could be urged in other terms too. The Bishop of London, Arthur F. Winnington Ingram, proved equal to the rhetorical challenge when he preached in St Paul's on 9 August 1914:

[5] Shirley, *Moral*, 3. [6] Ibid. 5. [7] Ibid. 7–11.

[8] Colonel Shirley, who had served in the Indian Army, was responsible for giving the Artists' Rifles a rather imperial flavour. They advertised commissions for 'gentlemen returning from abroad' (the advertisement which caught the attention of Wilfred Owen), and when Shirley set up the Artists' Rifles Regimental Association he affiliated it to the Royal Colonial Institute, intending the association to be in part 'a genteel Labour Bureau' which would help its members to settle and find jobs in the colonies after the war was over. See *Artists' Rifles Journal*, 1 no. 1 (Aug. 1916), 6.

Is it not possible that the terrors of death have been much exaggerated? . . . There is one thing at least far worse than death, and that is dishonour. If a heathen poet, with only a vague belief in another world, could say, 'Dulce et decorum est pro patria mori' (A sweet and pleasant thing it is to die for your country), with how much more conviction should a Christian parent say the same![9]

Later in the same month, Bishop Ingram addressed some units of the Territorial Army, called up for home service duties, with 'A Call to Arms'. 'What does England mean to you? What does it mean to all of us? It means everything we most value in the world—the purity of our homes, the safety and honour of our children, our sisters, our wives, and mothers.'[10] This assimilation of patriotism to family (and particularly family women) was to be a powerful trope of the recruitment campaign. 'Women of Britain say "Go!" ' But the bishop could find a higher endorsement yet. 'The motive of your drill and all your training,' he told the Territorials, 'is obedience to the call of your Country in response to an instinct planted in you by God.'[11] What matters is not that the bishop said these things, but that his utterances were made possible by an audience that wanted to hear them. 'A Call to Arms' was finalized (in the Bakhtinian sense) in a dramatic way, as a triumphant footnote to the sermon points out: 'In response to this appeal, given in the two camps at Cowshot and Bulswater, six more battalions volunteered for Foreign Service, and the Bishop received the thanks of the Commander-in-Chief.' Six battalions would contain five or six thousand men.

In another sermon the following year, the bishop returned to the theme of patriotism as a natural human instinct with a divine sanction. He reminded himself that Jesus had wept over Jerusalem. 'Yes, he loved his Jerusalem. He was a patriot at heart.' And consider how the empire had rallied round in the hour of need. 'And the reason of all this is that we have been the mother of free countries. We have grown free nations. There is no other country in the world that can make people so happy under its rule as our country.' How arrogant, in the face of this, 'the idea that the Germans are to conquer the world for its own good'. Of course Germans, the bishop had to allow, had a right to their own patriotism (natural

[9] Winnington Ingram, *A Day of God*, 4–5. 'Death sooner than dishonour, that's the style!' says the parent, doubtless 'a Christian parent', in 'S.I.W.'

[10] Ibid. 17. [11] Ibid. 25.

and God-given)—'if they would be content with loving their own country and not seek to dominate the world'. To those Anglicans embarrassed about going to war with Germany, a Christian nation after all and the cradle of the Reformation, Bishop Ingram was sorry to say that the Germans were 'a people who, for the time at least, are animated and dominated by pagan and unchristian ideas'.[12]

Owen quotes Bishop Ingram verbatim (on effeminacy) in a letter to his sister in February 1917 (*CL* 435), so even at the front he may have been sent (by his sister?) or have seen either a pamphlet or a newspaper report of the bishop's latest pronouncements.[13] But in any case, even after the Dunsden catastrophe Owen had remained a regular churchgoer, and furthermore a weekly church parade was a feature of army life everywhere except in the actual front line. He had had regular and ample opportunity to hear what the nation's Church had to say about the nation's war, and from preachers whose intellectual clarity was not likely, in the main, to be much more limpid than Bishop Ingram's.

Owen found offensive these rhetorical moves to dress the war effort in the robes of a godly crusade. A letter of May 1917 sets out to unpick the knot binding (as the Church of England did) the discourse of nation to that of Christ:

> Already I have comprehended a light which never will filter into the dogma of any national church: namely that one of Christ's essential commands was: Passivity at any price! Suffer dishonour and disgrace; but never resort to arms. Be bullied, be outraged, be killed; but do not kill. It may be a chimerical and an ignominious principle, but there it is. It can only be ignored: and I think pulpit professionals are ignoring it very skilfully and successfully indeed. (*CL* 461.)

A national church in wartime could only profess Christianity if it dismembered it, deliberately cutting some of the main Christian teachings by a practice Owen called 'selective ignorance' (*CL* 462). It was the kind of manœuvre by which the Revd Bernard J. Snell, for example, got round Christ's command to love your enemies.

[12] Ibid. 7–13, 46.

[13] These became increasingly feverish as in 1916 he launched in London the National Mission of Repentance and Hope, 'to purge the heart of the Empire before the boys come back', with a campaign against prostitution, vice, and 'lecherous and slimy theatrical productions' (Winnington Ingram, *Cleansing London*, 2).

'But what of loving the enemies of our nation? There is no reason to suppose that Jesus was thinking of international relations when he preached the Sermon on the Mount.'[14] But Owen—'more and more Christian as I walk the unchristian ways of Christendom'—insisted that Christ was the asset, and ally, of no nation or denomination. Nationalism could not lay claim to a Christian spirit, though other kinds of loyalty might.

> Christ is literally in no man's land. There men often hear His voice: Greater love hath no man than this, that a man lay down his life—for a friend.
>
> Is it spoken in English only and in French?
>
> I do not believe so.
>
> Thus you see how pure Christianity will not fit in with pure patriotism. (CL 461.)

As he tried to deny the discourse of 'England' the respectability it claimed from Christian principle, he also wanted to separate it from the power it drew from association with the family.

In 'It was a navy boy', written about the time of his enlistment, a connection between the war effort and a son's devotion to his mother seems to be the point that 'cleansed' the speaker of 'a cowardice', presumably about enlisting. Almost freezing to death in the advanced front line in February 1917, Owen thought of his mother and sister, he told them, without a break all the time (*CL* 430). And close to breakdown in April, he confessed he would give up 'the unequal contest' without a definite object for carrying on. 'And that object is not my Motherland, which is a good land, nor my Mother tongue, which is a dear language, but for my Mother, of whom I am not worthy to be called *The Son* xxx' (*CL* 449).

But although he felt love of the family protected him in battle, there is none of Bishop Ingram's sense that the battle was being fought to protect the family—on the contrary, as the encroaching shadow of war service swallowed Harold Owen and threatened the youngest brother Colin. Assent to what was being done in the name of England was a disgrace to the family: 'S.I.W.' dramatizes this, moving from the family's enthusiastic send-off of the lad to its eventual consequence in his breakdown and suicide. As we have seen, the letters written to Susan Owen, from the spring of

[14] Snell, *How are we to Love our Enemies?*, 4.

1917 onwards, conduct a delicate and determined campaign to prise his mother away from an unexamined patriotism to a critical understanding of the war. For her son's sake as much as for her own, you sense, she must be dissociated from the civilian nation which blithely sent its children to perish. 'The people of England needn't hope. They must agitate. But they are not yet agitated even' (*CL* 429). In the letters and poems he sent her, in which England is never named without hostility, he tried to win her over against the war. He seems to have succeeded. In October 1918: 'I am glad you are finding courage to speak. In a previous letter you said you kept quiet. I was not proud of that. The 4th Army General has had to issue an Order: "Peace Talk must cease in the Fourth Army."' (*CL* 584–5). And three days later, he told her: 'A Senior Lieutenant has turned up from Leave so I am now only Second in Command of D. Coy. He has returned from his first visit to London utterly disgusted with England's indifference to the real meaning of the war as we understand it' (*CL* 585). One can only guess at the extent to which, as far as he was concerned, his mother now no longer belonged in the word 'England' but was expatriated into its antagonist in the sentence, the pronoun 'we'—the other, dissenting nation.

The modality of that first-person plural pronoun in Owen's writing has really been the object of my whole enquiry, the sense of community from which his words speak. Something strange (but certainly not unique in his generation) happened to Owen's communal sense in the war years. A decisive motive for joining the army had been a sense of duty to his country, although, for reasons I have given, his sense of that country (and so his sense of obligations owed to it) was relatively weak. How much of a sense of what England might mean do you get from Owen's pre-war poems compared, not entirely unfairly, with contemporary poetry by Hardy, Kipling, Housman, or, for that matter, Sassoon? Once he had seen what war meant to the fighting soldier, and although he had been trained from childhood to obedient service, he turned in anger against the nation—its politicians and churchmen and leaders of opinion, its civilian population too lazy or too stupid to understand what was going on in their name, or too selfish to care. He experienced alienation in the sense of becoming an alien, uprooted, detached from the national community to which his loyalties were in any case not particularly strong. And his shell-shock makes relevant a parallel sense of alienation as a mental deracination. But the very circumstances that alienated him from England bound him into another community, a new nation.

The question of the nation is of the utmost relevance, I think, to the whole project of Owen's war-writing, for here in a word was a specific instance of his trying to renew and restore language which had become mendacious and corrupt. Much—everything—was demanded of soldiers in the name of England: but what did that name refer to? What (as Bishop Ingram had asked) did England mean? Patriotism drew on other loyalties; but how good was its credit? As he worked to cut the ideological lines of communication by which an unthinking patriotism sustained itself from sources of family loyalty, proprietorial pride, and Christian piety, Owen also hinted at what a true nation might mean.

When English officers went to war they ceased to *look* English, Owen said, bitterness changing their faces from their 'complacent English expressions' (*CL* 573). But the contrast was not simply between those in England and those in the army. It was a matter of knowledge and sympathy, of seeing, as he said to his mother, 'the real meaning of the war as we understand it' (*CL* 585).

> My last hours in England [31 August 1918] were brightened by a bathe in the fair green Channel, in company of the best piece of Nation left in England—a Harrow boy, of superb intellect & refinement, intellect because he detests war more than Germans, and refinement because of the way he spoke of my going away; and the way he spoke of the Sun; and of the Sea and the Air; and everything. (*CL* 570.)[15]

The nation Owen cared about was a community of sympathy, like a church or a political party. Returning to fight in September 1918, he passed a message to his brothers (now both in the armed forces) to tell them 'how peculiarly unreluctant I am to be back here with *the Nation*' (*CL* 574). It also happened that (discounting the Craiglockhart hospital magazine) the only poems of Owen's published in his lifetime appeared in the liberal weekly the *Nation*, edited by H. W. Massingham and one of the few publications prepared to question the prosecution of the war. Owen's cousin,

[15] This letter is to Susan Owen. He gives a very similar but mildly teasing account in a letter to Sassoon the next day: 'Moreover there issued from the sea distraction, in the shape, Shape I say, but lay no stress on that, of a Harrow boy, of superb intellect & refinement, etc.' (*CL* 571).

Leslie Gunston, also had a poem accepted by the *Nation*, in October 1918, and Owen wrote from France to congratulate him, but at the same time to reproach him; he was in the *Nation* in one sense but not in the other. 'You & I have always been open with each other: and therefore I must say that I feel sorry that you are neither in the flesh with us nor in the spirit against War' (*CL* 589).

Though Owen's editors and critics have tended to find 'Spring Offensive' a more tremendous conclusion, it seems likely that the last poem he wrote was this one:

'Smile, Smile, Smile'

Head to limp head, the sunk-eyed wounded scanned
Yesterday's *Mail*; the casualties (typed small)
And (large) Vast Booty from our Latest Haul.
Also, they read of Cheap Homes, not yet planned,
'For', said the paper, 'when this war is done
The men's first instincts will be making homes.
Meanwhile their foremost need is aerodromes,
It being certain war has but begun.
Peace would do wrong to our undying dead,—
The sons we offered might regret they died
If we got nothing lasting in their stead.
We must be solidly indemnified.
Though all be worthy Victory which all bought,
We rulers sitting in this ancient spot
Would wrong our very selves if we forgot
The greatest glory will be theirs who fought,
Who kept this nation in integrity.'
Nation?—The half-limbed readers did not chafe
But smiled at one another curiously
Like secret men who know their secret safe.
(This is the thing they know and never speak,
That England one by one had fled to France,
Not many elsewhere now, save under France.)
Pictures of these broad smiles appear each week,
And people in whose voice real feeling rings
Say: How they smile! They're happy now, poor things.

The central section, the speech, is a not particularly distorting parody of the discourse of official England, the public speech of the nation as state. The voice of England is a conspiracy of fathers, a patriarchal sermon delivered from a high place and laying down the law about wrongs and rights, in the panoply of institutional authority. It is clearly a parliamentary speech, though the poem attributes it casually to 'the paper', a distinction between press and government perhaps seeming pedantic at this time, when Northcliffe and Beaverbrook were in charge of political warfare and war propaganda.[16] Another difference is elided by the poem's drawing on a *Times* report of a speech by Clemenceau (*CL* 578, *CPF* 190–1). Owen manages the satire quite briskly, as you might expect from Sassoon's foremost disciple, allowing the voice of England the necessary length of rhetorical rope for his purposes. The interesting word 'integrity' is left to dangle on a pause, an invitation to consider the meaning and worth of that integrity, the probity (one meaning) of a nation on a spree of acquisition by armed robbery, and the singleness (another meaning) of a nation so thoroughly disintegrated, by its rulers' own words, into us and them. For the speech is all about pronouns, and England's 'we' does not include the soldiers' 'they'. (The persistent us/them organization of the speech in 'Smile, Smile, Smile' may recall the similar organization of Sassoon's poem 'They', a satire prompted, its author recalled, by a newspaper report of a sermon by Winnington Ingram.)[17] This England is a sketch for dystopia; it is the last of England, the cheap home of cynicism, greed, indifference.

It might have stopped there, or it might have gone on to pathos or anger. Something else happens. Out of the nation's disintegration a new 'England' is constituted, just as the collapse of Babel created new nations. This second England has turned against and away from home, reciprocating the cynicism of the home front. This England is a conspiracy of victims, and preserves its own integrity by keeping its counsel. It is a subculture of underground men, a nation whose nature is bound to remain a secret to outsiders.

There is more to this than a familiar theme of soldierly bonding, or the failure of civilians to sympathize. For while Owen often enough attacks civilian complacency, he is with plenty of other soldiers in insisting too that the experiential gap between the two nations *cannot* be bridged by language; and 'Smile, Smile, Smile' goes a step further in showing the soldiers *protecting* their difference like a secret, a dark one. Exploited and crippled as they

[16] Much to Owen's delight, Sassoon turned down the offer of a job under Beaverbrook in early October, saying he had no qualifications for war propaganda except that he had been wounded in the head (*CL* 588–9).

[17] Sassoon, *Siegfried's Journey*, 29–30.

are, the England of these men is closer to Utopia than the England they have fled from. (To Sassoon in England, Owen wrote at the end of August: 'I'm in hasty retreat towards the Front. Battle is easier here' (*CL* 571).) Their smile is exclusive, and it is complicitous —a badge and a mask.[18]

We may be literal-minded enough to ask (for the three lines in parenthesis do nothing to explain) just what the secret is that is guarded by that smile. Does it betoken past guilt, present delinquency, sinister intentions? Is the smile merely derisive or is it dismayed? Is it like a shared psychopathological symptom, indicating and masking trauma? Is it related to Owen's recent contact with the 'secret men' of the embattled homosexual community in London? Might the smile which deceives civilians conceal an intention of the betrayed to take revenge? Is it the germ of fascism, military coup, revolution? 'We' are not going to find out. If official language can appropriate tokens like 'England' and 'nation' to its rhetorical ends, others are at liberty to understand and inhabit these words differently, though they may not be free, or willing, to spell out that understanding. Silence is a shield; this is a nation which is not going to be betrayed because it cannot be known. And the poem itself with its triple smile colludes in the secrecy. The soldiers can read the language of 'us', but we can't read them, we can only see them smile (at each other, but also, you can't help feeling, at us). We may want to dissociate ourselves from lying speech (and speeches) uttered in our name, but that doesn't mean we belong with *them*, however 'real' our necessary but insufficient feeling. There is the official nation, and there is the secret nation. Where does that leave us?

In a letter of 22 October 1918 Owen reassured his mother, who was unwell at the time, that even if his letters ceased for a week or more, she should not conclude that he had been moved into the fighting zone. 'It is unlikely for a considerable time,' he lied, 'time even for the British Government & its accomplices to save their Nations' (*CL* 588).

[18] Desmond Graham's excellent discussion of this 'deeply disquieting' poem also leads him to reflect on the image of the smile elsewhere in Owen (Graham, *The Truth of War*, 68–72).

12

Morale and Breakdown

To refer to the condition and conduct of troops with regard to confidence, hope, zeal, and submission to discipline, you could use the word 'moral' or 'morale'. 'Moral' sounded more English, though in fact and confusingly the French word used in this sense is not *morale* but *moral*. The classic English exposition of the subject of an army's spirit is Shakespeare's *Henry V*, but the usage of the words moral and morale in this military application in English is post-Napoleonic, and probably marks the digestion by English minds of Napoleon's famous declaration: 'A la guerre, les trois quarts sont des affaires morales, la balance des forces réelles n'est que pour un autre quart.' Colonel W. Shirley not only agreed with Napoleon's words but thought that they explained why Napoleon had lost in the end. Shirley asked his lecture audience to mark that, in the Napoleonic wars, 'where the Frenchman had "Glory" in his mouth the Briton spoke of "Duty"'.[1] Colonel Shirley's lecture, as we have seen, was entitled *Moral: The Most Important Factor in War*, and his audience was made up of cadets undergoing instruction in the officers' course with the Artists' Rifles. I should apply in this connection a general point that I have made before: my case does not rest on Owen's having heard or read Colonel Shirley's lecture (though in my opinion he did know it, and I think Shirley is the unnamed colonel, described as 'an expert after the style of Belloc', whose 'brilliant lecture on the causes of the War' Owen admired at the Officers' School at Hare Hall Camp in January 1916 (*CL* 376)). What I do maintain is that Shirley's rhetoric is relevant and important data as part of the discursive environment in which Owen moved during his training. Indeed Shirley, as Commandant of the 2nd Artists' Rifles OTC, was the authoritative voice of that training programme in person.

Morale was to the group and the army what the 'soldierly spirit' was to the individual. It was a matter much emphasized in the

[1] Shirley, *Moral*, 31.

training of officers, since morale was particularly crucial in a large irregular army, serving in conditions that were far from conducive to high spirits; and the fostering of morale was the officers' job. The state of comparative inactivity which was the norm of life in the trenches was acknowledged to be very unfavourable to the maintenance of keenness in the men. 'There is an insidious tendency to lapse into a passive and lethargic attitude, against which officers of all ranks have to be on their guard, and the fostering of the offensive spirit, under such unfavourable conditions, calls for incessant attention.'[2] This talk of 'an insidious tendency to lapse' is the unmistakable trace of a Victorian discourse of vigilance against the moral dangers of idleness, a favourite Evangelical theme and a constant feature of warnings about intemperance and impurity. Bad morale was a mere letter away from bad morals. The military prophylactic against it is recommended in a headmasterly tone, by the author of *Notes for Infantry Officers*, as healthy and manly.

> Constant activity in harassing the enemy may lead to reprisals at first, and for this reason is sometimes neglected, but, if persevered in, it always results in an ultimate mastery, it gives the troops a healthy interest and wholesome topics of conversation, and it achieves the double purpose of raising the moral of our own troops whilst lowering that of the enemy's.[3]

It was this sort of thinking that was responsible for the dire reputation of the staff among the fighting troops. Owen's poem 'The Chances' suggests how troops might actually have dealt with the 'wholesome topics' that raids and attacks provided for their conversation.

The staff officer who compiled the *Notes for Infantry Officers* assimilated morale to discipline, aggression, and virtue. What is moral? asked Colonel Shirley on behalf of his Artists' Rifles audience, and then tried to pin it down with a whole chorus line of ideological angels. 'Moral forces are invisible, intangible, occult;—courage, intelligence, initiative, resourcefulness, training, discipline, pride, cheerfulness, temper, respect, tenacity, religion, patriotism, love, will-power.'[4] Morale was unselfish fellowship: love was one of its names. It was *esprit de corps*, anchored in each individual in a sense of duty, 'the greatest of all military, as of all civic

[2] *Notes for Infantry Officers*, 8. [3] Ibid. 8. [4] Shirley, *Moral*, 10.

virtues'. Owen had learned about duty and virtue (as Colonel Shirley had) from Ruskin, and (as Ruskin himself had) from an Evangelical upbringing. Here again, this time in uniform, was that language of self-denial and acquiescence that he had long been familiar with. 'Duty [Colonel Shirley explained] postulates the perfect subordination of self to constituted authority and the absolute consecration of self to the service of one's Country. It teaches one to be simple, straightforward, and humble.'[5] And John Baynes, a professional soldier and military historian writing in 1967 about the troops who fought at Neuve Chapelle in 1915, is making a similar approximation of good morale with goodness. 'The moral qualities which had an important effect on morale were sense of duty, kindness, and unselfishness,' says Baynes. 'In the really important moral qualities I believe the Armies in France were wonderfully rich.'[6] Moral qualities and the quality of morale are as indivisible for Baynes as for Colonel Shirley. For both, a collapse of morale is a moral failure.

Good morale was a strong communal sense among soldiers. All soldiers were encouraged to take pride in their regiments, and officers were advised to buy a regimental history and 'study it thoroughly', learning the regimental honours.[7] Colonel Shirley's introduction to the Artists' Rifles officers' course deals in turn with factors conducive to creating a group identity among soldiers, encouraging self-refashioning in communal terms by which the recruit will be so thoroughly absorbed into the body of the military that he will put the plural interest above his personal comfort, safety, and even survival. Military morale was binding together, quasi-religious, and above all socialization.

Shirley's lecture expounds eloquently and systematically what the manuals reveal diffusely—the good soldier must be prepared, and can be induced, to invest his life and if necessary his death in the community he feels he belongs to. Shirley, as we have seen, was not too shy to talk of love in this context, and he places comradeship first among the essentials of morale, a priority confirmed by Owen but also by virtually all the literature produced from the armies, for the Great War was an epoch in the history of love. Religion and patriotism were other powerful moral factors,

[5] Ibid. 31. [6] Baynes, *Morale*, 215, 217.
[7] 'Regular', *Customs of the Army*, 5.

Colonel Shirley thought. He pointed out that they go together, 'since every religion that is worth having teaches the principle of serving others rather than oneself'. Then he reached for the almost inevitable quotation:

'Greater love hath no man than this, that a man lay down his life for his friends'—readiness to sacrifice all, to live, or die for one's friends—that is one's neighbours—that is true patriotism, and the true patriot grudges nothing in the service of his countrymen and his Country. He is a foolish officer who scoffs at religion in his men, or who fails to encourage religion of the right sort.[8]

It is interesting to place this exhortation to patriotism next to Owen's recruitment of the same biblical text for an almost opposite purpose, in a letter of May 1917 from France:

Christ is literally in no man's land. There men often hear His voice: Greater love hath no man than this, that a man lay down his life—for a friend.

Is it spoken in English only and in French?

I do not believe so.

Thus you see how pure Christianity will not fit in with pure patriotism. (*CL* 461.)

Christ's words in John 15:13 are: 'Greater love hath no man than this, that a man lay down his life for his friends.' Owen's version uses a dash to detach the last phrase for emphasis, drawing the nucleus of attention along the sentence from the death to the friendship, whose object he makes singular. Self-sacrifice now sounds like an individual private transaction, exclusive, even romantic, and remote from matters of law or duty, public men or cheering crowds. Owen was writing this letter from his bed in the 41st Stationary Hospital, where he was awaiting evacuation, labelled 'Neurasthenia'. Colonel Shirley, on the other hand, had quoted the axiom accurately—'Greater love hath no man than this, that a man lay down his life for his friends'—but then further broadened its communal implications by adding the gloss: 'one's friends—that is one's neighbours'. By the end of the sentence the neighbours have swollen to 'countrymen' and finally 'Country'.

[8] Shirley, *Moral*, 18. But Ian Beckett reckons that religious belief was actually a factor of little importance for morale. See Beckett and Simpson (eds), *A Nation in Arms*, 23–4.

And so the Christian text is differently accentuated by the authoritative apologist of morale and by one of its failures.

Whatever his reluctance to join in the first place, once he was in the army Owen liked it and took a pride in it; the morale of his letters from late 1915 and 1916 is generally high. From the first drill sessions, the army worked hard to foster a sense of integration in the recruit, and although Owen had seen his own career hitherto as a struggle for independence from institutions and authority, it seemed now that he had found an institution he could respect, and even enjoy.

All our instruction is done by sergeants, who are as chummy between times as they are smart on parade. Impossible to get them out of temper. One is a rare wag, and gives plenty of exercise to the Risible Muscles. I never felt devotion, and not much respect, for any authority or individual in the world since I left the 3rd form of the Institute; but I am beginning again under these fellows. Astonishing what a changed meaning has a Captain or a Colonel for me. If a Major-General approached me I think I should fall down dead. (*CL* 362.)

Rudyard Kipling, another army poet, and something of an institution himself, was invited to visit the New Army in training in 1915. He gives a wonderful account of it as a working pastoral, a 'busy Eden' in which skilled and cheerful individualists co-operate on a project whose model is not the factory but the household, buzzing with domestic detail, and compensating its monosexuality with what Kipling calls 'housemaiding'.

In civil life men leave these things to their womenfolk, but where women are not, officers, inspecting tents, feet, and such-like, develop a she-side to their head, and evidently make their non-commissioned officers and men develop it too. A good soldier is always a bit of an old maid.[9]

It is possible that the absence of women, always a source of loud complaint among soldiers, was on balance good for army morale, since it turned men towards each other. When Harold Owen visited Wilfred in camp he was relieved to find that his normally reserved and 'socially immature' (*JFO* 3. 129) brother seemed quite at home with the general raillery of barrack-room conversation, 'shouting

[9] Kipling, *The New Army in Training*, 10. David Jones's *In Parenthesis* is a good place to examine the interaction between a humane, 'feminine', domestic discourse and the masculinity of the army's official language.

retorts in the best private's tradition in answer to the inescapable banalities' (*JFO* 3. 142). Ian Beckett, considering the general stability of British army morale during the war, thinks regimental tradition and identity were important producers of the adhesive of loyalty.[10] In spite of the dire predictions of some regulars, Kitchener's new soldiers seem to have acculturated quite quickly, absorbing traditional army usage and jargons; and most civilians (remarks Denis Winter) found 'a narcotic charm' in aspects of 'an institution so large, so all embracing, so old'.[11] Owen was especially delighted to find himself posted to the 2nd Manchesters, a Regular regiment of 'well-trained troops and "real-old" Officers' (*CL* 421).

He seems to have assented readily, perhaps even gratefully, to the army's socialization. Early references to men under his command as his 'little Family' (*CL* 403, 414) speak for his integration into military life as well as his familiarity with the quasi-parental role that came with his rank. If he was not simple enough to feel the almost mystic devotion that was Colonel Shirley's ideal of morale, there is no doubt that his strongest feelings for the army were of pride and loyalty. He was very anxious to do well. And belonging now to the army seemed at the same time to settle other relations that had been problematic, for it earned him admiring glances from young and old in the street in England (which would not have been conferred so long as he was in civilian clothes), and also won him 'spirited approbation' from his father, which embarrassed and pleased him (*CL* 430). Kipling made telling propaganda from the apparent power of war service to confer a kind of transcendental clubbability on the volunteer. The man in uniform was one of us.

> But what will be the position in years to come of the young man who has deliberately elected to outcaste himself from this all-embracing brotherhood? What of his family and, above all, what of his descendants, when the books have been closed and the last balance struck of sacrifice and sorrow in every hamlet, village, parish, suburb, city, shire, district, province, and Dominion throughout the Empire?[12]

'Sacrifice and sorrow' were the price that had to be paid for that self-respect, that unchallengeable right to belong. John Baynes

[10] Beckett and Simpson (eds), *A Nation in Arms*, 24.
[11] Winter, *Death's Men*, 52.
[12] Kipling, *The New Army in Training*, 64.

agrees: the hallmarks of good morale were cheerfulness, smartness, good health and discipline, aggression short of recklessness; 'but the final test is preparedness to sacrifice oneself.'[13] The sacrifice might be of the soldier's life; it would certainly be of his integrity as an individual. Good morale involved a willing subordination of freedoms to the interests of the collective. On this point the military manuals which deal with the soldierly spirit and matters of discipline often have to perform an ungainly balancing trick. Submission to discipline and unquestioning obedience were recognized as essentials. But a selfless automaton, with individuality and initiative drained and disciplined out of him, would not be a very useful soldier and was in any case not an ideal to admit to, especially as that was just how the British liked to imagine German soldiers. So the manuals usually find themselves saying that the army wants the soldier to be completely obedient but also, in Colonel Shirley's phrase, 'to be the creator and not the creature of situations, to set, not to solve the problems of life'.[14] Shirley gets into difficulties here which expose the paradox, or at least the dilemma. 'We have to steer between the Scylla of too much control and the Charybdis of too little,' he admits, allowing that 'the excellence of the mass must be founded on the excellence of the individual'. Still, 'officers and men must think and act for themselves only as far as that is compatible with concerted action for a common object.' It was an almost theological puzzle, at which Colonel Shirley waved a Pascalian flourish: 'The ideal at which we aim is "the thinking bayonet".' Of course an officer was expected to show more initiative than his men, but he would also have to learn to inhibit his intellectual integrity. Officers 'must imbibe their ideas from a common source of instruction, they must learn "to think alike on principles" and to curb individuality when they feel it might not harmonise with the design of their commander or the operations of their colleagues.'[15] Just such a sacrifice of individuality had been demanded—though in less totalitarian language—by the Keswick patriarchs in the name of Christ[16] as was now being exacted by the army. This time, Owen seemed willing to pay.

The soldier invested his person in the army. The linguistic sign of that integration is the first-person plural pronoun, the 'we'

[13] Baynes, *Morale*, 97. [14] Shirley, *Moral*, 26. [15] Ibid. 23, 24.

[16] 'The secret of Keswick is handing your individuality to Christ' (W. H. Griffith Thomas, in an address reported by the *Christian*, 25 July 1912).

which is larger than 'I' but at the same time less than 'I'. 'We' is, Benveniste points out, not a pluralization so much as a relationship.[17] 'We' could not mean 'I' plus 'I': it is an 'I' expanded beyond the strict limits of person, enlarged and at the same time amorphous; it is not a multiplication but a modification of 'I'. In 'Apologia pro Poemate Meo', you can observe the first-person singular at first observing (from outside) the soldiers as 'they', then immersing itself in them to constitute 'we', breaking (on the difference of rank, I think) and merging and separating again, finally standing on the singularity it started from, this time to deny to the *second* person (you readers, you non-combatants, perhaps you posterity) a free and easy honorary fellowship with the soldiers. To join them, 'you' have to change, and become worthy.

'The Next War', written two or three months before 'Apologia', is on the face of it a simpler matter. It might have been subtitled 'Good Morale'.

'The Next War'

War's a joke for me and you,
While we know such dreams are true.
Siegfried Sassoon

Out there, we walked quite friendly up to Death,—
Sat down and ate beside him, cool and bland,—
Pardoned his spilling mess-tins in our hand.
We've sniffed the green thick odour of his breath,—
Our eyes wept, but our courage didn't writhe.
He's spat at us with bullets, and he's coughed
Shrapnel. We chorused if he sang aloft,
We whistled while he shaved us with his scythe.

Oh, Death was never enemy of ours!
We laughed at him, we leagued with him, old chum.
No soldier's paid to kick against His powers.
We laughed,—knowing that better men would come,
And greater wars: when every fighter brags
He fights on Death, for lives; not men, for flags.

'The Next War' was written in Edinburgh in September 1917, and it looks forward to a postwar utopian internationalism of the sort advocated by H. G. Wells, whose proposals Owen took an interest

[17] See the essay 'Relationship of Person in the Verb', in Benveniste, *Problems in General Linguistics*, 197–210.

in at this time (*CL* 498). But enthusiasm for 'the international idea' (*CL* 497) was compatible with a vigorous attitude towards winning the war. It could indeed be seen as an asset to morale, giving its adherents a cause really worth fighting for, the war that will end war (as Wells himself had christened the conflict at its birth). And so 'The Next War' is stamped with the hallmarks of good morale—cheerfulness, comradeship, a belief in the task, willingness to sacrifice oneself. The epigraph couples 'me' and 'you', producing a first-person plural which dances jauntily through the sonnet, its variations appearing in almost every line. The themes of the poem are solidarity, faith, good humour, and courage, the themes of good morale. It would have satisfied Colonel Shirley. 'We' are unafraid of 'him', of Death. But it is worth enquiring who 'we' are. There is more than one answer.

One of the functions of the poem is as a sort of passport proffered for entry into the community of that pronoun of Siegfried Sassoon's. The epigraph gives the closing lines of Sassoon's 'A Letter Home' (the last war poem in *The Old Huntsman and Other Poems*), in which 'you' is 'Robert' (Graves), and the 'dreams' are elegiac intimations of the immortality of 'David' (Thomas), a friend whom Sassoon and Graves both loved and who had been killed. By appropriating and carrying on Sassoon's pronoun, Owen is setting about (or fantasizing about) taking the place of Graves as Sassoon's comrade-in-arms and fellow poet. On this level of the pronoun the sonnet is a sort of proposal. Owen considered beginning 'We two have walked' (*CPF* 335), but wisely decided against it. The conveniently amorphous pronoun had to be capable of a wider application.

Clearly 'we' are, as often in Owen, soldiers with experience of combat. 'We' are the army, whose morale is high. But all of this is given an extra poignancy by the circumstances in which the poem was produced. It was written in the Craiglockhart War Hospital where Owen had been sent for prolonged treatment after his neurasthenic crisis in France, at a time when he had been (or believed he had been) accused of cowardice by his commanding officer. 'I did not go sick or anything,' he told Susan Owen in a letter at the time (*CL* 453), but the doctor 'suddenly was moved to forbid' him to go into action again; so when his battalion next walked, friendly or not, up to death in the front line, Owen was in bed, though visibly unscathed, in Casualty Clearing Station 13.

The sonnet's testimony to comradeship, cheerfulness, and a steady nerve is, then, a sort of conjuring, a wishful rewriting of the past.

You may see this bragging of courage as dishonest and even comical, the strutting of the *miles gloriosus* who is always really a coward; but I don't think that does Owen justice. He listed 'The Next War' in his draft table of contents under the motive 'Cheerfulness' (*CPF* 539) and he recommended it to his teenage brother Colin, who was considering joining the Royal Flying Corps. But he published it in the *Hydra*, of which he was the editor, in September 1917, and this circumstance gives the sonnet's first-person plural a troubling and troubled modality. For the *Hydra* was the hospital's house magazine, and its readership consisted of men like Owen, the community of the hare-eyed and the jittery, neurasthenic officers who had fetched up at Craiglockhart because their courage had indeed writhed and was still writhing; what they had in common was that their morale had not been good enough. It was a complex and moving solidarity that the plural pronoun was signalling to them.

The opposite of good morale was breakdown. The crisis Wilfred Owen suffered in May 1917 had a medical name and status, but it was (or was inseparable from) a collapse of morale.

> There can be no doubt that, other things being equal, the frequency of 'shell shock' in any unit is an index of its lack of discipline and loyalty . . . Like all emotional disorders, shell shock is of a highly contagious nature; it may be rife in one unit, while rare, because regarded as a disgrace, in another.[18]

These were the observations of Charles S. Myers, temporary Lieutenant-Colonel in the RAMC and consulting psychologist to the British armies in France, and thus the voice of the army's professional opinion on nerves. He speaks of shell-shock rather as the temperance literature spoke of drunkenness, as primarily a moral failure; and a moral disorder required a rhetorical treatment. Myers recommended in the first instance a panacea familiar from the temperance project. The army medical officer's first recourse should be to 'moral suasion, in which he should have been trained', for 'It should be the physician's ultimate aim to convince the patient that he is fit for duty.'[19] Breakdown was a failure of that sense of

[18] Myers, *Shell Shock in France*, 39, 40. [19] Ibid. 51, 56.

duty which Colonel Shirley had equated with morale, and with the essence of being a soldier and being British. If morale meant courage, loyalty, manliness, integration, there could be no doubt of the judgement the army passed on the apparently unwounded Lieutenant Owen when he was told he was not fit to go into battle with his men.

He was being judged a failure as a soldier and as an officer. Everyone recognized the extra stresses that afflicted an officer at the front. Many, said 'One of Them' in 1915, had died of their wounds 'who would not have done so if their nerves had been in a normal state'.[20] But officers were supposed to be made of finer stuff than their men; by that right they were officers. W. H. R. Rivers (who was Sassoon's doctor at Craiglockhart) and Sir Frederick Mott believed that enlisted men were more liable to hysteria than officers were.[21] Myers agreed: he thought that the forces of 'education, tradition and example' gave officers greater self-control.[22] As you might expect, the ideological aspects of morale were equally inscribed in its opposite. Good morale was in any case normative, and still is for John Baynes, two wars later. 'I do not believe that the man of normal physical and mental development who has been properly reared in a good home with real love, affection, and interest is likely to break down under the normal strain of war.'[23]

'Do not for a moment suppose I have had a "breakdown",' Owen wrote from the Casualty Clearing Station. 'I am simply *avoiding* one' (*CL* 453). But he ended this letter with a request that his mother should not 'hawk it about', and asked her to tell no one that he was 'a Casual' again. When he dramatized a case of nerves in 'The Dead-Beat', he showed that the victim was assumed as a matter of course to be a malingerer and a coward. One Regimental Medical Officer complained in a report to Myers: 'We have seen too many dirty sneaks go down [i.e. from the front line] under the term "shell shock" to feel any great sympathy with the condition.'[24] The stigma was an extra source of anxiety and embarrassment to the wretched victim. 'It is quite likely that I

[20] 'One of Them', '*Out There!*', 14.
[21] See Beckett and Simpson (eds), *A Nation in Arms*, 22.
[22] Myers, *Shell Shock in France*, 40. [23] Baynes, *Morale*, 101.
[24] Myers, *Shell Shock*, 95. But Myers's own view was that '"pure" malingering was comparatively rare' (p. 40).

shall appear in the Casualty List,' Owen informed his mother, 'as Neurasthenia is marked W(ound) not S(ick)—not wrongly I think. I know . . . that some persons wear gold stripes for neurasthenia!' (*CL* 463). He was wrong about this, though the confusion reflects the difficulty of the army's attempts to categorize and deal with a condition that was physiological, psychological, and moral. Myers thought that recognition of shell-shock as a disease was liable to promote its frequency, and in fact he wanted the term 'shell-shock' discarded as the misleading catch-all it undoubtedly was. He suggested that the term should be changed to 'nervous shock', a less honourable-sounding condition which (he reasoned) fewer would be disposed to boast of, and which could also embrace those varieties of shock which were not directly due to the effects of shell-fire. The army did not adopt these recommendations. But in February 1917 GHQ issued instructions that patients should be labelled either 'shell-shock wounded' (where there was evidence of 'direct contact' with an explosion), or else 'neurasthenia', 'hysteria', etc. (specific terms to replace the old 'shell-shock sick', which indicated no evidence of explosion trauma, and conferred no entitlement to the status of a battle casualty or to a wound stripe). Owen was diagnosed in May 1917 as a case of 'neurasthenia'. If there was an honourable and a less honourable category of breakdown, Owen's case was not classed as the former.

The breakdown Owen denied in that letter was to become the great theme of the war poems. It was both metaphorically and metonymically associated with the image of the broken body. Owen himself dated his trauma from his experience at the railway embankment near St Quentin where he was literally blown up by a shell, and spent several days thereafter in a shallow hole just big enough to lie in, near the rotting remains of a brother officer 'who lay', he remembered, 'not only near by, but in various places around and about' (*CL* 456). Owen himself was not wounded, in a conventional sense, yet inasmuch as his collapse was involuntary (with its headaches, shakes, and terrible dreams), it was a unilateral initiative by the body through the unconscious; it was a mutiny of the singular body against the army's efforts to enslave it to plural interests and the absolute commands of the will. A feminist perspective can be illuminating here. Elaine Showalter makes the point that the expression of fear or protest was judged by the army to be a sign of weakness and unmanliness, and so severely repressed.

Shell-shock victims were then forced to express their conflicts 'through the body', their case (Showalter argues) being thus similar to that of countless women before them whose experience of repression and powerlessness was registered, and complained of, in symptoms of hysteria and neurasthenia. Shell-shock was 'the body language of masculine complaint'.[25]

Owen was no stranger to loneliness, but illness is a great isolator, and mental or nervous illness perhaps the most isolating of all. These feelings were made much worse by knowledge that he had 'outcaste himself' (to return to Kipling's phrase) by his unmanly unworthiness of the military community in which he had invested his self-respect. While the Dunsden breakdown had been entangled with his rejection of the Church, the neurasthenic crisis of 1917 was the occasion of his being rejected by the army. He had in spite of himself asserted his singularity, he had broken ranks, and now he belonged nowhere, except with other victims of breakdown. The rest of Owen's story is the story of his discovering just how large that brotherhood was. Its members were not to be found only in hospital wards for patients suffering from what was still sometimes called 'mental alienation'.[26] Owen created in his writing an understanding of his singular breakdown as, properly speaking, historic and cultural.

The details of the breakdown are as incomplete as the details of the Dunsden 'bust-up', and no doubt for the similar reasons that had made him reluctant to communicate his 'calm frenzy' to his family on the earlier occasion. It was to be fifteen months before the army judged Owen's nerves sufficiently restored to make him fit again for active service. You can't help wondering what it cost him to write with this sort of jollity, from CCS 13:

> My own dear Mother,
> I have been expecting every day to be moved from here, but nothing happens; only a great calm happiness. We are a cheery crowd here this time, and I like everyone as a great and interesting fellow. *Some* of us have been sent down here as a little mad. Possibly I am among them. (CL 454.)

When he made his way to Craiglockhart at the end of June, he admitted at first to a 'reserve and suspense' about everything he

[25] Showalter, *The Female Malady*, 172.

[26] Owen considered the title 'The Aliens' for the poem which became 'Mental Cases' (*CPF* 342).

did there, confessing in early July that he had made no friends in the hospital, and what he wanted most urgently was to see his mother (*CL* 472, 473). Meanwhile, the serious treatment began.

Owen was to spend four and a half months at the Craiglockhart War Hospital.[27] It provided him with an active physical life, the domestic company of men, a broadening of intellectual horizons, two influential mentors, and at least one intense romantic friendship. These amenities were usually supplied for the more affluent young Englishmen of his generation by more orthodox institutions of learning. Owen was not altogether joking when he said it was very kind of the army to provide 'this free-and-easy Oxford' for him (*CL* 482), and the following year at Ripon he reported having tea with 'an old Craiglockhartian', as one might say, an old Etonian or Wykehamist. But his first reactions to the place had not been enthusiastic. There was nothing attractive about this 'decayed Hydro', he thought (*CL* 472). There were too many inmates. The new arrival knew some of them already, but was shy of all of them. It is perhaps no wonder that Owen at first shrank from the society of his fellow patients. Admission to their twitching company was also admission to a moral or morale failure like theirs. Sassoon's Sherston writes of the uncomfortable notion that none of the patients in the war hospital respected one another. It was as though 'there was a tacit understanding that we were all failures', and he remembers wanting to singularize himself out of that pronoun, reassuring himself that 'I wasn't the same as the others.'[28] Sassoon wrote *in propria persona* to Ottoline Morrell that a great many of his fellow patients at Craiglockhart were 'degenerate-looking'.[29]

Owen's 1917 'breakdown' was double, or rather, it had an inner and an outer surface. Shell-shock was recognized as a condition similar or equivalent to a civilian nervous breakdown. Before the war Owen had told his mother that 'nerves' were the essential faculty of the creative artist, but that they might equally well be the cause of prostration or moral collapse (*CL* 256). His present

[27] See *WO* (189–234) and *OTP* (71–94). Samuel Hynes gives 'Dottyville' (as Sassoon called the place) a chapter in his cultural history, *A War Imagined*, though he is mistaken in thinking that Owen was a patient of Rivers (Hynes, 171–88). There is a fascinating treatment of the story of Rivers and Craiglockhart in Pat Barker's novel *Regeneration*, published in 1991.

[28] Sassoon, *The Complete Memoirs of George Sherston*, 532.

[29] Sassoon, *Diaries 1915–1918*, 183.

pass seemed an unwelcome proof of that rather complacently uttered formula. He had succumbed to nerves (the 'female malady' in Showalter's phrase), and the nerves that might have served the poet had ruined the soldier. He had become unbalanced, disorientated, unreliable, and withdrawn. His body was apt to rebel against his will. He was not a whole person, but subject to violent dissociation. Charles Myers explained the psychopathology of shell-shock by saying that the 'normal' personality goes into abeyance with the shock, and is replaced by the damaged 'emotional' personality. Thereafter the 'normal' person (usually without memory of the trauma) may alternate with the 'emotional' personality (who returns more or less frequently, in *crises des nerfs* and in dreams); the therapist's task is to reintegrate the two.[30] Owen's own doctor at Craiglockhart, Arthur Brock, spoke in similar terms; the essential element of shell-shock, he said, was 'fragmentation or "dissociation" of the mind'.[31]

But the other side of the nervous or psychological breakdown was the breakdown of morale, and this was a social failure. The Craiglockhart War Hospital was on the outermost margins of the army. Its officer inmates were there not only to receive therapy but also to isolate them from other soldiers, since (as we have seen Myers pointing out) their condition was 'highly contagious' and posed a threat to the morale of others. These were men in whom the socializing adhesive of morale had come unstuck under pressure; and all the patients at Craiglockhart had heard enough about good morale during their training to know that a breakdown of morale was a fundamental betrayal. Craiglockhart was not a prison, nor was anyone punished there.[32] Yet it was, and they were. It was a place for outcasts, a community of the ostracized.

But in spite of the strength of his early misgivings, and the habitual diffidence no doubt deepened by the state of his nerves, in a very short time after his arrival at Craiglockhart Owen was

[30] Myers, *Shell Shock*, 56–7. Following Myers's terms, you could read 'Insensibility' as the story of the splitting-off, repression, and eventual reintegration of the 'emotional' personality.

[31] Brock, *Health and Conduct*, p. xviii.

[32] Craiglockhart patients were relatively lucky. At Dr Lewis Yealland's clinic in Queen's Square, London, one shell-shock patient's treatment for hysteric mutism included electric shocks to the neck, throat, and pharynx, 'hot plates' in the mouth, and cigarette burns on the tip of his tongue. See Showalter, *The Female Malady*, 176–7.

immersed in a wider and busier social life than he had ever known. Through friends of his family, friends of friends, and friends of the hospital, he developed a considerable acquaintance in Edinburgh. He did some part-time teaching at Tynecastle School. No doubt inspired by the 'international idea', he started to learn German. There were long walks with friends in the Pentland hills south of Edinburgh. He attended a variety of Edinburgh churches and explored the city. Most of all, he threw himself with something like schoolboy enthusiasm into activities and associations based in the hospital itself—he was a founder-member of a natural history club, he took part in amateur theatricals, and became editor of the hospital's journal, the *Hydra*. This striking resocialization is not necessarily or simply evidence of his recovery from neurasthenia; it is evidence of his treatment, indeed it is the treatment itself.

It was Owen's fortune to come under the care at the Craiglockhart War Hospital of Dr Arthur Brock, who was treating his shell-shock patients with the ergotherapy or 'occupation cure' he had begun to develop before the war. Brock's theories were largely based on the principles of the celebrated Edinburgh sociologist, Patrick Geddes. The case for the importance of Owen's contact with Dr Brock, and through him with Geddesian sociology and the Outlook Tower Association in Edinburgh, has been very persuasively made in Dominic Hibberd's *Owen the Poet*, chapter 5 and appendix A4. Hibberd says:

> Geddes maintained that the ills of modern living were a result of people's having lost touch with their environment; work and life had become separated, towns had become shapeless, communities had fragmented. His formula 'Place—Work—Folk' expressed his belief that the crucial link between people and place is what they *do*, their work in its widest sense. One way to reforge that link was to encourage 'Folk' to undertake 'Regional Surveys' of their 'Place', studying every natural and civic aspect of their surroundings. Seeing the parallel between Geddes's formula and the biologist's 'organism–function–environment', Brock interpreted shell-shock as an extreme form of the social failings which Geddes had analysed: the organism had become violently detached from its environment and could no longer relate to it by means of its usual functions. Treatment had to concentrate on 'function' and 'work' if health was to be restored. (*OTP* 84.)

(Geddes himself wrote an early and rather eccentric book on Ruskin, whom he revered as the first social thinker to diagnose the fracture between modern modes of living and their environment.[33] It is notable how many of the ideas that touched Owen can be traced back, one way or another, to Ruskin.)

So Brock set his patients to work, and Owen was soon launched on his own 'regional survey' of Edinburgh, visiting schools and slums, factories and middle-class drawing-rooms, and exploring the topography and natural history of the area. In the brisk course of Brock's curriculum, he probably came to know Edinburgh in four months more comprehensively than he had ever known Birkenhead or Shrewsbury or Bordeaux. Dr Brock believed that the traumatic dissociation or fragmentation of the mind of the shell-shock victim was best treated by a programme of reintegrating him with his environment, restoring the damaged links that should bind him to community and place. His favourite myth was the classical legend of Antaeus, the giant whose strength was always magically regenerated when he touched his Mother Earth. He liked to use this story as a sort of parable of the neurasthenic's recovery, and he soon set his new patient to write a poem on the subject of the wrestling duel between Antaeus and Heracles (a subject which touched quite a number of the chords of Owen's imagination). Ergotherapy found a curative value in creativity: it was useful. 'The Craiglockhart patient must beware of Art for Art's sake,' advised an article by 'Acturus' (presumably Brock himself) in the January 1918 number of the *Hydra*: 'Our work must be constructive and productive, not merely critical and academic. It is when our heads are high in the clouds of unpracticality, our feet clean off the earth, that the Hercules of war will overcome us. *Labor omnia vincit.*' Dr Brock might have been gratified if he could have read what Owen wrote to his mother in late October, at the prospect of being 'sent away' from Craiglockhart. 'Strange, if you like, but I am seriously beginning to have aching sensations at being rooted up from this pleasant Region' (*CL* 503). Brock's influence has infiltrated this sentence: the capitalized 'Region' is Geddesian, and the image of the painfully uprooted man was one Owen used in his Antaeus poem 'The Wrestlers', written on doctor's orders.

It is not particularly difficult to like Edinburgh. But Dr Brock seems to have succeeded too in the much more tricky task of

[33] See Geddes, *John Ruskin*, 22–38.

integrating his shy and touchy patient into the community of the war hospital itself. After his initial flinching from the company of his fellow patients, Owen's letters soon became a catalogue of communal activities and quasi-public performances—debating, amateur theatricals, arranging expeditions with the Field Club and lecturing to them, the business of editing and writing for the *Hydra*.

The patients in the poem 'Mental Cases' are so stricken by horror that their eyeballs seem, in a revolting image, to 'shrink tormented | Back into their brains'. Owen was well acquainted with fear and shame. 'Life frightens him,' Dr Brock was to write of the post-shell-shock neurasthenic. 'He stands aside from things; literally he is in a state of Apostasy.'[34] Yet though he was diffident in the best of circumstances and now had every reason to be withdrawn, under Brock's guidance Owen became a prominent Craiglockhartian, a public figure in the hospital community and indeed, as editor of the *Hydra*, the community's voice. He recovered his morale, speaking to and for the company of those whose morale had broken. And this was possible because, though the army seemed to have singled him out as a shameful moral failure, with Brock's help he came to understand his condition as a shared, intelligible, and honourable predicament.

It appears that no records survive of the consultations Owen had in Dr Brock's study, under the picture representing Heracles and Antaeus. But Brock's ideas can be examined in his book *Health and Conduct*, published in 1923 with a preface by Patrick Geddes, which has much to say about war psychology and draws heavily on its author's Craiglockhart experience.

One of Brock's pre-war professional interests was (in the title of an article he published in 1912) 'The "Moral Factor" in Physical Disease'.[35] In *Health and Conduct*, thinking along Geddesian lines, he sought for social explanations of mental factors in illness, and drew upon what he called 'the parallels between human diseases and the diseases of the body politic'.[36] In industrial societies, he believed, specialization and the city had made modern life inhuman and modern citizens alienated, demoralized, and sick. 'Indeed neurasthenia may be taken as in a sense the mentality

[34] Brock, *Health and Conduct*, 143, 146.

[35] *Practitioner*, 88 (1912), 315–21.

[36] Brock, *Health and Conduct*, p. xv.

"normal" to the inhabitants of our great modern cities.'[37] Brock goes on to provide a psychological and medical dimension for an argument Geddes had first made in political terms in a lecture series in 1915.

What we were wont to call peace [Geddes had said] was really war-peace—thinly disguised but latent and potential war: in the dominant organisation and purpose of its administration, in the armaments which formed the first claim on its resources, latent war; in its diplomacy, at best delayed war; in even its philanthropic conventions, only mitigated war; and in the treaties, the results of wars put on record.[38]

Brock's view was that 'war-demoralisation' (of which shell-shock was a spectacular variation) was continuous with a pre-war mentality that was dissociated, debilitated, easily deluded, in flight from reality and prone to wasting diseases. The war exacerbated these tendencies, and the symptoms of shell-shock were 'extreme instances of the dissociation or separation of . . . pre-war conditions'.[39] In wartime civilians too suffered from 'general nervousness and restlessness', and there was an accelerated unravelling and dissociation of social as well as mental life, which included 'the continued disintegration of the family, the growing separation of man from woman, their coming together for mutual sexual exploitation, not for co-operation in the furtherance of life'.[40]

There is perhaps not much in Brock's ideas here, so far, to surprise the student of modernist gloom; yet such ideas would have been novel and even comforting to Owen in 1917. Brock encouraged his patients to think as he did in social, cultural, and historical terms. Shell-shock neurasthenics were neither unique nor culpable. Brock offered an explanation of their condition not as a shameful aberration but as a particularly sensitive, particularly tragic registration of a disease that was nothing less than the modern world; and his ergotherapeutic approach turned them back towards the world, rather than in upon themselves, for an understanding and some way out of their predicament.

On expeditions to and around the city, the convalescent Owen seems to have practised an imaginative reaching out to the lives of others. 'I am whatever and whoever I see while going down to Edinburgh on the tram' (*CL* 480), he informed his mother

[37] Ibid. p. xvii. [38] Geddes and Slater, *Ideas at War*, 39.
[39] Brock, *Health and Conduct*, 139. [40] Ibid. 181.

(perhaps mindful of what Keats had said about the protean identity of the poet); and the poignant 'Six O'Clock in Princes Street' imagines coming down to earth from flights of romantic fantasy to join or even to become the boy selling newspapers in the gutter:

> Neither should I go fooling over clouds,
> Following gleams unsafe, untrue,
> And tiring after beauty through star-crowds,
> Dared I go side by side with you;
>
> Or be you in the gutter where you stand,
> Pale rain-flawed phantom of the place,
> With news of all the nations in your hand,
> And all their sorrows in your face.

It was Dr Brock's belief that a neurasthenic—and a neurasthenic culture—had everything to learn from the lives of ordinary and simple people. 'With him lies the secret of psycho-sociological resynthesis and re-orchestration—with the plain man, and in his own immediate world.'[41] It would be good to know to what extent Owen's experiments with entering the perspective of common soldiers—he started to do this at Craiglockhart with poems like 'Disabled' and 'The Chances'—are related to the extraverting disciplines of ergotherapy.

Brock encouraged Owen's writing, for he took such things seriously. Poetry, like dreams, told the truth, every work of the imagination being (he was to write)

> a projection into sensory form of the artist's deepest personal experience . . . In the powerful war-poems of Wilfred Owen we read the heroic testimony of one who having in the most literal sense 'faced the phantoms of the mind' had *all but* laid them ere the last call came; they still appear in his poetry but he fears them no longer.[42]

But the work of art was more than just a menagerie for the display of private terrors and wishes. It is characteristic of Brock that he wanted his patient not just to write the Antaeus poem but also to publish it in the *Hydra*, where it would become as it were public discourse, hospital property. An amateur anthropologist and folklorist, Brock was alert to the social function of symbols and stories, and he believed with Geddes that art should serve the community, showing what was right and wrong with it. Poetry like everything

[41] Ibid. 251. [42] Ibid. 172.

else should be put to work and related to its environment. It should be communicative, responsible to the community.

Owen's first breakdown, at Dunsden, had involved a discursive dissociation. It isolated and almost silenced him, bringing him to a state of 'calm frenzy' which he felt he could not communicate to anyone (*CL* 181). The way out of his second breakdown, the breakdown of morale that sent him to Craiglockhart, was through working to reach out of isolation. To understand and share his predicament, and to understand it as a shared one, was a grim victory over it. In breakdown, as under Brock's care he started to understand it, Owen found his subject.

Breakdown in Owen's writing is not confined to images of nervous collapse or physical mutilation. The ideological ingredient in notions of morale and breakdown makes them protean, metamorphological. Good morale might mean something as trivial as whistling on the march, or as wide as good citizenship, or Christian virtue, or assent to what Kipling called 'order and the real'. Breakdown had equally many forms and applications, and in Owen's post-traumatic writings—which are the ones that matter most—breakdown is dispersed in multiple transformations. It is to be found in an early and bizarre form in the anarchic eruption of the biblical parody (*CL* 458–60) he wrote at CCS 13, where '*some* of us' had been sent 'as a little mad' (*CL* 454). More generally in the poetry of 1917 and 1918, it is to be found in brutal and cynical language, positioned to fracture unsuspecting lyric grace in many poems, and it is to be heard in the broken-down rhyme Owen developed at Craiglockhart. It is dramatized in communicative breakdowns (of which the poems are full), failures to speak or to listen at the right time, misunderstandings, imposed or stubborn or deceiving silences, unwitting or deliberate lies; in social breakdowns, the splintering of fighting units by death or injury, the social burial of the physically and mentally crippled, and in the difficult relations with the reader that complicate the community-creating act of many of Owen's war poems. Its traces are in the patterns of betrayal and contempt that sour relations between Owen's people, alienating those who carry out orders from those who give them, the nation in arms from the nation at home, men from women, young from old, and putting enmity even between men and the natural world, men and God. There is nothing singular about breakdown in Owen's poems; the blinded man in

'The Sentry' is the only one who does not know that everyone is in the dark.

The Waste Land comes irresistibly to mind as an exposition (by another convalescent) of a dissociation and fragmentation that has many dimensions, personal and historical. This is not the place for a prolonged comparison, but one point of contrast may be worth making. Owen has much to say about the breakdown of morale, but the letters and poems show that he also knew from experience—before, during and after his time at Craiglockhart—what good morale was. That is to say, there are images in Owen's work (as I do not think there are in Eliot's) of a decent and humane community, united in shared experience by loyalty and respect for one another. Another name for this good morale (as Colonel Shirley knew) was love, and it is part of its meaning that the war both created and destroyed it.

Owen's last letter evokes, in the manner of Barbusse, a scene in the domestic life of soldiers. It was written in a place he calls 'The Smoky Cellar of the Forester's House'. It ends like this:

So thick is the smoke in this cellar that I can hardly see by a candle 12 ins. away, and so thick are the inmates that I can hardly write for pokes, nudges & jolts. On my left the Coy. Commander snores on a bench: other officers repose on wire beds behind me. At my right hand, Kellett, a delightful servant of A Coy in *The Old Days* radiates joy & contentment from pink cheeks and baby eyes. He laughs with a signaller, to whose left ear is glued the Receiver; but whose eyes rolling with gaiety show that he is listening with his right ear to a merry corporal, who appears at this distance away (some three feet) nothing [but] a gleam of white teeth & a wheeze of jokes.

Splashing my hand, an old soldier with a walrus moustache peels & drops potatoes into the pot. By him, Keyes, my cook, chops wood; another feeds the smoke with the damp wood.

It is a great life. I am more oblivious than alas! yourself, dear Mother, of the ghastly glimmering of the guns outside, & the hollow crashing of the shells.

There is no danger down here, or if any, it will be well over before you read these lines.

I hope you are as warm as I am; as serene in your room as I am here; and that you think of me never in bed as resignedly as I think of you always in bed. Of this I am certain you could not be visited by a band of friends half so fine as surround me here. (*CL* 591.)

13
Officers and Others

The last letter Owen wrote, from 'The Smoky Cellar of the Forester's House', evokes an unexpected and poignant idyll: the scene is an officers' billet, yet in the snug physical proximity and social promiscuity of the cellar the distance between officers and other ranks is reduced almost to nothing, in an underground community in which everyone is within reach (*CL* 590–1). It was a rare moment. For it was never really possible to forget that the fundamental fact of life in the army rested on that distinction between the two classes that constituted it, officers and men. It is hard to imagine what sort of war poems Owen might have written if he had not been an officer and specifically a junior officer of infantry; yet the question of how he became an officer has not seemed to deserve much attention.

The distribution of rank had been simple enough in the pre-war regular army. The 'other ranks' were drawn from the poor and relatively uneducated, some 70 per cent of them from what Baynes calls 'the real lower class', the urban poor only intermittently employed in civil life, for whom enlistment was the only way out of the slums or vagrancy. Of these people, according to Baynes, 'one could almost say that for them the whole of their lives had been a conditioning for the trenches.'[1] Of the officer corps, meanwhile, the overwhelming majority were products of the public schools, and passed through training at Sandhurst or Woolwich, or in some cases through the 'back door' of the militia. It was, says Keith Simpson, 'almost impossible for someone who had not been through this system to become an officer and a gentleman',[2] though General (later Field-Marshal) Sir William Robertson, who had risen from the ranks, was a famous exception. But when a European land war came in 1914, conditions and needs changed

[1] Baynes, *Morale*, 162.

[2] Beckett and Simpson (eds), *A Nation in Arms*, 65. Data in this paragraph and the next about recruitment comes from Keith Simpson's essay 'The Officers', in ch. 3 of this volume.

dramatically, to the chagrin of many old soldiers. Thirty thousand new recruits in a single day of September 1914 exceeded the pre-war total for the regular army in a whole year. These troops had to have officers. Some candidates for a commission were taken from military colleges in the dominions, and numbers were taken directly from public school and university OTC's through the Special Reserve and sent straight to France. This was still not enough, so it was decided to waive the preliminary training (at military college or in the ranks) and offer temporary commissions to 'suitable young men'.

But who was suitable? An officer was a gentleman in uniform. Not everyone who applied for a commission was judged to be of the right quality. The War Office itself offered very few guidelines, preferring to leave considerable latitude to the raisers, perhaps on the grounds that in the most class-conscious nation in Europe gentlemen needed no instructions on how to recognize one another. All candidates were interviewed by regimental officers, and no doubt a candidate's accent and manners, and the name of his school, were quickly decisive in most cases. But qualifications, luck, and influence could play a part too, and there were regimental and no doubt individual variations. R. C. Sherriff was refused a temporary commission when he first applied to his county regiment, because he had been to a grammar school. Clement Attlee was told he was too old (at thirty-one), but influence secured him a commission in another regiment. Harold Macmillan trained with the Artists' Rifles (like Wilfred Owen), but when he was commissioned into the disappointing King's Royal Rifle Corps, his mother arranged an interview with the regimental lieutenant-colonel of the Grenadier Guards, and in due course Macmillan went to war as a Guards officer.

Owen's own background had not dealt him a very strong hand. He had no powerful friends or relatives, and no connection with the army. His father was an assistant railway stationmaster. He had not been to university or to a public school, and he had no professional qualifications. He could ride a horse, but was no sportsman. He was well-spoken (but 'perceptibly provincial' to Sassoon's ear),[3] and very well-mannered though socially fairly inexperienced. He thought of himself as a gentleman, of course, and an awareness

[3] Sassoon, *Siegfried's Journey*, 58.

of his family's gentility had been an important factor in his upbringing. But socially he was somewhere close to an important class frontier whose exact position was a matter of opinion. Relevant to this is Harold Owen's career at sea, first as an apprentice and then as an extremely junior officer on merchant ships, and later—in wartime—as midshipman and then junior officer in the navy, and his recourse to a succession of labouring jobs in hard times in the 1920s. Also relevant is the fact that, after a series of very young and slatternly servant girls, Mrs Owen insisted on acquiring, in 1910, an experienced and trained housemaid whose services the family could not really afford (*JFO* 2. 223). These social circumstances meant that, for Wilfred Owen, an officer's commission was both a matter of urgency and a focus of some insecurity. The socially assured might choose, at least at first, to serve in the ranks (as Sassoon did). But such men had nothing to prove. In the event, Owen's expatriation, and his choice of regiment, both worked to his advantage. Keith Simpson observes:

> After the outbreak of war thousands of men who had emigrated or were working abroad came back to enlist. Many of them were quite happy to serve in the ranks, but a considerable proportion were awarded temporary commissions. Regular officers believed that even given a wide range of social and educational backgrounds these men made good officers, 'for they had taken some risks, they had been on their own responsibility, and had generally had men under them and experienced dangers by flood and field'.[4]

Owen was no John Buchan hero, and his tutoring in Bordeaux had not exposed him to many dangers by flood and field (nothing worse, at least, than the attentions of Mme Léger), but it did seem to make him eligible for the opportunity offered by an announcement he saw in June 1915 to the effect that 'any gentleman (fit, etc.) *returning to England from abroad* will be given a commission —in the "Artists' Rifles"' (*CL* 340). That reassuring guarantee may have been at least as alluring to Owen as the regiment's romantic-sounding name.

The shade of class insecurity, which had dogged the family ever since the loss of Plas Wilmot, meant that Owen was inclined, at least at first, to stand on his dignity as an officer and a gentleman.

[4] Beckett and Simpson (eds), *A Nation in Arms*, 72. The quotation is from Williams, *Raising and Training the New Armies*, 63.

After his first drill with the Artists' Rifles, he wrote with satisfaction to his mother: 'Fortunately our Sergeant is a gentleman, and, what is more, considers us as such' (*CL* 361). The same rather anxious touchiness is responsible for the apparently contradictory presence, in the letters, of indignation at the snobbery of officers—like the Major who would not board a train that had no separate accommodation for officers, declaring (said Owen): 'Aw I decline. I *eb*solutely decline, to travel in a coach where there are—haw—*Men*!' (*CL* 467)—alongside a selective snobbery of his own. Arriving at camp in Ripon in March 1918, he found most of the officers to be 'privates and sergeants in masquerade', and said he would prefer to be among 'honest privates' (*CL* 539). At Scarborough, in July, most of the officers were 'glorified N.C.O.'s' but there was 'an element of gentlemen left' (*CL* 563). Returning to France, he was pleased to have 'an intellectual gentleman for Captain'; the Colonel too was 'a mild, honourable gentleman', but at least two of the officers in his company were 'quite temporary gentlemen' (*CL* 579).

'Temporary gentlemen' (on the irresistible analogy of the 'temporary officers' commissioned into Kitchener's army) was a jibe frequently heard, and not only among regular officers; it spoke for a justifiable feeling that the war was unsettling the social categories of the *status quo ante bellum*. In the event, in giving him a commission the army confirmed for Owen (as the navy did for his brother) the social rank which he felt was rightfully his, and he seems to have been both proud and jealous of his status. He took his training seriously and worked hard at it. Cadets would be judged on their gentlemanly conduct as well as on their soldierly skills, and there were manuals of instruction for both kinds of accomplishment, for those who needed them. 'When out of camp remember that in uniform you must never do anything which is not becoming to an officer and a gentleman,' warned the author of *Customs of the Army: A Guide for Cadets and Young Officers* (1917). As examples of unseemly conduct he cited getting drunk, standing about on street corners, or smoking a pipe in public places, as well as being seen 'walking about with one of the opposite sex with whom you would not care for your Colonel or men to see you'.[5] 'Your Colonel or men': the manuals advised the junior

[5] 'Regular', *Customs of the Army*, 11.

officer that he would be under constant scrutiny from above and from below.

What was more, when he arrived in France Owen found himself posted, at the very beginning of 1917, to the 2nd Manchesters, which meant that his first combat experience was to be in a regular army regiment among professional soldiers, 'well-trained troops and genuine "real-old" Officers' (*CL* 421). This was a distinction that still mattered in January 1917, though continuing heavy losses and organizational upheavals were soon to erode the remaining differences between regular, Territorial, and 'service' (i.e. wartime recruit) battalions. He declared that this posting to the 2nd Manchesters was a stroke of luck, but it must also have been daunting; the temporary officer would have to measure up to professional standards. It was in a regular regiment that he received his baptism of fire, and from a regular regiment that he was sent out of the line, at the end of April 1917, as unfit to lead his men in battle. Both before and after his breakdown, there was every reason for Lieutenant Owen to be continuously conscious of the meaning of his military rank.

The dreadful discovery at the end of 'The Show' is one of the consequences of this awareness. In this poem, 'My soul looked down from a vague height, with Death,' on a ruined and rotting battlefield, where squads of soldiers looking like caterpillars squirmed about and slaughtered each other:

> Whereat, in terror what that sight might mean,
> I reeled and shivered earthward like a feather.
>
> And Death fell with me, like a deepening moan.
> And He, picking a manner of worm, which half had hid
> Its bruises in the earth, but crawled no further,
> Showed me its feet, the feet of many men,
> And the fresh-severed head of it, my head.

In this moment of authentic horror, the image is more complicated than it might seem. The officer is the head of his platoon: if their leader is incapacitated—killed or wounded, or shell-shocked and useless—they are helpless. But decapitation is a mutilation with a meaning. With or without a Freudian gloss, beheading is the punishment of a crime; it is an execution. Here it is the 'manner of worm' that is so punished, that is, the body of soldiers with its many members, suffering retribution, perhaps like their counterparts the attacking troops in 'Spring Offensive' when the sky 'turned | In fury against them' and the earth swallowed them up. The collective body of these soldiers is beheaded of its leader; but he too, the speaker, is individually beheaded. Did Owen remember that he had lost his head (his nerve), causing the men under his command to lose their head (their leader), in those several days when he was alone and sheltering in a hole on the railway embankment—near the remains of a dismembered brother-officer—in the fighting at Savy Wood the previous April?[6] The severing of the head can be construed as a condensed image of both punishment and the offence it punishes (a dereliction of duty), and another meaning of the already ambiguous title points to the exposure of a terrible half-buried crime. This nightmare vision is a dream not only of terror but also of guilt, the disguised confession of a failure to meet the inexorable demands made on an officer whose duty was to show no fear himself, and somehow to protect his men from the danger into which he was responsible for leading them.

But what kind of language was exchanged between a junior officer and his men? The social profile of the ordinary British infantryman in the middle and later years of the Great War was somewhat changed from that of the career rankers Owen had dismissed loftily, in a letter of August 1914, as 'all Tommy Atkins, poor fellows' (*CL* 282). Now the ranks of the British forces, like those of their continental allies and adversaries, were likely to contain men from all walks of civil life, while the officer corps was having to rely increasingly on replenishment by promotions from the ranks, even in the field. The postwar consequences of this loosening of caste were to be quite considerable. But meanwhile military culture was slow to adapt to the changes, and maintained the great gulf fixed between the two classes of an earlier evolutionary phase of the British army, the sporting class who officered it and the poor who manned it. Intercourse across that gulf may have come more easily to officers whose home background had accustomed them, better than Owen's had, to dealing with servants and subordinates and employees. As it was, when he joined the

[6] Shell-shock cases usually involved some degree of repression of the memory of the trauma (Myers, *Shell Shock in France*, 56–7). It is more than likely that Owen found it hard to face consciously the memory of what preceded his 'coming-to after the Embankment-Shell-Shock' (*CL* 475) and afterwards he may simply not have known at all clearly what had happened.

5th Manchesters at Milford Camp and had men under his command for the first time, Owen felt self-conscious and isolated, describing himself as 'marooned on a Crag of Superiority in an ocean of Soldiers' (*CL* 395).

Officers were expected to make the welfare of their men a duty second only to carrying out their orders; but they were advised that an essential distance should not be blurred. 'Always treat men with kindness, and do everything you can to help them. Be cheerful yourself and keep them cheerful. Talk to them individually, and get to know each one of them, but never be familiar with them.'[7] Formality and a literal distance were the usual conditions of discourse between officer and men. 'When a soldier addresses an officer he will halt two paces from him, and salute with the right hand.'[8] A soldier could never on his own initiative be alone with an officer; if he wished to speak with one, the regulations said he could do so only in the presence of a non-commissioned officer.[9] This meant that such dialogue as there could be between officers and men (other than personal servants) was likely to be in the nature of public speech, and most of an officer's dealing with his soldiers was monologic and, of course, official—words of encouragement or reprimand, lectures, instructions, and the language of command in which young officers and NCO's were frequently practised. Colonel Shirley took a quite liberal line on intercourse across the ranks, but he said this could only be relaxed so long as officers could demonstrate that their authority did not depend on rank alone.

> The soldier's best friend is, or ought to be, his officer; but, if officers are to mix freely with their men and still maintain their position, they must see to it that they are as superior to their men in all moral qualities as they are in rank—for 'rank is but the guinea stamp' which may be impressed as easily upon dross as upon gold.[10]

An officer must not forget or allow his men to forget that he held his authority from on high. There is hardly any distance between this and the advice Griffith Thomas had given to young clergymen

[7] 'Regular', *Customs of the Army*, 10. [8] *Infantry Training*, 24.

[9] *What Every Soldier Ought to Know*, 5. Sergeants in particular were the linchpin of the British army as well as its great dialogic intermediaries. It is a misfortune that they seem, by and large, to have had little interest in adding to the literature of the war. [10] Shirley, *Moral*, 16.

on their pastoral duties, in *The Work of the Ministry*. 'Three characteristics of dealing with men must be constantly kept in view,' he had said. 'We must be manly, brotherly and godly.'[11]

All sorts of prescriptions and circumscriptions, then, set limits on the speech exchanged between officers and men, and these limits could only rarely be surmounted or transgressed. There is a curious moment in a letter of October 1918 when Owen is telling Sassoon about his battalion's part in recent savage fighting. His name had been put forward for a Military Cross.

> I'm glad I've been recommended for M.C., & hope I get it, for the confidence it may give me at home. Full of confidence after having taken a few machine guns (with the help of one seraphic lance corporal,) I held a most glorious brief peace talk in a pill box. You would have been '*en pamoisons* [*sic*]'. (*CL* 582.)

Jonathan Cutbill has suggested in his *New Statesman* article of 16 January 1987 that what Owen is talking (or hinting) about here is a sexual encounter. It is a speculation that seems to underestimate the potency of language itself to thrill the poet. Surrounded as they were by carnage and destruction, the extraordinary drama of war had provided the briefest of opportunities for officer and soldier to speak in privacy and as equals, as they could never have done in ordinary circumstances, and to discover that they were of like mind about what mattered most—although merely to say so was to disobey an order forbidding any 'Peace Talk' in the Fourth Army (*CL* 585). Owen was surely right: the vertiginous contrast between the subject of this discourse and its circumstances would have been enough to cause Siegfried Sassoon, connoisseur of ironies, to go into a swoon (*en pâmoison*).

That moment of communion (if my interpretation is right: not for nothing did Owen call himself 'a master of elision' (*CL* 521)) was rare, perhaps unique, and purchased by extreme circumstances. As a rule, the army kept officers as a class apart from their men (with their own eating and living arrangements, for example, even in the line). Both sides were encouraged to keep the distance between them, and furthermore they were to a greater or lesser

[11] W. H. Griffith Thomas, *The Work of the Ministry*, 283.

extent separated (to adapt Oscar Wilde) by a common language. Vernacular speech was not just a social barrier between the middle-class officer and his largely working-class troops; it also presented Owen, as it presents any serious realist, with a stylistic problem. The dominant style of Owen's poetry is the elaborated code of educated written English. Within such discourse, the representation of the vernacular has to be marked as different, and thus must appear abnormal—at best stylistically deviant, but possibly also quaint, comic, or incomprehensible. As soon as he decided to write poems about the army, at Craiglockhart, Owen started experimenting with ways of showing how ordinary soldiers spoke:

A low voice said,
'It's Blighty, p'raps, he sees; his pluck's all gone,
Dreaming of all the valiant, that *aren't* dead:
Bold uncles, smiling ministerially;
Maybe his brave young wife, getting her fun
In some new home, improved materially.
It's not these stiffs have crazed him; nor the Hun.'

This speech from 'The Dead-Beat', a poem drafted immediately after his first meeting with Siegfried Sassoon, shows that Owen's touch was unsure when it came to the demotic. His few previous efforts in this vein had been, like the 1913 fragment 'I Began to Run' (*CPF* 423–4), in the idiom of *Punch*'s comic working class. The words of the 'low voice' in 'The Dead-Beat' are not a caricature, but alongside the quite persuasive rhythm and diction of 'It's not these stiffs have crazed him' Owen could not resist serving up the leftover joke about ministerial smiles, which dated from a letter he had written two years before (*CL* 353) and clearly belonged to a different order of speech, so that the result is neither one thing nor another. Another Sassoonish effort, 'The Letter', is more consistent. It contains the sort of language ('Mother might spare you half a sov') Owen must have been very familiar with, for a platoon commander had to read and censor all his men's letters; but, in a surprising solecism, it confuses the conventions of written and spoken language. No one ever wrote 'We don't see much of them square-'eaded 'Uns' in a letter. 'The Chances', a dramatic monologue, is Owen's most successful rendering of the speech of the ranks.

I 'mind as how the night before that show
Us five got talkin'; we was in the know.
'Ah well,' says Jimmy, and he's seen some scrappin',
'There ain't no more than five things as can happen,—
You get knocked out; else wounded, bad or cushy;
Scuppered; or nowt except you're feelin' mushy.'

One of us got the knock-out, blown to chops;
One lad was hurt, like, losin' both his props;
And one—to use the word of hypocrites—
Had the misfortune to be took by Fritz.
Now me, I wasn't scratched, praise God Almighty,
Though next time please I'll thank him for a blighty.
But poor old Jim, he's livin' and he's not;
He reckoned he'd five chances, and he had:
He's wounded, killed, and pris'ner, all the lot,
The flamin' lot all rolled in one. Jim's mad.[12]

Owen's relative failures elsewhere show how difficult this apparently casual mimicry was to get right. This is a steady and sure-footed poem, neither patronizing nor sentimental, and its vocality is not at the expense but at the service of its wit and drama.

'The Dead-Beat' and 'The Chances', and probably 'The Letter' (*OTP* 101, 204), were drafted at Craiglockhart, in the phase of Owen's military career when he was most isolated from the actual speech of soldiers of the 'other ranks' (Craiglockhart was a hospital for officers only) but in almost daily contact with Siegfried Sassoon, whose 'trench life sketches' (*CL* 484) Owen took as a model.[13] He did not attempt any other sustained dramatic speech in the vernacular. There are other poems in Sassoon's style which date from this period and deal with the lives of ordinary soldiers, but in them Owen contrives to find ways round the stylistic problem of speech representation. In 'Inspection' (as we have seen), the soldier punished for having a blood-stained uniform voices his bitter commentary in the speaker's (the officer's) own idiom, as if

[12] This version tones down a little some of the earlier drafts' conventional notations of vernacular speech—''Ad the misfortoon to be took be Fritz', etc. (*CPF* 345–6).

[13] Another possible model for the poetry of soldiers' lives and language seems not to have tempted him: 'I have written *no Barrack Room Ballads*!' (*CL* 493). This suggests at least that he knew what Kipling's *Barrack Room Ballads* were like. But there seems, perhaps surprisingly, to be no trace of Kipling's soldiery in the language of Owen's poems.

the officer now lends the soldier his language as a kind of reparation for not having listened to him in the first place; a fascinating dialogic transaction. 'S.I.W.', which is related to Sassoon's 'The Hero', is a curious case. Its protagonist is an anonymous infantryman (he writes letters on the butt of his rifle, so he can't be an officer) yet his story is decked out with an aesthetic self-consciousness unusual in Owen at this stage, graced not only with an epigraph from one of Yeats's symbolist dramas but also with headings entitling its four unequal parts respectively 'The Prologue', 'The Action', 'The Poem', and 'The Epilogue'.[14] Why this rather dandified metapoetic apparatus, for this subject? One answer may lie in its very inappropriateness. The wretched soldier is caught up in an exalted discourse of honour which is quite over his head and grotesquely inapplicable to actual circumstances, a discourse which hands him over to an oppression of body and spirit that imprisons and crushes him until suicide is his only way out. He is sent off to war by the chattering of his family; worn down by bombardment and constantly under fire, as both death and life torment him (by speech-acts: promises, scoff, riling), in this noisy poem only the victim himself is silent. It is part of his hopelessness that he has no speech of his own, and opens his mouth only to stick a gun in it, making a grim literal mockery of the organ of eloquence:

> With him they buried the muzzle his teeth had kissed,
> And truthfully wrote the mother, 'Tim died smiling.'

It is a noticeable feature of Owen's later poems that ordinary soldiers in them have little to say. The men in 'The Calls' have no speech, only sighs which it is the officer-poet's vocation to interpret. 'The Last Laugh' catches only their dying exclamations, while in 'The Sentry' the blinded man can only whine, sob, moan, and shout. The draft in 'The Send-Off' are heard to sing but not to speak, and in any case they are soon 'hushed-up' and despatched. These are all 1918 poems. The discourse of the amputee in 'Disabled' (drafted in late 1917) is a third-person narration of the unspoken thoughts and memories that are a function of his isolation; whereas his officer counterpart, the dying man in 'A Terre',

[14] In an earlier version the divisions are: 'The Prologue—a satire; The Incident—narrative; The Apology—a poem; The Epilogue—a cynicism' (*CPF* 329).

at least still has his voice and addresses a dramatic monologue to the poet. Only one word, an officer's command, is spoken in 'Spring Offensive'. And in the very late and Sassoonish 'Smile, Smile, Smile', the pompous rhetoric of press and politicians is met, and mocked, by the silence of the wounded troops, and a smile that is as easily misread by the ignorant—'They're happy now, poor things'—as the rictus of the suicide in 'S.I.W.' which is reported 'truthfully' as a consolation to his mother.

It was possible, then, to exploit the reticence of the ranks for the purposes of pathos or irony, or even to render them heroic. 'Apologia pro Poemate Meo' found music in 'the silentness of duty'. But this was to make a virtue of something like a necessity. A certain diffidence, after Craiglockhart, about representing the speech of the troops was an acknowledgement of a stylistic insufficiency; it was something he could not trust himself to do well. The implication seems clear, and it is an important one. Owen was not confident that he could speak (or hear) the language of the ranks well enough to reproduce it. Though the whole project of his war poetry was to speak for the common soldier, that distance between officers and men was a barrier—erected by class consciousness, maintained by regulations, and doubtless guarded by Owen's own social uneasiness—which his compassion, his fellow-feeling, could flood over but did not wash away. The silence (the relative silence) of the troops in Owen's poems admits that their speech was in important ways foreign to an officer, a gentleman, and a poet, with the best will in the world. Yet that relative inaudibility becomes an eloquent image in the poems, and that distance acquires a pathos of its own.

He was a man set in authority over others; his authority made him responsible for his men but it also made him different from them. The institution which brought an officer and his soldiers together also kept them apart. Of all officers, an infantry subaltern such as Owen saw his men at closest quarters. But, as I have suggested, he himself had reasons to nurse his authority carefully, for it must have seemed a little precarious. These reasons had to do with a long-standing touchiness about his social class, his youth (he was twenty-two when he enlisted), and his being a temporary and very junior officer, first an untested soldier in command of battle veterans, and later, at least in his own eyes, a man whose courage under fire was not beyond question. The slenderness of his authority was an old story, of course, the story of the junior 'third parent', the pupil-teacher, the parish drudge at Dunsden, and the young tutor of adults at Bordeaux.

He was used to finding himself the executive or contact point at which a higher authority worked on a lower order. This position of mandated intermediacy, facing both ways, had on occasion in the past allowed or obliged him to speak out against the authority whose surrogate he was, when it seemed unjust or irresponsible. This goes back to the junior parent's running battle with his father, and to his later indignation at the negligence of Mr Wigan and the Keswick preachers, and the meanness of his employer at the Berlitz School; in a sense his turning against Tennyson and what he stood for belongs to the same series of insurrections. In so far as there is a pattern here, it should lead us to expect an indignation directed up the military hierarchy towards the plump and tempting array of sitting ducks, the scarlet majors and bungling generals, that had already—and the precedent was another incentive for Owen—provided targets for Siegfried Sassoon's *Counter-Attack*. But no such indignation is expressed in Owen's verse or letters. It was a phase of family discourse that did not repeat itself in his relations with the army; here was one aspect of the father that he never challenged. At no point does he criticize or mock a senior officer, regimental or staff (except for the snobbish major on the train, (*CL* 467) and—in 'Inspection'—Field-Marshal God). He seems to have had little but admiration, not unmixed with fear, for the ones he knew. The colonel who ordered him out of the line at the beginning of May 1917 features alongside Christ and Keats in a list of his heroes drawn up that November (*CL* 505). He had too wholehearted an investment in army discourse to bring the institution into any sort of disrepute. It is as if he is constrained by a religious orthodoxy or political loyalty, as if he stands in the same awe of the army as he had held in adolescence for poetry, when his enjoyment of the old *Quarterly Review*'s mockery of Tennyson filled him, he said, with 'all the guilty consciousness of infidelity' (*CL* 96).

It is of considerable interest that criticism of senior officers, and even of the staff officers usually so resented or despised by regimental soldiers, was a move that was not in Owen's repertoire. Yet the pattern of contraversion does get repeated, even so. Though any attack on the army establishment was off the limits of his discourse, Owen's anger at the wastage of the war went round his military superiors in a sort of flanking movement to assault what lay behind them, the civilian political authority and public opinion at whose bidding, ultimately, the army did what it was told. The slaughter was futile, to be sure, but the culprits were not in uniform.

> Did I tell you that five healthy girls died of fright in one night at the last village. The people in England and France who thwarted a peaceable retirement of the enemy from these areas are therefore now sacrificing aged French peasants and charming French children to our guns. Shells made by women in Birmingham are at this moment burying little children alive not very far from here. (*CL* 590.)

Owen wrote nothing like Sassoon's 'The General', where it is the incompetence of the commander and his staff that leads to the soldiers' deaths. He was inclined to place the blame further back, and was more ready to take 'Field-Marshal God's' name in vain than that of any human senior officer. On Easter Sunday 1918 he told his mother: 'God so hated the world that He gave several millions of English-begotten sons, that whosoever believeth in them should not perish, but have a comfortable life' (*CL* 544). His strongest outburst against religion turns, before the sentence is over, to an attack on civilian selfishness. The pattern of insurrection, which is one of Owen's basic structures of feeling, bypasses military authority and settles on more long-range targets, targets closer to home.

Platoon commanders like Owen were told that they were 'the keystone of the arch' in the structure of command (and therefore had to bear the most stress). The subaltern mediated between the ordinary soldier and higher authority, for 'he acts not only as a Platoon Commander, but also as a go-between.'[15] It was his job not only to pass on commands from above, but also as far as possible to represent the interests of his men and to see that these were taken note of in the army's scheme of things, for the junior officer could see at close quarters what these interests were. At the end of 1917, in England, Owen remembered the 'blindfold look' on the faces of the troops at Etaples: 'to describe it,' he told his mother, 'I think I must go back and be with them' (*CL* 521). It was after the action in which he won the Military Cross, a month

[15] 'One of Them', '*Out There!*', 6.

before his death, that he wrote: 'I came out in order to help these boys—directly by leading them as well as an officer can; indirectly, by watching their sufferings that I may speak of them as well as a pleader can. I have done the first' (*CL* 580). Here was a broad but reasonable interpretation of the lieutenant's duty to act 'not only as a Platoon Commander but also as a go-between', though it is not to a higher military command, but to the civilian public, that he must represent the common soldier's case. It is a crucial moment, a statement of vocation that is a convocation, bringing together, in his self-dedication to 'these boys', the voices of the brother, minister, officer, and poet.

The army could not speak to the people whose instrument it was, any more than a private soldier could address a commanding officer. There had to be a mediator. Although few of them speak directly (like 'Dulce et Decorum Est', 'Greater Love', and 'Apologia pro Poemate Meo') to a second-person addressee, all Owen's war poems are for civilians, to make audible to them the authentic experience of the army. 'I don't want to write anything to which a soldier would say No Compris!' (*CPF* 193). The poet was continuing the officer's function as go-between. Owen frequently talks about his fellow officers in his letters, but remarkably few of them are portrayed in the poems. Nevertheless, the voice itself of the war poems—even when it mimics the language of the troops—is the voice of the officer doing his job. An officer regularly had to give an account of the strength, status, and morale of his men, give a hearing to their complaints and take any necessary action on them, write reports on combat experience, requests for support, commendations of courage, and letters to the bereaved. The list covers most of what Owen's war poems do. The roles of poet and officer meet in the function of representation, both in the mimetic and in something like the democratic sense of the word. The war poet was a realist in his representations of the experience of soldiers. The officer too had a duty to make representations on behalf of his men; to see that their situation was understood, and if possible helped, by the people who had put them where they were. He was their representative. There was nobody else. And they must be properly represented: a true officer must be truthful.

But to mention the democratic aspect of representation is to expose a nest of difficulties. There was nothing democratic about the army or its chain of command. What gave someone like Lieutenant

Owen the right to assume spokesmanship for ordinary soldiers? His answer was to rest that claim on a shared experience, a sort of blood-brotherhood, 'Bound with the bandage of the arm that drips'. He had been there too, and was a witness.

> But what say such as from existence' brink
> Ventured but drave too swift to sink...
> Why speak not they of comrades that went under?

What was more, he went back a second time. The great theme of soldierly fellowship that runs all through the war poems is also strategic, for it is a legitimation of Owen's representativeness, his escape from *ex officio* singularity, and the basis of his moral authority. But it does not fully exempt him from the embarrassment of belonging with the officers (the sort of embarrassment which was to afflict Owen's admirers of the next generation, the upper-middle-class leftist writers of the 1930s, who did not always face the problem with Owen's honesty). How could the young officer speak for the common soldiers when, as we have seen, he did not really speak their language? He was, surely, not one of them, and his representation could be at best paternalistic, at worst patronizing or even in bad faith.

Owen could see and feel these difficulties. If they could not really be overcome, he could at least make them (as we have seen him make the necessary brutalizing effects of battle) a part of his theme. They are dramatized in poems where the officer is shown as helpless to alleviate the misery of his men, or even as a cause of it. They are a recurrent issue in the letters too. He might devote himself to 'watching their sufferings', but it was his job to punish his soldiers if they flinched from them. The anomaly of his position is caught in a letter written in October 1918, when he describes how his shattered company, coming out of the line, has been reinforced by a draft of young conscripts just arrived from England. 'Some of them look pretty scared already, poor victims.' Owen as company commander was distressed that he was not able to provide enough food for these exhausted and unnerved newcomers, but he had something for them; he had to stand in front of them that evening and promulgate a General Order forbidding all soldiers to talk of peace (*CL* 583). It was as if they had asked for bread and been given a stone.

In curtailing his men's freedom of speech Owen was behaving

properly as the conduit of the official and monologic word of army command to its lowest subordinates; this after all was the other and busier track of his function as go-between. At this stage his own feelings about the prospect of peace were not in doubt, but they had to take second place to the priority of that word, whatever he may have thought about it privately. He lends his voice to the discourse of a higher command whose commission he holds, and in so doing he makes himself identical with what Bakhtin calls 'the authoritative word'.

> The authoritative word demands that we acknowledge it, that we make it our own; it binds us, quite independent of any power it might have to persuade us internally; we encounter it with its authority already fused to it. The authoritative word is located in a distanced zone, organically connected with a past that is felt to be hierarchically higher. It is, so to speak, the word of the fathers.[16]

Bakhtin mentions religious dogma and acknowledged scientific truth as types of authoritative discourse, but it is a formulation in which the language of military command sits very comfortably. Bakhtin is inclined to see a struggle between this inflexible and externally powerful word and a discourse which is 'internally persuasive',[17] and to think of human (and perhaps social) development as a gradual conquest of the former by the latter. But in the circumstances in which Owen found himself the word of authority was not to be contradicted or adapted; it was unthinkable to challenge it wholesale, and impossible to choose which orders to execute and which not. As long as he held office in a totalitarian military hierarchy and discourse, he was bound to promulgate 'the word of the fathers', and to give orders which might leave the sons with hell to pay. From the authoritative discourse of Christianity, Owen had clung on to what he found 'internally persuasive'—the moral example of Christ's compassion—and rejected most of the rest; he could not have done this if he had held office in the Church, just as he was not now free as an infantry officer to select which aspects of the army's *logos* to endorse.

As a soldier he described himself ruefully as 'a conscientious objector with a very seared conscience' (*CL* 461), but as an officer he was more than that—he was the voice and instrument of an

[16] Bakhtin, *The Dialogic Imagination*, 342. [17] Ibid. 342 ff.

authority whose words could have terrible meanings for the people in his charge. The secret irony of 'The Parable of the Old Man and the Young' (which retells the story of the sacrifice of Isaac) was that Owen himself was cast as Abram, the patriarch commissioned to execute an order by a higher command whose word he could not question. Wilfred thought, sourly, how Tom Owen would relish and recognize the prospect of the kind of authority his son now wielded as a company commander. 'Father would like to see me on my Charger; or sitting at my Orderly Room Table, where I can inflict Field Punishment!' (*CL* 583). Number One Field Punishment allowed an offender to be attached by straps, irons, or ropes to a fixed object, often a large-spoked wagon-wheel, for up to two hours a day over a maximum period of twenty-one days.[18] It was known colloquially as crucifixion. 'Then Abram bound the youth with belts and straps,' in 'The Parable', before slaughtering him. Owen's rank put him among the patriarchs and the crucifiers. For him the obverse or dark side of an officer's responsibility was guilt. It is explicit in the elaborate conceit, in the letter to Osbert Sitwell in which he likens training recruits to preparing Christ for his crucifixion (*CL* 562); already implicit, perhaps, when he meets his inert and lumpish troops in January 1917 and declares like some Ancient Mariner that the officers 'feel the weight of them hanging on us' (*CL* 422).

An officer had absorbed all he could of the advice of the training manuals and of his instructors, and he learned on the job. Owen's work is full (if not as obsessively full as Kipling's) of casual evidence of old-soldierly 'shop' or the knowledge of professional experience:

Courage leaked, as sand
From the best sandbags after years of rain.

But beyond the ordinary experience of front-line conditions—the materials for the binding (and exclusive) freemasonry of those who had seen combat—officers had another kind of knowledge, that went with their power: they were in the know. Private soldiers

[18] It was a punishment for minor transgressions. Private Frank Richards, for example, was given eight days' Number One Field Punishment for being found drinking after hours in a café, and considered that he had got off lightly, no doubt because he had just been awarded the DCM (which is what he had been celebrating). Richards, *Old Soldiers Never Die*, 161.

had little idea what was going on beyond their very limited line of vision, though Rumour, as in *Henry IV Part II*, always played chorus to their drama. But even junior officers were to some extent privy to tactical intelligence and even decisions, and were kept (at least in comparison with their men) in the picture as far as their own sector of the line was concerned. So in this extra sense, an officer was a man of knowledge. But there is another and more profound way in which the officer is a man set apart, in Owen's work, by a special knowledge. By virtue of that responsibility and guilt I have been discussing, which inheres in their rank and perhaps in their social class, officers were possessed by something like a biblical knowledge of good and evil, a sense of their own damnability which, I think, the other ranks in Owen are spared. This at least is one way of reading those groups in the poems who seem singled out by a special doomed self-consciousness, as in 'Insensibility':

> Happy the lad whose mind was never trained:
> His days are worth forgetting more than not.
> He sings along the march
> Which we march taciturn, because of dusk,
> The long, forlorn, relentless trend
> From larger day to huger night.

These watchful and haunted individuals share a guilty secret, as 'We wise, who with a thought besmirch | Blood over all our soul', which is why they know that their destination is 'huger night'. We see them again set apart at the beginning of 'Spring Offensive', disbarred by their knowledge from sharing the innocent sleep of the other ranks:

> Halted against the shade of a last hill
> They fed, and eased of pack-loads, were at ease;
> And leaning on the nearest chest or knees
> Carelessly slept.
> But many there stood still
> To face the stark blank sky beyond the ridge,
> Knowing their feet had come to the end of the world.

These men too know that they are going to hell. Army discourse invested the officer with privileges of knowledge and power, but in doing so it loaded him with a burden that could not be shrugged off like a pack-load, and gave him a fallen language to speak.

You can hear it in 'The Sentry', which starts like this:

> We'd found an old Boche dug-out, and he knew,
> And gave us hell; for shell on frantic shell
> Lit full on top, but never quite burst through.
> Rain, guttering down in waterfalls of slime,
> Kept slush waist-high and rising hour by hour,
> And choked the steps too thick with clay to climb.
> What murk of air remained stank old, and sour
> With fumes from whizz-bangs, and the smell of men
> Who'd lived there years, and left their curse in the den,
> If not their corpses.

It begins with a favourite Owen motif, the entry underground. A comparison with the same motif at the start of 'Strange Meeting' (with its grandiloquent 'granites which titanic wars had groined' and the like) shows this poem electing a lower style, closer to the language of the army. The speech genre is the combat anecdote and it makes a conversational, even debonair start:

> We'd found an old Boche dug-out, and he knew,
> And gave us hell.

This was the tone of sang-froid that *Punch* liked to believe was typical of the British soldier, but the casual and even faintly sporting idiom introduces a metaphorical hell which a wealth of detail is quick to realize—the torments of fire and freezing, the noisome and weltering darkness, the curse, and the corpses. Still, there is no flinching from this, and indeed the catalogue of horrors serves to confirm the soldierly toughness with which it is faced. So far for the officer who narrates it, the ordeal in the dug-out is not a personal hell but a professional hazard, in the line of duty, to be dealt with as it is narrated, without personal feeling. He has got this far without mentioning himself individually. This will soon change:

> There we herded from the blast
> Of whizz-bangs; but one found our door at last,—
> Buffeting eyes and breath, snuffing the candles,
> And thud! flump! thud! down the steep steps came thumping
> And sploshing in the flood, deluging muck,
> The sentry's body; then his rifle, handles
> Of old Boche bombs, and mud in ruck on ruck.

We dredged it up, for dead, until he whined,
'O sir—my eyes,—I'm blind,—I'm blind,—I'm blind.'
Coaxing, I held a flame against his lids
And said if he could see the least blurred light
He was not blind; in time they'd get all right.
'I can't,' he sobbed. Eyeballs, huge-bulged like squids',
Watch my dreams still,—yet I forgot him there
In posting Next for duty, and sending a scout
To beg a stretcher somewhere, and flound'ring about
To other posts under the shrieking air.

This is a crime story and there is a body, revealed after due suspense ('came thumping . . . sploshing . . . deluging . . . The sentry's body'). At first the wounded sentry is buried or immersed in the freezing mud and slush. When he has been pulled out of it he is presumed to be dead and is not dignified with a human pronoun, but he will not be cancelled out.

> We dredged it up, for dead, until he whined,
> 'O sir—my eyes,—I'm blind,—I'm blind,—I'm blind.'

His first act is to single the officer out from the group (though he can see none of them) in an appeal *de profundis*, but the officer hears his voice as a whine, an undignified, unpleasant, and unwelcome noise. By addressing him, the blinded man flushes the officer out from the communal pronoun he has inhabited up till now, demanding a singular response from him or making a demand on his individual responsibility; the officer somehow has to answer for what has happened. Why? The soldier turns to him instinctively, like a hurt or frightened child to its parent or elder brother, for help and comfort; and although the officer has neither of these to give, we can see him desperately assuming the authoritative word of a medical expertise he does not possess, for this is expected of his commanding role, just as a young child expects his elders to have all the answers.

But the officer narrator is answerable in another way too. The sentry has been hurt because the officer ordered him into a vulnerable position; indeed, it is at the officer's command that this soldier became 'the sentry' and consequently a casualty. It was sometimes a platoon commander's job to put a life at risk. In a rough working draft of this poem the point is made more brutally, for no sooner has the first sentry's body tumbled down the steps than the officer replaces him ('Whose turn for sentry? . . . up you go' (*CPF* 372)), *before* paying attention to his injury. So the officer hears in the blind man's whining not just an irksome demand for help he cannot give, but also an accusation. This is the meaning of the incident that will not be buried, but returns from the dead and from the dead past in spite of efforts to repress it. The officer 'forgot him there | In posting Next for duty' (thereby adding a kind of insult to the man's injury), but in his dreams, when his own eyes are closed, the blinded sentry keeps a dreadful watch on him.[19]

> Those other wretches, how they bled and spewed,
> And one who would have drowned himself for good,—
> I try not to remember these things now.

The speaker's rank, and his responsibility for what has happened, effectively isolate him and alienate him from the group, not only from the gibbering sentry with his repulsive blind eyes 'huge-bulged like squids'', but also from the other soldiers, no longer 'we' but 'they', and now perceived with indifference or hostility as 'wretches', their bleeding and vomiting more disgusting than pitiful. But part of this disgust must surely be transferred or pre-emptive, for these are simply victims, and their case is different from that of the man who knowingly led them down the slippery descent to this place and now cannot lead them out again.

The letter of 16 January 1917, which recounts the incident that provided the raw material for this poem, also shows that there were actually two particular casualties that day for which Owen felt a kind of personal responsibility:

> In the Platoon on my left the sentries over the dug-out were blown to nothing. One of these poor fellows was my first servant whom I rejected. If I had kept him he would have lived, for servants don't do Sentry Duty. I kept my own sentries half way down the stairs during the most terrific bombardment. In spite of this one lad was blown down and, I am afraid, blinded. (*CL* 428.)

[19] 'Dulce et Decorum Est' reports another haunting by the face of a man who has been led into danger and struck down. The deathly staring face was an image from Owen's pre-war poems and presumably nightmares. 'The face was a projection of his own imagination and unspoken urges, arousing guilt, fear and helplessness' (*OTP* 18).

The blinded sentry was a man under Owen's direct command as an officer, whereas the other man went to his death as a consequence of Owen's exercising a definitive (and recently acquired) class privilege, the prerogative of a gentleman to engage and dismiss personal servants. It was a graphic and cruel illustration of class power. That Owen could not reasonably be blamed for either tragedy was beside the point; his verdict on himself is to be read in his language, the guilty language of the officer and gentleman that implicates its speaker. In the poem the case against the officer is indeed damning by implication. He plays down his role as leader ('We'd found' is disingenuous) and does not mention his posting of the sentry (though there is a suspicious and unexplained gap, after 'corpses', in his testimony). His confidence that the main witness has been silenced ('We dredged it up, for dead') is misplaced, his alibi in the first-person plural pronoun is broken, his coaxing reassurances carry no conviction, his revealed lack of sympathy for the others counts against him, he flounders in his guilt, and his repeated attempts to dismiss the case from his own mind are thwarted by the dreams in which he returns obsessively to the scene. And if we admit evidence from the January 1917 letter ('I nearly broke down and let myself drown in the water' (*CL* 427)), the action of 'one who would have drowned himself for good' speaks for itself.

This then was what it could mean to be a junior officer of infantry—to carry the double burden of victim and self-accused, and to seek and fail to find oblivion from memories that were both torment and confession. This is what brought Owen to Craiglockhart, which is where he began this poem. But in a sense 'The Sentry' is woven into all his experience as a serving officer, as the story of an incident from his first week in the front line, first drafted in the war hospital, continued at Scarborough in May 1918, and completed in France that September (*CPF* 189). It is a kind of autobiography of his army career, from its jaunty if nervous beginnings, through the explosive violence of his baptism of fire, the self-lacerating sense of failure, and his haunted effort to put it behind him. But it points beyond that too, beyond collapse and isolation to a deliberate return in memory to the terrible scene, where there was still a job to be done, a report to be made.

> I try not to remember these things now.
> Let Dread hark back for one word only: how
> Half-listening to that sentry's moans and jumps,
> Renewed most horribly whenever crumps
> Pummelled the roof and slogged the air beneath,—
> Through the dense din, I say, we heard him shout
> 'I see your lights!'—But ours had long gone out.

He had originally thought to end 'The Sentry' by a Sassoonish cut to bridge-playing club-men glancing at the war news in the paper (*CPF* 372), before he settled on the extraordinary *coup de théâtre* of the lights, where hope is suddenly glimpsed and snatched away. The focus in the end moves beyond the individual to a collective tragedy; but tragedy itself has become a community, and the officer is not alone in his failure any more than the sentry is alone in his blindness now. As the officer's voice reaches silence, the poem surrenders to the dark (in the end, darkness does comprehend the *logos*), a darkness that ripples out from the centre through that infinitely expansible possessive plural. For Owen, at the story's end, all 'our' leading lights have failed—officers, ruling class, institutions, traditions, the enlightenment of science, and the kindly light of religion—all authorities and beliefs, all ranks and all distinctions are blotted out in the dark, where the blind lead the blind.

IV

Poetry

14
A History of Poetry

Wilfred Owen, aged perhaps sixteen, wooed his muse in an invocation 'To Poesy', in which he said he realized that he would have to travel over 'the vasty seas | Of learning' before he could hope to win Poesy's favour. He reckoned he would have to become learned and fluent in classical and modern languages,

> And, in my own tongue, with no word amiss,
> For all its writers must be known to me.

Poetry was a community he could join by learning its language and getting to know its denizens. But not all of English writing was equally useful, attractive, or indeed available to the young man who set himself this ambitious curriculum. The literary history which can be inferred from what we know of Owen's reading is no smooth chronological procession but a bunched and straggling affair, with knots of concentration and great empty gaps, dictated by fashion, accident, his own developing taste, and the knack that poets have of finding what they need. No less earnestly than Keats did Owen desire to be among the English poets after his death. But the community of poetry, the tradition in which he set himself, was an order whose shape and membership changed with his changing literary theory, his sense of what poetry was and what it was for.

Every poet writes his own history of poetry. I shall deal with Owen's more or less chronologically, though it is important to be aware, of course, that this is not how it was formed; in Owen's literary education, Keats and Dickens come before Dante. And there is another kind of priority too. We can be pretty sure Owen would have agreed that Byron was a great poet and his own first cousin, Leslie Gunston, was not. But Gunston was a much more important poet for Owen than Byron was. His cousin's work may be fairly mediocre, but Owen's knowledge and judgement of it were important factors in his own stylistic formation, for it helped him to see and become the poet he wanted to be. So Leslie Gunston has a place in Wilfred Owen's history of poetry, while Byron does not.

First the classics. Owen studied Latin at school but it was already becoming 'tarnished' after a few months at Dunsden; an enthusiasm to learn classical Greek came to nothing (*CL* 140–1). He would have had to translate passages from the Latin authors at school,[1] but there is no evidence that he studied the classics outside the classroom, either in the original or in translation, or that he ever looked into Homer or Virgil on his own account. Still, he was well-versed in classical mythology, and had some Roman history from Shakespeare and Macaulay, as well as from his archaeological investigations. Physical beauty, especially that of boys, was often Greek to him, and so was the desire that beauty aroused, as in the fragment headed 'The cultivated Rose (from the Greek)' (*CPF* 465–6). An early sonnet, 'Perversity', claims to be able to see 'More loveliness in Grecian marbles clear | Than modern flesh', though at this stage it is unlikely Owen had seen very much of either. Nineteenth-century aesthetes, from Keats to Swinburne and Wilde, declared an allegiance to Hellenic art (and sometimes morals) partly as a strong alternative to Christian forms and standards. Owen too could be strategically pagan. 'The time was aeon' presents a conflict between classical Eros and Christian denial. In Bordeaux in 1914 Owen went to Midnight Mass on Christmas Eve, but wrote to reassure his mother that 'it would take a power of candle-grease and embroidery to romanize me. The question is to un-Greekize me' (*CL* 311). If there is here a disguised confession of a preference for 'Greek love', it was probably safe enough from Mrs Owen.

The next space in Owen's imaginary anthology or palace of art is for Dante, and this is really the first sign that something unusual is afoot. Although there was an English Romantic taste for Dante—at its most romantic and most English in Tennyson's 'Ulysses'—it is surprising, in view of the provincialism of the young Owen's cultural and religious horizons, to find Dante on his shelves so early, by 1913 if Harold Owen's memory serves (*JFO* 2. 71). Both the reason and perhaps the date of his coming to Dante may well be found in the period of his most sedulous aping of Keats, in

[1] In 1911 he won second prize from *Bible Society Gleanings* in a competition for translating a hymn from the Latin (*CL* 94).

1911–12. He read Dante, as Keats had done, in Cary's translation, entitled *The Vision, or, Hell, Purgatory, and Paradise of Dante Alighieri.*[2] In Owen's copy there are marks in the margin of cantos X to XIV of the *Inferno,* where Dante is in the seventh circle, the punishment of those who have done violence against their neighbour, themselves, God, or nature. It seems fairly certain that Owen had read canto XV too, Dante's meeting with Brunetto Latini, which seems to be remembered in 'Strange Meeting'. How much more he read, and whether he ever got beyond the *Inferno*, must be a chance to guess.[3]

The Dante whose presence is felt in Owen's writings is the poet of visionary descent and reporter of anguish. Owen's work keeps returning to images of a bodily descent into hell. 'Supposed Confessions of a Secondrate Sensitive Mind in Dejection', drafted in 1911 or 1912, had imagined being dragged off to torment by 'vile devil-broods', and the theme of an underground (or its variant, an underwater) descent into horror runs all the way through to the late 'Spring Offensive'. Dominic Hibberd describes Owen's underworld as 'an obsessive but not very scholarly compound of the classical Hades, Dante's *Inferno*, Tannhäuser's Venusburg, and the Hell familiar to an ex-Evangelical' (*OTP* 166), and already before the war it seems to have been a recurring image in the poet's dreams. Of course the Evangelical child knew plenty about hell before he had heard of Dante. Dante leaves his particular mark on Owen, I think, in vocality—in the bold use of dialogue (actual or implied), the pattern of prompting and explication or narrative found in 'Inspection', 'Mental Cases', 'A Terre', 'Strange Meeting', and even in the quiet interrogation of the dead in 'Miners'. Such exchanges are the motor of Dante's drama. There is a good deal of speaking in Owen, and especially later, in the form of Dantesque confrontations in which a life is weighed in the balance. Dante's example had been one way out of the droning Romantic monologues of Owen's adolescence. (The forty-one poems which Owen's cousin, Leslie Gunston, published in 1917 as *The Nymph and Other Poems* contained, in all, a single line of speech.)

Another aspect of Dante which seems to be remembered creatively

[2] Owen's copy, with the rest of his books, is in the English Faculty Library, Oxford University.

[3] Dominic Hibberd (*OTP* 215) notices that Owen confused *Inferno* and *Purgatorio*, using both terms to describe the war zone (*CL* 425, 440).

in Owen's poetry is physical. Dante is the most bodily of poets and the fierce body language of the *Inferno*—there is not really anything like it in English—is also spoken in Owen's notations of intense staring, vivid and ghastly faces, stretching out of arms, writhing, rolling, flinching, shrinking, clutching, wounding, and mutilation. Owen could learn from Dante that pain was a subject for poetry. He could further learn from Dante's high seriousness that the poet was a witness, and his words could be a matter of life and death. Owen's inferno, however, lacks the triumphant faith that overarches Dante's.

The Dantesque in Owen was not all imbibed at source. Some of it came filtered through the latter visions of Keats's Hyperion poems and Shelley, and even through the genteel piety of Lewis Morris's *The Epic of Hades* (1879).[4] But it was the sights, sounds, and smells of war that must have seemed the most powerful reminders of Dante. Owen would have read this, in the great battle chapter of Henri Barbusse's novel *Le Feu*, which Sassoon put into his hands at Craiglockhart, in the translation by Fitzwater Wray.

> We arrive at last on the summit, which is marked as with a signal by a wounded and frightful man. He is upright in the wind, shaken but upright, enrooted there. In his uplifted and wind-tossed cape we see a yelling and convulsive face. We pass by him, and he is a sort of screaming tree.[5]

Owen (and doubtless Barbusse) had first met the image of a screaming human tree in the *Inferno*, in canto XIII (one of those marked by Owen) in which Dante comes to the forest of suicides. But Barbusse offers the image as neither allegory nor dream, but a documentary detail in a realist narrative.[6] George Steiner discusses in *In Bluebeard's Castle* the way twentieth-century European history has sometimes seemed both to parody and make literal the medieval imaginings of hell. When Owen made a poem of a memory or a dream of the terrible war landscape of 1917, beginning 'My soul looked down from a vague height, with Death,' he described the exhausted, stinking, calamitous prospect with the

[4] See Bäckman, *Tradition Transformed*, 104.

[5] Barbusse, *Under Fire*, 273. Owen seems to have read the novel first in the Fitzwater Wray translation, and later in the original French. Jon Glover discusses Owen's reading of the novel in his article 'Owen, Barbusse and Fitzwater Wray'.

[6] See Jonathan King, 'Henri Barbusse: *Le Feu* and the Crisis of Social Realism', in Klein (ed.), *The First World War in Fiction*, 43–52.

kind of appalled fascination with which Dante, with Virgil, looks down from 'the utmost verge of a high bank' (canto XI, Cary's translation), through the 'horrible excess | Of fetid exhalation', at the dreadful country before him. It is the seventh circle of hell. Owen called his poem 'The Show', but he had originally entitled it 'Vision', perhaps in recognition not only of the first chapter ('The Vision') of Barbusse's novel but also of the book he possessed which bore the title *The Vision . . . of Dante Alighieri.*[7]

He found Chaucer 'delightful', he said (*CL* 344), but Owen's Middle Ages are almost entirely the product of the nineteenth century, the picturesque and costumed romance on which British Romanticism rests. Walter Scott had been an early favourite. It seems from an 'Extract from ye Chronicles of Wilfred de Salope, Knight', a jocular piece which appeared in the *Hydra* in September 1917, that Owen could churn out medieval pastiche with the same facility as pseudo-biblical stuff. The previous month he had been working on a 'Ballad of Lady Yolande', an imitation of Scott's manner which soon turned into a facetious parody.[8] There is as much enjoyment in the 'Ballad' of 'archaic' language as of the colourful properties, the bowers and chargers and silken vests and 'falding-stool', which provide its pre-Raphaelite furniture.

Owen had first studied Spenser's *Faerie Queene* at school, but it was more often in latter-day romances like *Marmion*, 'The Eve of St Agnes', and especially Tennyson's Arthurian poems that he found and enjoyed the glamour of chivalry. It was a romance which, since its nineteenth-century revival, was still embedded in the western European imagination of war. Owen tried it out half-humorously for a moment in a letter from Bordeaux, in the second month of the war.

Fifty thousand extra people are here! It is easy to recognise Parisians. In certain streets pass a dream of fair women. The populace grumbles that *chic* toilets should still be worn; but if not for such gentle ladies, what on earth is the Fighting about? It is the old story of the Lists: the Princess sits in flowers, while the warriors scuffle about in the ring. (*CL* 284.)

[7] Jon Stallworthy makes the convincing case that the poem referred to in two letters (*CL* 512, 514) as 'Vision' is what came to be called 'The Show' (*CPF* 156).

[8] Owen was in the romantic habit of adapting his reading to places: thus he read Scott at Kelso and again in Edinburgh, Shelley by the Thames, Wordsworth at Keswick.

An all too familiar arc of disillusion leads from the rhetorical question here to the cripple in 'Disabled' who enlisted to please his girlfriend, and the doomed soldiers in 'The Send-Off' who 'mock what women meant | Who gave them flowers'. The innocent Princess who sits in flowers was to have a disturbing metamorphosis in the late poem, 'The Kind Ghosts', as the dreaming lady in her terraced and tapestried palace, where roses flower out of the blood of boys and the walls are made of corpses; the image had become *fin de siècle* as the politics had become cynical.

The young Owen read and studied more of Shakespeare than of any other poet, and this is not surprising. Shakespeare was the glory of English, an important symbol of national prestige and a pillar of the curriculum; what was more, his supremacy was endorsed by Owen's admired Keats. Owen studied the plays at school—an exercise book mentions at least ten in only three months of 1907 (*WO* 40)—and seems to have used the essay topic 'The Ideal English King' to show off his knowledge of *Henry V* in his matriculation exam for London University in September 1911 (*CL* 79–80). In France in 1915 he was teaching Shakespeare—*Richard III* and *Hamlet*—to his pupils at Mérignac (*CL* 320). He saw a number of Shakespeare productions on stage—the national poet seems to have been exempted from Susan Owen's Evangelical distrust of the theatre—and even had a walk-on part in a scene of *The Merchant of Venice* at the Craiglockhart Hospital in July 1917, though his mother had to be prudently reassured that the two professional actresses in the production were 'model wives, no less than model women' (*CL* 479). It would be satisfying to report that Portia's plea for compassion (say), or the fortunes of the expeditionary force in *Henry V*—a play Owen had 'read, and learnt, and spouted' in his last two years at school (*CL* 82)—left a legible mark on Owen's own writing. But in fact, though Bäckman may be right to say that Owen studied some of Shakespeare's sonnets very closely,[9] Shakespeare is not an important visible presence in Owen, however deeply interfused in the rhythmic bloodstream of the English iambic line which Owen favoured. He is infrequently mentioned and quoted in the wartime letters. Discovering *The Old Huntsman and Other Poems* in 1917, Owen declared that nothing like Sassoon's trench-life sketches had ever

[9] Bäckman, *Tradition Transformed*, 37–8.

been written. 'Shakespeare reads vapid after these. Not of course because Sassoon is the greater artist, but because of the subjects, I mean' (*CL* 484–5). And no doubt he means just what he says. Sassoon's influence starts to pour into Owen's work from this point; 'The Dead-Beat' was drafted less than a week later, in a deliberate imitation of Sassoon. If we look for Shakespeare in Owen's war poetry, it must be for less obvious and perhaps less conscious echoes, of which I offer a single instance as an example.

The worldly Mme Léger, Owen's pupil in France in 1914, seems to have found her young tutor attractive. At thirty-one, and the mother of an eleven-year-old daughter with whom Owen liked to play, she was 'a surpassingly fair and dangerous woman' in his opinion (*CL* 279), and she alarmed and excited him with her 'Coquetterie' (*CL* 278). But a couple of months later, describing his pleasure when sometimes a boy playing in the Jardin Public would come up to him, hat in hand, just in order to talk to him, Owen wrote that such incidents gave him hope 'that the Léger episodes have not taken the bloom off my innocency' (*CL* 288). 'Bloom'—in the idiom 'to take the bloom off' something—refers to the greyish powdery deposit on the skin of a grape or plum, which comes off when the fruit is touched; but it is difficult to see or hear the word and completely ignore its more common meaning of 'blossom'. Now this tiny drama of young male innocence, in the emblem of 'bloom', threatened by older female corruption, must have been quickly forgotten, but not completely. Three years later at Craiglockhart, Owen was engaged in the serious business of working out the climax of a poem, 'Dulce et Decorum Est', about a gassed soldier, his dying body flung into the back of a wagon:

> If you could hear, at every jolt, the blood
> Come gargling from the froth-corrupted lungs,
> Obscene as cancer, bitter as the cud
> Of vile, incurable sores on innocent tongues,—
> My friend, you would not tell with such high zest
> To children ardent for some desperate glory,
> The old Lie: Dulce et decorum est
> Pro patria mori.

Four complete drafts of this poem survive, all with corrections (*CPF* 292–7). The earlier versions have the lines:

And think how, once, his face was like a bud,
Fresh as a country rose, and pure [also *clean/clear/keen*], and young,—

which Owen eventually cancelled, substituting:

> Obscene as cancer, bitter as the cud
> Of vile, incurable sores on innocent tongues,—

and this is an improvement, to be sure. But if we assemble these images—the youth like a pure unopened rose; the painful and revolting blemish on innocence; and (from the earlier and unrelated passage) the immodest attempt to 'take off' innocency's bloom—if we assemble these pieces as a palaeontologist assembles his finds we can posit, I think, a single buried textual ancestor. It is *Hamlet* III. iv., 40–4:

> Such an act
> That blurs the grace and blush of modesty,
> Calls virtue hypocrite, takes off the rose
> From the fair forehead of an innocent love
> And sets a blister there.

Thus Hamlet, in his mother's bedroom, accusing her of an act of betrayal which has corrupted the whole world for him. Who is responsible for the disfiguring and death of Owen's soldier? The poem was originally inscribed 'To a certain Poetess', Jessie Pope, who specialized in verse that exhorted lads to join the forces. Here (though painted out of the later version) was another specimen of the corrupting older woman, and she can be glimpsed again in a mother-and-child group at the end of the poem:

> you would not tell with such high zest
> To children [also *small boys*] ardent for some desperate glory,
> The old Lie . . .

When she should be protecting their innocence she is telling them lies, and will hand them over to be despoiled. The confusion and hurt and reproach of Hamlet's words, in their perhaps unconscious haunting of the second part of 'Dulce et Decorum Est', seem to shine a momentary light into the depths of Owen's feelings about women and about his mother in particular. Who really stands accused in this poem, and of what betrayal? If my textual speculation is justified, the over-determined return of this moment in *Hamlet* points to ways in which the codes of poetry and of family were entangled at a profound level of language, complex and perhaps in the end inexplicable. It is also a reminder of how blunt an instrument is encased in our usual assumptions about literary 'influence'.

Owen showed few signs of interest in the writers of the sixteenth and seventeenth centuries—Elizabethan lyricists, Ben Jonson, Jacobean dramatists, and metaphysical poets—who were gaining a renewed respect from the makers of modernist poetry and modernist taste in England before and during the war. After Shakespeare, for Owen, came Milton, for whom he showed not much enthusiasm. Milton is brushed aside in a letter to Leslie Gunston in July 1915: 'I still hold the violin capable of "better" i.e. more essential, music than the organ, and *shall do* while I hold Keats a more poetical poet than Milton' (*CL* 350). This musical preference encodes the idea that essential, 'poetical' poetry is a lyrical and expressive instrument rather than an epic and public one: the choice of violin over organ, the pagan Keats over the Christian Milton, is also a restatement of allegiance to what was secular and pleasurable in art rather than to what was religious and improving.

Whether or not he laboured through *Paradise Lost* in his copy of Milton's *Poetical Works*, Owen's annotations and marginal markings (as Sven Bäckman noticed)[10] are confined to shorter, lyrical pieces—the 'Nativity Ode', 'Il Penseroso' and 'L'Allegro', and 'Lycidas'. The last was an important poem for him, and I shall discuss it later, along with Gray's 'Elegy Written in a Country Churchyard', when I turn to Owen's rewriting of elegy. It is a reflection of the middlebrow taste of his time that Gray's 'Elegy', the most famous poem in the English language, is the only one to have left a mark on Owen between Milton and the *Lyrical Ballads* of Wordsworth and Coleridge. He possessed, and so probably knew, some of the poetry of Pope, Swift, Johnson, Cowper, and Burns; yet with the exception of Gray's 'Elegy', the poetry (and the novels) of the decorous and unromantic eighteenth century might as well have been a closed book.[11]

[10] Ibid. 40.

[11] It was a long-standing prejudice. On the evidence of the exercise books of 1907–8, according to Hibberd, 'His teacher seems to have had a particular interest in the Romantics, although she wrote "Too strong!" against a 1908 comment that the eighteenth century had lacked "imagination and moral nature"' (*OTP* 1).

The history of English writing, if we were to infer it only from the evidence of Owen's reading, could be seen to swell out to its full stretch only in the nineteenth century, filled with the Romantic afflatus of Wordsworth and Coleridge, Scott, Keats and Shelley, Tennyson, the Brownings, Swinburne; for prose there were Dickens, Ruskin, Stevenson, the Victorian men of letters. The taste of Owen's generation was formed in what Bäckman describes and discusses as 'the Romantic–Victorian poetic tradition' in English,[12] and there was nothing in Owen's education and early experience (if we discount for the moment his reading in French), and next to nothing in his own writing before 1917, to unsettle Romantic–Victorian tastes and practices. Everyone knows that Owen's war writings eventually came to take a challenging and sometimes hostile posture towards that tradition, but it took his first-hand experience of warfare to expose what came to seem its inadequacies and dishonesties. The war was the bleak unforgiving critic that caused the foliage of Romanticism to wither for Owen; without that experience, he might have been as content to sport in its comfortable shade as his cousin, and fellow poet, Leslie Gunston.

There is, as a matter of fact, a document that can give some idea of the sort of poet Owen might have become in different (and, it might be said, luckier) circumstances. The amiable Leslie Gunston was Owen's first cousin and his closest boyhood friend. They had family circumstances, religious upbringing, and poetic enthusiasms in common. The Gunston parents and four children were rather better off than the Owens, but Leslie and Wilfred had been brought up to the same habits and values—Leslie's Evangelical mother was Susan Owen's sister—and were often together; they shared a taste for natural history, music, and the arts, they corresponded about poetry, and, in 1916 and 1917, they wrote and exchanged sonnets on at least ten chosen subjects.[13] Leslie's health ruled out enlistment, and he was working as a trainee architect. He was a conventionally patriotic young man. His first and only book, *The Nymph and Other Poems*, published in November 1917 and dedicated to Wilfred Owen, is the nearest we could hope to an experimental control. Not too fancifully, this might be the work

[12] Bäckman, *Tradition Transformed*, 23–62.

[13] See Hibberd, '"Rival Pieces on a Chosen Theme"' and *OTP* 62–3. Olwen Joergens, a friend of the Gunstons and at the time 'a slight, dreamy girl of nineteen' (*WO* 126) was the third partner in this scheme.

of Wilfred Owen without experience of the life and language of the army.

The forms and feelings of *The Nymph*, and its furniture of imagery, constitute a small but pretty representative anthology of the sweeter tastes of the Romantic–Victorian tradition. Its emphasis is on music. There are several poems on musical subjects, and a constant attention to a lyrical melopoeia which Owen would have called 'poetical', and which is above all the mark of Swinburne, whose fingerprints are, as it were, all over *The Nymph*. One of the more accomplished poems in the book is entitled 'Ode, in Memory of a Birthday, April 5th 1837', and it ends with a flourish:

> April buds and the flowers of Maytime
> Weave him a crown that will not fade;
> All the colours and scents of the daytime
> All the seas at his feet are laid.—
> So give praise for a gift not mortal,
> Love-songs sweeter than love could be,
> Hitherward heard of the purple portal,
> Sung this side of the sea.

Owen told his cousin that this 'Ode for A.C.S.' was one of his favourites (*CL* 510). It is a small but perhaps telling point about this genteel volume that, although Leslie Gunston celebrates (and imitates) Swinburne, he does not quite dare to speak his name, but enciphers his master coyly in that birth-date. The well-brought-up young author of *The Nymph* was not ready to claim kin, in a public way, with the still not quite respectable author of 'Dolores'.

Swinburne was an Owen enthusiasm too; he was still reading him at the very end of his life. All the poetic ancestors that haunt *The Nymph* are Owen's also, but Leslie Gunston shows no sign of having read either Dante, or anything much written since 1900, though he did, apparently, take some interest in contemporary verse. Swinburne gives Gunston some metrical variety and the occasional happy bounce (but not the risk-taking in matters of taste which Owen took from him). He is probably also responsible for *The Nymph*'s besetting vice of relentless alliteration ('Such sylvan solitudes of shine and shade!' ('An Incident'); 'Rich, radiant, royal, rapturous and romantic!' ('Purple')). There are other phrases that show what else Gunston (and Owen) liked to read—'long level wastes of sandy earth' recalls Shelley's 'Ozymandias';

'Full-throated harmonies' is a half-echo of Keats's 'Nightingale'; 'pearl-pale light' is borrowed from early Yeats. These are individual instances; but the whole collection is struck through with the aesthetic of Romantic poetry (and painting and music), as the sunlight creates the scene in this not untypical stanza from the poem 'Sea Pictures':

> A saffron shimmer shines above the sun,
> A rosy glow suffuses all the pearl
> And strikes upon their outermost edge and rim
> Great banks of cloud, plum-colour, out at sea.
> A streak of molten gold slips through the pearl
> And smites the sea as with a magic wand,
> And glitters from the sea-line to the beach
> In a long bright line of lucent light,
> Shining and sparkling on the soft moist sand
> As burnished copper in the noonday sun.

Owen does not have this sort of patience with an unpeopled landscape, but he was quite capable of writing as poetically as this, and more. From its alliterative opening, Gunston's stanza is overdressed, loaded down with poetical properties and all too predictable epithets. Although he has tried to describe carefully the scene before him, he ends up with a cliché in almost every line; an established kind of poetic language is guiding his pen and perhaps his gaze. It would take a larger talent to do something new with a subject—actually two subjects, seascape and sunrise—so exhausted by Romantic artists that it virtually writes itself, running on smooth rails from rosy glow to burnished copper (or something very like it). 'Sea Pictures' belongs, as the title almost confesses, to the genre of the holiday water-colour; and the subject has been selected because this is the sort of thing people write poetry (or paint pictures) about.

And so were these: 'Spring Time', 'The Sea', 'Harmony', 'Le Baiser', 'Mountains at Sunset', 'The Colosseum', 'Chopin', 'Thine Eyes', 'Remembrances', 'L'Amour', 'Nippon', 'A Hymn of Love to England', among other titles in *The Nymph*. When the two cousins had agreed in 1916 to write sonnets together, the topics they thought appropriate were 'Purple', 'Music', 'The End', 'Golden Hair', 'Happiness', 'Sunrise', 'How do I love thee?', 'Fate', 'Beauty', and 'Attar of Roses' (*OTP* 62). These titles indicate the scope of the poetic for the two young men, the kind of things poets ought to be attending to. To be fair, Owen's range (as the teleological poems testify) was never quite as short as Leslie Gunston's, who never ventured far from the shallows of the proven poetical—colours, jewellery, England, perfumes, vegetation, the sea and the mountains, the happy past, romantic places, classical legend, and thinking about kissing girls. Gunston's subjects are, without any exception, beautiful things, and his emotional reach is confined to enjoying, remembering, anticipating, and sometimes missing what is beautiful. There are very few people in *The Nymph*, and they do not have very much to do—those girls, for example (usually 'maids') synecdochically shrunk, more often than not, to a pair of lips (or, in a phrase Owen said he admired (*CP* 510), 'Her lips! red as the dawn of doubtful days'). There is (with one momentary exception) only one voice in *The Nymph*; and I am not sure there are any ideas at all. The whole collection, it is quite accurate to say, is purely lyrical.

Leslie Gunston was preparing these poems for print just at the time when his cousin was rejecting, in theory and in practice, many of the qualities they embodied so cheerfully. In August 1917 he had declared for Sassoon over even Shakespeare, 'because of the subjects' (*CL* 484). *The Nymph* was published in November. In January Owen was defending in a letter another Georgian, whom Leslie Gunston seems to have disparaged. 'Graves's technique is perfect. Did Poetry ever stand still? You can hark back if you like, and be deliberately archaic, but don't make yourself a lagoon, salved from the ebbing tide of the Victorian Age' (*CL* 526). At this time, Owen's allegiance within the company of poets was shifting with his practice. Gunston's *The Nymph* was published in the same month as Graves's *Fairies and Fusiliers*, and Owen was in correspondence with both authors. 'Apologia Pro Poemate Meo' has both in mind. It may be in part a response to Graves's advice, in a letter in December, that Owen should 'For God's sake cheer up and write more optimistically—The war's not ended yet but a poet should have a spirit above wars' (*CL* 596). It is certainly a self-assessment prompted by his young cousin's launching as a published poet (Owen had published nothing), and by his recognition at the same time of the inadequacies of his cousin's work. It was a recognition sharpened—perhaps enabled—by seeing *The Nymph* through the eyes of his new fellows (he sent Sassoon a copy); but it was a painful recognition too, because it involved in some measure disowning his own past as a poet, and the snapping of another link that bound him to his family. 'Apologia' is audibly in dialogue with two poets and two kinds of poetry, the 'old song' of Leslie Gunston and the Georgian realism of Graves. You can hear the negotiations as Owen distances himself from one and orientates himself by the other. Leslie Gunston's volume had included a poem on love, 'L'Amour':

> Love is the binding of souls together,
> The binding of lips, the binding of eyes,
> As great as the sea in windy weather,
> As strong as the breeze that sweeps the skies.[14]

But Owen had been reading a poem in *Fairies and Fusiliers* which he knew was addressed to Sassoon, and which used a different kind of language. 'By wire and wood and stake we're bound', Graves had declared in 'Two Fusiliers', and 'Show me the two so closely bound | As we, by the wet bond of blood.' In his own 'Apologia' Owen brought these discourses together in a dialogue with both poets:

> I have made fellowships—
> Untold of happy lovers in old song.
> For love is not the binding of fair lips
> With the soft silk of eyes that look and long,
> By Joy, whose ribbon slips,—
> But wound with war's hard wire whose stakes are strong;
> Bound with the bandage of the arm that drips;
> Knit in the webbing of the rifle-thong.

So Gunston is silenced by Graves, within Owen's style (as is the Keats of the odes, the poet of 'happy love' and personified Joy), but not absolutely:

> I have perceived much beauty
> In the hoarse oaths that kept our courage straight;
> Heard music in the silentness of duty;
> Found peace where shell-storms spouted reddest spate.

[14] 'L'Amour', with its infelicitous 'binding of eyes', is again trumped in Owen's 'Greater Love'—'O Love, your eyes lose lure | When I behold eyes *blinded* in my stead!' [my italics].

'Beauty' and 'Music', both titles in *The Nymph* which had been among the topics the cousins agreed to write about, were still on Owen's agenda, but on his own terms and in his own time.

The importance of Leslie Gunston for Owen sits rather untidily in the textualist framework in which literary 'influence' is usually considered, for the dialectic between the two poets was a tangle of highly personal, social, aesthetic, and political factors. Owen's lack of enthusiasm for *The Nymph* was related to his having found a friend at last, Sassoon, who meant more to him than his family. His disappointment with his cousin had as much to do with a growing impatience with Leslie's conduct—his non-combatant support of the war—as with his style, his traditionalist 'Victorian' lyric complacency, with its subliminal assurance that everything was all right in an England that Owen was coming to think was all wrong.

Owen's relationship with Gunston in 1917–18 was not only with the author of the poems but with the whole man—naturally, since they were cousins and old friends. But for the romantically educated and biography-hungry Owen, a response to any poet that mattered to him was likely to mean a conscious personal relationship with the whole man, or with what he could know of the whole man (or woman). It was not simply a textual encounter; or rather, the text encountered was not only a poet's poems but everything that could be known or surmised about him, from his extra-literary opinions to his handwriting and his physical appearance. Arguably, Keats's tuberculosis was a more important factor than his 'Ode on a Grecian Urn' in the formation of what Keats meant to Wilfred Owen. Owen first turned against Tennyson in 1917, not out of dissatisfaction with his poetry but after reading his biography (*CL* 482). In studying poetic influences on Wilfred Owen we shall have to be ready to dig for a phenomenon more earthbound and less clean-cut than the angelic psychomachia investigated by Harold Bloom in *The Anxiety of Influence*, in which the poem of the poet engages with (by misreading) the poem of his precursor, in a vacuum of circumstances. Bloom announces from the start that he is interested in poetic influence as 'the story of intrapoetic relationships'. He is quite willing to acknowledge that poets are subject to influences not purely poetical, but his concern, he says, 'is only with *the poet in a poet*, or the aboriginal poetic self'.[15] In the terms of my enquiry this is an essence that does not really exist.

In assessing the importance of (say) Keats for Owen, it would hardly be possible to separate the impact of the poems from the impact of the life, or to separate either of these from the impact of the reputation. It was an influence which was interpoetic (not just intrapoetic), circumstantial, and contextual, and it had a communal dimension too. A poet rarely comes either single-handed or empty-handed to an encounter with a precursor. Owen first read Keats under the guidance of an enthusiastic schoolteacher, and his subsequent reading was itself influenced by accounts of Keats's life (Owen knew at least three) and by the way his work was presented and judged by biographers, literary historians, anthologists, and other men of letters. For Owen's generation the great writers of the Romantic-Victorian tradition were served up gently simmering in the climate of taste they had helped to form.

It was a taste that recognized little distinction between the poet's life and his writings. The age of Romanticism was also the age of heroes and hero-worship. Poets were great and exemplary men and women, as Stopford Brooke explained in the first sentence of a book which Owen read at Dunsden in 1912:

> The History of English Literature is the story of what great English men and women thought and felt, and then wrote down in good prose and beautiful poetry in the English language . . . Every English man and woman has good reason to be proud of the work done by their forefathers in prose and poetry.[16]

As Stopford Brooke lucidly shows, an essentially expressive theory underlay a largely biographical criticism (supporting, incidentally, a nationalistic history), and it is not surprising to find Owen responding aesthetically and emotionally as much to the person of his poets as to their writings. He greatly admired Elizabeth Barrett Browning, and claimed to be able to hear her voice as he read her poems, and to have seen her 'palpably in visions' (*CL* 481). He underlined physical descriptions of the young poets in books on Keats and Shelley.[17] He told his mother that he was 'in love

[15] Bloom, *The Anxiety of Influence*, 1, 11.

[16] Stopford Brooke, *English Literature*, 3.

[17] See Owen's copies of Colvin's *Keats* and Symonds's *Shelley*, in the English Faculty Library, Oxford.

with' Keats (*CL* 187). You could dismiss that 1913 confession as mawkish (he was just past his teens), but the phrase seems as good as another to describe what he would come to feel about Siegfried Sassoon in 1917.

So in considering the impact of other writers on Owen we have to go beyond the hunt for verbal reminiscences and even the transmission of images and ideas, not into the Bloomian realm of the textual unconscious but out into a form of virtual social activity. Naïve as it may appear, Owen took his poets for friends and, occasionally, enemies. For the lapsed Evangelical, the company of poets began to bear a resemblance to a sort of secular communion of saints. They were exemplary figures (which was why 'the true poets must be truthful') but they were not only examples of how to write. The history of English poetry inscribed in Owen's writing becomes, as it enters the Romantic period, biographical and ethical. In his troubling contact with the poor at Dunsden, for example, he seems to have looked to Wordsworth and Shelley for guidance. Poets could teach you how to live. Owen remembered that even as a boy he had guessed 'that the fullest, largest liveable life was that of a poet' (*CL* 325). His admiration for Sassoon—which cannot be exaggerated—was as much for the older poet's conduct as for his poems. Owen's return to the front line in 1918 was a most fatal tribute to Sassoon's example, as well as a recognition that sometimes the authority (and so the meaning) of a poet's writing could not be independent of the circumstances—in this case the military circumstances—of his life.

In turning now to the case of Keats and Shelley, Owen's most important poets before Sassoon, my concern will be less with textual echoes and adaptations (an area in which Owen scholarship has been particularly strong)[18] than with the impact on Owen of the lives of these poets and of the critical and literary-historical accentuation in which their voices came wrapped. Owen came to Keats as a teenager, and his youthful enthusiasm took the form of identification. He persuaded himself that Keats's handwriting, in manuscripts on display in the British Museum, resembled his own (*CL* 82). I would not rule out the possibility that Owen was drawn to Keats partly because they were both small. He certainly

[18] For example in Breen's 'Wilfred Owen's "Greater Love"', Bäckman's *Tradition Transformed*, *CPF*, Graham's *The Truth of Poetry*, and *OTP*.

felt he knew all about the financial constraints that set a frustrating limit on Keats's education, and he may also have fancied a sympathetic echo in Keats's social insecurity. Owen marked, in his copy of Colvin's *Keats*, Leigh Hunt's opinion that 'Keats, being a little too sensitive on the score of his origin, felt inclined to see in every man of birth a sort of natural enemy.'[19]

For many Victorians Keats was both the high priest of beauty and a cult object himself. Owen was eighteen when he read Sidney Colvin's rather dangerous advice to young poets to learn from Keats's example 'the endeavour after a continual positive poetic richness and felicity of phrase'.[20] Two years later he came across Stopford Brooke's work, which attributed to Keats's 'the love of loveliness for its own sake', and declared that 'in the singleness of worship which he gave to Beauty, Keats is especially the ideal poet.'[21] It is in this role that Keats is often present, as a subject and as a model, in Owen's juvenilia in the years before he went to France.

But if Keats stood for beauty, he also and equally stood for friendship or brotherhood. This is the second great theme of the Victorian account of Keats, and is still prominent in the first and longest chapter, 'Keats and his Friends', of Edward Thomas's study of Keats, which Owen read during his army training. The story of Keats was a story of suffering and of loyalties—loyalty among the circle of like-minded young friends that Owen in his intellectual isolation had reason to envy; the loyalty of John Keats to his dying brother Tom; of the faithful Severn to Keats himself in his last illness; and of Shelley in his tribute to Keats's spirit in 'Adonais'. The emotional meanings of Keats's life were profoundly imprinted on the young Owen's imagination; and Keats, Severn, and Shelley provided him with a repertoire of roles that his own later career would assume. He himself was to become the doomed youth, the ministering comrade, the indignant memorialist. Poetry was bound up with friendship. Colvin had praised Keats's 'beautiful unselfishness and warmth of sympathy'.[22] Keats inspired love to the last. 'Two friends alone,' exclaimed Stopford Brooke, 'but they, tender as Cordelia, lived for him and tended him to the last; but it is beyond all noble compassion to think that the lover of beauty died in his youth, while as yet his revelation to us was but

[19] Colvin, *Keats*, 39. [20] Ibid. 219.
[21] Stopford Brooke, *English Literature*, 161. [22] Colvin, *Keats*, 213.

begun.'[23] These are the sentiments, though not quite the language, of 'Greater Love' and 'Strange Meeting'. And in his *Life and Writings of John Keats*, William Michael Rossetti, after quoting Severn's harrowing account of his friend's last days, concludes: 'No words of mine shall be added here to tarnish upon the mirror of memory this image of a sacred death and a sacred friendship.'[24]

There was ample and authoritative precedent, then, for thinking of Keats's death as a tragic play or a religious image, as Owen was to do. That death itself was a thing of beauty for the young Owen; it excited him.

> Last week . . . I got W. M. Rossetti's *Life of Keats*, and, though he is horribly crabby over the early poems, throws more light on the Life & Character than I have obtained from Sidney Colvin. I cannot read either for long without getting wound up. I have more than once turned hot and cold and trembly over the first haemorrhage scene; and sobbed over Severn's 'He is gone . . .'
>
> But I never guessed till now the frightful travail of his soul towards Death; never came so near laying hold of the ghastly horror of his mind at this time. Rossetti guided my groping hand right into the wound, and I touched, for one moment the incandescent Heart of Keats. (*CL* 160–1.)

This feverish passage belongs to September 1912, two years before Owen's visit to the war hospital in Bordeaux and more than four years before he himself went to war. The hand groping into the wound probably comes from the story of the doubting apostle Thomas and the resurrected Christ in St John's gospel, chapter 22 ('reach hither thy hand, and thrust it into my side; and be not faithless, but believing'). In this way Keats in agony is linked to what we have seen as the earlier source of Owen's imagery of the wounded body in Christian iconography. But the combined elements of this complex of image and feeling, which was to be so vital in the history of Owen's imagination—the stricken body of the beautiful young man, done to death (Shelley had claimed) by the envious and unimaginative old; the blood-coughing 'scene' (imagery of bloody mouths recurs in 'Long ages past', 'Has your soul sipped?', 'I saw his round mouth's crimson', 'Dulce et Decorum Est', 'S.I.W.', 'Greater Love', 'The Kind Ghosts'); the love and the helplessness of the friend who is minister and witness; and finally

[23] Stopford Brooke, *Studies in Poetry*, 253.
[24] Rossetti, *Life and Writings of John Keats*, 63.

the mixture of arousal and horror, of pity and terror and fascination, of death itself—all these themes first became present to Owen in his reading of Victorian biography, years before he saw a battlefield. Keats's overt influence was to dwindle after a few years, but the important lines of communication had been established in Owen's imagination, the lines linking the themes of which Keats's last illness was a sort of abiding allegory—poetry and pathos, male friendship and beauty and death.

After Keats came Shelley—because of 'Adonais', and because a comparison between the two was almost obligatory among writers on Keats. Setting them beside the work of Shelley, Stopford Brooke had to admit that Keats's masterpieces had 'no political, religious, social elements'.[25] W. M. Rossetti decided Shelley was 'superior beyond all reasonable terms of comparison'.[26] It was inevitable that the admirer of Keats should become curious about Shelley, especially when he found himself living not far from Shelley's cottage at Marlow in the Thames valley. Indeed Shelley was Owen's most important poet in the Dunsden period, and Owen scholars from Welland to Bäckman and Hibberd have given due attention to the presence of Shelley in the war poems (most notably in 'Strange Meeting'). But what kind of poet was the Shelley that Owen knew? As Paul Foot vigorously shows in *Red Shelley*, the poet's reputation was and remains an ideological battlefield.

Owen first mentions Shelley in a letter from Dunsden at the beginning of 1912:

> I find that Shelley lived at a cottage within easy cycling distance from here. And I was very surprised (tho' really I don't know why) to find that he used to 'visit the sick in their beds; kept a regular list of the industrious poor whom he assisted to make up their accounts;' and for a time walked the hospitals in order to be more useful to the poor he visited! I *knew* the lives of men who produced such marvellous verse could not be otherwise than lovely, and I am being confirmed in this continually. (CL 106.)

Again, the poet was a model of conduct as much as of writing, for the two things were really one. Here was proof that, as John Addington Symonds said elsewhere in the book that Owen quotes here, 'Shelley's life and his poetry are indissolubly connected.'[27]

[25] Stopford Brooke, *Studies in Poetry*, 202.
[26] Rossetti, *Life and Writings of John Keats*, 232.
[27] Symonds, *Shelley*, 182.

The Shelley whom Owen was coming to know was a member of that Romantic generation whose 'soft Lydian airs' were at this time his poetic ideal (*CL* 136), and before long Owen had to admit that Shelley was 'the brightest genius of his time', Keats notwithstanding (*CL* 112). The elevation of this new hero coincides (but it is not a coincidence) with Owen's disaffection at Dunsden. For him, part of the point of the story of Shelley's charitable works lies in its contrast with the lordly and aloof vicar of Dunsden. The example of Shelley gave important support to Owen's rebellion against the Church (which he was to liken to Shelley's 'running away from College' (*CL* 175)) and particularly to his hostility to St Paul's strictures. The clash, in 'The time was aeon', between Hellenic beauty and Pauline repression, in a dream landscape, owes a good deal to Shelley both in imagery and ideas. Owen read, in Symonds, Leigh Hunt's remark that Shelley 'drew a distinction between the Pauline presentation of the Christian creeds, and the spirit of the Gospels ... His want of faith in the letter, and his exceeding faith in the spirit of Christianity, formed a comment, the one on the other, very formidable to those who choose to forget what Scripture itself observes on that point.'[28] But this acknowledgement of Shelley's running battle with the Church is carefully put, and it becomes the basis for an act of recuperation. A Victorian taste in love with his lyricism found ways of negotiating the awkward problem of Shelley's militant atheism. It seems not to have rippled the serenity of the Revd Stopford Brooke, who declared in the inaugural lecture of the Shelley Society in 1886: 'The world will always be drawn to Shelley for the religious gravity of his teaching.'[29]

While Shelley's example gave Owen courage in his own quarrel with the Church, the Victorian version of Shelley (as a sort of honorary Christian nevertheless) also helped him to qualify his apostasy and leave the church door ajar behind him. Owen could console himself (and he could console his mother, which was just as important) with the idea that, like Shelley, he was not rejecting true religion but searching for it. In the late days at Dunsden he

[28] Ibid. 100.

[29] Foot, *Red Shelley*, 244. Buxton Forman (1886), and A. G. Ross (1887) both used the word 'reverence' of Shelley, in speeches to the Shelley Society (ibid. 244, 246). Brooke's lecture was reprinted in his *Studies in Poetry* (1910); Owen had a copy.

felt he had the powers to challenge the Church openly and 'shake the foundations of many a spiritual life', but he immediately reassured his mother:

Think not I would use those Powers. Shelley scrupled not to play their whole force upon *his* young friends. But because the *Religion* he had met with was hollow, it does not follow that no religion is solid. He and all his thousand tribes may never have struck the real thing. It exists none the less, you say. Only I haven't met it—to know it—yet. (*CL* 179.)

It is probable that the Victorian fudging of the issue of Shelley's radical atheism was in a practical way useful to Owen, enabling him to understand his own rebellion as being against the letter (and institution and personnel) of Christianity without quite being against Christianity itself. This prepared his later position—as he walked 'the unchristian ways of Christendom' (*CL* 461)—of restating Christian ethics and imagery while denying Christian teleology.

The Victorian fudging of Shelley's revolutionary politics, on the other hand, may have deprived Owen of an orientation which could have helped him. Shelley's radicalism was another awkwardness which had to be negotiated before he could be taken to the bosom of the Victorian reading public. Here anthologists and men of letters laid their emphasis on Shelley the poet of nature, and of private dejections and hopes. *The Revolt of Islam*, thought Stopford Brooke, was written in the hope that men were starting to recover from the proven failure of revolution and to seek new directions, while the 'Ode to the West Wind'—'the lyric of lyrics', Brooke calls it—had the theme of a private rededication of the self after disappointments and disillusion.[30] Matthew Arnold had set the tone by famously describing Shelley in *Essays in Criticism* as 'a beautiful and ineffectual angel, beating in the void his luminous wings in vain'. Shelley was a dreamer, an idealist; his theories were hopelessly, and fortunately, impractical. Owen read in J. A. Symonds's *Shelley* that 'The blending in him of a pure and earnest purpose with moral and social theories that could not but have proved pernicious to mankind at large, produced at times an almost grotesque mixture in his actions no less than in his verse.' Still, Shelley was to be valued because his real lesson 'is not to be

[30] Stopford Brooke, *English Literature*, 159; *Studies in Poetry*, 175.

sought in any of his doctrines, but rather in his fearless bearing, his resolute loyalty to an unselfish and in the simplest sense benevolent ideal'.[31]

The more Shelley's nineteenth-century admirers invested him in a cloak of idealism, the more they muffled his alarming politics, and presented him as the poet of romantic love, natural religion, and the weather. This was the Shelley Owen encountered at Dunsden—the contemplative and unworldly idealist (and not the satirist and polemicist) which Victorian taste had selected to admire.[32] Though Owen was clearly drawn to Shelley when his social conscience troubled him at Dunsden—and Shelley does seem to have helped change his opinion of working people (*CL* 109)—Shelley's example seemed to have little to offer him beyond private acts of charity and a rededication to beauty. The pattern of 'Deep under turfy grass' is the paradigm of this impasse, moving as it does from indignation at the lot of the poor to the consolations of the beautiful. There is virtually no satire, no polemic, and nothing but private life in Owen's poetry before his meeting with Siegfried Sassoon in 1917. 'The qualities in Shelley that obviously appealed most to him were his fervent idealism, his compassionate sympathy with the poor, and his revolutionary zeal,' says Bäckman;[33] but the last of those qualities was one that left very little impression on Owen, who had been trained to admire Shelley the aesthete and to ignore the zealot. Symonds, for example, was patronizing about the pacifist ideas in Shelley's *The Revolt of Islam*; but the fifth canto (where Owen was to find the impetus and the title of his 'Strange Meeting') he recommended to readers as 'lovely'.[34]

The Victorian reading of Shelley is symptomatic of the Victorian taste and literary history that conditioned Owen's own. Nineteenth-century poetry was lovely; its poets, as Elizabeth Barrett Browning wrote in *Aurora Leigh* (1: 859), were 'the only truth-tellers now left to God', but it was a spiritual truth they sought, beyond appearance; their eyes were fixed on matters beyond the affairs of the contemporary actual world. Other than sturdy nationalism,

[31] Symonds, *Shelley*, 183.

[32] An influential version of Shelley as unworldly lyricist is constructed by Palgrave's (and Tennyson's) selection for the *Golden Treasury*. This unworldly Shelley is briefly mocked in Owen's 'A Terre', but his real nemesis awaited him in Leavis's *Revaluation* (1936).

[33] Bäckman, *Tradition Transformed*, 49.

[34] Symonds, *Shelley*, 97.

political views in a poet were most likely signs of immaturity, an impression which found support in the long careers of the century's two great laureates, Wordsworth and Tennyson. (Laurie Magnus's *Introduction to Poetry* entitles Wordsworth 'A Repentant Rebel'.)[35] Stopford Brooke's history of English literature saw modern poetry in steady retreat from the recalcitrance of the modern world until, in about 1860, 'the poets grew weary of the whole struggle' and sought escape, as he said Keats had done, in the past and in art for art's sake.[36]

Laurie Magnus, whose *Introduction to Poetry* (1902) Owen studied at Dunsden, tended to be scornful of poets who embraced the modern world. Whitman 'had nothing rare enough to offer in exchange and compensation for the beauty which he had abandoned,' and as for Robert Browning, 'we do not count his original utterance as a welcome innovation.'[37] Magnus explicitly linked poetic innovation to liberal views, and he thought both were dangerous. 'Novelty in poetry, like liberty in politics, must be governed by law.'[38] He himself was an enthusiast for the 'imperial race sentiment' (this probably meant the poetry of W. E. Henley) which was bringing about a movement 'backward in a sense to aristocracy', and he hoped the poetry of the new age would reflect this 'permanent and uplifting' change.[39] It was Magnus who noted with satisfaction that the spirit of the French Revolution had flourished for a time among the British Romantics, 'till its fires have died down today'.[40] 'Have they!' protested Owen (*CL* 131), who read this at Dunsden at a time when he was losing patience with the vicar's conservatism. But the protest is followed by a confused paragraph—'Am I for or against upheaval? I know not; I am not happy in these thoughts;'—whose rebellious mutterings peter out in a quotation from Tennyson's *Guinevere* on the satisfactions of religious retreat and charitable works, a conclusion that might seem to make Laurie Magnus's point.

Symonds, Brooke, Magnus, and the like were Owen's tutors in literary history and taste. The history of the Romantic poetry he loved, as Owen came to know it in these conditions, appeared to offer him virtually no help in the task of telling the truth about the

[35] Magnus, *Introduction to Poetry*, 112.
[36] Stopford Brooke, *English Literature*, 165.
[37] Magnus, *Introduction to Poetry*, 109, 111.
[38] Ibid. 119. [39] Ibid. 131. [40] Ibid. 146.

war he plunged into in 1917. In fact, it seems to have given him no precedent for considering that such experience could be a subject for poetry in the first place. He was to come to believe that romanticism, in cultivating a language of mood and beauty, had developed a mendacious way of seeing, or not seeing, what was in front of it. The poet on his pedestal was as myopic as the preacher in his pulpit. Romantic poetry, like the Church itself, claimed to know the truth about the world, but knew less than a common soldier about what the world was like.

The other day I read a Biography of Tennyson, which says he was unhappy, even in the midst of his fame, wealth, and domestic serenity. Divine discontent! I can quite believe he never knew happiness for one moment such as I have—for one or two moments. But as for misery, was he ever frozen alive, with dead men for comforters. Did he hear the moaning at the bar, not at twilight and the evening bell only, but at dawn, noon, and night, eating and sleeping, walking and working, always the close moaning of the Bar; the thunder, the hissing and the whining of the Bar?

Tennyson, it seems, was always a great child.

So should I have been, but for Beaumont Hamel. (*CL* 482.)

Poets (as tormented Ivor Gurney was to write) were luckier once.

Yet of course Owen could no more forget Romanticism than he could resign from his family. Romantic ideas and language saturate the war poems, and by no means always as a subject for mockery or anger. The blinded cripple in 'A Terre' is the smashed remnant of a Wordsworthian tradition, a Romantic natural philosopher with his nostalgia, his dejection over his loss of potency, his meditations on the place of mankind in nature, his longing for regeneration. He can be 'poetical', but it is a poetry that has gone bad:

> I have my medals?—Discs to make eyes close.
> My glorious ribbons?—Ripped from my own back
> In scarlet shreds. (That's for your poetry book.)

His dramatic monologue drags his listener through a most unromantic actuality, the prospect of death without any dignity, to which the life of a muck-man or even a rat or a germ would be preferable. Amid this hopeless hymn to the vitality of dirt, the allusion to Shelley's 'Adonais' sounds gratingly incongruous, and yet Shelley's words are not there simply to be despised for their distance from what this poem shows actual experience to be. Shelley's Romantic fancy of becoming 'one with nature, herb and stone' is (when translated into the demotic as 'pushing up daisies') the only meagre consolation left for dying soldiers to clutch at. And after its unromantic insistences—on the crippled body and the jokes, the muck-man and the cheese-mites and the rats—'A Terre' in the end (like 'Insensibility') returns to Romantic language, the language of pastoral and the 'soul' (thrice in the last eight lines), of tears but not idle tears:

Friend, be very sure
I shall be better off with plants that share
More peaceably the meadow and the shower.
Soft rains will touch me,—as they could touch once,
And nothing but the sun shall make me ware.
Your guns may crash around me. I'll not hear;
Or, if I wince, I shall not know I wince.

Don't take my soul's poor comfort for your jest.
Soldiers may grow a soul when turned to fronds,
But here the thing's best left at home with friends.

My soul's a little grief, grappling your chest,
To climb your throat on sobs; easily chased
On other sighs and wiped by fresher winds.
Carry my crying spirit till it's weaned
To do without what blood remains these wounds.

Here was another rewriting of the deathbed scene of the stricken friend. An earlier version of 'A Terre' had a title—'Wild with all Regrets'—from Tennyson and a dedication to Sassoon (*CPF* 355), another of Owen's challenging antiphonies. He was trying not to destroy but to restore a debilitated tradition by confronting it with a subject to test it and to expose where it was still alive and where it was atrophied. 'These men are worth | Your tears', says 'Apologia pro Poemate Meo'. He was giving Romanticism something worth crying about.

15
A Modern Voice

Writing some thirty years after Wilfred Owen's death, Osbert Sitwell was to remember in his young contemporary a quality of reverence for literature which struck him as being not entirely English:

> With his contemporaries he talked with ease. Only in the presence of such literary nabobs of the period as Wells and Bennett could he scarcely bring himself to speak; and this silence, apart from being rooted in his natural modesty and good manners, was due, I think, to the immense esteem in which he held literature and those who practised the profession of author. His residence in France may have deepened this attitude of respect, and almost awe, which had in it nothing of the Englishman's casual approach to books. To him they were all-important, while poetry was the very crown of life, and constituted its meaning.[1]

Owen's romantic dedication to poetry—to poets, and to the 'life . . . of a Poet' (*CL* 325)—had, to be sure, put down its roots some years before he went to live in France in the autumn of 1913, but it is still true to say that his residence in France was a determining factor in his understanding of 'the profession of author' and hence in the shaping of the poet he was becoming. The young man who arrived in Bordeaux to teach at the Berlitz school was, by and large, provincial in outlook and conservative in taste. (The year before, he had had a copy of Meredith's *Poems* 'foisted' upon him, but rejected it as being poor stuff, to his ear 'a jumbled barrel-organ', unmelodious and vulgar 'after the soft Lydian airs I have heretofore heard from his predecessors' (*CL* 136).) But of course a decisive motive in the move to France was precisely to try to shake off provincialism and conservatism. At the age of twenty and with the prospect of getting to university looking increasingly forlorn, Owen had taken his education into his own hands. France became his school of modernity. Far from Shrewsbury and Dunsden (farther still from Keswick) he would have his coming of age; and in his reading of French, more than of English, he was to begin to

[1] Sitwell, *Noble Essences*, 104.

think about what it meant to be a writer in the modern world. The importance to him of French writing can be investigated and assessed in terms of his understanding of that question.

He arrived in Bordeaux with good schoolroom French, though he was to complain that this was a poor grounding for the actual communicative needs of life in a French city. He worked hard on the language, in the little time there was to spare from teaching English—as at Dunsden, and later in the army, there was never enough time to do the work that was most important to him—and it is not surprising to find, from conscientiously underlined items of vocabulary in many of his French books, that the reading of literary works was a part of his autodidactic programme. It seems to have worked. Before long his French was good enough to earn compliments from Laurent Tailhade, on both his conversation and his writing.

It was a busy time, and a happy one. In January 1914 he informed his mother that he was 'writing' nothing at the moment, 'but,' he added cheerfully, 'I prosecute my Enquiries in Human Nature, and learn Philosophy, as I teach Speech, by the *Direct Method*' (*CL* 227). It would not be quite right to say that he was learning about French literature by the direct method, if 'direct' means 'unmediated'. Although no one was directing his studies, he was encountering French writers (as he had encountered English ones) not in some ideal non-space, but already framed, lit, exhibited in company or contrast with others, catalogued, recommended (or deprecated)—intertextualized, in a word, by the critical opinion (not always unanimous) and the climate of taste that formed their reputations. For this reason it is worth looking briefly at the literary entrepreneurs who guided Owen's studies in French writing. The most important of these was Laurent Tailhade himself, whom Owen was to meet in August 1914, but there were plenty of others—schoolteachers, friends, anthologists, literary historians and men of letters—and some of these can be identified as they are to be found among the books in Wilfred Owen's library.

He would certainly have studied some classical French at school, but from his time in France there is not much evidence of an interest in any French writing before 1800. But he read as much as he could of the writers of the nineteenth century, and particularly of its latter half. And reading his anthologies and brief histories, he could not fail to realize that here was contentious matter.

The writing (not to mention the lives) of major figures in this period in France—Baudelaire, Flaubert, Verlaine—was problematic, controversial, even scandalous, in a way that had no real equivalent across the Channel in the kingdom of Dickens, Tennyson, and Ruskin.

The critical story that Owen's texts were telling him was of a battle between the traditional and the modern, and although where you drew the line was a matter of opinion, you had to stand on one side of it or the other. The compiler of an anthology of *Les Cent meilleurs poèmes (lyriques) de la langue française* declared unequivocally that the hundred most perfect poems in French would be found 'presque uniquement parmi les oeuvres des quatre ou cinq grands maîtres du XIXe siècle' (Owen underlined this in his copy). It was with Lamartine and Hugo that 'le grand siècle de la poésie lyrique française' began (and was, presumably, still going on).[2] But another of Owen's books, the similarly titled *Anthologie des Poètes lyriques français*, told a quite different story: most of the masterpieces of French poetry were classical, maintained Charles Sarolea in the introduction to this volume, and he claimed that 'la poésie tout autant que la prose classique occupe le domaine étroitement circonscrit de la réalité humaine,' whereas modern poetry was increasingly mannered in language and remote—exotic or private—in subject.[3] There was a widening gap, of experience and of sympathy, between the poets and the public. In a textbook of literary history, René Canat traced a debasement of Romanticism for which Baudelaire was largely to blame. 'Baudelaire est le poète des frissons malsains et macabres; il a voulu expérimenter les "décompositions" et les pourritures de la société.'[4] He thrust what was rotten about society in society's face. In Canat's opinion, Baudelaire's nastiness combined with Flaubert's heartless depictions of ugliness to create the climate for 'la littérature brutale' in the later nineteenth century, writing at odds with literature's traditional public, antagonistic to social norms and decent feelings, dwelling on what was morbid, sickening, and lost.[5] An English academic, H. H. Johnson, was similarly hostile to the French

[2] Dorchain, *Les Cent meilleurs poèmes*, pp. v, vii. All volumes quoted in this paragraph are to be found among Wilfred Owen's books, housed in the English Faculty Library, Oxford. There is an annotated checklist in *WO* 308–23.

[3] Sarolea, *Anthologie*, 10.

[4] Canat, *La Littérature française*, 686.

[5] Ibid. 687.

moderns in *A Short Introduction to the Study of French Literature*; the charge was not that they wrote badly, but that they wrote improperly. 'The spirits of the cynics and lewder Epicureans dominate Gaul's latest literature . . . The French literary decadence can be readily explained on Ruskin's system: confusing art with literature and both with morality.'[6]

It was a battlefield indeed, and Owen (to cut a long story short) took sides and aligned himself with the French moderns before he really belonged among the English. It was an alignment possibly brought about, but most likely confirmed, by the guidance and example of Laurent Tailhade. And while there are stylistic consequences of Owen's espousal of late-Romantic and realist models from the French, its lasting effects were probably more importantly felt in the way French writers opened to him a field of possibility, not readily available in English, for the relation between a poet's work and the society in which that work took place. When the occasion arose in 1917, Owen was not completely unrehearsed for the production of his own 'littérature brutale', a bulletin from the very margins of society, combining a troubling and exquisite sensationalism with a brutal notation of squalid fact and scant respect for its reader.

He was acquainted, then, with the main issues of the critical (and moral) debate about what was considered modern French writing, though it is not possible to say how far he was acquainted with its leading poetic exponents, beyond the standard anthology pieces, which might in any case have given him all he needed. The resources he had would have agreed in pointing him to Baudelaire as a sort of godfather of the modern, for better or worse, and Baudelaire was to leave his mark on the young English poet, both directly and through his pervasive presence in the writings of late Romantic and Decadent poets who followed. The sonnet 'The city lights along the waterside' (which may be a Bordeaux poem) expands, a little woodenly, some rich hints from the imagery of Baudelaire's 'Harmonie du Soir'; and there is a glimpse of Baudelaire again in the interesting late fragment 'The roads also have their wistful rest' (*CPF* 531), another civilian piece. It can only be conjectured how much, and how directly, Baudelaire is a presence in Owen's war poems; I would suggest he is a considerable one.

[6] Johnson, *A Short Introduction to the Study of French Literature*, 147–8.

There seem to be no verbal echoes, but there are no verbal echoes of Dante either.

In France Owen acquired a Baudelairean taste for city wandering, which he indulged in a visit to London in the summer of 1915, his last civilian summer.

On Sat. being now tired of the West End, I thought a little ugliness would be refreshing; and striking east from the P.O. walked down Fenchurch St. and so into the Whitechapel High Street, & the Whitechapel Road. Ugliness! I never saw such beauty, in two hours, before that Saturday Night. (*CL* 341.)

The pose is that of the slumming *flâneur* ('The Jews,' he continues, 'are a delightful people, at home'), but the Baudelairean themes here, of the relationship between beauty and ugliness, and common cause with the marginalized and underprivileged, are the themes of the 'Apologia pro Poemate Meo' and other war poems. And to turn from Baudelaire to late Owen is to remain in some sense in a Baudelairean world, with its troops of living ghosts, its night landscapes, its strange and disturbing beauties and corruptions, the martyrdom (and exhaustion) of sensibility, the contempt for the insensible, the alienation. And as in Baudelaire the *poète maudit* makes, as it were, a spectacle of himself for his public both to shrink from and to recognize ('Hypocrite lecteur,—mon semblable,—mon frère!'), so in Owen the image of the soldier, weltering in his own and others' 'superhuman inhumanities', stands as a challenge to the reader's honesty, imagination, and responsibility. To make this kind of challenge in the essentially confessional mode of many of his war poems required a kind of courage Owen could have found in Baudelaire but perhaps nowhere else.

Not all examples are for following, and France's greatest war poet seems to have cast no spell on Owen. Victor Hugo was not only a monumental figure but a monumentally respectable one. His reputation in the Third Republic was that of an almost superhuman sage and genius. Owen enjoyed Hugo's prose romances but he did not share his cousin Leslie Gunston's veneration of this poetic colossus, a veneration which he seems to mock elliptically in a 1914 letter where he says that he is not going to 'babble of Victor Hugo, and why he is the greatest possible of all the grandest, and also the highest, deepest, and thickest, and toughest' (*CL* 252). In 1913 Gunston had submitted to a publisher some translations of Hugo (*CL* 208), and although these were not accepted, one of them turned up in *The Nymph* in 1917. It is a version of the first part ('Il neigeait . . .') of 'L'Expiation' from *Les Châtiments*, the famous and much-anthologized description of Napoleon's winter retreat from Russia:

—Sortira-t-on jamais de ce funeste empire?
Deux ennemis! le Czar, le nord. Le Nord est pire.
On jetait les canons pour brûler les affûts.
Qui se couchait, mourait. Groupe morne et confus,
Ils fuyaient; le désert dévorait le cortège.
On pouvait, à des plis qui soulevaient la neige,
Voir que des régiments s'étaient endormis là.
O chutes d'Annibal! Lendemains d'Attila!

Hugo's poem is an exercise in the grand epic style and although it evokes the terrible suffering of the troops this is essentially background to the brooding figure of the commander-in-chief, the Romantic tragic hero and his expiation. Owen read Leslie Gunston's English version in the late summer of 1917 (he had probably seen it before) with an eye sharpened by his own experience on the Somme and the examples of Sassoon's and Graves's recent war poems. He knew more about poetry (and French) than Leslie Gunston and more about winter campaigning than Victor Hugo. It is satisfying to think of grim, spare, late poems like 'Exposure' and 'Futility' ('Qui se couchait, mourait') as part of his answer to both of them, exposing Gunston as slack and trite and Hugo as verbose and star-struck.

His sources had warned him that a disreputable note had entered French writing around the middle of the century, and this was the mark of what was most self-consciously modern in French. It is congruent with his new sense of independence that Owen found in himself an affinity with writing stemming from the alienated and notorious Baudelaire, rather than the nationalistic and celebrated Hugo. This affinity set him, as far as one can judge, on the path to the aesthetic movement, Verlaine, and the French Decadents, among whom Tailhade was to be his guide. And it was to send him back in a sort of loop to English work which he was just starting to be aware of when he left the country in 1913—the poetry of Swinburne (Baudelaire's first English champion), and of the aesthetic and Decadent writers grouped around the figure of

Oscar Wilde. Individually and independently, and a little late, Owen was enriching his poetic world from the same heady French sources as English poetry had drawn on in the late century before the downfall of Wilde.[7] Hibberd's *Owen the Poet* makes a persuasive and detailed case (*OTP*, chapters 3, 4, 9 and *passim*) for the profound effect on Owen's work of literary ideals and models, French in origin, of aestheticism and the Decadence. (It also points to an uncanny consonance between certain recurrent motifs of Decadent art—the petrifying Medusa's stare, for example—and recurrent features of Owen's psychic life, a consonance that suggests that such images belong to a discourse with long roots in the unconscious.) Hibberd's reading, in this as in other matters, has significantly broadened our modern understanding of Owen's writing. Owen's poetry after 1914, including the war poems, is the work of a poet fluent in the language of what Mario Praz entitled the Romantic Agony.

As the war began, Owen in France was educating himself in the modern sensibility in French writing. His reading told him that this modernity was the intertwining of two strands. One was a late Romantic exploration of the extremes of sensation and 'the wildest beauty in the world', an aestheticism associated with beliefs, tastes, and conduct widely considered scandalous and immoral. The other strand was of a meticulous realism—shocking, satirical, mocking or indignant—which was equally a challenge to the sensibilities of the bourgeois Third Republic. René Canat attacked the naturalism of Zola in terms almost identical to his condemnation of Baudelaire, quoted above: 'Il n'a voulu voir dans l'humanité que les laideurs, et il les a peintes, cyniquement, brutalement, sans y mêler la moindre pitié.'[8] His reading in French told Owen something simple but important. To be a modern writer might entail an elective or helpless alienation from the culture's prevailing opinions and values. Such a writer could well find himself profoundly at odds with the public from which his readership must be drawn. French modernity was scandalous, in art and in life. Baudelaire, Flaubert, Verlaine, and Zola could be considered (Hugo apart) as

[7] Baudelaire was a patron saint of the English as of the French Decadence. In his copy of Robert Sherard's book about Wilde, Owen could have read: 'I owe it altogether to Oscar Wilde that I became familiar with the most wonderful verse which was written in France in the nineteenth century [i.e. the poetry of Baudelaire]' (Sherard, *Oscar Wilde*, 45–6).

[8] Canat, *La Littérature française*, 689.

the masters of French writing in the second half of the nineteenth century; they had all been in trouble with the police, as of course had Wilde.[9]

Owen's expatriation placed him mentally as well as geographically outside England for two important years (and his later war experience too was, of course, the experience of an exile). He had been driven abroad by disaffection with the way things were at home. There were many facets to this, as we have seen: his loss of faith and the 'bust-up' with the Church at Dunsden; his discontent with small-mindedness at home and the frustrations of his family's relative poverty; his feeling that further education and career opportunities were barred to him, in spite of his talents, in a country where money counted for everything and imagination and beauty for nothing; probably also his awareness of an illicit sexual orientation. All of these disaffections added up to a sense of his own difference, of feeling uncomfortable and impatient in the moral and intellectual climate (such as it was) of home—a feeling of alienation that expressed itself in his seizing the opportunity of exile when it came. Now he was finding there was a whole literature, distinguished and modern, which was both much to his taste and indifferent or hostile to what bourgeois respectability held to be important and true. Writing could create—and might have to create—an alternative or adversary culture.

It seems to me that the example of Siegfried Sassoon by itself is not enough to explain one of the mysteries of Owen's war poetry, the confidence and courage with which this conventionally and narrowly educated young man, brought up in a class and faith that emphasized above all modesty and deference, respectability and duty, was to produce a radically alienated and critical body of poetry, at a time and in circumstances when there were very powerful pressures on poets—and everyone else—to rally round and keep their disaffections and differences to themselves. I have in mind not only the more or less official organs of patriotic discourse, in the Church, the press, etc., but also such phenomena of indirect pressure as Robert Graves's well-meaning advice to Owen at the end of 1917 to 'cheer up and write more optimistically' (*CL* 596). There are textual and thematic traces, as Dominic

[9] Apollinaire, leader of a modernist generation Owen probably knew nothing about, continued the tradition by being arrested in 1911 on suspicion of having stolen the *Mona Lisa*.

Hibberd shows, of the French moderns in Owen's writing, but I think they provided him with a discursive example too, a way of thinking about the relationship of a writer with his society. There was a body of work in French—and nothing really comparable in English, though there were English imitations—that was proud to operate as a kind of ideological opposition, a counter-culture. Such an idea is a modern cliché, but it was French before it was English, and I believe the French example helped give Owen the courage to think of what he and Sassoon were doing in the same terms. And when Sassoon sent Owen with an introduction to Robert Ross in the autumn of 1917, he was introducing him to the circle of another, overlapping counter-culture, that of English literary homosexuality. What is more, Owen seems towards the end of his life to have been developing an idea of *the army itself* as an adversary to the home culture, an alternative 'nation' with its own different and superior sensibility, experience, and language. Misunderstood by (and scornful of) a hidebound and hypocritical public at home, the army is intriguingly described, in the late 'Smile, Smile, Smile', as having collectively performed Owen's own gesture of transfer of loyalties and 'fled to France'. The true war poets spoke for a *génération maudite*, which had done damnable things and plumbed the extremes of sensation, but had found in a terrible world truths that lay—as 'Strange Meeting' puts it—'too deep for taint'. This is the burden of poems, like the 'Apologia', 'Dulce et Decorum Est', and 'Insensibility', which measure a scornful distance from conventional views and ordinary (civilian) experience.

It is also clear that the 'strange friend' in 'Strange Meeting' is generically modern, in the way his reading in French had taught Owen to understand modernity in a writer; a nonconformist aesthete who devoted his life to hunting a dangerous and elusive beauty, an outsider with the courage and wisdom to break ranks with the majority and resist the drift of the modern world towards false refuges of vanity and lies, a martyred saint (perhaps a Christ figure) stigmatized and ruined yet witness to the truth.

> Whatever hope is yours,
> Was my life also; I went hunting wild
> After the wildest beauty in the world . . .
> Courage was mine, and I had mystery,
> Wisdom was mine, and I had mastery:

To miss the march of this retreating world
Into vain citadels that are not walled.
Then, when much blood had clogged their chariot-wheels,
I would go up and wash them from sweet wells,
Even with truths that lie too deep for taint.
I would have poured my spirit without stint
But not through wounds; not on the cess of war.
Foreheads of men have bled where no wounds are.

One of the first things Laurent Tailhade did for the young Wilfred Owen, to whom he had taken a fancy, was to present him with a copy of Flaubert's baroque and meticulous *La Tentation de Saint-Antoine*, with an introduction by Emile Faguet, having carefully amended the title page to read: 'le stupide Emile Faguet de l'Académie Française qui déshonore ce chef d'oeuvre'. Under a single cover the older poet was making him a gift of French aestheticism, realism, and hostility to official authority. Owen took the hint. He went on to read at least *Salammbô* and *Madame Bovary*, and to announce to his cousin: 'Flaubert has my vote for novel-writing!' (*CL* 350). In the current of French literary history, something of Flaubert flows into the macabre and orientalist fantasies of late nineteenth-century Decadence, and something into the 'brutal' realism of Zola and, later, of Barbusse's *Le Feu*. Flaubert is an ancestor of Owen poems like 'Long ages past' and 'Has your soul sipped', as well as of 'Dulce et Decorum Est' and 'Disabled'.

Laurent Tailhade was an old friend of the theatrical M. Léger, who asked him to stay at Bagnères-de-Bigorre in August 1914, while Owen was tutor there. Tailhade at sixty was no longer a practising poet but he was still a dandy, whose vividly lived past included numerous duels, close friendships with Verlaine and other lights of the Decadence, membership in the nineties of the Ordre Kabbalistique de la Rose-Croix, and a spell in prison for his political views (see *OTP* 194–5). He was the author of stylish lyric poems and satires against bourgeois philistinism. He sounds, from Owen's letters, inclined to be fussy, self-centred and snobbish, but Owen was delighted and fascinated by him, describing him as 'a charming old gentleman to meet', and flattered by the attention Tailhade paid to him.

I called at his Hotel this morning to know his mind about the day of his removal. I saw him up at his window in shirt-sleeves, mooning. He received me like a lover. To use an expression of the Revd H. Wigan's, he quite slobbered over me. I know not how many times he squeezed my hand; and, sitting me down on a sofa, pressed my head against his shoulder. [*Two lines illegible*] It was not intellectual; but I felt the living verve of the poet . . . who has fought *seventeen duels* (so it is said). (*CL* 282.)

There is an amusing discursive vengeance in forcing 'the Revd H. Wigan' to cohabit in that sentence with this alarmingly unrestrained continental, and an interesting associative transition from feeling the living verve of the poet in his embrace to his reputation as a duellist. This is a moment of intimate contact and discursive communion to be placed alongside Owen's fervent imaginary touching of 'the incandescent Heart of Keats' while reading of his last illness two years before (*CL* 161). But here was 'the life . . . of a Poet' in the very proximate flesh. Although Owen was to read Tailhade's *Poèmes élégiaques* and *Poèmes Aristophanesques* it was Tailhade's person more than his writings that made the more profound impression, for Owen's first friendship with a well-known poet was with this veteran aesthete who had dedicated his career and his life to convictions which Owen felt, so far in a theoretical and tentative way, he shared. His own father's attitude had been Owen's first indication that poetry had to make its way in the teeth of the world's misprision. He described Tailhade admiringly as 'too Parisian to care' what people might think about him (*CL* 281). For Owen he was a first and most unrepentant example—the second would be Siegfried Sassoon—of a poet who lived by his beliefs, regardless of the hostility or incomprehension of what he called (in the poem 'Paysages I') 'la foule stupide à l'accoutumée' and (in 'Ballade élégiaque pour le morose après-midi', which Owen started to translate (*CPF* 435–6)) 'la plèbe immonde et forcenée'.

Tailhade was in any case an ageing literary lion enjoying the role of metropolitan celebrity in provincial Bagnères. Some of the lofty arrogance of his manner and writing rubbed off on Owen, who informed his family at this time that the new war would 'effect a little useful weeding' (*CL* 282), and sent Harold a description, with Flaubertian relish and realism, of the wounded in Doctor Sauvaître's hospital, adding coolly that he was 'not much upset' by what he had seen there (*CL* 284–6). This capacity for an elective indifference seems to have been alien to Owen's inclination, though it may be related to his later self-protective insensibility in battle. It is a short-lived phenomenon in his letters, but it was to be a valuable literary weapon (as it was for Tailhade) for later satire and invective, where Owen was able to summon up a ruthless single-mindedness which can be disturbing (as in the treatment of women in his poems, for example). It was part of the assurance and poetic self-respect that Owen was learning by example in France, as Osbert Sitwell was later to suggest. With his French models, for a time becoming modern for Owen meant becoming un-English; yet it was not in the nature of his education to replace one thing with another, but to enrich the field of discourse. If Owen learned from Tailhade's boldness, which could sound disdainful and heartless, he did not unlearn the lessons of Dunsden parish, of Shelley's sympathies, and Ruskin's social conscience. At Mérignac in 1915 he completed 'Nocturne', a gentle lyric in his Dunsden style, full of compassion for 'all souls' who toil through the night, exhausted or driven mad by manual labour.

For a while in Laurent Tailhade Owen could study at privileged range a man who seemed the embodiment of modern ideas and practices in writing. Tailhade the satirist and enthusiast for Flaubert and Zola certainly helped purge some of the besetting vagueness from Owen's work and showed him the uses of realism and sharp observation. Tailhade the lyricist and aesthete and friend of Verlaine emphasized the importance of prosody and music, as well as putting on display the fashionable Decadent properties—beautiful wounded bodies, apocalyptic sunsets, fatal women, gloomy landscapes, erotic languor, ghosts, and so on—which were often to furnish Owen's war poetry. And Tailhade in person could simply show him what he had never seen before, that it was a possible and proud thing to live as a poet. Here, extending a hand of welcome was the living proof of a community of poetry, and Owen's isolation, hitherto virtually complete, was broken.

Two Tailhade themes, his pacifism and his homoeroticism, need attention before we follow Owen back to England. Tailhade had argued against war in his *Lettre aux Conscrits* (1903) and his address *Pour la Paix* (1908), published as one volume in 1909, and D. S. R. Welland in his pioneering study of Owen was the first to suggest that these pieces 'anticipate Owen so markedly in sentiment and even on occasion in turns of expression that it is impossible that Owen should not have known them'.[10] It is prima

[10] Welland, *Wilfred Owen*, 89.

facie an attractive speculation: Tailhade was a pacifist, Owen was to become an anti-war poet, and they became friends in 1914. But Owen shares no anti-war ideas with the Tailhade pamphlets that he could not have found instead in *The Old Huntsman* and the New Testament (assuming he was not able to work them out for himself). And I do not find Welland's textual evidence convincing.[11]

But more to the point is the absence of any real anti-war (still less pacifist) sentiments from Owen's writing before 1917. To this must be added the high improbability that Tailhade would have been dispensing his former pacifist opinions and handing out copies of his anti-war pamphlets in the heady atmosphere of August 1914 (when Owen met him), or at their later meeting in May 1915, after the terrible French losses in Champagne and at St. Mihiel. Tailhade's opposition to war did not extend to this conflict, when his country had been invaded, again, by the still unrequited aggressor of 1870. Before 1914 was over the portly Tailhade was in uniform, in company with the equally ex-pacifist Anatole France (their aggregate age 130), 'shouldering a rifle' as Owen reported in a letter which goes on to broach for the first time the possibility that he too might be 'led into enlisting' (*CL* 295). French was not the language of pacifism for Wilfred Owen. On the contrary, he used it for his only excursion into patriotic war poetry, drafted in 1914 on the back of a sheet of paper on which he had transcribed Verlaine's 'Mon Rêve familier' (*CPF* 444).

Nous ne nous fions pas à la multitude d'une armée.
Les nations qui ont grandement construit, grandement se soutiennent[.]
Dans ces heures ténébreuses, la splendeur d'une main
S'est remuée derrière l'obscurité, jusqu'à ce que cette côte
Où la haine et la faction semblaient le plus triompher
Se revèle—un bouclier et un brandon.

[11] One example: Welland (ibid. 90) traces back to a moment in *Pour la paix* ('Des larves rampent sur le sol') the imagery of 'The Show' and its somewhat uncommon use of the verb 'ramped'. But Owen uses 'ramped' in a pre-Tailhade letter ('I ramped about all day, and gave my pupils the dickens of a time' (*CL* 239)): in the letter and the poem, 'ramped' seems to have an aggressive sense for Owen, which the verb *ramper* does not have in French. The immediate source of this aspect of 'The Show' is generally agreed to be the first chapter of Barbusse's *Le Feu* ('On voit, en bas, des choses qui rampent!'). For another possible echo I would suggest the famous outburst of Perdican in Musset's *On ne badine pas avec l'amour*, II. v: 'le monde n'est qu'un égoût sans fond où les phoques les plus informes rampent et se tordent sur des montagnes de fange.'

This commonplace fragment is about Britain (with its small army, and its outline on the map fancifully likened to an arm upraised with buckler and torch); and it is in dialogic *entente cordiale* with the discourse of French patriotism that surrounded Owen in the early months of the war. For all his professed indifference to the mob, Tailhade was not a dissenter from this discourse. Indeed Owen's poem may have been intended for his eyes. For whom else, other than his admired *maître*, would the young English poet have been writing French verse at this time?

Tailhade's sometime pacifism may have made no impact on Owen: his homoeroticism was another matter. *Poèmes élégiaques*, which Tailhade gave to Owen with a friendly inscription in May 1915, has a number of moments like this 'Sonnet':

> Ton col surgit du sein comme une tour d'ivoire,
> Jeune homme! Les anneaux sombres de tes cheveux
> Flottent sur son pâleur, liquides et plus bleus
> Que la Nuit aux yeux d'or, en sa robe de moire.
> Sous le maigre habit noir, tes flancs purs et nerveux
> Des marbres consacrés éternisent la gloire:
> Et ta bouche sanglante est le tiède ciboire
> Où revit la senteur des chrêmes fabuleux.
> Ton beau corps cependant, aux lignes cadencées,
> Jamais n'assouvira l'amour des fiancées:
> Tes larges yeux, pareils aux gouttes de la mer,
> Ne descendront jamais de leurs ciels poétiques
> Où rêvent, fraternels, les éphèbes antiques
> Et Narcisse au grand coeur qui mourut de s'aimer.

There may be a memory of 'tes flancs purs et nerveux' in another tenderly evoked body, in 'Futility', with its 'sides | Full-nerved, still warm'. But if Owen's reading in aesthetic, decadent poetry had any breadth, he would not have found anything particularly surprising or original in Tailhade's sonnet, and this is an important point. The male body as erotic icon was a favoured theme of the Romantic agony. It was a theme profoundly congenial to Owen before he came to France—the spell of male beauty links 'The Little Mermaid' with 'The time was aeon', for example—and it seems to be at the centre of the project of a long poem on the theme of Perseus, which Dominic Hibberd has tried to piece together from fragments mostly written in 1914–15 in France (*OTP* 42–54). It was in the writing of the French moderns (of whom

Laurent Tailhade was the focal point for him) that Owen found homoeroticism unabashed and as it were legitimated as a theme for poetry. Because of the extreme stigma attached to homosexuality in England—at its most despised in the quarter-century after the Wilde disaster, in other words in Owen's lifetime—literary homoeroticism, except of the most ingenuous kind, tended to protect itself in elaborate coding and private editions. But Tailhade was responsive in an unembarrassed way to male beauty, as is suggested by this and other poems, and by his obvious physical admiration for Owen. Susan Owen quoted from (and probably repunctuated) a letter Wilfred sent her in September 1914 which has since been lost (or 'lost').

The poet Tailhade calls my eyes 'So very lovely!!!' etc. and my neck 'The neck of a statue!!!! etc.'—because he is a poet and unconsciously appreciates in me, *not* the appearance of beauty but the Spirit and temperament of beauty, Tailhade says he is going to write a Sonnet on me.[12]

Would it be cynical to suppose that Tailhade was economically flattering Owen with the sonnet he had already written about a young man with beautiful eyes and a statuesque neck? Owen in any case responded to the example of Tailhade's writing and his affection. In this as in other ways, the French poet was encouraging him in a direction he had already tentatively embarked on. The male body becomes established as a central theme of his work, a focus for his curiosity, desire, and pity. And for him the question of writing modern poetry was henceforth never quite to be separated from the question of sexuality. The homoerotic and the poetic were a mark of difference, hence of identity.

Owen returned from France in 1915 with his vocal range considerably extended, though that range would not be fully exploited until he began to write about the war, in 1917. In the modern French writers he had discovered that he had company in some of the emergent issues of his imagination: in the poetic dissidence from orthodox views he had started to voice at Dunsden but had kept secret, in his excitement at male beauty and hunger for male companionship, in the dedication to his art, which was accompanied by a troubling fascination with what was painful, squalid, and brutal; and in a certain self-dramatization as an outsider—

[12] Hibberd, 'Wilfred Owen's Letters', 286.

'I was always a mad comet' (*CL* 505), he was to boast to Sassoon—who was nevertheless part of a company and could speak for others. This added up to a modern accent that helped free Owen's voice from the 'soft Lydian airs' (*CL* 136) to which it had been apprenticed. As an emancipated modern, he would later speak scornfully of all things Victorian (*CL* 426, 558), though this was not a term fixed by mere chronology: Leslie Gunston's *The Nymph* (1917) was 'Victorian' (*CL* 526), Oscar Wilde presumably was not. When Owen started reading Wilde, probably at the time of his meeting with Wilde's friend Robert Ross in late 1917, he encountered the same modern accent.

'The Ballad of Reading Gaol' is in many ways remarkably close to Owen's compassionate and indignant poetry of war:

> A prison wall was round us both,
> Two outcast men we were:
> The world had thrust us from its heart,
> And God from out his care.

Wilde's speaker makes common cause with his fellow-sufferer, the anonymous prisoner who has 'killed the thing he loved' and now, doomed to die, lives out his last days in the power of unpitying professionals—prison officers, the gloating 'coarse-mouthed Doctor', the chaplain with nothing to offer but tracts. The ballad, like so much in Owen, is mostly about hopeless waiting. The hour of execution is at last announced by 'God's dreadful dawn', the condemned man dies, and his death is felt by his fellow outcast (guilty himself, yet 'each man' is guilty too) with his burden of sensibility.

> For he who lives more lives than one
> More deaths than one must die.

The ballad, with its far from poetical setting and subject, is unusually raw and shocking. But there is much that is close to Owen in Wilde's pre-prison poetry too, with its gallery of admired and martyred youth, its impressions of nights and dawns populated by secretive phantoms, its humanitarian gestures, its music, and even its favourite colours (purple, crimson, black). The similarities are less a sign of 'influence' in a direct sense than a consequence of both poets having learned their modernity from writers like Baudelaire, Flaubert, and Verlaine. Much of Wilde would have been *déjà vu* for Owen.

There was another aspect of modernity in the French fashion that was to be important for the poet Owen was becoming. To write and live in a self-consciously Decadent manner was, as the name suggests, to speak from a cultural situation supposed to be in a state of organic decomposition. The lights are constantly going out in Decadent literature and painting; the machine is running down, the end is at hand. Bourgeois society smothers in its own greed and vulgarity. The official faiths are empty; there is nothing to believe in. The individual, alienated, hypochondriacal, and sad, can keep at bay his share of a cosmic *ennui* only by retreating into the artificial paradise of art 'for its own sake' or by the pursuit of novelty in sensations, the more bizarre the better. No one, perhaps, took this absolutely seriously all the time. But the melancholy shadow of an impending end looms over late Romantic modernity from Baudelaire's 'Chant d'Automne' to Verlaine ('Je suis l'Empire à la fin de la décadence') and Wilde ('This modern world is grey and old'), and to Yeats (who traversed a *fin de siècle* twilight and then decided to embrace what he saw as the coming darkness) and Owen himself, poet of endings, of 'The End', 'Exposure', 'Futility', and 'Strange Meeting'. A theme of entropy and a historical melancholy were part of the condition of modernity Owen learned in France. This is important for his war poetry, but there were alternative discourses too.

The fact is that Owen had modernized himself in a somewhat old-fashioned way. He returned to England in 1915 equipped to become a poet of the nineties, and seems to have known next to nothing about contemporary English poetry. There was an important exception. As early as October 1911 he had chanced upon Harold Monro's *Before Dawn: Poems and Impressions*, published earlier that year, and had read it carefully (*CL* 96; *OTP* 14–15). Now a month after his return to England he went to the Poetry Bookshop in London and introduced himself to its proprietor, Monro. He had made contact with a different modernity, that of the English Georgians. In March 1916 he was again at the Bookshop, and he asked Monro to read his sonnets. 'He went over the things in detail and he told me what was fresh and clever, and what was second-hand and banal; and what Keatsian, and what "modern"' (*CL* 384).

Owen read Monro's *Children of Love* (1914) and later his *Strange Meetings* (1917), but Monro's chief lesson in 'what was . . . "modern"' was already there in the remarkable *Before Dawn*. This volume, published in the year before the foundation of the Poetry Bookshop and the first anthology of *Georgian Poetry*, can be read as a sort of Georgian manifesto, inaugurating a counter-discourse to challenge a debilitated late Romanticism. If late Romantic decadence was fascinated by what was morbid, sterile, and sad, *Before Dawn* was vigorously different. Its title looks forward, beyond the shadows of the *fin de siècle* to something new. Its dedication makes a pledge to 'obey the beautiful future, which alone we may call God'. It is a poetry of frankness and daylight. 'The pale moon-worshippers must waste away,' declares a poem ('The Moon-Worshippers') which seems an allegory of the passing of the Decadence and the moon-drenched 'Fantaisies décoratives' of Wilde. 'The Swamp' is another allegory, populated by figures sunk in despond with a weariness which is recognizably part of a nineties syndrome—'voice-weary priests', 'love-weary lovers', 'pleasure-weary harlots'—but which the poet himself breaks free from, his spirit soaring above the mud in a moment remembered (but made thoroughly ambiguous) in Owen's 'Apologia' and 'The Show':

> My eager spirit breathlessly took wing . . .
> Strong with the beautiful resolve to dare,
> Welcome the unaccustomed and the new,
> Wing the high spaces of the liquid blue.

The voice of the modern poet could be the voice of hope, welcoming 'the beautiful future' without fear.

It is not hard to see how this could become tiresome and inanely jolly, a reputation the Georgians would later suffer from. But *Before Dawn* is an intelligent book, and Monro had an important lesson for Owen, showing a fresh modern idiom—plain, realist, above all not concerned with poetical decoration—and a role for the socially responsible modern poet, facing the future with the confidence of his progressive views. *Before Dawn* is full of generation, of births and rebirths. There is a return of Christ, a 'Return of Arthur', the poet's own escape from the swamp of deadly *anomie* (and, in another poem, from the life-denying gloom of Tolstoy); even the hero of 'Don Juan in Hell' (which rewrites Baudelaire's sombre 'Don Juan aux enfers') is confident he will 'rise for another spell, | Fierce as summer, and fresh as dew'. And there is a liberating theme of simple bodily enjoyment—of love, food, fresh air; in 'Paradise' Monro's Adam is a humanist *homme moyen sensuel* and God is the spoilsport snake in the grass. Owen seems to have sensed early what Monro could do for him, and he adapted an image of liberating beauty from Monro's 'Two Visions' for his own 'The time was aeon', only to show it still threatened with repression by his own Evangelical feelings of guilt. Monro's satirical verse portraits left their mark on him too, as Hibberd has argued (*OTP* 15–16).

Owen was to read widely the work of poets in the Georgian movement which Monro helped to inaugurate; some became his friends. The plainer style they favoured was a useful corrective to Owen's tendency to efflorescence and bookishness (which Tailhade's example had, if anything, encouraged); useful too was their willingness to find poetry in the experience of ordinary people and things. And yet, for better or worse, Monro's social and historical optimism is a discourse that can be found in Owen only as a fleeting and feeble voice. It did not offer him an issue from the darker, alienated modernity of his French models. The reason is not far to seek. That optimism was to falter in Monro himself under the pressure of the war. Already in *Children of Love* (1914), a 'happy boy' ('Youth in Arms') succumbs to the forces of decaying age—'Greybeards plotted. They were sad. | Death was in their wrinkled eyes'—and he ends up as carrion in a ditch, in a pattern that was to become familiar in Sassoon, Graves, and Owen. Monro's *Strange Meetings* (1917) is much possessed by death, and seems to withdraw finally into a weekend-cottage pastoralism, a refuge from the tide of history which *Before Dawn* had been confident of taking at the flood. As for Owen, he was to find the Western Front a world much closer to the nightmares of the Romantic agony than to the utopian prospects of *Before Dawn*. That Georgian optimism (which Graves was still urging on Owen late in 1917) is a note that sounds in Owen's war poetry only to deepen its poignancy. Like the spasm of the dying man in 'Asleep', it is the quaking of an aborted life. 'The Next War', written at Craiglockhart, manages to sound cheerful; it is the only one of the war poems that can imagine a future worth having. Elsewhere, we can observe the characteristic Monrovian images of generation and hope being dialogically worsted—as comprehensively, it might seem, as Monro in *Before Dawn* had contradicted the favourite imagery of the Decadence. In Owen dawn itself becomes a 'poignant misery', worse than the dark, to be greeted with dismay. No one is healthy, for to be at war is to be part of a disease. The 'aborted life' of the soldier killed asleep quakes for an instant and then subsides, dead before it can be born. The abandoned fields in 'Futility' will remain unsown, the sun generates nothing, no one comes back from the dead. Even that Georgian last hope, the domestic idyll, is closed off to the soldiers in 'Exposure', its cheerful fire now ashes.

Georgian modernity represented itself as a youthful renewal, a fresh start, whereas the modernity of Verlaine's (and Wilde's) poetry was performed and understood as a belated and even pathological phenomenon, outcast voices issuing from a decaying world. The fate of modernity in Owen can be read in his imagery, where the tokens of youth and promise fight a losing battle against weariness and decay. There is no mystery about why Owen found a theme in the doom of youth; in the demographic circumstances of the Great War it was simply part of his realist agenda, but it is a theme which also has implications for his reading of the literary and cultural history of the still-new century, with its images of young men grown unnaturally old and decrepit (in 'Disabled', 'A Terre', 'Mental Cases', 'S.I.W.', 'Dulce et Decorum Est'), its dawns and springtimes that do not come, or come but bring no renewal. 'We Georgians,' Owen told Leslie Gunston casually in 1918, 'are all so old' (*CL* 526). To be modern in 1918 meant, for him, to be the voice of a world as ill and decaying as the landscape seen from on high in 'The Show', 'a sad land, weak with sweats of dearth'. There was a need for satire and elegy here, but no place for a poetry of hope.

16
English Elegies

The prospect of publishing a book of his poetry—a prospect that seemed to be becoming real in the last winter and spring of his life—caused Owen to think in a new way about his work. He was well aware that something extraordinary was happening to him. With Sassoon's help he was rapidly creating for himself a new and more powerful poetic personality, and as rapidly becoming dissatisfied with the old. He said in 1918 that for every new poem he added to his list he subtracted one from the beginning of it (*CL* 554), and indeed in the lists of contents he drafted that summer there is virtually no piece of work more than a year old. (Versions of the titles of 'The Unreturning', 'A New Heaven', and 'With an Identity Disc' appear in the first of two longer lists, are relegated to a 'Doubtful' category in the second, and have disappeared altogether from the later, shorter list (*CPF* 537–540.)) It was clear that he had found a voice, or rather (since there had never been a lack of voices) a way of orchestrating the different discourses of his experience to produce together a polyphony both expressive and urgent. At the same time, in thinking about the editorial decisions that preparation of a book would require, he was having to think about the shape of his work as a whole, and the relation of poems to one another. A clue to these deliberations lies in his search for the best title for this book which would introduce him to the public. He considered *With Lightning and with Music* and *English Elegies*, before settling on *Disabled and Other Poems* (*WO* 265).

A poet cannot choose his name or his relatives but he can do these things for his book, and Owen's titles are intertextual manoeuvres to define the place of his work in the community of poetry. 'With lightning and with music' is a quotation from 'Adonais' (stanza xii), Shelley's elegy for Keats. Owen seems to have first considered using it for a collection of his sonnets, before 1917 (*OTP* 63). It is a title that would place the war poems, as it were, at the deathbed of Keats, which was the imaginative centre of Romanticism for Owen, while signalling that his own Romantic project would combine the music of poetry with the lightning of war. The hint of elegy contained in the 'Adonais' quotation is explicit in the graceful title *English Elegies*, which places itself in relation to Tennyson's *English Idylls* while managing to suggest that the Tennysonian idyll has been overtaken by catastrophe. Owen may have decided that both these titles sounded over-romantic, and besides *English Elegies* was not (on the face of it) an accurate description of many of the poems intended for the book. And so he chose instead the unadorned *Disabled and Other Poems*, following even in the matter of his title the example of Sassoon's *The Old Huntsman and Other Poems* and *Counter-Attack and Other Poems*, and perhaps for his own satisfaction also providing an eloquent and grotesque contrast with his cousin's *The Nymph and Other Poems*. But elegy was much in Owen's mind, and the preface drafted at Ripon, probably in May 1918, refers to the contents of his book as elegies. 'Yet these elegies are to this generation in no sense consolatory.' Dominic Hibberd comments:

> He had probably begun to think about the poetry of 'pity' before the end of 1917, since it is clear that he set himself to read several famous elegies during the winter and following spring. He may have had no very scholarly idea of what an elegy was, remembering only from reference books that it originally meant a song of grief over a dead man and from Tailhade's example that *élégiaque* meant something other than *aristophanesque*, but when he described his war poems as 'These elegies' he did not use the word at random. (*OTP* 140.)

That programme of reading is an important clue to the way Owen worked. He had always thought of himself as being scholarly by nature. He had had consistently good reports at school, and to his family, who were not particularly well-educated themselves, his bookishness was legendary. But his failure, for financial reasons, to get to university was a disappointment that still rankled, and now he was moving into the orbit of people (like Sassoon, Graves, and later Robert Ross and his friends) for whom a sophisticated level of literary culture could be taken for granted. It is not surprising to find him a little overawed in this company, keeping himself unobtrusive, minding his manners, and listening carefully.

Meanwhile, in his autodidacticism there is something of the earnest self-improvement of the socially humble Victorian. But although the poetry he set himself to read, from his arrival at Craiglockhart onwards, was liberal in its range, it was selected with a purpose, as Hibberd suggests. The evidence is overwhelming that in these months, and for his own purposes, Owen set to work to make himself an expert on elegy. This is the only instance in which we can see him placing his own work in intertextual relation not to other individual poets, but to a genre.

He read the classical elegies of Bion and Moschus in Andrew Lang's translation. Traces have been found of Milton's 'Lycidas' in Owen's 'Asleep' and of Gray's 'Elegy' in 'The Send-Off'. 'A Terre', and one of his proposed titles, as we have seen, quote Shelley's 'Adonais'. Tennyson's *In Memoriam* is remembered in 'Futility' and probably in 'Strange Meeting'. 'Hospital Barge' was written after reading 'The Passing of Arthur'. On the back of a draft of his 'Elegy in April and September' Owen scribbled a note about Matthew Arnold's 'Thyrsis' and 'The Scholar Gipsy', while other poems have traces of the elegies in Housman's *A Shropshire Lad* and possibly (though I am not convinced of this) Hardy's *The Dynasts*. Laurent Tailhade, of course, had given Owen an inscribed copy of his *Poèmes élégiaques*. And Dominic Hibberd, from whom I have purloined this formidable list (*OTP* 140–1), might well have added two more titles. One is Sassoon's collection *The Old Huntsman*, especially 'The Last Meeting' and section three of 'A Letter Home'. The other is Swinburne's elegy for the poet Baudelaire, 'Ave atque Vale'. Owen had known Swinburne's poetry since 1912, and had been reading him in 1916 and again at Craiglockhart in 1917. He certainly knew this famous poem, although it is not in Swinburne's *Poems and Ballads,* which he bought in August 1918 and took with him on his last journey to France. (Leslie Gunston's book, besides its 'Ode' to Swinburne, has a poem entitled 'Ave atque Vale'.) Many of these poems were old favourites of Owen's and undoubtedly he had first met some of them in the schoolroom. But that they were all in his mind in the last year of his life indicates no casual browsing but a self-imposed discipline, the curriculum of the trainee elegist.

It might seem unnecessary to ask why Wilfred Owen was so interested in elegy in 1917 and 1918; but the answer is not as straightforward as might be expected. For one thing, Owen was in pursuit of the level of education that his social circumstances had denied him. Anyone who had not much time and wanted to make a study of the history of poetic language might find it hard to improve on Owen's curriculum for convenience, variety, and quality. Elegy had elicited some of the highest flights of the English genius. Was there something especially elegiac about that genius? In elegy could be read an epitome of English poetry, and in the development of English elegies might be traced a spiritual history too. These ideas were not new to Owen in 1917, for he had come across them in the course of his earlier studies in poetry, in time snatched from theology and parish duties at Dunsden in 1912.

In April 1912 he was making a careful study of Laurie Magnus's *Introduction to Poetry* of 1902. Part 3 of that book, entitled 'The Progress of Poetry', starts with a long discussion of the role of tradition and the need for a poet to bend to it. Magnus had a suspicion of innovation, modern poetry, and liberal views. 'The Progress of Poetry' examines the poetic tradition in its continuity and change, and in one section Magnus asks his reader to consider 'The Example of Elegy'.[1] This section gives seven quotations, as follows:

Fourteen lines of Moschus' lament for Bion, translated into English heroic couplets by the Revd Richard Polwhele, including the famous section 'But we, the great, the valiant, and the wise, | . . . Slumber, to wake no more, one long unbroken sleep!'

Four stanzas about the spirit's immortality, from 'Astrophel', Spenser's lament for Sir Philip Sidney. 'Ah no! it is not dead, ne can it die . . .'

Twenty-one lines of Milton's 'Lycidas', beginning 'Weep no more, woeful shepherds, weep no more, | For Lycidas, your sorrow, is not dead . . .'

From Shelley's 'Adonais', stanzas xli ('He lives, he wakes—'tis Death is dead, not he'), xlii ('He is made one with nature') and the opening of stanza xliii ('He is a portion of that loveliness | Which once he made more lovely').

The last three stanzas of Tennyson's *In Memoriam* lxxiv, beginning 'I care not in these fading days | To raise a cry that lasts not long'.

[1] Magnus, *Introduction to Poetry*, 132–7.

The antepenultimate stanza of Matthew Arnold's 'Thyrsis', 'Thou too, O Thyrsis, on like quest wast bound . . .'

Seventh and last, a stanza from William Watson's lament for Tennyson, 'Lachrymae Musarum'. 'He hath returned to regions whence he came. | Him doth the spirit divine | Of universal loveliness reclaim. | All nature is his shrine. | Seek him henceforward in the wind and sea,' etc.

Laurie Magnus comments:

These extracts speak for themselves. The pagan resignation of Moschus at the loss absolute of his friend, with its elaborate pretence in the earlier part of the elegy that all nature has gone into mourning; the dogmatic theology of Spenser and Milton, with the consolation they derive from the scriptural view of immortality; the natural religion of Shelley at the century's dawn, repeated almost verbally at its close by Mr William Watson— the identity of thought and language is remarkable—who find comfort in the belief, new a hundred years ago, but familiar and less sustaining today, that death is not absolute, nor heaven literal, but that immortality implies an unconscious continuation of faculties. And between the two the reserved creeds of Matthew Arnold and Tennyson, on the century's noon, that we cannot dogmatise, but must believe. Is there not in this visible movement of poetry an epitome of the history of religion, culminating in the spiritual tenuities of today, hardly discernible from chill despair? For, according to the mellifluous language of our latter-day poets, the hope of immortality has been reduced by a rationalising process to the less comfortable prospect of impersonal survival in the colour of a rose or in the sound of a wind.[2]

Sven Bäckman considers Magnus's *Introduction to Poetry* the most important, for Owen, of the general books about poetry that he set himself to read.[3] We have seen Owen quoting, indignantly, Magnus's view that the ideals of the French Revolution are waning in English poetry (*CL* 131). This claim is made in the chapter following 'The Example of Elegy', which may have been fresh in Owen's mind three weeks before, when he suggested teasingly that his sister should 'compose a short Elegy' on her canary, recently deceased (and perhaps the bird whose voice he was to remember under rifle-fire in 1917, the day the sentry was blinded) (*CL* 127–8). Edmund Blunden in his memoir quotes part of a verse letter (since lost) written early in the Dunsden period, apparently in December 1911, and invoking the region's associations

[2] Ibid. 136–7. [3] Bäckman, *Tradition Transformed*, 147.

with three of the elegists from Magnus's list—Shelley, Arnold, and Tennyson—in company with the definitively elegiac Gray (*EB* 6–7). That may be no more than a coincidence. But it is a fact that at Dunsden in the spring of 1912 Owen was studying a book that drew his attention to the genre of elegy, as a classical form that had been constantly reinterpreted in English poetry by the changing light of religious faith, or the lack of it.

1912 and 1913 were momentous years in the history of Owen's own faith (he left Dunsden in February 1913), some of which is inscribed in the teleological poems that belong to this time and are related, I believe, to his thinking about elegy as Laurie Magnus's book prompted him to do. He was to return to elegy in the latter part of 1917, quite deliberately, as the evidence of his systematic reading shows. He may have taken another look at the Laurie Magnus chapter. He certainly remembered it, for in December 1917 in Scarborough he got his hands on a copy of Andrew Lang's translation of poems by Theocritus, Bion, and Moschus, where he was able to read in full the first poem quoted in Magnus's list, Moschus' lament for Bion.

Before examining what sort of elegiac writing Owen produced in these two phases, 1912–13 and 1917–18, there is time to consider what he understood by the term elegy. Elegy was the poetry of loss and mourning. It was an expression of grief at the death of a friend (in all of Magnus's examples, the lost friend is himself a poet). It was likely to contain a description of the corpse (like 'Astrophel') or a meditation on it (like *In Memoriam*). The death would usually be carefully placed in or related to a landscape. Magnus had pointed out in Moschus' lament 'its elaborate pretence . . . that all nature has gone into mourning', and Owen could follow the elegiac convention of the desolated landscape through the 'widow state' of the fields in 'Astrophel' to more modern instances. Elegy recorded the bitterness of bereavement, a double grief which mingled a sense of the waste of a life lost too young (Watson's elegy for the octogenarian Tennyson may be allowed to be an exception: the elegies Owen knew, from Moschus to Sassoon, usually mourn *young* men) and the grief of the bereft survivor.

But there was often a plot in elegy too: and if Owen had not seen this, there was Magnus to point out to him its usual denouement. For elegy is not only an expression of grief but also a management of grief. It explores loss but it is in search of consolation, and often finds it.[4] From 'the pagan resignation' of Moschus to 'the reserved creed' of Arnold and Tennyson, Magnus ticks off the various strategies with which different elegists have sought to cope with their grief, to find in themselves the resources of faith or imagination that will enable them to deny death its triumph, with more or less confidence. This is what interests Magnus most about elegy, and he presents the genre in such a way as to suggest that its principal issue is that of survival. (The question of survival is surprisingly ambiguous in Gray's elegy, which is perhaps why it is surprisingly absent from Magnus's list.) Moschus and Shelley find the spirit of their dead friend ever alive and powerful in nature and in song. Spenser's and Milton's 'dogmatic theology', as Magnus says, gives them unshakeable faith in the resurrection. Even Tennyson and Arnold have some such faith, though it has lost its former virility. But does this exemplary genre have a future in English? It seems, on the evidence, unlikely. Magnus's placing of Willian Watson's ludicrously derivative effusion has a polemical bathos, for it is part of Magnus's case against modern poetry that it has lost or misplaced its faith, and is foundering in 'spiritual tenuities'; and without the faith to ground some sort of survival, how can you have elegy?

Laurie Magnus is of some especial interest in the history of Owen's intellectual development since he is, I believe, the first written authority that Owen felt confident enough to challenge, in his letters. He took issue, as we have seen, with Magnus's rather smug claim that the fires of the 'Revolutionary Ideals' had died down in modern English poetry. Owen declared that they had certainly not died down in his own breast, for he was increasingly liberalizing and liberating his thought, he said, 'spite of the Vicar's strong Conservatism' (*CL* 131). Magnus and Mr Wigan, an intellectual and a spiritual authority here interlinked, both presented a challenge to the young poet, a challenge taken up in the 1912 and 1913 poems of teleological doubt, which can be read as being in dialogue with both of them. While these poems (which Owen appears to have kept to himself at the time) make it clear why this 'unofficial curate' could never in good faith enter the Christian ministry, they also show why this newcomer among what Magnus

[4] Peter M. Sacks discusses how the genre performs 'the work of mourning' in *The English Elegy* (a title Owen would have savoured, though he appears only fleetingly in Sacks's book). See also Smith, *By Mourning Tongues*.

calls 'our latter-day poets' could never write a consoling elegy of the kind Magnus admired as exemplary of the genius of the English poetic tradition.

'Deep under turfy grass' is a non-elegy in a country churchyard, a funeral poem which declares that belief in any kind of afterlife is a mockery (though its speaker turns to the beauty of the living for comfort). The consolation of immortality is specifically denied again and again in the poems of this period—in 'The Dread of Falling into Naught', 'Science has looked, and sees no life but this', 'Impromptu' or 'I have no other thought of peace', 'Sonnet' or 'Daily I muse on her', 'But it is not enough to look upon a rolling main', and 'The Unreturning'. In the last-named poem, a sonnet, the 'young Dawn' which restores Shelley's Adonais to 'presence' (in the stanzas quoted by Magnus) is now senile, not a herald of resurrection but of death and nothing but death:

> There watched I for the Dead; but no ghost woke.
> Each one whom Life exiled I named and called.
> But they were all too far, or dumbed, or thralled,
> And never one fared back to me or spoke.
>
> Then peered the indefinite unshapen dawn
> With vacant gloaming, sad as half-lit minds,
> The weak-limned hour when sick men's sighs are drained.
> And while I wondered on their being withdrawn,
> Gagged by the smothering Wing which none unbinds,
> I dreaded even a heaven with doors so chained.

Owen's religious crisis issued in his choice of 'the fullest, largest liveable life . . . of a Poet' (*CL* 325) over that of a minister of the Church, but it also helped to determine the sorts of poetry he could and could not write. The poetic denial, in 'The Unreturning', of the conditions for a reassuring poetry of consolation is inseparable from his rejection of an orthodox life of Christian faith—literally so, for on the back of the earliest sheet of rough working for this poem Owen drafted a letter to the vicar of Dunsden setting out his objections to 'The Christian life' (*CPF* 107). He could be neither the kind of priest Herbert Wigan wanted, nor the kind of poet Laurie Magnus wanted. Of course, as Owen's later reading showed him, elegies do not have to be consolatory; but his introduction to the genre, by way of Magnus's selections and comments, had suggested that they do. The teleological poems live in two discourses. They are a record of Owen's religious doubts, but also, in the words of his slightly ungrammatical original title for a later poem, an 'Apologia lectorem pro Poema Disconsolatia Mea' (*CPF* 278).

Laurie Magnus was a minor man of letters, a publisher with parliamentary ambitions, but to the self-educating nineteen-year-old he was an authority. I have emphasized the importance of Magnus's construction of the idea of the English elegy to show that Owen's 'disconsolation' was a rebellion in poetic as well as religious terms. The teleological poems start what the poems of 1917 and 1918 accomplish—the breakdown of that idea of elegy.

None of these 1912–13 poems of doubt quite belongs to the genre of elegy, although taken as a whole they perform the obsequies for Owen's dead (and unreturning) Christian faith. They can be described as poems in the elegiac mode, however, and their elegiac themes, moments, and images anticipate the 1917–18 poems—in 'Deep under turfy grass', the body in earth, the chill of death, 'stretcher after stretcher of our dead'; in 'The Dread of Falling into Naught', a winter landscape, youthful death; in 'Science has looked', the death of the world, and 'eternal sleep'; in 'Sonnet' or 'Daily I muse on her', doomed youthful beauty again; in 'But it is not enough', 'I must . . . sleep for ever'; in 'The Unreturning' the spirits of the dead are invoked but will not or cannot come home. Owen's elegiac mode was disconsolate, refusing a comforting closure in reassurances of the survival and return of the spirit in some form or another. The generic dawn, whose promise of renewed life starts to heal the elegist's grief in 'Lycidas' and 'Adonais' and several times in *In Memoriam*, is a time of renewed anxiety and suffering in Owen, the dawn that in 'Mental Cases' 'breaks open like a wound that bleeds afresh', but which was already creeping up in 'The Unreturning' only to shed its weak light on a deathbed.[5]

There are close connections between the poems of 1912–13 and the war poems, 'these elegies' which were to be 'to this generation

[5] Paul Fussell's excellent discussion of the ironizing of the meaning of dawn (and sunset) in English writing is a little too inclined to derive the change simply from the experience of the Great War, with its dusk ritual of 'stand-to' and the danger of attack. See Fussell, *The Great War and Modern Memory*, 51–63. Owen's hopeless dawn in 'The Unreturning' is pre-war, civilian, and somewhat Decadent. But there are also ironic as well as hopeful dawns in *In Memoriam*, most famously in vii ('Dark house, by which once more I stand').

in no sense consolatory'. In September 1917, about a fortnight after meeting Sassoon, Owen wrote from Craiglockhart asking his mother to forward from Shrewsbury three portfolios of his writing which he had kept locked in his desk at home, binding her on her unimpeachable honour not to look at their contents. 'This sounds mysterious; but I am serious. Some of these verses will light my cigarettes, but one or two may light the darkness of the world. It is not a question of wheat and chaff, but of devils and angels' (*CL* 492). It is reasonable to suppose that in this way the poems of teleological doubt, parcelled up but still unread by the pious Mrs Owen, made their way to Craiglockhart, and that the poet had them to hand in the autumn of 1917. In his next letter he had another request: would his mother please also send his copy of Laurent Tailhade's volume, *Poèmes élégiaques* (*CL* 493)? No doubt he wanted to show his manuscripts, and the poems of his old French friend, to his new friend Sassoon; but also he wanted to immerse himself in 'elegiac' writing, including his own, as he embarked on the project of his elegies of disconsolation.

The recurrence of the elegiac mode in Owen's war writing can be illustrated by the case of 'Futility', which also carries a trace of his earlier elegiac phase.

> Move him into the sun—
> Gently its touch awoke him once,
> At home, whispering of fields half-sown.
> Always it woke him, even in France,
> Until this morning and this snow.
> If anything might rouse him now
> The kind old sun will know.
>
> Think how it wakes the seeds—
> Woke once the clays of a cold star.
> Are limbs, so dear achieved, are sides
> Full-nerved, still warm, too hard to stir?
> Was it for this the clay grew tall?
> —O what made fatuous sunbeams toil
> To break earth's sleep at all?

I discussed 'Futility' earlier as a moment in family discourse, an exposure of the inadequacies of the father. That reading is not contradicted if we now consider how the poem makes a place for itself in the discourse of English poetry. It starts from the situation of elegy—reaction to the death of a young man. Indeed it is a small compendium of elegiac themes. There is the corpse, and the sympathetically desolate landscape, the dead of winter, the death of nature. There is an evocation of the swain in the prime of his youth, living the life of nature in his home landscape, when like Bion he was the darling of the Apollonian sun. There is the grief of the bereaved over the young body, ruined but still beautiful. There is the invocation of a divine or natural power. There is a dawn, or at least a sunlit morning, the usual figure of renewed life in traditional elegy. There is even, as in 'Lycidas' and 'Adonais', the awakening of a star. But these are fragments of a broken mode; they do not add up, at least not to elegy. The poem, like the dead man, is without issue. Instead of reaching an elegiac resignation, 'Futility' quarrels with resignation and will not be comforted. Why *should* this death be accepted with resignation, still less with hope? The three increasingly aggressive interrogations leave the poem rudely open. An evolution that leads merely to extinction is nothing to be thankful for. Owen knew that the same nihilistic sense of futility was the subject of Tennyson's *In Memoriam* lv, which concludes like this:

> O life as futile, then, as frail!
> O for thy voice to soothe and bless!
> What hope of answer, or redress?
> Behind the veil, behind the veil.

But Owen's questions are not to be fobbed off, or misted up, like this. He believed, as the teleological poems had already shown, that behind the veil was nothing. There are similar forebodings of extinction in 'Strange Meeting', 'Asleep', 'The End', and 'A Terre'. Owen's work in the last year or so of his life is the God-forsaken *In Memoriam* of his generation. And this reminder of the connection between the breakdown of elegy and Owen's loss of faith brings to light another curious feature of 'Futility'. It encodes a narrative of Owen's own apostasy—his inability to believe in the promises of resurrection was a decisive factor in his abandoning his faith (*CL* 176)—which is also a narrative of his Dunsden rebellion against the vicar, 'dear Mr Wigan', whose character he thought 'on a higher plane than myself' at first (*CL* 92), but who before long was to be seen as the fatuous hypocrite who would not lift a finger to help the afflicted of the parish for whom his assistant felt an increasingly angry pity. 'Futility', then, has four discursive dimensions, of family, Church, army, and poetry.

Only two of Owen's poems are elegies by title. The fragment 'An Imperial Elegy' (*CPF* 453–4), subtitled 'Libretto for *Marche Funèbre*' and written during army training, imagines the front line as 'a titan's grave' but gets not much further. The piece has no people in it and its only elegiac element is an allusion to Gray's 'paths of glory'. The later 'Elegy in April and September', written in two parts in those months of 1918, is, as it stands, a pleasant little exercise in assonance and alliteration:

> Close, rose, and droop, heliotrope,
> And shudder, hope! The shattering winter blows.
> Drop, heliotrope, and close, rose . . .

This would not be at all out of place in *The Nymph*, and this is partly because it is all form, and has nothing much to say. In its first part there is a search through the natural world for the lost friend, and in the second part nature mourns; both are themes of classical elegy. But this poem too peters out. Owen is tinkering here with a form for which he clearly does not yet have a subject. One draft is entitled 'Ode for a Poet reported Missing: later, reported killed' (*CPF* 363), but the poet friend in question has not been identified. My own guess is that the subject with which this elegy is waiting (perhaps without knowing it) to be filled, is the death of Sassoon, Owen's Astrophel.

The largely musical exercise of 'Elegy in April and September' is the closest Owen came to traditional pastoral elegy, in direct line from Bion and Moschus. There are straightforward elegiac moments—the ending of 'Insensibility', for example, or the last line of 'Anthem for Doomed Youth', 'And each slow dusk a drawing-down of blinds', a beautiful refreshment of the theme of mourning nature—elsewhere in the war poems. But there is no straightforward elegy. The elements of the genre get entangled with other things, and are sometimes roughly treated by the company they have to keep. 'Asleep', for example, begins as a trench life sketch. Owen told Leslie Gunston it was 'written *as from* the trenches' (*CL* 508):

Under his helmet, up against his pack,
After so many days of work and waking,
Sleep took him by the brow and laid him back.

There, in the happy no-time of his sleeping,
Death took him by the heart. There heaved a quaking
Of the aborted life within him leaping,
Then chest and sleepy arms once more fell slack.

And soon the slow, stray blood came creeping
From the intruding lead, like ants on track.

The death over, the poem turns to address the consolations of elegy:

Whether his deeper sleep lie shaded by the shaking
Of great wings, and the thoughts that hung the stars,
High-pillowed on calm pillows of God's making,
Above these clouds, these rains, these sleets of lead,
And these winds' scimitars,
—Or whether yet his thin and sodden head
Confuses more and more with the low mould,
His hair being one with the grey grass
Of finished fields, and wire-scrags rusty-old,
Who knows? Who hopes? Who troubles? Let it pass!
He sleeps. He sleeps less tremulous, less cold,
Than we who wake, and waking say Alas!

Sven Bäckman noticed the way the 'Whether . . . Or whether' construction echoes a passage in 'Lycidas' (156–67),[6] a passage which comes just before the injunction 'Weep no more, woeful shepherds, weep no more, | For Lycidas, your sorrow, is not dead.' It is characteristic of Owen's intertextual habits that he has this great Christian elegy at the back of his mind as he dismisses with a shrug the kind of comfort it has to offer, the assurance of the dead man's assumption into paradise. And the other, pagan version of post-mortem survival—the formula 'He is made one with Nature' from 'Adonais', alluded to in 'A Terre'—is given a run too, but exposed to and immediately withered by Owen's wintry realism.

—Or whether yet his thin and sodden head
Confuses more and more with the low mould . . .

[6] Bäckman, *Tradition Transformed*, 40–1.

This traditional consolation, of the re-absorption of the body into the vitality of nature, is revealed as only a sort of poetical disinfectant applied to the fact that dead bodies decompose and rot in the ground. Owen had seen ('and in the darkness, *felt*' (*CL* 429)) decomposing human remains as Shelley had probably not. It is the usual story: Owen confronts a genre (elegy) of one discourse—that of poetry—with the experience of another—that of the army. He is in grim, covert, antagonistic dialogue with the genre. The insolence of his undermining of elegy here is disguised by the gentle, dreamy movement of that long sentence, till its rude stop; for these *are* dreams, and 'we' have to wake up. In the end the poem dismisses the consolations of elegy not because they are untrue but because they are irrelevant. What does it matter what becomes of the dead? 'Asleep' not only refuses to be comforted, it is also a refusal to mourn—an anti-elegiac motif that links it to 'S.I.W.' with its Yeats epigraph ('that man there has set his teeth to die . . . I cannot mourn him') and to the speaker in 'Strange Meeting' who, though he knows he is in hell itself, finds 'no cause to mourn' because he also knows he is 'out of battle'. In the last line of 'Asleep' (which in an earlier draft lengthens to twelve syllables like the last line of the Spenserian stanza used in 'Adonais' (*CPF* 314)), the survivors have failed to reach elegy's usual destination, a determination to 'weep no more'. But they do not mourn for the dead man. Only in their own death will they weep no more.

There were, to be sure, poetic precedents for Owen's stubborn disconsolation, though it was a tone excluded from even the 'modern' texts in the list Laurie Magnus had presented as exemplary, canonical, English elegies. The refusal of false comfort, in 'Asleep', and its suggestion that the unrising dead are better off than the embattled living, is close in tone (if not in style) to the last stanzas of Swinburne's 'Ave atque Vale':

> There is no help for these things; none to mend
> And none to mar; not all our songs, O friend,
> Will make death clear or make life durable . . .
> Content thee, howsoe'er, whose days are done;
> There lies not any troublous thing before,
> Nor sight nor sound to war against thee more,
> For whom all winds are quiet as the sun,
> All waters as the shore.

But Swinburne (no favourite of Laurie Magnus) still had something of a reputation for being disreputable, dangerous, and un-English (and his elegy was for the still more scandalous—for those who had heard of him—Baudelaire). The preference Owen had developed for Swinburne over the monumentally respectable Tennyson was congruent with his choosing to venture into what he allegorized as 'the untravelled world' seen 'over the hedges of Dunsden Garden' (*CL* 553). But as a matter of fact even the most respectable elegy could show Owen the possibility of mixing the issue of grieving, as the war poems do, with indignant and topical satire and protest. 'Lycidas' after all contains an attack on corrupt clergy, in a passage which Owen had seen carefully expounded in his beloved *Sesame and Lilies*, itself an example to him as it examines and treats with equal seriousness the elegiac verse of Milton and the report of an inquest on a working man who had died of starvation in London.

Owen explores the resources and limits of elegy. He takes issue, and takes liberties, with the elegiac mode, drawing on the elegiac conventions to break the genre down and mix it up, confront it with testing experience, modernize it. Compared with Owen's rough handling of elegy, Siegfried Sassoon's exercise in the genre, in 'The Last Meeting' (in *The Old Huntsman*), is respectful to the point of timidity, and extremely English. Carefully insulated from the demotic and satiric modes rampant elsewhere in the volume, and scarcely mentioning the war, 'The Last Meeting' is a very conventional pastoral elegy: the loved one is mourned, sought, and missed in his home landscape, but is rediscovered as a spirit diffused throughout a very Wordsworthian nature and survives, predictably, in the light of stars and the returning loveliness of a summer dawn. It is against this that Owen's sometimes unmannerly experiments with elegy can be judged radical. Meanwhile it is an odd sort of paradox that it was the influence of Sassoon that ensured that Owen would never write a poem like this.

His fruitful quarrel with the genre bends and batters it into some odd transformations. An elegy is, in plain words, a send-off, and 'The Send-Off' is a kind of elegy, and another disconsolate one:

> Down the close darkening lanes they sang their way
> To the siding-shed,
> And lined the train with faces grimly gay.

Their breasts were stuck all white with wreath and spray
As men's are, dead.

Dull porters watched them, and a casual tramp
Stood staring hard,
Sorry to miss them from the upland camp.

Then, unmoved, signals nodded, and a lamp
Winked to the guard.

Bäckman, who identified traces of 'Lycidas' in 'Asleep', detects in the third stanza of 'The Send-Off' 'a couple of ironic echoes' of Gray's 'Elegy', where the swain who used 'To meet the sun upon the upland lawn' is one morning 'miss'd . . . on the custom'd hill'.[7] English elegy again is at the back of this poem's mind, and flowing underneath its account of a draft of soldiers starting their journey to the front is a covert drama, an underground elegy. The plucking and strewing of flowers and garlands for the dead is a generic convention, honoured at the start of 'Lycidas' and 'Ave atque Vale', for example. These soldiers who march singing to the railway in the evening are their own funeral procession. They are as good as dead already, and the rituals of their passing are laconically depleted to the operation of the signals and the lamp, just as the plangent troop of generic and allegorical figures who turn up to mourn in traditional elegy have dwindled, in these reduced circumstances, to a single casual tramp who is 'sorry to miss them':

So secretly, like wrongs hushed-up, they went.
They were not ours:
We never heard to which front these were sent;

Nor there if yet they mock what women meant
Who gave them flowers.

Shall they return to beating of great bells
In wild train-loads?
A few, a few, too few for drums and yells,

May creep back, silent, to village wells,
Up half-known roads.

There is another story going on here, of course, already hinted at in the sly collusion of signals, lamp, and guard. It is a story about betrayal, of which the soldiers are both the victims and the evidence. The betrayal—and this is really Owen's whole case against

[7] Ibid. 42–3.

elegy in the war poems—turns elegy sour, problematic, and ironic, making a mockery of its forms. Whether the blithe gesture of the 'women . . . Who gave them flowers' was hypocritical or just ignorant, it is treated with cynicism by the soldiers. And of course the usual elegiac trope or turn to consolation, in the figure of survival and return, is put literally into question. Neither apotheosis nor resurrection awaits these swains, and it is far from certain that anyone really cares what has become of them, or wants them back. The few who may survive will return as bewildered and lost souls, creeping back guiltily to a place half-recognized as home. At the point where elegy might be expected like 'Adonais' to record the spirit's triumph, 'outsoaring the shadow of our night', or at least like Gray's 'Elegy' lay it to rest in peace 'upon the lap of earth', 'The Send-Off' comes to an inconclusive end, haunted by restless and unappeased ghosts.

Although I am suggesting that something like violence is done to elegy in this poem, it is nonetheless, and for all its laconic coolness, itself in the elegiac mode, a poem of grieving. At the same time it dramatizes with a brutal economy an urgent social and political issue, the gap felt to have opened up between an exploited and alienated nation under arms and an indifferent and selfish nation at home. There seems little point, then, in quarrelling over whether Owen should be read as primarily a satirical poet of anger or an elegiac poet of pathos.[8] Owen's rewritings of elegy are inseparable in the war poems, as they had been at Dunsden, from his inability to accept hypocrisy, injustice, and complacency. And his preface meant what it said: the war poems were elegies, and were not to be comforting. How could poems about the death of soldiers be comforting in a time of compulsory military service?

Owen, then, had been aware at least since 1912 of elegy as an established genre in English poetry, one which registered the changing linguistic and spiritual resources of the poetic tradition. He had also come across the genre at a time and in circumstances that led him to associate it with English complacency. His earliest experiments in elegiac writing challenge its traditional movement towards

[8] See Silkin's preface to *The Penguin Book of First World War Poetry*, Hibberd's 'Silkin on Owen', Silkin's 'Owen: Elegist, Satirist or Neither', and Glover's 'Whose Owen?' The argument is still rumbling in Silkin's essay 'Sassoon, Owen, Rosenberg', in Roucoux (ed.), *English Literature of the Great War Revisited*, 84–107.

calm acceptance and its tropes of survival and return, and those challenges were taken up and extended when in 1917 he turned his hand to a large-scale project, putting elegy to the exacting test of modern war.

In many ways the genre suffers badly at Owen's hands. Elegy is inclined both to glamourize death and make it acceptable, and Owen was inclined to do neither. But although the war poems are the grounds of a quarrel with traditional elegy, they also immeasurably extend the constituency of the genre, and they do this simply by breaking its fundamental rule and making the living, and not just the dead, its subjects. It is this that enabled Owen to describe all the poems in his projected volume as elegies, in the draft preface. The rite of passage in 'The Send-Off' is, as we have seen, a kind of funeral. Here, as elsewhere, Owen imagined those who were sent with the army to war as having passed over (as Eliot's Hollow Men were to do) to death's other kingdom. There at the front they dragged out an existence exiled from the life they had known, often in the dark and under the ground, or in a God-forsaken landscape submitted to tortures for which no end could be foreseen. It was unearthly, like 'the eternal place of gnashing of teeth' or like Sodom, Gomorrah, and Babylon, cities of the damned (*CL* 429). There could be no communication between the land of the living and this place at the end of the world whose inhabitants, even when nothing was happening, could not believe they were alive, and who knew that from this country they could never return. Owen envisaged war itself as a kind of death which only death could end.

These men were worth the tears of elegy, but they could not be consoling tears. The poems ruthlessly abort any comfort that might be born from elegy. The idea that the men's suffering has its rewards, and they have gone to a place where they are 'content' or even 'happy now', is disallowed in 'Apologia' and in 'Smile, Smile, Smile'; that God is still looking after them is dismissed in 'Spring Offensive' with a shrug—'Some say God caught them even before they fell.' That there will come a time, (at least in 'this generation') to weep no more for them is angrily denied and denied again.

'These elegies' celebrate and mourn these anonymous men, but they exclude any consoling hope. Consistently the poems raise only to contradict the possibility of survival and return, whether the return of 'wild train-loads' at the end of 'The Send-Off', of the blinded sentry's eyesight, of another spring for the young cripple in 'A Terre', or the return home, even in dreams, of the soldiers in 'Exposure', condemned to a life indistinguishable from death. The favoured rhetorical tactic in Owen's campaign of disconsolation is a dramatic irony of false expectation. Its characteristic sound is heard in pararhyme, a broken promise to return, which he began to use frequently when he embarked on his elegiac project.

Harold Owen repeatedly avers that his brother did not expect to survive and return from the war. If army service was envisaged as already a kind of death, then Owen's elegies are written, in a sense, *d'outre-tombe*. When he arrived back at the front line in September 1918, he soon acquired a nickname among his fellow officers. 'They call me The Ghost,' he reported, '(which is a point in favour of their latent imaginations)' (*CL* 579).

17
Soldiers and Poets

'Disabled' was drafted at Craiglockhart in October 1917 and revised at Scarborough in July 1918. Robert Graves was shown an early draft and declared it 'a damn fine poem' (*CL* 595). Owen himself must have thought highly of it too, for he intended to make it the flagship of his first book, *Disabled and Other Poems*. It is an appropriate place, having come this far, to study the operation of the forces that shaped the language of Owen's war poetry.

The title itself, arresting in its severity, is a category from the language of the military medical institution, the bureaucratic equivalent of a cliché. It is the last word that official language has to spare for the human subject of the poem, and the poem itself is left to supply him with what that language cannot confer or recognize—a human meaning. Owen does the same with 'S.I.W.' ('self-inflicted wound') and 'Mental Cases', other category title poems in which the bare bones of official nomenclature are brought to troubling life. These poems wage war on the emotional paucity of their titles. 'Dulce et Decorum Est' simply exposes its title to a flat contradiction in narrative: this is what dying for your country is really like. 'Disabled' is adversarial in a different way. Like 'The Dead-Beat', its title is not dismissed but grimly expounded. And Owen's intention to entitle his book *Disabled* seems to suggest he found a truth in this word that went a considerable way beyond the particular young man in this poem. Telling his family about a consumptive child at Dunsden five years before, Owen had exclaimed: 'This, I suppose, is only a typical *case*; one of many *Cases*! O hard word! How it savours of rigid, frigid professionalism! How it suggests smooth and polished, formal, labelled, mechanical callousness!' (*CL* 126). 'Disabled' was another dead and pitiless word, which this poem restores to life and feeling. The language of the poet must redeem the language of the professionals. The poetry would be in the pity.

He sat in a wheeled chair, waiting for dark,
And shivered in his ghastly suit of grey,
Legless, sewn short at elbow. Through the park
Voices of boys rang saddening like a hymn,
Voices of play and pleasure after day,
Till gathering sleep had mothered them from him.

About this time Town used to swing so gay
When glow-lamps budded in the light blue trees,
And girls glanced lovelier as the air grew dim,—
In the old times, before he threw away his knees.
Now he will never feel again how slim
Girls' waists are, or how warm their subtle hands.
All of them touch him like some queer disease.

'He sat . . .': it begins in the manner of one of Harold Monro's satirical verse sketches in *Before Dawn*, with its 'impressions' of characters like a priest, a butcher, an armaments king; a simple opening move also favoured by Sassoon for his sketches of similarly anonymous men, and used six times to open war poems in *The Old Huntsman* ('He turned to me', 'He staggered in', 'He woke', and the like). But just as Owen soon moved beyond the Sassoon-like quatrains of his first draft (*OTP* 101) to these paragraphic stanzas, so too his portrait poem quickly becomes larger in scope than anything of Monro's or Sassoon's. The wheeled chair in the first line announces a brisk Georgian realism—writing, as Sassoon did, of things like prostheses and liver pills was one way for the true poets to be truthful. But the next phrase, 'waiting for dark', opens another dimension, placing the human figure in that generic, historical twilight that so often bathed the late Romantic poetry Owen had come to admire in France, and enlisting him in the grey company of those weary, defeated spectres that have their being in (for example) the Paris and London of Verlaine's poems. Here the young man grown unnaturally old is helpless in a world which is as the Decadents felt the actual world to be (indeed it might be 'le vieux parc solitaire et glacé' of Verlaine's 'Colloque sentimental')—grey and darkening, chilling, futureless. And for Owen the individual tragedy stands, obviously enough, for a tragic history, the wrecked and truncated body figuring the soon-broken promise of the new century. (How old is the man in the chair? We will be shown that he was visibly under age when he joined the army, presumably before 1917.) Owen now measures what has been lost, in innocence and pleasure, by evoking his favourite image of children but placing it out of reach and sight. Many of his own happiest memories, as his letters show, were of time spent in the company of children, especially of boys. Distance makes the image poignant (and it is possible he may have remembered 'Et O ces voix d'enfants', from Verlaine, as Eliot too was to remember it in *The Waste Land*). The park is not private property but common ground, a place of public enjoyment. The amputee may be 'in the park' (as he is described in an early draft (*CPF* 351–3)) but he is segregated and cut off (the poem makes this metaphor unavoidable) from its communal life. He can hear but cannot enter into its pleasures. The wheelchair is both a post-lapsarian exile and a social limbo. 'Voices of boys' are heard, in a context of sadness, evening and bell-ringing,[1] in two Craiglockhart fragments (*CPF* 485–8), which also provided ideas for 'Anthem for Doomed Youth'. But the simile of voices that ring 'saddening like a hymn' is of particular interest because it implicates Owen's loss of faith with the other losses this poem deals with.

The sound of worship is heard in the poem, but heard as a figure for melancholy. The hymn, a song of praise, has been swallowed into the discourse of elegy, a song of mourning. Hymn-singing now can evoke nothing but sadness; it is the voice of a community of faith from which the man in the wheelchair is exiled as absolutely as he is from his childhood. And even the poor comfort of these elegiac-sounding voices (for classical elegy represents itself as a sad hymn sung out of doors by swains lamenting a young man's loss) is soon itself lost. Children at play must go home to bed when the day ends. The ideas of sleep and of mother had long been associated in Owen's mind, as we have seen. Sleep like a mother is what is desired here (and at the poem's end), promising shelter, peace, relief; she gathers the children to herself, forming the nucleus of a community, a family. Yet the ambiguities of the figure have to be noted too. She it is who puts a stop to the play and pleasure of the boys, for her gathering of her charges is also a segregation, taking them from the common

[1] Ringing is usually a saddening sound in Owen, an association no doubt reinforced by the curfew that starts Gray's 'Elegy', the tolling of 'forlorn' in Keats's nightingale ode, and a phrase he remembered from *Madame Bovary* about the *lamentation pacifique* of a bell. (See Bentley, 'Wilfred Owen and Gustave Flaubert', 456)

ground and company of others, and a silencing—temporary, but death-counterfeiting—of their voices. And to the wounded man himself she has nothing to offer but unappeased exclusion. The grammatical oddity of the phrase 'sleep . . . mothered them from him' turns mothering into a kind of deprivation, like stealing or (transitive) alienation. This gentle maternal sleep is also, then, the first of the poem's female traitors. In this way, registrations of the comfort of both home and Church are present in the first stanza, but both are present as contradictions. Glimpses of the life of congregation and of family now reinforce the isolation and helplessness against which they ought to be a defence. And like many of the soldiers Owen wrote about, the young cripple has no voice of his own in the poem; his disability is a kind of excommunication.

The second stanza opens with a move to recover a different meaning in the dusk that was so full, in the opening stanza, of intimations of loss and ending. There is an effort of memory, conjuring up a past in which the day's end meant not sadness but glamour, the beginning of excitement and the quickening of erotic possibilities. As this happens, a momentary jauntiness enters the poem ('Town used to swing so gay') which will recur as the signature of the cripple's former self. This signals or confirms a shift of point of view towards the interiority of the young man who was first observed dramatically, from the outside. As the poem enters his memory it moves into something like free indirect style and picks up traces of his accent, acquiring a double voice in which the literary English of the observer (the poet, if you will) forms a sometimes untidy dialogic partnership with the more oral, casual style of the young man. Here Owen's recurring sociolinguistic problem with the representation of soldiers' language is met with just enough demotic-sounding phrasing—in the first and last lines of the second stanza, for example, and early in stanza four—to establish the characterization and social register, but Owen does not make a consistent attempt (as in 'The Chances') to mimic how a soldier would speak, even to himself. Part of the victim's disability is linguistic in any case—in his speechless isolation he has become like an infant, a foreigner or a ghost—and the poem supplies that lack, giving him language (and people, readers, to attend to it). This was the vocation of the officer poet in 'The Calls', which itself anticipated Owen's resolve to help 'these boys', as he told his mother in a late letter, 'by watching their sufferings that I may speak of them as well as a pleader can' (*CL* 580). So in the terms of 'The Calls', the poet-pleader brings his own 'skill' to articulate the 'distress' of the soldier. Here, then, it is the poet nurtured on Keats who evokes the glow-lamps as portents of vernal fertility, budding in the trees, and the aesthete rather than the soldier who manages the consonantal glides of 'girls glanced lovelier as the air grew dim'; and it is the student of elegy who knows perfectly well that to hark back to the happy old times before bereavement (usually an obligatory passage early in elegy) is only to deepen the sense of subsequent loss.

There is in the contrast of pictures of 'before' and 'after'—the carefree lad about town and the friendless wreck at death's door—a rhetorical pattern of a kind often used for didactic, advertising, and propaganda purposes, a pattern Owen had been familiar with since his early exposure to temperance parables, and one that provided a favourite theme for *Punch* in the metamorphosis of the mild or fastidious civilian into the grubby and formidable Tommy (and, later, the flapper into the land-worker). The 'Disabled' narrative of the lad's progress reverses the militarist myth that the army turns boys into men. The poem exhibits the picture of 'after' before we see 'before', and it is clear that the lad after battle is in every sense less of a man than he was before. His dancing days are done. The first stanza saw him exiled from the paradise of boys, and now he is locked out from whatever Eden girls might have to offer. Here matters start to get complicated. For one thing, a young man's exclusion from the love of women is a frequent topos in the homoerotic poetry of the Decadence (and of the Uranians),[2] where it is by no means seen as a tragic matter. The statuesque ephebe in the Tailhade sonnet, for example, was to be congratulated because his young body would not have to satisfy 'l'amour des fiancées'. For Owen the sexual disabling of the youth is certainly presented as an aspect of his tragedy, yet his loss of the attentions of women cannot be seen as quite unequivocal. What is more, the indifference to women exemplified in the Tailhade poem was an attitude that had a more violent, phobic relative, an obsessive mistrust and fear whose symbols are the frightening

[2] D'Arch Smith, *Love in Earnest*, 163–201. See also the introduction to Martin Taylor's anthology, *Lads: Love Poetry of the Trenches*.

sisterhood of Lamias, Medusas, and Salomes that slink through the art of the Romantic agony. Keats's Lamia, one of the type's earlier incarnations, was a beautiful woman who proved to be a snake. Owen's girls, with their lovely glances and slim waists, have hands which are at first 'warm' but then immediately 'subtle'. There is an unresolved confusion between sexual tragedy (budding young love cut down before its prime) and sexual treachery (the man beguiled and destroyed by the woman, a theme which will become explicit later). For the second time, a stanza about loss hints at an under-story or subtext of betrayal by a woman, a betrayal that has left the young soldier, like Keats's knight-at-arms, haggard and woebegone. A Romantic literary theme meshes with Owen's own already ambiguous feelings about women, and becomes entangled with a not uncommon tendency among morale-bonded soldiers in wartime to treat the other sex with suspicion and even hostility. 'You love us when we're heroes, home on leave, | Or wounded in a mentionable place,' begins Sassoon's 'Glory of Women'. But Owen's amputee has no such luck. His honourable wound is treated by the women like a shameful disease.

There is a cancelled stanza with a further description of the lad in civilian times, loafing in the evenings in an old soft cap, 'Proud of his neck, scarfed with a sun-burn band, | And of his curl, and all his reckless gear, | Down to [the] gloves of sun-brown on his hand' (*CPF* 353). The idea of suntan as clothing links this doomed youth with the young working-class man of godlike beauty vividly remembered in the unfinished 'Lines to a Beauty seen in Limehouse' (*CPF* 481–4), and also to the poet's younger brother. 'Let your hands be gloved with the dust of earth,' Wilfred had written cheerfully to Colin Owen the year before, 'and your neck scarved with the brown scarf of sunshine' (*CL* 407). Dominic Hibberd, adducing both these connections, makes the point that there may also be 'something of the poet himself' in the soldier in 'Disabled' (*OTP* 79–82). The figure is certainly of complex genesis, compounded of different discourses, and an example of the way Owen's language in the creative process is usually doing several things at once. Thus in the disabled figure one thing that has been ruined is the kind of male beauty that was the ideal subject of the homosexually inclined aesthete, a beauty related to that of the classical ephebes of Wilde (and Tailhade), the unattainable red-coats and sportsmen of Housman, and the guardsmen and stokers and schoolboys admired by the Uranians. At the same time, as we shall see, there was a thrilling pleasure to be felt in contemplating the very ruin of that beautiful body, its martyrdom. Meanwhile 'Disabled' is equally caught up with Owen's helplessly protective feelings for his younger brother Colin, as he approached and then reached the age of active service. (Colin Owen was born in 1900, an *enfant du siècle* indeed: he joined the RAF in June 1918, shortly before 'Disabled' was finished. Johnny de la Touche, Wilfred's Mérignac pupil, became at about the same time 'a creature of killable age' (*CL* 544).) Here what I have called the double voice of 'Disabled'—half identified with its subject, and half a kind of elder advocate for him—goes right back to the discursive positions of the junior 'third parent' at Birkenhead and Shrewsbury, the child shouldering responsibility for 'the children'. And at the same time again, the poem is a bleak elegy for Wilfred Owen's own youth, his amputated civilian future, the social independence and sexual self-confidence which he was starting to develop, too late to enjoy. The youthful promise of the flesh was threatened with crucifixion in 'The time was aeon', and the sentence has now been carried out on the young man immobilized and forsaken in his wheelchair. (But from this tableau of Crucifixion the usual attendant figures have absconded.)

'Disabled' continues:

> There was an artist silly for his face,
> For it was younger than his youth, last year.
> Now, he is old; his back will never brace;
> He's lost his colour very far from here,
> Poured it down shell-holes till the veins ran dry,
> And half his lifetime lapsed in the hot race
> And leap of purple spurted from his thigh.

There may be a hint here of Wilde's Dorian Gray, with his portrait and his unnaturally youthful appearance; and the artist 'silly for his face' might recall Tailhade's fulsome compliments about Owen's 'lovely' eyes and 'neck of a statue', or be related to the fact that at the time of writing 'Disabled' Owen was having his picture painted by a Mrs Steinthal in Edinburgh (*CL* 500). But the artist also sounds like Owen himself, with his erotic and aesthetic enthusiasms for the beauty of lads. The artist's infatuation introduces a blurring of the aesthetic and the sexual; but the catastrophe that has now overtaken the young man—he has 'lost his colour', a bold use found for a familiar phrase from the register of chat or gossip—has drained him at once of pictorial vividness and of passion. His body has been emptied and will never stand again. And his wounding in battle is described in a language redolent of the Decadence, for it sounds very much as if (continuing the theme of sexual treachery) he has been ravished by the vampire or succubus of war, that has drained his potency and left him pale and unmanned. There is a fascination too with the extreme excitement of that devastating moment—it would not be inaccurate to call it ecstatic—an extraordinary climax (and the sad years of disablement will be the anticlimax) which is both an extreme example and, surely, a dreadful indictment of those moments of overwhelming sensation which Romantic and Decadent writers liked to exalt as being worth any purchase. Men who had been to war knew better the price of romantic gestures. Yeats, who had not been to war but had served his own apprenticeship to late Romantic fashions, was to imagine the pilot in his 'An Irish Airman Foresees his Death' coolly and deliberately exchanging 'half his lifetime' for the romantic intensity of life and death in battle. Beneath that great poem runs an aristocratic fantasy, a dandyism for the sporting class. For Owen's soldier the 'hot race | And leap' are the sensations of the blood leaving his broken body, a moment of intensity which does not release him from the grey world but condemns him to it. The body streaming blood might be Bion's Adonis or Spenser's Astrophel (both wounded in the thigh), but the afterlife that this unconsoling elegy awards him will not be one fit for heroes.

Next:

> One time he liked a blood-smear down his leg,
> After the matches, carried shoulder-high.
> It was after football, when he'd drunk a peg,
> He thought he'd better join.—He wonders why.
> Someone had said he'd look a god in kilts,
> That's why; and maybe, too, to please his Meg,
> Aye, that was it, to please the giddy jilts
> He asked to join. He didn't have to beg;
> Smiling they wrote his lie: aged nineteen years.

Germans he scarcely thought of; all their guilt,
And Austria's, did not move him. And no fears
Of Fear came yet. He thought of jewelled hilts
For daggers in plaid socks; of smart salutes;
And care of arms; and leave; and pay arrears;
Esprit de corps; and hints for young recruits.
And soon, he was drafted out with drums and cheers.

This longest of the poem's paragraphs addresses the question of its original title, 'Why he joined' (*CPF* 352). It also reveals that its intertextual next of kin is A. E. Housman's poem, in *A Shropshire Lad*, called 'To an Athlete Dying Young':

The time you won your town the race
We chaired you through the market-place;
Man and boy stood cheering by,
And home we brought you shoulder-high.

The Housman lyric congratulates the young champion on dying before the 'garland briefer than a girl's' has time to fade on his brow. He will never know failure or the loss of his youth. Owen for once has no quarrel with his precursor; his own sportsman's story confirms and illustrates the point of the earlier poem that, even or especially for the young and beautiful, there are fates worse than death. The presence of Housman here is a reminder that Owen's relationship with this poet was a curiously personal one, and not just because both of them found a theme in their feelings about lads. Though Housman was not in fact a Salopian, for the poet from Shrewsbury he was something of a local hero. It is also interesting to see Wilfred Owen in a 1916 letter lightly referring to his brother Colin as 'the Shropshire Lad' (*CL* 399). Later, in 1918, he nicknames him 'my Immortal Innocent' (*CL* 559). The Housman intertext, then, also leads back to Shropshire and home. And if one of the propellants of 'Disabled' is Owen's anxiety about his young brother's safety (much on his mind in 1917) under the threatening shadow of war, it may be more than coincidence that sends this poem's victim to his fate along a path already taken by that paradigm of disaster in Owen family discourse, Susan Owen's brother Edward, the champion footballer who under the influence of drink left home and never found his way back.

But in the case of Owen's athlete, the blame for what becomes of him is now laid explicitly to the charge of women:

> to please his Meg,
> Aye, that was it, to please the giddy jilts
> He asked to join.

It is not possible to say just what is being avenged, or warded off, in that rush from 'his Meg' to the contemptuous judgement on the entire sex in the following line. Owen's own feelings about women in general were no more simple, and no more fully articulate, than his feelings for the mother and sister who were probably the only women he knew well. The rights (and therefore the nature) of women had become a widely debated political issue in his lifetime—there was a women question as there was a social question—and he cannot have been unaware of the suffrage movement and the enthusiasms and hostilities it aroused. Then there were those who felt that women's pre-war agitation for social equality, and their exemption from service when war and conscription came, made an equation that did not add up. It is not hard to understand how the non-combatant role of women in wartime could embitter a misogyny latent in all-male institutions like the army, and in any case evident as a presence in pre-war culture (not least in some of the poetry Owen most admired, which gave him plenty of precedents for a distrust of women). At this point of the poem, hostility to women is an attitude expressed by the disabled man himself, since the oral style of the language ('Aye, that was it') shows we are in his thought processes here. But that being the case, Owen's choice of the words 'giddy jilts' becomes of great interest. Did he really suppose it was a phrase that would occur spontaneously to the mind of a teenaged private? Why, exigencies of rhyme apart,[3] did he resort to this stiff Victorian cliché in this context? At a point where, presumably, he wanted to mount the decisive assault in the poem's attack on women, his rhetorical armoury turns out to be antiquated and inappropriate. Words have failed him. Owen here seems to reveal a blind spot, a moment of discursive indecision or inexperience, and has to issue his young

[3] Still, although Owen's innovations in rhyme are justly admired, the weakest moments in his mature verse tend to happen when rhyme is too demanding—whether conventional rhyme, as in 'Greater Love', or pararhyme, which pulls some of the couplets of 'Strange Meeting' towards awkwardness and banality.

soldier a phrase that belongs not to the speech of pub and dance-hall but, if anywhere, to Dunsden vicarage. And it is particularly interesting that this momentary stumble involves the formulation of an attitude to women, always a difficult question for Owen. He immediately regains his footing, however, when it is a question of taking aim at his other, less problematic target, the callousness of the authorities:

He didn't have to beg;
Smiling they wrote his lie: aged nineteen years.

The whole drama, and scandal, of under-age enlistment, is placed with an expert economy;[4] Owen had learned this sort of thing from *The Old Huntsman*, but here he out-Sassoons Sassoon in laconic pace. The lad's lie about his age has a kind of innocence, but there is nothing innocent about the way 'they' cynically pretend to believe him. The adversary of 'the true poets' was, as 'Dulce et Decorum Est' ambiguously puts it, 'the old Lie'.

Although he has been somehow manipulated (those subtle hands!) into going to war, the boy has gone willingly, collaborating in his own downfall. Parliamentary or editorial pronouncements in justification of the war mean next to nothing to him; the nation speaks a language that is foreign to both his mind and his feelings. But though he does not buy the official arguments for the war, he cannot resist investing in its imagery. He fantasizes about 'jewelled hilts | For daggers in plaid socks', believing the uniform will make him yet more beautiful and thus fatally falling in love with an image of himself, like that favourite myth of the Decadents (invoked in the Tailhade sonnet), 'Narcisse . . . qui mourut de s'aimer'. Recruitment propaganda, and the whole thrust of army training with its instillation of discipline and fostering of morale, urged the neophyte to make himself over, fashioning a new and desirable self in the army's image. Owen knew about this kind of allure, for he too had at least in part assented to it. The lad's eagerness to show off his legs to advantage might be laughable (though tragic too in view of the mutilation in store for him), but *esprit de corps*—

[4] 'OFFICER (to boy of thirteen who, in his effort to get taken on as a bugler, has given his age as sixteen): "Do you know where boys go who tell lies?" APPLICANT: "To the Front, sir."' In this *Punch* cartoon (11 Aug. 1915), two of the three recruiting staff are indeed depicted as smiling (*Mr Punch's History of the Great War*, 51).

even if we may suspect Owen of a gruesome pun here—was not something he was inclined to take lightly; indeed, it takes its place among the things the cripple in his solitude has now lost. The army offered a community with its own activities, bonding rituals, values, and hierarchy. And one thing it offered its juvenile recruit was the satisfaction of himself in due course playing the father, giving an admiring new army generation the benefit of a veteran's experience. It is of some interest that Owen gives this the last place, and therefore the greatest rhetorical weight, in the list of the army's attractions. And so with this luggage of mixed motives, some foolish and some not, the young man is sent 'out', into the exposed world, as if he really were the hero he thinks he is.

He returns:

> Some cheered him home, but not as crowds cheer Goal.
> Only a solemn man who brought him fruits
> *Thanked* him; and then enquired about his soul.

Mr Wigan's assistant had done his share of visiting the sick and dying in the parish of Dunsden, and here is a wry memory of the embarrassment and futility of some of those visits. The fate of the soul, agonized over during the months of Owen's religious crisis, is now an enquiry which is not even worth pursuing—in the circumstances, an impertinence and a bore. And the 'solemn man' is also a kind of premature and fatuous elegist: he brings an offering, he praises the subject's achievements, and wants to reassure himself about the spirit's destination. It is an approach which, however well-meaning, has nothing to offer the desperate question of the poem, the fate of the body.

> Now, he will spend a few sick years in institutes,
> And do what things the rules consider wise,
> And take whatever pity they may dole.
> Tonight he noticed how the women's eyes
> Passed from him to the strong men that were whole.
> How cold and late it is! Why don't they come
> And put him into bed? Why don't they come?

The final paragraph begins in a tone which is, in a manner familiar by now, both authoritative and guilty. 'Now, he will spend a few sick years in institutes,' is the voice of one professionally in the know, an insider who is well acquainted with the system and how it works, and who does not even pretend that it speaks with a human voice. This is an account of the 'rigid, frigid professionalism' Owen knew from Dunsden, a bloodless discourse in which it is 'the rules' that determine what is considered wise, and allocate pity like a ration.[5] Much as its failures of feeling disgusted him, Owen was (and had sought to be) apprenticed to that ruling discourse and its class in his roles of junior authority—clerical, pedagogic, and military. He had also at various times felt unsure of his place in it, hostile towards it, patronized and even rejected by it. Hence the two voices that confront each other in this last paragraph, both of them Owen's—the voice of knowledge and rank, uttering its comfortless prognosis and prophecy, and the voice of inadequacy, helplessness, and alienation.

The last four lines move back fully into the point of view of the disabled man, already becoming invisible as a ghost, and yet not dead but living out a tragic duration in a cold and belated world. The story is over but the end has not come: narrative is dead, but not the subject. There are suggestive parallels in Tennyson's images of desolation—Mariana in the moated grange, oddly enough, and the abandoned 'infant crying in the night' in *In Memoriam*. Other correspondences lay in the as yet unwritten modernism of Eliot's *The Hollow Men* and Beckett's endgames of disablement. Owen reads the historical tragedy in the image, hardly to be avoided in the towns of wartime Britain, of a young man whose life is finished before his youth is over. He sits, impotent as the very old, and neglected, in a grey world in the evening, waiting for extinction. Late Romantic artists and poets in the *fin de siècle* were fond of imagining that the world was ending—'our sense of epoch,' Frank Kermode observes, 'is gratified above all by the ends of centuries'[6]—in a blood-coloured sunset or lingering melancholy twilight. Owen in the autumn of 1917 did not find the death of the future difficult to imagine, or indeed particularly imaginary. If there is a palpably personal urgency and grief to be felt in the pity and anger of 'Disabled', it is enough to recall that it is a poem

[5] In a 1912 letter Owen had quoted the resolution of Tennyson's *Guinevere* to 'distribute dole | To poor sick people' (*CL* 131), in relation to his own charity visiting for Mr Wigan. But the word 'dole', as a noun, had a precise social meaning, having become the everyday name for unemployment benefit since the passing of the National Insurance Act in 1911, the year Owen went to Dunsden and started his work among the poor of the parish.

[6] Kermode, *The Sense of an Ending*, 96.

written in hospital when the war had entered its fourth year and there was little to suggest that it might not go on for years more, and when the poet—himself in the army, with one brother in the navy and the third soon destined for the air force—could contemplate the real possibility that the young men in his family would be wiped out, to be survived by two old people and a girl.

The disabled man is not Wilfred Owen and yet the whole story of Owen's life is inscribed in the poem, for the discourses in which the poem is written are the discourses in which the life was lived, ways of speaking and understanding made available to him through his participation in the linguistic system—the English language—he shared with countless others, but forming unique combinations shaped by a quarter-century of particular experience. Poetry, Wordsworth said, brings the whole soul of man into activity—and, we might add, all his history too, if we could read it.

A first draft of 'Disabled' was finished by the second week of October 1917 at Craiglockhart (*CL* 499), and Owen revised it in Scarborough, the following July, the month before he embarked on his last journey to France. All of his best work in poetry belongs to the year that brackets the composition of 'Disabled' and starts in August 1917, with his meeting with his fellow patient at the war hospital, Siegfried Sassoon. It was this encounter—not the war, his enlistment, his baptism of fire, or his breakdown—that released that remarkable surge of creativity in Owen, and it did so with a dramatic suddenness, although (as I have tried to show) that creativity found for its resources the discursive formation of a whole lifetime.

Sassoon mobilized Owen's imagination by showing him that he could write poetry about the army (and thus enabling him to write about much else in doing so). It does not seem to have occurred to Owen to do this before his encounter with Sassoon. He had already written a handful of poems about the war—'1914', 'A New Heaven', and 'With an Identity Disc' are examples—but they do not appear to be, in any interesting way, what he was later to declare every poem ought to be, 'a matter of experience' (*CL* 510). Still, it was not that Owen had to wait for Sassoon to give him the idea of writing verse about the war. In Bordeaux, when the war was a year old, he had read with great interest the supplement of war poems published by *The Times* on 9 August

1915, and containing work by Bridges, Hardy, Kipling, Newbolt, and others (*CL* 355). Verse came to enjoy something of a boom in the war years, when a nation hitherto not notably keen on poetry other than Kipling's and Owen Seaman's (the editor of *Punch*) was treated to an outpouring of war verses in newspapers and magazines, memorial volumes, and fund-raising anthologies. Some of this was written by soldiers, and some of them were men who had seen fighting for themselves. It was inevitable that Owen should take an interest in this writing—poems by soldiers were a regular feature of *Poetry Review*, for example, of which he was a regular reader[7]—but puzzling, surely, that he did not find a subject in his own experience of service until he read, and met, Sassoon. Owen had been both a poet and a soldier for some considerable time before that meeting. Why had he not become a 'soldier poet', as was the fashion? Military training in England was perhaps not the most promising raw material for a poet. But not a shred of his searing experiences at the front in 1917 made its way into a poem before August. What was the catalyst that Sassoon provided?

One clue may lie back in early 1913. In the eye of the storm at Dunsden, in the crisis of faith, which was also a *crise des nerfs* and soon to become a breakdown in health, Owen had withdrawn into himself, not wanting (he told Susan Owen) to communicate his 'calm frenzy' to anyone (*CL* 181). At its height the crisis silenced him; yet the months before and after the 'bust-up' itself were his most productive phase thus far, as he worked on the teleological poems that laboured with his burden of unbelief. His creativity seems to have been stirred by discursive conflict; it throve on contradiction or dialectic, a struggle going on between ways of speaking and seeing. Thus, those Dunsden poems carry on a quarrel that pitches the faith of the Church against the doubts of 'science' and the competing claims of art. Thus too, the later work that assaults Romanticism was to be livelier than the early work that imitates it. He needed not only something to write about but also something to write against.

Now Sassoon in 1917 was a controversial and iconoclastic figure. That, after all, was why he was sent to Craiglockhart. Owen was presumably repeating hospital gossip when he said the new arrival had been sent there because he had been 'too outspoken'

[7] Norgate, 'Wilfred Owen and the Soldier Poets', 516–7.

(*CL* 485). The poems in *The Old Huntsman*, which first impressed Owen by their accuracy, were also adversarial, already a counter-attack against complacency, cruelty, and lies. Sassoon made articulate the kinds of anger which hitherto, to judge from the letters, were only timidly or incompletely formulated in Owen's mind. A new boldness, which can be read in his letters in attacks on Tennyson ('always a great child' (*CL* 482)) and the Church ('Send an English Testament to his Grace of Canterbury' (*CL* 483)), coincides with his excited discovery of *The Old Huntsman*, early in August 1917. First and last Owen admired Sassoon for his courage, and he drew on it. The older poet's work spoke of horrors which he had seen, and which Owen recognized as true because he had seen them too; they were the very things he had found unbearable, which had led to his breakdown and brought him to Craiglockhart. Owen's sense of horror had been called cowardice and had caused the army to declare him unfit to do his job. No one believed Sassoon was a coward—he was a soldier with a reputation for conspicuous gallantry—and yet his writing protested against the war and cried out for it to stop. Sassoon's story showed that to hate and speak out against the war was not necessarily an act of cowardice; on the contrary. For Owen, still diffident and jittery in the moral quarantine of Craiglockhart, it was a liberating example, at a time when (it is important to remember) he knew of no others.

The second aspect of Sassoon's example that loosed the tongue of Owen's war poetry is related to this. *The Old Huntsman* is a book in love with soldiers. Glum or cheerful, courageous or cynical or just pitiful, its collective hero is the army itself, and the book constructs a fierce loyalty to the men whose lives and deaths it represents and pities. An attack on the war, then, was not an attack on the army; on the contrary. To write of the war in the way Owen now realized he wanted to—the way Sassoon had now shown to be possible—was neither shameful nor disloyal. And so another self-doubt and inhibition was removed. Even, perhaps, before Owen summoned up the courage to go and knock on his door, Sassoon had pointed the way out of the brooding lack of self-respect and the miserable isolation of shell-shock. To give a voice to the anguish, the sense of terrible unfairness, and even the fear, was not an act of weakness. It did not mean letting others down, but speaking up for them. A poet could warn, if he could do nothing else. And so Owen entered the company of soldier poets with Sassoon's sponsorship and encouragement, and his great productive phase began. Sassoon unwittingly, and Dr Brock deliberately, led him back to community and communication.

Reading *The Old Huntsman*, Owen told his mother, left him 'feeling at a very high pitch of emotion', and he added, characteristically, 'I think if I had the choice of making friends with Tennyson or with Sassoon I should go to Sassoon' (*CL* 484–5). The new poet was already thought of as a new friend, although they had not yet met. Once they had met, the friendship immediately became, at least on Owen's part, whole-hearted. His entire social and mental life was rearranged, and a new world for him crystallized around Sassoon at its centre. Everything was passed in review. He gathered all the manuscripts he had left at home or entrusted to his cousin to show Sassoon his work (he had no poems in print yet, not even in the *Hydra*). Books by his friends Tailhade and Leslie Gunston were submitted to Sassoon's inspection. Almost all of the new friends and new writing that Owen encountered in his last year of life he owed, directly or indirectly, to Sassoon. His life had moved into the strong gravitational field of his friend. 'And you have *fixed* my Life—however short. You did not light me: I was always a mad comet; but you have fixed me. I spun round you a satellite for a month, but I shall swing out soon, a dark star in the orbit where you will blaze' (*CL* 505).

Sassoon here is a wholly benign version of the sun, that father-associated image we see as fatuous in 'Futility' and hostile in 'Spring Offensive'. Indeed, he is almost the fathering God of creation: 'Oh! world you are making for me, Sassoon!' (*CL* 511). Other planets in the system soon swam into Owen's ken: Graves, Robert Nichols (though Owen could see that Nichols was closer to Graves than to Sassoon), and Robert Ross, who had satellites of his own.

Sassoon's voice became a strong and for a short while (in poems like 'The Dead-Beat') an almost overwhelming presence in Owen's writing, but it may be that as time went on he was more important to Owen as a reader—actual or, as it were, introjected—than as a writer. It was a function which in earlier days had been assigned within the family, to Susan Owen and Leslie Gunston. Owen was now submitting his poems to Sassoon, who responded with praise, censure, criticism, suggestions for amendment, and advice on publication. Sassoon's reading was participatory and fully dialogic, whereas Susan could probably offer nothing more useful than admiration. The ascendancy of his new friend was to some degree accomplished at the expense of the old exclusive intimacy with his mother. She was forbidden to look at manuscripts he no doubt intended to show Sassoon (*CL* 492). The letters became aware of and a little embarrassed about his newly divided loyalties. At Scarborough in December he told Susan he was so busy and distracted that he had 'not even written to Sassoon or anyone' (*CL* 515), but this was not actually true, for he had sent Sassoon at least two letters from Scarborough already (*CL* 510–12, 514–15). The following July Sassoon was back in London, wounded in hospital, and Owen was very anxious to visit him when he had a few days' leave, but was committed to meeting his mother. 'If only you'd come to Scarborough I might see him' (*CL* 567). It is an almost unique moment of impatience with her. But he also wanted to share Sassoon with Susan Owen, sending her a day or two later 'a precious letter, from the Greatest friend I have' (*CL* 567), and towards the end of his life asking, if he should not survive, that his friend try to go and visit his mother (a commission which Sassoon did indeed carry out).

It had seemed natural from the first to introduce Siegfried Sassoon to his family, at least textually. He praised Sassoon's poems in letters to both his mother and his sister in August 1917 (*CL* 484, 489), but it was, significantly, to Tom Owen that he sent a copy of *The Old Huntsman* (recommending, a little patronizingly, a poem about a railway station), with this rather aggressive testimonial:

> My dear Father,
> I think this work of Sassoon's will show you to the best possible advantage the tendencies of Modern Poetry. If you don't appreciate these then it's Na-poo. There is nothing better this century can offer you. I've marked the pieces for first reading, and those underlined are specially good. (*CL* 488.)

'Please send me your Criticisms,' he instructed; but it is the reader and not the writer who is being put to the test here. Owen is trying to organize in life what he often arranged in his poems, a discursive confrontation. He is setting up a dialogue in which his father must either endorse Sassoon's views on the war, or reveal himself to be a war-mongering, out-of-date philistine. He enquired twice more about 'Father's views' of Sassoon (*CL* 490, 494), but Tom Owen seems not to have given him the satisfaction of supplying them (if he had any). Although his father could not be expected to appreciate Sassoon, it was important that Susan should, and Wilfred reassured her that although she might be 'a little shocked by Sassoon's language', he never swore conversationally, and was 'simply honest about the war' (*CL* 493). Owen also emphasized—his mother may have voiced some suspicion about Sassoon's name—that his friend was 'eminently *English*' (*CL* 494). In these ways Owen sought an accommodation between the old life of his family and the new life Sassoon was opening for him, just as in his poems the language of Sassoon's disciple is also the language of the son of Susan and Tom Owen.

The major revelation that Sassoon's writing vouchsafed Owen was, as I have suggested, simple, immediate, and profound. *The Old Huntsman* moved and impressed him, he said, 'because of the subjects' (*CL* 484–5). Sassoon liberated for poetry a tract of experience in which Owen had most urgent things to say. The only 'influence' Sassoon himself claimed on Owen, in *Siegfried's Journey*, was that he 'stimulated him towards writing with compassionate and challenging realism'.[8] That compassion and realism speak for themselves, but the challenge must be expounded a little further.

'How to Die' is a fairly typical Sassoon war poem, published in *Counter-Attack* in July 1918 (though Owen may have seen it earlier in manuscript):

> Dark clouds are smouldering into red
> While down the craters morning burns.
> The dying soldier shifts his head
> To watch the glory that returns;
> He lifts his fingers toward the skies
> Where holy brightness breaks in flame;
> Radiance reflected in his eyes,
> And on his lips a whispered name.
>
> You'd think, to hear some people talk,
> That lads go West with sobs and curses,
> And sullen faces white as chalk,
> Hankering for wreaths and tombs and hearses.

[8] Sassoon, *Siegfried's Journey*, 60.

But they've been taught the way to do it
Like Christian soldiers; not with haste
And shuddering groans; but passing through it
With due regard for decent taste.

'How to Die' is not a complicated piece, but it is one that illustrates clearly the 'challenging' nature of Sassoon's realism, for of course what is challenged by the realism of the second stanza here is the non-realism of the first. That highly pictorial first stanza presents a myth of the dying soldier composed of language that is thoroughly corrupt—sentimental, clichéd, and mendacious. On a first reading it takes (if we are honest) several lines before we realize we are in a minefield of irony; then we may look back and recognize that there was something suspiciously trite about that romantic dawn 'smouldering into red', and an altogether too composed arrangement of dying soldier and returning glory. Stock properties of Christian piety and self-deluding romanticism (the 'whispered name' on a dying man's lips was already a venerable romantic cliché when Conrad nailed it at the end of *Heart of Darkness*) are trundled out to support a myth of war as noble, painless, tidy, and gratifying, and each of these properties is then confronted with a contradiction in the second stanza, the colour of dawn with the colour of scared and sick faces, glory and holiness with curses, and so forth. When the comforting version of death in battle is thoroughly discredited, the poem delivers the *coup de grâce* by appearing to reaffirm it at the end, and in fact unmasking it as not only mistaken but wickedly so, not a misconception but a lie uttered to protect civilian complacency from rude embarrassment.

Again and again, Sassoon's war poems like this one are produced out of a paradigm of discourse clash, a contrast and contradiction between different ways of speaking and seeing. It was not enough, in 'Lamentations', to describe the indignity and uncontrollable grief of a soldier crazed by the death of his brother; the portrait had to be framed by a pig-headed commentary—'In my belief | Such men have lost all patriotic feeling.' The rhetoric of a Sassoon war poem depends on such contrasts, linguistic and structural. Unless he is being simply sentimental, there is almost always a double perspective, a challenge of discourses which quite often involves actual speakers. It was a lesson Owen learned immediately, and his first effort 'in Sassoon's style' was 'The Dead-Beat' (*CL* 485–6), a polyphony of satirical contrasts in which, in its revised form, four voices are to be heard. Sassoon's poems were dispatches from a battlefield of languages, the struggle between words that flattered and fed the war and words that tried to expose it for what it was. His public statement of 1917 was specifically not a protest against the military conduct of the war, but against the 'deception' (a language crime) that prolonged it. On 19 June, a few days after composing that statement, Sassoon pondered the relation between war and language in a diary entry which is as close as he came to a manifesto for his war poetry, and whose ideas he is more than likely to have repeated to the deferential young officer and poet he was to meet at Craiglockhart a few weeks later.

The diary entry[9] is bitterly sarcastic about 'the destruction of Kaiserism and Prussianism'. This slogan, masquerading as Britain's peace terms, is merely 'empty words (so often on the lips of the Jingos) [that] mean the destruction of Youth'. And if language can kill in this way, silence can be deadly too. The army is 'dumb', the soldiers 'willingly entrapped by the silent conspiracy against them'. Meanwhile 'the ruling classes do all the talking', and can rely on the ignorant and credulous crowd not to question them. Women are party to the conspiracy, in public praising the soldiers as 'dauntless warriors' while secretly enjoying a sexual thrill in the bloodshed perpetrated and suffered by their lovers. 'The soldiers are fooled by the popular assumption that they are all heroes.' Old men glory in 'senseless invective against the enemy', in the mock heroism of their young men, and in the 'mechanical phrases' of the Northcliffe Press, 'cackling about "attrition", and "wastage of man-power", and "civilisation at stake"'. Soldiers conceal their hatred of the war, and civilians conceal their liking for it. It is this chorus of untruth, Sassoon concludes, that is responsible for the slaughter. Examples of bad language were everywhere to be found, but particularly on the lips of the established and powerful.

'How vastly the spiritual gain of those who are left behind outweighs the agony and loss of those who fight and die . . . the everlasting glory and exaltation of war.' (From a review in *The Times Literary Supplement*)

[9] Sassoon, *Diaries 1915–1918*, 175–6.

This is the sort of thing I am in revolt against. But I belong to 'a war-wearied and bewildered minority which regards "victory" and "defeat" as rhetorical terms with little precise meaning'.[10]

If all this was 'the sort of thing' Sassoon was in revolt against, it also articulates in almost every particular (including its hostility to women and the old) the campaign Owen too was to undertake. The war in France depended for its continuation on a war of language at home, and in this other war the truth was losing. The true poets had to combat lies. Sassoon gave him all he needed of both a theory and a method of war poetry, a poetics of contradiction (or counter-attack) in which the discourse battle is carried out by and within the poetry. Owen, of course, was no stranger to discourse rivalry.

Sassoon was to remember having 'eager discussions of contemporary poets' with Owen at Craiglockhart,[11] and it was through Sassoon's eyes, as it were, that Owen read other literary responses to the war. His admiration of Sassoon gave him both a perspective and a criterion by which to judge others. And his relationship with Sassoon also gave his work its entrée into the busy dialogic life of Great War poetry, where a steady intertextual conversation was kept up with friends and sometimes enemies. Graves's *Fairies and Fusiliers* contains a poem 'To Robert Nichols', and another, 'Two Fusiliers', addressed to Sassoon. Sassoon's 'A Letter Home' is addressed to Graves, and is quoted as the epigraph to Owen's 'The Next War', and 'Two Fusiliers' is paraphrased in Owen's 'Apologia', while his 'Wild with All Regrets' (the title is from Tennyson) is dedicated to Sassoon. Sassoon gave his *Counter-Attack* an epigraph from Barbusse's *Le Feu*, a book he lent (in English translation) to Owen and whose subsequent impact is felt in several Owen poems, including 'Dulce et Decorum Est', a poem originally addressed to Jessie Pope, authoress of several volumes of war poems. And so on.

The letters and his own library reveal that Owen was acquainted with a good deal of war writing. While compiling a list of individual 'influences' and echoes would not necessarily be time well spent, it is worth pointing out that he was well-informed in the varieties of the proliferating discourse of war literature, in its political range from the jingoism of Jessie Pope to the socialist

[10] Ibid. 176. [11] Sassoon, *Siegfried's Journey*, 60.

internationalism of Barbusse, and in its formal range from the stately dirge of Péguy's 'Heureux ceux qui sont morts'[12] to the jolly anecdotes of Ian Hay and the hysterical but oddly banal grammatical breakdowns of Nichols's 'The Assault'. It is not always easy for the student of Owen to remember that the mixture of pathos, realism, and satire that Owen found so liberating in Sassoon, and so creative, was a literary option that was neither an inevitable nor necessarily an obvious response to the experience of the war. There were soldier poets in Galloway Kyle's popular anthologies, for example, who had seen more action than Owen and whose poems were interested in none of these qualities.

At the end of 1917 Robert Graves was exhorting Owen to 'outlive this War' so as to 'help S.S. and R.N. and R.G. to revolutionize English Poetry' (*CL* 596). Owen had already made a point of getting to know Robert Nichols's work. He had reservations about it, telling Sassoon that he found Nichols 'self-concerned and *vaniteux* in his verse' (*CL* 511), but Sassoon, whose own feelings about Nichols were not simple, was soon promising to put Nichols in touch with Owen, 'for' (said Owen) 'he likes him much' (*CL* 520). About Graves's work, meanwhile, Owen had no doubts. He was full of admiration for *Fairies and Fusiliers*—'I should never stop if I started to rejoice over these poems' (*CL* 511)—and grateful for Graves's sometimes bracing criticism of his own work. But the poem that Owen singles out as 'too glorious' is Graves's 'The Legion', a Kiplingesque piece which, in thin Roman disguise, makes the point that military tradition is safe in the hands of the new armies—a poem with a theme that would have been reassuring to Owen as a 'temporary' officer, but a tone that is very far from that of the war poems he himself was writing at this time. He admired Graves, then, and liked him (though Graves could be alarming) but was not tempted to imitate him as he imitated Sassoon. Graves's stance was an option Owen respected but did not share.

Graves's recommendations (in correspondence and in his poetry)

[12] This famous and beautiful elegy for soldiers, part of Péguy's long religious poem *Eve* (1913), is reprinted in the first volume of Larronde's *Anthologie des Ecrivains français morts pour la Patrie*; Owen had a copy. Péguy's line 'Heureux ceux qui sont morts sur un dernier haut lieu' may have helped to suggest a phrase in 'Spring Offensive', with its doomed soldiers running on 'that last high place'. Péguy's elegy is certainly predicated on a faith that 'God caught them even before they fell.'

of cheerfulness and a stiff upper lip—for, as he told Owen, 'a poet should have a spirit above wars' (*CL* 596)—were chiefly useful to Owen in helping to clarify just why he thought it important that a poet's spirit should *not* be above war, but (as Isaac Rosenberg said) saturated in it. In the war poems of Graves—and, for that matter, of Nichols—there was a certain amount of trench realism, but there was neither satire nor protest of the kind Owen was learning from Sassoon. Graves did not have much patience for protest against the war while the war was still going on. Owen probably knew that Graves more than any other individual had made possible the official interpretation of Sassoon's public 'protest' as a 'breakdown', an insufficiency of morale to which the authorities could respond by sending the delinquent/patient to hospital. He may not have known that Graves was of the opinion that such a protest did reprehensible damage to the morale of others. Graves commanded Owen's respect, as a poet and a soldier. An awareness of Graves among his putative readership caused Owen to examine and to defend what he was doing in the war poetry, most notably in 'Apologia pro Poemate Meo', which echoes 'Two Fusiliers' but pointedly refuses Graves's advice to 'cheer up':

> You shall not hear their mirth:
> You shall not come to think them well content
> By any jest of mine.

Owen probably had as much to learn from Wilfrid Wilson Gibson, whose *Battle* he read in the same month as Nichols's fashionable *Ardours and Endurances*, December 1917 (*WO* 242). The lyrics in Gibson's volume speak in, as well as about, different characters. They touch on the madness and fear of battle, as well as on life's (and death's) little ironies, like that of the soldier entrusted with the dying words of three men but unable, now, to remember which was which. The longest poem, 'Between the Lines', imagines what passes through the mind of a soldier lying wounded in no man's land. Drifting between present and past, it inaugurates a little sub-genre of its own, to be followed by Sassoon's 'The Death-Bed' which was followed, in turn, by Owen's 'Conscious' and 'Disabled'. Although Gibson had never been in combat, his war verse is animated by the same sympathies that can be read in his pre-war poems about the lives of the poor. Established political convictions lay behind the poetry of Lady Margaret Sackville, whom Sassoon took Owen to meet in Edinburgh.[13] Sassoon thought her work 'fairly rotten',[14] but Owen was more enthusiastic about *The Pageant of War*, a collection of poems dwelling on the plight of war's victims; some of these he considered 'very fine' (*CL* 497). He must have been interested in 'Nostra Culpa', in which Lady Margaret laid the blame for the war on those who had sowed its seeds—women, 'We mothers and we murderers of mankind'. He sent his copy, autographed by the author, to Susan Owen (*CL* 500).

Sassoon, Graves, Nichols, and Gibson (and Harold Monro) were represented in *Georgian Poetry 1916–1917*. Owen boasted at the end of 1917 that he was 'held peer by the Georgians' (*CL* 521). Gibson, Sackville, Sassoon, and Graves (and Osbert Sitwell, whom Owen met and corresponded with in 1918) all had war poetry published in the *Nation*, which took 'Miners' in January and 'Futility' and 'Hospital Barge' in June 1918. It was hardly a movement and certainly not a school, but Owen was identifying himself with a company of fairly like-minded poets and adding his voice to theirs in the creation of a poetry of modern war.

His growing realization of the sort of poetic identity he wanted can be read in his draft tables of contents for *Disabled and Other Poems* (*CPF* 537–40). With the partial exception of 'Miners' (which gets 'mixed up with the War at the end' (*EB* 125))[15] the volume was to exclude completely his 'civilian' verse. This is, surely, remarkable self-discipline in a poet anxious to make his name with his first published book; but Owen had placed himself, and found himself, confidently in the discourse of a war poetry that sought to tell the truth, and there must be no distractions. Sassoon was responsible for this, though he had not 'lighted' but '*fixed*' Owen's star (*CL* 505). Through Sassoon, Owen found himself sharing an order of friendship which was also a brotherhood in arms.

> But there is no denying to myself that he is already a *closer* friend than, say, Leslie. Just as this assertion is not the result of having been with him so much lately, neither is it derogated by the shortness of our acquaintance-time. We have followed parallel trenches all our lives, and have more friends in common, authors I mean, than most people can boast of in a lifetime. (*CL* 494.)

[13] Welland, *Wilfred Owen*, 157–8. [14] Sassoon, *Diaries 1915–1918*, 187.
[15] Edmund Blunden quotes from this letter in his edition but it is not in *CL*.

The inseparable themes of poetry and friendship, of language and community, go back of course to Owen's teenaged rhapsodies over Keats. In the early days, the 'friends' Owen found he had in common with Sassoon would have been mostly among dead poets, but before long Owen could think of himself as belonging to a company of living authors, all (to adopt his figure) in the same trench system, his comrades, and his peers. These were 'the true poets', honoured and challenged in his draft preface. They were the prophets and witnesses of a community bound together, like a church, by revelation, a community whose body was the suffering victims of the war, 'of ours or Theirs'. As the ties had loosened that bound him to Church and nation, and to some extent even to his family, now in the last year of his life his feeling of belonging to this other communion gave him strength—even happiness—and gave his work the authority that speaks in poems like 'Futility', 'Exposure', and 'Spring Offensive'.

The antagonist that this 'truthful' discourse confronted was many-headed. For Owen its most familiar voice was that of his own father, the conventionally patriotic civilian of an older generation, blusteringly uncaring of his children's sensibilities (or so it seemed, an impression not dispelled by his message of congratulation to Wilfred on his becoming 'normal again' after his shell-shock (*CL* 562)), and far too ready to make terrible demands on his sons as the price of his own failures and romantic fantasies. Tom Owen is the prototype of all those patriarchs in the poems 'whom no cannon stuns', who cannot see or do not care about what the war is doing to young men, but remain tucked up cosily in the narrow limits of their imaginations. Their 'paucity' could not be forgiven.

The written form of this antagonist discourse was to be found in the slogans of the recruitment campaigns, the sanitized and dishonest dispatches of war correspondents, all official and semi-official *bourrage de crâne*, the complacencies of the likes of *Punch*—Owen's favourite magazine, but much of it (by October 1918) condemned as 'dastardly' (*CL* 587)—anything produced by Beaverbrook's Ministry of Information (so memorably snubbed by Sassoon (*CL* 589)), all newspapers (in the end) but the *Daily News* (*CL* 587, 590), and all civilian apologetics for the war, whether by the high and mighty 'milord Winnie Ingram' (*CL* 435), the otherwise admirable Belloc, or the absolutely hated Bottomley (*CL* 468, 525, 585).

There was also a war poetry that had to be combated. Owen's most direct adversary proceedings are taken against the 'certain poetess', Jessie Pope, named in early drafts as the addressee of 'Dulce et Decorum Est' (*CPF* 292–7), and accused of perpetrating 'the old Lie' that will lure children to hideous death in war. Here an unsparing realism that evokes the gassed soldier's agonies is the best answer to the fatally uninformed jollity of Jessie Pope, who earned Owen's hostility because her verses were widely read (she published her poems in *Punch* and the daily press, and also had a loyal readership among children) and she actively encouraged recruitment, whether directly in verses like 'The Call' ('Who's for the trench— | Are you, my laddie?') or indirectly, as in 'The Beau Ideal':

> The lad who troth with Rose would plight,
> Nor apprehend rejection
> Must be in shabby khaki dight
> To compass her affection.
> Who buys her an engagement ring
> And finds her kind and kissing,
> Must have one member in a sling
> Or, preferably, missing.[16]

Female, civilian, a pro-war propagandist and (in Owen's view) criminally ignorant, Jessie Pope was in every way his opposite. 'Dulce et Decorum Est' is the most straightforward example of that challenging realism Owen learned from Sassoon. To see it as a riposte to work like 'The Beau Ideal' helps to explain its vehemence; it would not be easy to decide which of the two poems is the more revolting. But the quieter 'Arms and the Boy' can be seen as another kind of answer to Jessie Pope, an alternative version of what ought to be taught to innocent youngsters on the brink of war.

If Owen's work was a voice raised against civilian ignorance and callousness, it was in contrast, too, to the bulk of war poetry written by soldiers; and here a real problem raised itself. It was understandable, if not excusable, that the likes of Jessie Pope and the editor of *Punch* had no idea what the war really meant: they had not been there. Yet there were large numbers of men who had seen the fighting and who, even so, produced war poetry that

[16] Hibberd and Onions (eds), *Poetry of the Great War*, 109–10.

endorsed the official view that the war was necessary, and the civilian belief that it could be glorious. And standing behind them were countless other soldiers who, at least, offered no protest. This problem—that there were soldiers for whom the war seemed not to be a problem—was one which, I think, Owen never resolved. It is the question that remains unanswered at the end of the late 'Spring Offensive'—'Why speak not they of comrades that went under?' The unprotesting silent majority of soldiers could be seen as simply having no skill to speak, and no access to authoritative discourse: that is the point made in 'The Calls' (which admits, however, that most soldiers also lack 'the will' to make their voices heard). But there were others who could speak, but did not protest.

R. A. Vernède was one. He was a novelist turned soldier, who died of wounds in April 1917. Later that year Owen bought his posthumous *War Poems and Other Verses*, published by Heinemann (who had brought out *The Old Huntsman*)[17] with a laudatory preface by Edmund Gosse. Partly because of his literary connections, and partly because he had sportingly joined the ranks in 1914 when he was nearly forty, Vernède became well known as a war poet.[18] To read him alongside Owen is to become aware of how much of the stock-in-trade of what might be called orthodox English war poetry is simply missing from Owen. Vernède's war is placed in a context of English national history, and national identity, which seem completely foreign to Owen's historical and cultural sense. It is, for example, difficult to imagine Owen ever invoking the name of Nelson, as Vernède is fond of doing. And Vernède's loyalties, like Kipling's, have an imperial dimension ('Canada, Canada, is not thy face most fair?' etc.) and, fascinatingly, a racial dimension too, for at one point Germany's delinquency is likened to the imperialist nightmare of the white man who goes crazy 'in some hideous ju-ju place', and must be put down, to preserve the supremacy of the race. These were concerns and anxieties that did not feature at all in Owen's idea of what it meant to be English.

As might be expected in a man who had had several war poems

[17] Sassoon was not impressed. 'Vernède's poems are wretched stuff, aren't they?' Sassoon, *Diaries 1915–1918*, 189.

[18] See the biographical note in Hibberd and Onions (eds), *Poetry of the Great War*, 226.

published in *The Times* in 1914 and later, Vernède seemed to have no difficulty in interpreting the war in terms of the institutional and linguistic equipment of official culture—he is patriotic, imperialistic, gentlemanly and Christian. Owen was not, in any straightforward sense, a patriot or a Christian, and he was certainly not an imperialist; and the colloquialisms, the cursing, the brutality, and the slang in his poems are there (as they are in Sassoon) because he has no wish to sound genteel. Owen's anti-war poetry—in view of the disclaimer in his draft preface, we might call it his war anti-poetry—inverts the kind of Victorian certainties that sustain Vernède, and empties them out. Consider what damage is done to the well-worn formula 'England, home, and beauty' (from John Braham's 'The Death of Nelson') by Owen's 'Smile, Smile, Smile':

> England one by one had fled to France,
> Not many elsewhere now, save under France...

and 'Exposure':

> Slowly our ghosts drag home...
> Shutters and doors, all closed: on us the doors are closed...

and the fragment 'Beauty':

> A shrapnel ball—
> Just where the wet skin glistened when he swam—
> Like a full-opened sea-anemone.
> We both said 'What a beauty! What a beauty, lad!'

The last example of this campaign in semantics—the redefinition of 'Beauty'—is at once unpatriotic (the wound is 'a beauty' because it will exempt the soldier from battle), Decadent (erotic attention to the male body, and a Wildean simile), and subversive (in dialogic contradiction of Kant's lofty definition of the beautiful which is quoted at the start of the poem, 'We both'—a collective, demotic, spontaneous, alternative voice, momentarily 'carnivalesque' in Bakhtin's terms—seem to know better).

The reading public could find in a poet like Vernède—and even late in the war there were many more poets like Vernède than poets like Owen—a reassurance that all was well with the war, which was being fought and would be won by men who believed it was a necessary, just, and honourable prosecution of a cause worth dying for. This coincided with the official line also espoused by the Church and almost all of the press. The poetry which tended to endorse this view of the war found one literary institution, of a kind, in the popular anthologies of work by 'The Soldier Poets', edited by Galloway Kyle. Many of the poems in Kyle's *Songs of the Fighting Men* (1916) and *More Songs by the Fighting Men* (1917) had first appeared in the *Poetry Review*, of which Owen was a regular reader. Throughout the two volumes, as Paul Norgate says, 'the verses of the Soldier Poets complement each other to articulate a "voice" which is remarkably consistent.'[19] This is not fortuitous. Galloway Kyle, the editor, and Erskine Macdonald, the publisher (it was not widely known that these were one and the same person) had learned from the success of Marsh's Georgian anthologies the commercial advantages of an identifiable movement with a name. Macdonald had indeed cheekily profited from the reputation of the Georgians by publishing his own series of Little Books of Georgian Verse (one of his authors was Olwen Joergens) (*OTP* 62–3). Now in launching his Soldier Poets, Kyle stressed their homogeneity. In his preface to *Songs of the Fighting Men*, he went to some lengths to establish his poets as a group or movement, with recognizable and marketable qualities in common.

> Even a cursory glance at this volume will show the authors are soldiers whose military service dates back in most cases to the early days of the war, if not earlier, and not conscript poetasters who have found a new stimulant to jaded literary exercises. The note of pessimism and decadence is absent, together with the flamboyant and the hectic, the morose and the mawkish . . . The spirit that has turned our soldiers into poets is the spirit of the V.C.—brave and debonair, but neither melancholy nor mad. It is not a new spirit, but a new bright efflorescence—a survival and a revival.[20]

The Soldier Poets, in other words, were being advertised as patriotic, manly, amateur in the attractive English way (for they were not poetasters but soldiers turned into poets), optimistic, healthy, not given to excess, respectful of tradition. Kyle goes on to quote approvingly the relief that Rupert Brooke had claimed to feel in leaving behind 'half-men, and their dirty songs and dreary' upon

[19] Norgate, 'Wilfred Owen and the Soldier Poets', 518.
[20] Kyle (ed.), *Songs of the Fighting Men*, 8, 9.

entering the war. This profile of the generic Soldier Poet could hardly have been further removed from the Wilfred Owen of 1917–18, a homosexual neurasthenic with decadent continental tastes, unpatriotic and more than disinclined to be cheery about the war. By this account he was certainly not worthy, and nor was Sassoon, to be numbered among the Soldier Poets, this title which Kyle had bestowed upon his men.

Owen and Sassoon seem to have shared what Paul Norgate calls 'a dismissive familiarity' with the writings of the Soldier Poets.[21] In a letter to Sassoon in October 1918, Owen speaks of having been given 'a book of Erskine MacD's Soldier-Poets' by 'one of these amalgamations' (Murray McClymont) whom he had met at the Base: he has now had to lend this book to the Adjutant, and asks Sassoon to send him more copies of *Counter-Attack* which he proposes to apply as a sort of antidote. He needs more ammunition in the battle of the books (*CL* 582). Sassoon's kind of challenging realism would be a riposte or antiphon—as it so often is *within* a Sassoon or an Owen poem—to a false representation of the war. Here the challenge of language was a matter of literary politics. It is not hard to imagine Owen and Sassoon being scornful or resentful of the exclusive definite article with which Kyle's books claimed to contain the work of 'the' Soldier Poets. What was at stake in this literary rivalry was the right to that title, and so to a particular authority in the discourse of war poetry. Who really spoke for the experience of soldiers? Who was telling the truth about the war? What kind of poet should a soldier be? 'All a poet can do today is warn,' Owen wrote in his draft preface. 'That is why the true War Poets must be truthful.' But on second thoughts, he struck out the word 'War' from the sentence (*CPF* 535).

The way Owen engages with the ideas and the literary habits of the Soldier Poets has been examined in some detail by Paul Norgate. He points out, for example, that both Kyle's anthologies have poems unironically entitled 'Dulce et Decorum est Pro Patria Mori', with which Owen's similarly titled poem can be seen as contending; that the hospital poem was a popular 'sub-genre', invariably optimistic in the hands of the Soldier Poets (pointing to recovery, or at least to serene death) but problematized in Owen's inconclusive 'Conscious'; that in contrast to the practice of the Soldier

[21] Norgate, 'Wilfred Owen and the Soldier Poets', 519.

Poets, Owen in general refuses to invest every action of the ordinary soldier with positive significance, and resists sealing his war poems in the kind of neat and satisfying closure that would suggest the experience has been somehow mastered. 'Wilfred Owen's experience on the Somme was of conditions and circumstances which conformed to no "meaning" or "plot" such as might be conceived in traditional or conventional terms.' The result, says Norgate, is the development in Owen of 'a more subtly provisional discourse' than either the Soldier Poets' unquestioning reference back to religion, tradition, sacrifice and so on, or for that matter Sassoon's essentially simple counter-assertion and satirical inversion of such ideas.[22]

This account of Owen's intertextual relations with the work of other soldier poets seems substantially right. Paul Norgate sometimes overestimates the unquestioning serenity of the Soldier Poets' belief in the war; but it is remarkable how potentially quite dangerous doubts (in Evan Morgan's 'The World's Reward' in *Songs*, or Jarvis's 'At a Wayside Shrine' in *More Songs*, for example) do not prevent these poems reaching a conclusion that confirms orthodox interpretations of the war and systems of belief. Owen, whose first independent work had been a poetry of doubt, seems to have been increasingly ready to leave the painful questions of his work without resolution, dark and unsettling. The instinct that drew him to the ill-fitting conclusions of pararhyme also abandoned 'Strange Meeting' in mid-line, and would not allow even death to release the aching tensions of 'Exposure' or the brooding hopelessness of 'Disabled'.

Dreadful as Owen's ordeal in the trenches had been, it has to be said that it is unlikely to have been very much more terrible than that of *all* the soldiers whose verse—so free of the 'note of pessimism and decadence'—appeared in Galloway Kyle's anthologies. And if it was, as I would suggest, at least as much his reading of Sassoon as his experiences on the Somme that showed Owen the inadequacies of the Soldier Poets, it is right to add that his admiration for Sassoon's work was not, or not for long, completely unqualified. Norgate suggests that Owen's 'subtly provisional discourse' is an implicit rebuke to Sassoon's frequent recourse to a black-and-white polemic. Owen did not share that

[22] Ibid. 526, 530.

public-school mixture of establishment loyalty and cynicism that led Graves to deprecate Sassoon's protest; he considered the protest an act of courage, and said Sassoon's poems were 'perfectly truthfully descriptive of war' (*CL* 489). There is no reason to suppose that he ever revised these opinions, formed at Craiglockhart. His warning to Leslie Gunston, to remember that 'Poetry with him [Sassoon] is become a mere vehicle of propaganda' (*CL* 520), was given partly to soften the news of Sassoon's negative reaction to Gunston's *The Nymph*. It is a reservation worth considering none the less, for if Owen moved beyond Sassoon's orbit it was not to leave behind such 'truthfully descriptive' representations of the war, but to present and understand them in a different context.

The context of the war, as Sassoon saw it, can be read in the careful architecture of *The Old Huntsman and Other Poems*. The title poem was not just (as Owen told his father) 'put in . . . to catch the hunting-people, and make 'em read the rest' (*CL* 488). It also evokes a traditional world which the war had come to disrupt, a world personified in the elderly, already superannuated but wholly admirable old huntsman, with his lifetime's experience in the service of the squire and of leisurely, sporting, rural England. Then come the early poems that register the romantic excitement and idealism of war, then the ugliness and agonies and disillusions, the angry satire and the bitterness, culminating in 'The Death-Bed', Owen's early favourite and Sassoon's too (*CL* 486). Next comes 'The Last Meeting', a classical elegy of consolation in a Georgian idiom and landscape; and finally the jaunty (or brave) recovery of 'A Letter Home', addressed to Graves, with its anticipation of an *après la guerre* of country walks and sporting holidays. The second half of the book consists of Sassoon's mostly rather weak lyrical poems 1908-16. This scheme seems to suggest that the war is a rude interruption. To put it crudely, all was well before the war came along and all will be well once it is stopped. Even the more single-minded *Counter-Attack and Other Poems* ends, with the poem 'Together', looking forward to a peace which is also a nostalgic looking-back, a reconstitution of the fox-hunting English pastoral first met in 'The Old Huntsman'—a virtually eighteenth-century world, equestrian, rural, subject to no change but the seasons:

Splashing along the boggy woods all day,
And over brambled hedge and holding clay,
I shall not think of him:
But when the watery fields grow brown and dim,
And hounds have lost their fox, and horses tire,
I know that he'll be with me on my way
Home through the darkness to the evening fire.

When the war has been left behind, and pre-war conditions restored, the mourned past will return (after the usual elegiac pattern) as a friendly presence. To measure the distance between this and Wilfred Owen is to see how far, in the end, Owen's understanding of the meaning of the war, and his representations of it, differ even from those of the poet he most admired.

Sassoon's poetry of protest has a background in time and space. His anger is directed against a war which disrupts a basically benign continuity, and prints a blot on a natural world traditionally viewed as a source of pleasure. But in spite of the war there are reminders of that other, better, idyllic England throughout Sassoon's war poetry. It is glimpsed again by the soldier on leave or invalided home, recreated in memory, reverie, and dreams, looked forward to as a reward when the war shall be over; even the afterlife imagined in 'The Investiture' and 'Invocation' looks like a Kentish pastoral. The war is abominable because it is an aberration, a malignant spell cast on a kindly world. It has made a murderous incompetent of the cheery old gentleman in 'The General', and set the generations unnaturally against one another, so the poet must treat as enemies those 'impotent old friends of mine', the arm-chair warriors in 'The Fathers'. It is all a mistake, a terrible interruption; stop the war, and the pastoral may be regained. And indeed much of Sassoon's postwar writing, in verse and prose, is a poignant effort to make that idyll live again.

Strikingly, Owen's war poetry has almost no such background, in place or time, landscape or history. The England his own history had dealt him was not Sassoon's comfortable 'weald of youth', but Shrewsbury, Birkenhead, and Dunsden parish, an England that had denied him the education and prospects that he wanted, but expected him to offer his services in war. It was not a community where everyone from squire to tinker seemed to know their place and be content, but a country where the child of poor parents could be left by the callousness of 'rigid, frigid professionalism' to die of consumption without hospital care. (*CL* 126). The insensibility of stone-hearted 'dullards' could not be a complete surprise after this. Owen had romantically dramatized his own life, in that letter of late October 1914 (*CL* 289–90), as a struggle against a series of dominating tyrants, and he certainly saw his own father as the first of the series. In the unjust and sometimes fatal demands that old men made on the young in wartime, and the authoritative made on the helpless, Owen could read not the disruption but the continuity of a pattern, a war that neither 'propaganda' nor military action could turn into peace.

Sassoon carried on his courageous campaign of 'propaganda' out of a clear sense of values and arrangements that the war had violated, and that must be restored: though he ended the war a socialist, his protest is essentially conservative. (The Sherston memoirs make the matter even clearer.) Owen was in full agreement with Sassoon's denunciations of the war, and yet Owen's war is in a sense more terrible than Sassoon's, as no alternative to it is to be found, in space or in time. No landscape untouched by war can be imagined in the poems Owen chose for *Disabled and Other Poems*. To rise above the earth in 'The Show' or to plunge beneath it in 'Strange Meeting' is only to come more closely face to face with horror. There is no escape anywhere—when Owen 'crossed the long backs of the downs' after visiting his cousin in Winchester in November 1917, he realized he 'could almost see the dead lying about in the hollows of the downs' (*CL* 508)—and no sense (in the poems) of a decent home life being continued somewhere or ready to be resumed when peace comes. With the exception of 'From My Diary, July 1914' there is no pre-war idyll against which the war is measured, and the poems show no faith in the prospect of ever seeing an end to the fighting. The war has swallowed the world: there is no world elsewhere. That immensely reassuring (and English) line from the final poem of *Counter-Attack*—'Home through the darkness to the evening fire'—is unimaginable in late Owen: indeed it is just what the bleak 'Exposure' tries, but fails, to imagine. There, the soldiers' ghosts 'drag home' painfully, only to find that home is locked and the evening fire sunk. There is nothing to do but to turn back to their dying.

Owen, then, learned from Sassoon how to be a war poet. But he brought, to the realistic treatment of war subjects he had learned from Sassoon, an understanding of war and a discourse of war poetry that was more radical and more desolate than his friend's.

That different understanding had more to do with Owen's discourse history than with the ways his actual military experience had differed from Sassoon's. It had had its origins long before the war, in the domestic frustrations, educational disappointments, and social alienation of his earlier years. It was related to his Dunsden apostasy, when declaring his independence had meant refusing a comforting faith which promised that in the end all tears should be wiped away. It was related to Dr Brock's Geddesian reading of the war as not a disruption of continuity but itself a continuation of the prevailing malaise of modernity, a malaise from which Owen could foresee no recovery:

> Now men will go content with what we spoiled,
> Or, discontent, boil bloody, and be spilled.

(The conditions of warfare stretch ahead as far as the imagination can reach. Or, as 'Exposure' has it, 'war lasts . . . But nothing happens.') And it was related to the 'sense of an ending' Owen had learned from late Romanticism, where Baudelaire's images of *ennui* and damnation had inaugurated a teeming, Decadent fantasy of termination—the end of the world, in hopeless entropy or bloodstained apocalypse—which seems to be coming true in the God-forsaken landscapes of Owen's war poems. He had looked this nightfall in the face:

> I saw his round mouth's crimson deepen as it fell,
> Like a sun, in his last deep hour;
> Watched the magnificent recession of farewell,
> Clouding, half gleam, half glower,
> And a last splendour burn the heavens of his cheek.
> And in his eyes
> The cold stars lighting, very old and bleak,
> In different skies.

In 'Spring Offensive' the feet of Owen's soldiers have brought them 'to the end of the world', and no narrative of return or salvation can bring them back. There they lie, in 'Exposure', in a dying world. There is nowhere else. This is where words have led them—others' words, and their own—and in the end words will be all that remains of them.

All of Owen's history is inscribed in his language, and it is out of the whole of his language—formed from all the speech and writing he had encountered—that the poems come: 'Exposure', 'Disabled', and the rest. Whistler, in the Ruskin trial in 1878, declared famously that a picture painted in two days contained the knowledge of a lifetime.[23] Owen's language contains his life, both what Dominic Hibberd calls 'the strangeness and secrecy of his genius' (*OTP* 192), and the social and cultural history of which he was a part. There it can be read now that his words belong to other voices.

[23] Walker, *Whistler*, 82.

Bibliography

AUSTIN, ALFRED, *Songs of England* (London: Macmillan, 1898)

BÄCKMAN, SVEN, *Tradition Transformed: Studies in the Poetry of Wilfred Owen*, Lund Studies in English 54 (Lund: C. W. K. Gleerup, 1979)

BAKHTIN M. M., *The Dialogic Imagination*, ed. Michael Holquist (Austin: University of Texas Press, 1981)

—— *Speech Genres and Other Late Essays*, ed. Caryl Emerson and Michael Holquist (Austin: University of Texas Press, 1986)

Band of Hope Outline Addresses, series 1–3 (London: Church of England Temperance Society, 1892–1902)

Band of Hope Entertainer, The: Dialogues and Recitations (Manchester: Abel Heywood, 1893)

Band of Hope Lesson Album, The (London: Church of England Temperance Society, n.d.)

BARBUSSE, HENRI, *Le Feu: suivi du Carnet de Guerre* (Paris: Flammarion, 1965; first published in 1916)

—— *Under Fire,* tr. Fitzwater Wray (London: Dent, 1917)

BARKER, PAT, *Regeneration* (London: Viking, 1991)

BARROW, ANDREW, *The Flesh is Weak: An Intimate History of the Church of England* (London: Hamish Hamilton, 1980)

BAYNES, JOHN, *Morale* (London: Cassell, 1967)

BECKETT, IAN F. W. and SIMPSON, KEITH, eds. *A Nation in Arms: A Social Study of the British Army in the First World War* (Manchester: Manchester University Press, 1985)

BENTLEY, CHRISTOPHER, 'Wilfred Owen and Gustave Flaubert', *Notes and Queries*, 17 (1970), 456–7

BENVENISTE, EMILE, *Problems in General Linguistics*, tr. Mary Elizabeth Meek (Coral Gables: University of Miami Press, 1971)

BERGONZI, BERNARD, *Heroes' Twilight* (London: Constable, 1965)

BLOOM, HAROLD, *The Anxiety of Influence* (London and New York: Oxford University Press, 1973)

BORLAND, MAUREEN, *Wilde's Devoted Friend: A Life of Robert Ross 1869–1918* (London: Lennard, 1990)

BOSTOCK, J., *How to Instruct in Aiming and Firing* (Aldershot: Gale & Polden, 1909)

—— *Notes on Visual Training and Judging Distance in Relation to Musketry* (Aldershot: Gale and Polden, 1915)

BRADLEY, IAN, *The Call to Seriousness: The Evangelical Impact on the Victorians* (London: Cape, 1976)

BREEN, JENNIFER, 'Wilfred Owen: "Greater Love" and Late Romanticism', *English Literature in Transition*, 17 (1974), 173–83

BROCK, ARTHUR J., *Health and Conduct* (London: Williams and Norgate, 1923)

BROOKE, RUPERT, *1914 & Other Poems* (London: Sidgwick and Jackson, 1915)

BROOKE, STOPFORD A., *English Literature from A.D. 670 to A.D. 1832* (London: Macmillan, 1905)

—— *Studies in Poetry* (London: Duckworth, 1910)

BROPHY, JOHN and PARTRIDGE, ERIC, *The Long Trail: What the British Soldier Sang and Said in the Great War of 1914–1918* (London: André Deutsch, 1965)

CANAT, RENÉ, *La Littérature française par les textes* (Paris: Librairie Classique Paul Delaplane, n.d.)

CARPENTER, EDWARD, *Love's Coming-of-Age* (London: Methuen, 1914)

CARTER, HENRY, ed. *The Church and the Drink Evil* (London: Epworth Press, 1922)

CARTER, HENRY, *The English Temperance Movement: A Study in Objectives*, vol. 1 (London: Epworth Press, 1933)

CLARK, ALAN, *The Donkeys* (London: Hutchinson, 1961)

COLVIN, SIDNEY, *Keats*, English Men of Letters Series (London: Macmillan, 1887)

CUTBILL, JONATHAN, 'The Truth Untold', *New Statesman*, 16 January 1987, 22–4

CUTT, MARGARET NANCY, *Ministering Angels* (Wormley, Herts.: Five Owls Press, 1979)

DANGERFIELD, GEORGE, *The Strange Death of Liberal England* (London: MacGibbon and Kee, 1966)

DANTE ALIGHIERI, *The Vision, or, Hell, Purgatory and Paradise of Dante Alighieri*, tr. H. F. Carey (London: Frederick Warne, n.d.)

D'ARCH SMITH, TIMOTHY, *Love in Earnest* (London: Routledge, 1970)

DICKENS, CHARLES, *Christmas Books*, New Oxford Illustrated Dickens (London: Oxford University Press, 1954)

DORCHAIN, AUGUSTE, ed. *Les Cent meilleurs poèmes (lyriques) de la langue française*, (Paris: A. Perche, 1913)

ELKIN, ROGER, 'Hunting Wild', *Stand*, 30 no. 2 (1988–9), 48–57

Field Service Manual (London: HMSO, 1913–16)

Field Service Pocket Book (London: HMSO, 1914; repr. with amendments, 1916)

FLAUBERT, GUSTAVE, *La Tentation de Saint-Antoine*, introd. Emile Faguet (Paris: Crès; London: Dent, n.d.)

FOOT, PAUL, *Red Shelley* (London: Bookmarks Publications, 1984)

FOUCAULT, MICHEL, *Discipline and Punish: the Birth of the Prison*, tr. Alan Sheridan (New York: Vintage Books, Random House, 1979)

FUSSELL, PAUL, *The Great War and Modern Memory* (New York and London: Oxford University Press, 1975)

GEDDES, PATRICK, *John Ruskin: Economist* (Edinburgh: William Brown, 1884)

GEDDES, PATRICK and SLATER, GILBERT, *Ideas at War* (London: Williams and Norgate, 1917)

GEDDES, PATRICK and THOMSON, J. ARTHUR, *Sex* (London: Williams and Norgate, 1914)

GIBSON, WILFRID WILSON, *Battle* (London: Elkin Matthews, 1915)

GLOVER, JON, 'Owen and Barbusse and Fitzwater Wray', *Stand*, 21 no. 2 (1980), 22–32

—— 'Whose Owen?', *Stand*, 22 no. 3 (1980–1), 29–31

GORDON, LAWRENCE L., *Military Origins* (London: Kaye and Ward, 1971)

GRAHAM, DESMOND, *The Truth of War: Owen, Blunden and Rosenberg* (Manchester: Carcanet, 1984)

GRAVES, ROBERT, *Over the Brazier* (London: Poetry Bookshop, 1916)

—— *Fairies and Fusiliers* (London: Heinemann, 1917)

GUNSTON, E. LESLIE, *The Nymph and Other Poems* (London: Arthur H. Stockwell, 1917)

HALLIDAY, M. A. K., *Language as Social Semiotic* (London: Edward Arnold, 1979)

HARRISON, BRIAN, *Drink and the Victorians* (London: Faber, 1971)

HIBBERD, DOMINIC, '"Rival pieces on a chosen theme": A Note on Some of Wilfred Owen's Minor Poems', in *Four Decades of Poetry 1890–1930*, vol. 1 (Merseyside, 1976), 70–5

—— 'Wilfred Owen and the Georgians', *Review of English Studies*, 30 (1979), 28–40

—— 'Silkin on Owen: Some Other War', *Stand*, 21 no. 3 (1980), 29–32

—— ed. *Poetry of the First World War: A Casebook* (London: Macmillan, 1981)

—— 'Concealed Messages in Wilfred Owen's Trench Letters', *Notes and Queries*, 29 (1982), 341

—— 'Wilfred Owen's Letters: Some Additions, Amendments and Notes', *Library*, 4 (1982), 273–87

—— *Owen the Poet* (London: Macmillan, 1986)

—— *The First World War* (London: Macmillan, 1990)

HIBBERD, DOMINIC and ONIONS, John, eds. *Poetry of the Great War: An Anthology* (London: Macmillan, 1986)

HOOD, B. R. N., *Duties for All Ranks* (London: Harrison, n.d.)

Hydra, The: Journal of the Craiglockhart War Hospital (The Oxford English Faculty Library has a complete set of nos 1–12 (fortnightly, 28 Apr.–29 Sep. 1917) and nos 1–3 and 7–9 of the monthly new series (Nov. 1917–July 1918).)

HYLSON-SMITH, KENNETH, *Evangelicals in the Church of England 1734–1984* (Edinburgh: T. and T. Clark, 1989)

HYNES, SAMUEL, *A War Imagined: The First World War and English Culture* (London: Bodley Head, 1990)

Infantry Training (London: HMSO, 1914)

JOHNSON, H. H., *A Short Introduction to the Study of French Literature* (London: Francis Griffiths, 1910)

JONES, DAVID, *In Parenthesis* (London: Faber, 1963)

KERMODE, FRANK, *The Sense of an Ending* (New York: Oxford University Press, 1967)

KERR, DOUGLAS, 'Wilfred Owen and the Social Question', *English Literature in Transition,* 34 no. 2 (1991), 183–95

—— 'The Disciplines of the Wars: Army Training and the Language of Wilfred Owen', *Modern Language Review,* 87 (1992), 286–99

—— 'Brothers in Arms: Family Language in Wilfred Owen', *Review of English Studies*, 43 (1992), 518–34

KIPLING, RUDYARD, *The New Army in Training* (London: Macmillan, 1915)

KLEIN, HOLGER, ed. *The First World War in Fiction* (London: Macmillan, 1976)

KYLE, GALLOWAY, ed. *Songs of the Fighting Men* (London: Erskine Macdonald, 1916)

—— *More Songs by the Fighting Men* (London: Erskine Macdonald, 1917)

LARRONDE, CARLOS, *Le Livre d'Heures* (Paris: Eugène Figuière, 1913)

—— *Anthologie des Ecrivains français morts pour la Patrie*, 4 vols (Paris: Larousse, 1916)

LIDDELL HART, B. H., *A History of the World War 1914–1918* (London: Faber, 1930)

MACKENZIE, E. G., *Notes on Mess Etiquette* (London: Heath Cranton, 1918)

MAGNUS, LAURIE, *Introduction to Poetry* (London: John Murray, 1902)

MARWICK, ARTHUR, *The Deluge: British Society and the First World War* (London: Macmillan, 1965)

MONRO, HAROLD, *Before Dawn: Poems and Impressions* (London: Constable, 1911)

—— *Children of Love* (London: Poetry Bookshop, 1914)

—— *Strange Meetings* (London: Poetry Bookshop, 1917)

MOORE, E. W., *Wanted, a Man! or Bible Characteristics of the Ideal Man* (London: Religious Tract Society, 1912)

MORRIS, JAMES, *Heaven's Command: An Imperial Progress* (Harmondsworth: Penguin, 1979)

—— *Pax Britannica: The Climax of an Empire* (Harmondsworth: Penguin, 1979)

MORRIS, LEWIS, *The Epic of Hades* (London: Henry S. King, 1877)

MYERS, CHARLES S., *Shell Shock in France 1914–18* (London: Cambridge University Press, 1940)

NICHOLS, ROBERT, *Ardours and Endurances* (London: Chatto and Windus, 1917)

NORGATE, PAUL, 'Wilfred Owen and the Soldier Poets', *Review of English Studies*, 40 (1989), 516–30

Notes for Infantry Officers on Trench Warfare, compiled by the General Staff (London: HMSO, 1916)

Notes on Field Defences, compiled by the General Staff (London: HMSO, 1914)

'ONE OF THEM', *'Out There!' or The Platoon Commander in Warfare* (London: Sifton, Praed, 1915)

OWEN, HAROLD, *Journey from Obscurity*, 3 vols (London: Oxford University Press, 1963–5)

—— *Aftermath* (London: Oxford University Press, 1970)

OWEN, WILFRED, *Poems by Wilfred Owen*, ed. Siegfried Sassoon (London: Chatto and Windus, 1920; repr. Imperial War Museum, Arts and Literature Series no. 1, 1990)

—— *The Poems of Wilfred Owen*, ed. Edmund Blunden, with a memoir (London: Chatto and Windus, 1931)

—— *The Collected Poems of Wilfred Owen*, ed. C. Day Lewis (London: Chatto and Windus, 1963)

—— *Wilfred Owen: Collected Letters*, ed. Harold Owen and John Bell (London: Oxford University Press, 1967)

—— *Wilfred Owen: War Poems and Others*, ed. Dominic Hibberd (London: Chatto and Windus, 1973)

—— *Wilfred Owen: The Complete Poems and Fragments*, ed. Jon Stallworthy, 2 vols (London: Chatto and Windus, Hogarth Press, and Oxford University Press, 1983)

Palgrave's Golden Treasury/Poetry and the Drama, Introd. Edward Hutton (London: Dent, Everyman's Library, 1906)

PARFITT, GEORGE, *English Poetry of the First World War: Contexts and Themes* (London: Harvester Wheatsheaf, 1990)

PENNYMAN, W. G., *The Collapse of Convention* (London: Fisher Unwin, 1924)

PRAZ, MARIO, *The Romantic Agony*, 2nd edn. (London: Oxford University Press, 1951)

PUNCH, *Mr Punch's History of the Great War* (London: Cassell, 1919)

QUILLER-COUCH, Sir Arthur, ed. *The Oxford Book of English Verse* (Oxford: Clarendon Press, 1900)

'REGULAR', *Customs of the Army: A Guide for Cadets and Young Officers* (London: Harrison, n.d.)

REILLY, CATHERINE W., ed. *Scars Upon My Heart: Women's Poetry and Verse of the First World War* (London: Virago Press, 1981)

RICHARDS, FRANK, *Old Soldiers Never Die* (London: Faber, 1933)

RIVERS, W. H. R., *Conflict and Dream* (London: Kegan Paul, 1923)

ROSMAN, DOREEN M., *Evangelicals and Culture* (London: Croom Helm, 1984)

ROSSETTI, W. M., *Life and Writings of John Keats* (London: Walter Scott, n.d.)

ROUCOUX, MICHEL, ed. *English Literature of the Great War Revisited* (Picardie: Presses de l'UFR Clerc Université, 1987)

RUSKIN, JOHN, *Lectures on Art*, 8th edn (London: George Allen, 1898)

—— *Sesame and Lilies* (London: Allen and Unwin, 1919)

SACKS, PETER M., *The English Elegy: Studies in the Genre from Spenser to Yeats* (Baltimore: Johns Hopkins University Press, 1985)

SACKVILLE, LADY MARGARET, *The Pageant of War* (London: Simpkin, Marshall, n.d.)

SAROLEA, CHARLES, ed. *Anthologie des Poètes lyriques français* (Paris and New York: Nelson, n.d.)

SASSOON, SIEGFRIED, *Siegfried's Journey 1916–1920* (London: Faber, 1945)

—— *Collected Poems 1908–1956* (London: Faber, 1961)

—— *The Complete Memoirs of George Sherston* (London: Faber, 1972)

—— *Siegfried Sassoon: Diaries 1915–1918*, ed. Rupert Hart-Davis (London: Faber, 1983)

SHERARD, ROBERT H., *Oscar Wilde* (London: Greening, 1909)

SHIRLEY, W., *Moral: The Most Important Factor in War* (London: Sifton, Praed, 1916)

SHOWALTER, ELAINE, *The Female Malady: Women, Madness, and English Culture 1830–1980* (London: Virago Press, 1987)

SILKIN, JON, *Out of Battle: The Poetry of the Great War* (London: Oxford University Press, 1972)

—— ed. *The Penguin Book of First World War Poetry* (Harmondsworth: Penguin, 1979)

—— 'Owen: Elegist, Satirist, or neither; a reply to Dominic Hibberd', *Stand* 21 no. 3 (1980), 33–6

SIMCOX, KENNETH, *Wilfred Owen: Anthem for a Doomed Youth* (London: Woburn Press, 1987)

SITWELL, OSBERT, *Noble Essences or Courteous Revelations* (London: Macmillan, 1950)

SMITH, ERIC, *By Mourning Tongues: Studies in English Elegy* (Ipswich: Boydell Press, 1977)

SNELL, J. BERNARD, *How are we to Love our Enemies?* (London: Simpkin, Marshall, 1915)

SPEAR, HILDA D., *Remembering, We Forget: a Background Study to the Poetry of the First World War* (London: Davis-Poynter, 1979)

SPURGEON, C. H., *Fifty Most Remarkable Sermons* (London: Passmore and Alabaster, 1908)

—— *Sermons*, Sir W. Robertson Nicoll ed. (London: Thomas Nelson, n.d.)

STALLWORTHY, JON, 'W. B. Yeats and Wilfred Owen', *Critical Quarterly*, 11 (1969), 199–214
—— *Wilfred Owen: A Biography* (London: Oxford University Press and Chatto and Windus, 1974)
STEINER, GEORGE, *In Bluebeard's Castle: Some Notes Towards the Re-definition of Culture* (London: Faber, 1971)
SWINNERTON, FRANK, *The Georgian Literary Scene 1910–1935*, rev. edn. (London: Hutchinson, 1969)
SYMONDS, JOHN ADDINGTON, *Shelley*, English Men of Letters Series (London: Macmillan, 1909)
TAILHADE, LAURENT, *Poèmes élégiaques*, 3e édition (Paris: Société du Mercure de France, 1907)
—— *Pour la Paix: suivi de Lettre aux Conscrits* (Paris: Albert Messein, 1909)
TAYLOR, A. J. P., *The First World War: An Illustrated History* (Harmondsworth: Penguin, 1966)
TAYLOR, MARTIN, ed. *Lads: Love Poetry of the Trenches* (London: Constable, 1989)
Theocritus, Bion and Moschus, tr. Andrew Lang (London: Macmillan, 1889)
THOMAS, EDWARD, *Keats* (London: T. C. and E. C. Jack, n.d.)
THOMAS, W. H. GRIFFITH, *The Training of Candidates for Holy Orders* (London: SPCK, 1908)
—— *The Work of the Ministry* (London: Hodder and Stoughton, n.d.)
THORPE, MICHAEL, *Siegfried Sassoon: A Critical Study* (Leiden: Universitaire Pers Leiden; London: Oxford University Press, 1966)
TODOROV, TZVETAN, *Mikhail Bakhtin: The Dialogic Principle* (Manchester: Manchester University Press, 1984)
Trench Warfare: Notes on Attack and Defence, collated by the General Staff (London: HMSO, 1915)
TURNER, E. S., *Roads to Ruin* (London: Michael Joseph, 1950)
VERNEDE, R. E., *War Poems and Other Verses* (London: Heinemann, 1917)
VOLOŠINOV, V. N., *Marxism and the Philosophy of Language*, tr. Ladislav Matejka and I. R. Titunik (Cambridge, Mass.: Harvard University Press, 1986)
WALKER, JOHN, *James Abbott McNeill Whistler* (New York: Harry N. Abrams, 1987)
WATSON, WILLIAM, *Excursions in Criticism* (London: Elkin Matthews and John Lane, 1893)
What Every Soldier Ought to Know, compiled from the Official Manuals (Humphrey Milford: Oxford University Press, 1915)
WELLAND, D. S. R., *Wilfred Owen: A Critical Study* (London: Chatto and Windus, 1960; repr. with a postscript, 1978)

WEST, ARTHUR GRAEME, *The Diary of a Dead Officer* (London: Allen and Unwin, 1918)

WHITE, GERTRUDE M., *Wilfred Owen* (New York: Twayne, 1969)

WILLIAMS, BASIL, *Raising and Training the New Armies* (London: Constable, 1918)

WINNINGTON-INGRAM, ARTHUR F., *Social Purity* (London: Wells, Gardner, Darton, 1909)

—— *A Day of God: Being Five Addresses on the Subject of the Present War* (London: Wells, Gardner, Darton, 1914)

—— *The Church in Time of War* (London: Wells, Gardner, Darton, 1915)

—— *Cleansing London* (London: C. Arthur Pearson, 1916)

WINTER, DENIS, *Death's Men: Soldiers of the Great War* (Harmondsworth: Penguin, 1979)

WOOD, FRITZ P., *Facing Facts: A Series of Addresses on the Foundation Truths of Christianity* (London: Bagster, 1913)

Index of Owen's Poems

Index of poems and fragments quoted or referred to in the text.

General Index